The Live Food Factor

A COMPREHENSIVE GUIDE TO THE ULTIMATE DIET FOR BODY, MIND, SPIRIT & PLANET

SUSAN SCHENCK, L.AC., M.T.O.M.

Disclaimer

The purpose of this book is to dispense information. It is sold for informational purposes only. The publisher and author of this book cannot be responsible for your health. As this book teaches, only you can be responsible for your health. This book is not intended as medical advice because the author is not a medical doctor and does not promote the use of medical drugs.

Because there is always some risk of detoxification involved when one pursues the path of true health and switches to a healthful lifestyle and diet, the author, publisher, and distribu-tors of this book are not responsible for any adverse effects or consequences resulting from the use of any recipes, suggestions or procedures described in this book.

Printed in the USA

First Edition, Second Printing, 2006

Published by:
  Awakenings Publications
  P. O. Box 712423
  San Diego, CA 92171-2423

Front cover artwork by Joe Alexander (www.joealexander.net)
Back cover photo by Joseph Peiri (j-pieri@sbcglobal.net)
Cover design by Bob Avery (bobavery@umich.edu)

Editing and production by Bob Avery

ISBN 0-9776795-0-0

Library of Congress Control Number: 2005911302

Health   Weight Loss   Beauty   Nutrition/Diet

To Dad,
whose love of healing
inspired me...
You always said
I'd make a great lawyer;
I rest my case with this book.

Table of Contents

3 Radically Raw: My Story 84

Section Two — *Raw Proof: The Science*
   99

4 A Paradigm Shift in Our View of Disease and Its Treatment............ 101

5 Cooked vs. Raw Diet Experiments . 121

6 Man's Fatal Chemistry Lab: The Great Cooked Food Experiment............ 145

7 The Raw Ingredients 159

Section Three — *Raw Pioneers: History & Leaders*... 173

8 A Brief History of the Raw Food Movement 175

9 Modern-Day Leaders of the Raw Food Movement 183

12 Controversial Nutritional Issues... 233

13 Common Pitfalls to Avoid 275

14 Frequently Asked Questions 289

Table of Contents

Bibliography and Other Resources... 441

Glossary... 485

Index 491

Acknowledgements

I would like to acknowledge the following people for the parts they played in making this book possible:

First of all, I wish to acknowledge Bob Avery for assuming the role of chief editor and production manager, as well as his vetting of factual information. He even found grammar and punctuation errors in the writings of this former college English teacher! Without his persistent work and dedication, this book wouldn't have been possible. Most of all, I thank him for the Herculean feat of converting me to uncooked eating! Bob deserves a lot of credit for working tirelessly on the computer, educating people via e-mail on the benefits of a living foods diet, one person at a time.

My heartfelt thanks go out to all of you who contributed testimonials, notably Jacqueline Nash, who also provided much-needed professional editorial input.

Additional editorial assistance, proofreading and textual suggestions were contributed by Joan Kurland, Sara Pess, Lynn Pollock and Barbara Vensko, for which I am very grateful.

I am also very grateful to Joe Alexander for his wonderful painting and calligraphy for the front cover and his enthusiasm for the project.

Thanks for donated recipes are due to Buddy and Cherrie, as well as Lorenzo and Marycie Haggarty, who also contributed their inspiration and advice for improving this book.

I must also express my deep appreciation to every raw food author or teacher quoted or profiled in this book, especially Victoria Boutenko for her study on cooked food addiction, Dr. Gabriel Cousens for his research into the scientific aspects of the diet and David Wolfe for his zeal to convert the world.

I am pleased to thank Joan Kurland, Dana Pettaway and other raw friends for hosting raw, alternative, social activities locally and Helene Idels for promoting them.

I am thankful to Cilantro Live, Kung Food, Rancho's, Life Restaurant and Couleur Alive Café for making live food available in San Diego restaurants.

And *most of all,* I wish to thank *Allen, my husband,* for following me on this raw journey and for being the biggest fan of my writings. Thank you for all the encouragement and emotional support that made this happen!

Note to Reader

This book is intended to be read from cover to cover, as many of the facts, concepts and ideas presented are built upon from chapter to chapter. So the first time it is read, it is best read chronologically. But if you find a part you're not interested in and end up skipping parts, that's certainly better than putting the book aside and not finishing it at all.

If you come across something that you find hard to believe or you believe is not true, please do not let this keep you from learning what the book has to offer. Rarely is there a book that is free from error or opinion, and indeed, many of the greatest history and so-called factual books are full of errors, half-truths or slants of the authors and/or publishers.

While newspapers may employ "fact combers," the truth is that they, more than anyone, are guilty of "sins of omission" by disallowing information that offends the corporations that pay for their advertisements. For instance, we cannot read in newspapers about the effects of all the harmful food additives mentioned in Appendix A or about research on the ill effects of cell phones on the brain because that could offend the food and mobile phone advertisers.

As Mark Twain once said, "If you don't read the newspaper, you are uninformed; if you do read the newspaper, you are misinformed."

Therefore, I invite you to read this book with an open mind so that you may be able to receive whatever assistance or helpful insights it may provide.

Preface

I _had_ to write this book because the raw food diet is _the best-kept secret_ on the planet.

The results of my years of research into the raw diet via reading, talking to people, attending lectures and workshops, experimenting on my own, and coaching others are summarized in this book.

I debated, however, about how to present the material. Some people advised me to avoid a lot of science because it makes for dull reading; on the other hand, facts backed by science are what convince most people. Without research backing it up, many will reject theory based on case studies as "mere anecdotal evidence." If hard science turns you off, _simply skip Section Two_, but please at least read Chapter 4, which is the most important science chapter.

This book will also arouse some disagreement among my friends and colleagues. Acupuncturists I know will think I am a heretic since Chinese medicine advocates a macrobiotic diet, a diet of whole foods, most of which are cooked, especially when a patient has what is known in Chinese medicine as a "cold condition."

A number of my friends and family in the medical profession may be put off by some of the facts I point out about the pharmaceutical companies. I don't mean to offend _any_ of you; I am just sharing the facts. While drugs apparently do _some_ good, there is a much higher, much healthier and simpler way.

One thing I can say with nearly 100% certainty: My mother would still be alive if I had known about this diet six years ago because she wanted to live and would have been willing to change her diet. I wrote this book in the hope that perhaps the information might spare somebody else's mother or loved one from _senseless and needless death by cancer or from some other dread disease._

Even my raw food friends and fellow authors who are strict vegans (see the Glossary) may think I am a heretic to present a small bit of favorable evidence for eating raw animal foods, at least for certain people with certain conditions. This was the most difficult chapter for me to write, as I was trying not to offend any of my vegan colleagues and friends, since vegans make up the vast majority of raw fooders.

I pondered about whether or not to omit certain chapters. I decided that certain things, however, just had to be said. I am really a "truth warrioress" at heart, with a voracious appetite for seeking and teaching the truth.

I have always been a pioneer, although — I believe Stuart Wilde was the one who said this — a pioneer is often someone with an arrow in her back! But I can also be a bit of a wimp at times when it comes to having an arrow in my back. I therefore put the truly, majorly controversial — *and therefore juiciest!* — things in the appendices. That way they won't detract from the main message, which is pure and simple: Let (raw) food be your medicine!

Oh, and by the way, I have always been annoyed by footnotes. I don't like having to flip to the back of the book looking for the reference to something so totally unbelievable that I just have to know the source. So, for your convenience, I have included the references in parentheses within the main body of the text. (Okay, it was also easier for me to write it this way.)

Introduction

There is one custom dating back five hundred to one thousand generations prevalent in virtually every culture on earth — cooking. What if you could attain an infinitely stronger immune system, a clearer mind, a happier emotional state, and even a more highly developed spiritual level merely by omitting this custom?

The raw food diet has been portrayed by the media as the latest diet craze. Out of ignorance, some "experts" will even recommend that this diet could be "unsafe" for children. Hmmm... I wonder how all those children survived for eons before cooking was invented?

Yet this diet is here to stay. People discovering its benefits develop such a zeal that they want to tell the world. It is so much more than a weight-loss diet. It is truly the diet that unveils our latent capacity to live in peace and harmony with mental and spiritual clarity.

I will always recall my first introduction to the world of living food: In 1989, I had a housemate who ate 80% "live" food, as she called it. Why wasn't I convinced after a year of living with her?

Hmmm, live food? Well, that's fine, I thought, but I would just as soon eat what I love and spend money on supplements (enzymes and vitamins) for the things lost in the fire of cooked food. Besides, her diet was *so boring*! Just fresh juice, salad and "health-food" chips for the 20% of allowed cooked food.

Little did I know that supplements could never compensate for ingredients in live food that are impossible to put into a tablet or liquid supplement; and little did I know at that time how to make raw food more appealing than cooked food. I had no idea of the variety of tastes that I was missing out on!

As I explain in Chapter 3, I was searching for the elusive "fountain of youth," the "silver bullet" that would give me more energy and halt or reverse aging. I thought it would be something that would probably cost a lot of money.

When I discovered the living food diet, and experienced it firsthand, I realized that this was *it*! I quickly read everything I could find on the topic, frequently "google-ing" the words "raw food" into the Internet search engine, as well as at the Internet bookstore Amazon.com. I read about 70 books related to nutrition, including everything on raw food that I could find, within a year and another 30 the next two years. I attended numerous workshops and lectures by long-term raw fooders.

Usually when we think of a diet, we think of weight loss. This book will show you that the power of what you eat — and refuse to eat — goes far beyond weight control. When properly nurtured, the body can heal itself of cancer, infertility, thyroid problems, asthma, diabetes and even sleepwalking, in addition to obesity. Surgery can almost always be avoided. You will read testimonials like these, and more, in Chapter 2.

Even if you have already begun your journey into living foods, you will have with this book a compilation of nearly all the scientific studies that have been done on the raw diet (Chapter 5) as well as many studies that implicate cooking in disease (Appendix D).

In this book, I have answered the most frequently asked questions about the living foods diet. Is cooked food *really toxic*? And more importantly, could it be that relieving the body of the toxicity of cooked food (explained in detail in Chapter 6) would give your immune system a big enough boost to *heal disease*? What personal testimonials and experiments support this claim? (See Chapters 2 and 5.) Could it really be that a raw food diet can boost your mental ability, as well? (See Chapter 5.)

Won't a raw food diet make me feel cold and be impossible to do in winter? How can I get my family to go raw? Does my pet also need this diet? And one of the most frequently asked questions: *How do you get enough protein?* (See Chapter 14.)

In this book you will find answers to all those questions and many more, as well as how the raw food diet is a huge benefit for the environment and future generations. (See Chapter 1.) You will discover various ways to transition, choosing the way that is most comfortable for you. (See Chapter 10.) You will learn how to make the diet work for you in practical terms, such as while traveling and in social situations. (See Chapter 11.) There is even a chapter with over 60 delicious raw recipes to get you started. (See Chapter 15.)

What, you say? You've already tried this diet, but failed? In Chapter 13, you will learn of many of the pitfalls that trip people up when starting a living foods diet and how to avoid them. You will learn about the addictive nature of cooked food, as I have experienced myself, and how to break the addiction.

But wait — if this diet is so great, why isn't it making the news? One would think that such a dietary change that can enable the body to heal itself of diseases thought to be incurable (such as cancer and even AIDS) would be all over the front pages of newspapers and on the 6 o'clock news. Why do the media make it seem like just another Hollywood diet fad?

You will discover, as I have, that there are powerful financial interests behind the cover-up and why this movement will never have big money to support its research. (See Appendices A and B.) You will learn why it may never be more than a grass-roots movement — at least for a long time to come.

In this book, you will learn how to empower yourself, taking back control of your health from the giant food processors and drug corporations.

As I mentioned earlier in the Preface, my mom would still be alive if she'd had this information. And it is worthy of repetition to restate that I simply *had to write this book*. I have never been fully convinced of the idea of predestination, but I can state with firm conviction that this book was born of forces beyond my control. I couldn't sleep at night knowing that I was not sharing with others the *best kept, best secret you may ever learn in your lifetime!*

"I'm prescribing a low-carb diet for your diabetes, a high-carb diet for your colon, a low-fat diet for your heart and a high-fat diet for your nerves."

Section One

Raw

Power:

Reasons to Go Raw

"My job is giving me migraines, high blood pressure, chest pains, and bleeding ulcers. I'd quit, but I like their health plan."

1
Ten Reasons to Stop Cooking

If cooking becomes an art form rather than a means of
providing a reasonable diet, then something is clearly wrong.
—Tom Jaine, British editor of *The Good Food Guide*

Imagine you have discovered the most incredible secret
formula that has completely transformed you. You are now at
your ideal weight. Your hair is thick, your skin soft and smooth.
You have recovered the vitality and energy levels of your youth,
and you don't recall feeling such mental clarity and bliss *since
pre-adolescence.* Your body heals itself of all disease, even minor ailments such as athlete's foot, acne, premenstrual syndrome (PMS), constipation and allergies. You feel *alive, in the
zone, in the flow.* You have discovered the magical formula, the
fountain of youth.

Well, such a formula does exist. Only it is not a pill, potion,
drug or lotion. It is simply a return to man's original diet: raw,
natural, basic food — the lost art of non-cooking, just eating
food in its natural state.

Many who have tried the raw food diet feel such a mental,
physical, emotional and spiritual shift, indeed, such a *radical
transformation,* that they find it easy to believe that the "fall
from grace" referred to in the mythology of numerous cultures
arose from the cooking of food.

There was a time, eons ago, which most ancient cultures
spoke of, when people lived in harmony with nature and in tune
with many of our untapped mental abilities, living in peace with
all other creatures. Could the end of these times have resulted
from the invention of widespread food cooking, thus damaging
the fuel we depend on for our optimal health and well-being?

In some traditions, heavenly images include a garden of
paradise, abundant with luscious fruit, whereas the image of
hell is one of fire and brimstone.

Perhaps we don't have to wait until the afterlife to experience these states. Could it be that those archetypes were generated from earthly observations? Eat a diet of fruit and other botanical abundance from the garden, and you'll have "heaven on earth." Eat a diet prepared over fire, and you'll manifest hell on earth!

When God threw Adam and Eve out of the Garden of Eden, he said to Eve, "I will greatly multiply your pain and your conception; in pain you shall bring forth children" (Genesis 3:16).

Interestingly, women on raw food diets do not experience nearly as much pain in childbirth, and often their menstrual bleeding is scanty to nonexistent and painless. Could it be that Adam's and Eve's legendary fall from the Garden of Eden was not from *eating* the apple, but rather from *cooking* it?

We are told that *Homo erectus*, who may have been the first to tend fires on a regular basis, first appeared on Earth about 1,800,000 years ago. For those of you who think we should have adapted to cooked foods by now, author Severen L. Schaeffer presents an excellent analogy: "If we were to imagine the course of evolution as a road 25 miles long, men would be coming into existence only 70 yards from the end, the discovery of cooking 25 feet from the end, and the development of agriculture about five inches before our time. Coca-Cola would appear roughly $1/200^{th}$ of an inch into the past" (*Instinctive Nutrition*, Severen Schaeffer, p. 9).

Truly, the vast majority of our evolution as humans has been spent eating food in its pure, natural, whole state — unheated, unprocessed, unsprayed with chemicals. You still may think, "Well, couldn't we have adapted by now?"

If we have only been cooking for ten to twenty thousand years, it would be impossible to have genetically adapted so quickly to these chemical changes in the food, which will be discussed in more detail in Section Two. Widespread genetic changes of significance need a million or several million years to occur.

The use of fire for cooking may have begun roughly 400,000 years ago. Agriculture and cattle ranching, with the consequent consumption of grains and dairy, began only about 10,000-20,000 years ago. The widespread use of cooking began about the same time, although it has only been within the past century that such a large percentage of cooked food has been consumed — for some, 95-100% of the diet.

The belief that early paleolithic man routinely cooked his food is incorrect. Anthropologist Dr. Vaughn Bryant studied the fossilized excrement of early paleolithic people and concluded they were primarily raw food eaters and, from studying the skeletons, that they were in excellent health. Thus, it appears that cooking became customary only after the Stone Ages.

Why did man start to cook? There are many theories. Some anthropologists suggest that as man migrated to colder climates, the only way he could eat the frozen food he found was to thaw it out with fire. Since then, cooking has become an art form and is now thought to be a near necessity.

Culinary arts have been a part of virtually every historical culture, dating back thousands of years. Every country's inhabitants have generated recipes that swell their pride, just as they are proud of creativity in the literary or musical arts.

Now I am going to suggest something *very radical.* Maybe cooking is not only unnecessary, but also deadly. Could this be one case in which creativity is not progress and in fact is sending people to premature deaths? You may think, "Well, my grandfather ate cooked food and lived to be 100." What if our natural life span is much greater than 100? And what if we have the potential to be very, very healthy even as we get closer to the end of our lives?

A diet of raw, living food is not just another weight-loss diet. This is about energy transferred from the sun to the food to your body. This is about the life force and the enzymes in the food nourishing your body — hence the terms "living food" and "live food," often used to describe uncooked food in its pure, original state. If merely giving up the heating of food could transform your health and well-being, extend your life and youth, and raise you to a level of health you never even envisioned, wouldn't you gladly throw out the pots and pans?

Let us now take a closer look at some of the main benefits that a live food diet can bring you. In fact, let's look at *ten reasons to stop cooking.*

1. Super Health

The Greek doctor Hippocrates, considered to be the founder of modern medicine, uttered the famous words, "Let food be thy medicine."

How far we have fallen from his wisdom! First, let it be made clear that nothing, no outside object, "cures" or "heals" the body. *The body always heals itself,* and it alone has the wisdom to do so. As French philosopher Voltaire (1694-1778) once observed, "The art of medicine consists in amusing the patient while nature cures the disease."

But in order for nature to do the healing, it must be aided by the right nutrients, or building blocks. Thousands of modern-day people have enabled their bodies to heal themselves from all kinds of degenerative diseases using raw food diets. As we shall see in Chapter 9, many have written books (or have been written about) describing their journeys to health and full recovery from cancer, diabetes, heart disease, AIDS and other ailments.

A number of doctors have recognized the therapeutic value of raw diets in treating a host of conditions, including diabetes, ulcer, cancer, jaundice, Grave's disease, arthritis, fibromyalgia, asthma, ulcerative colitis, menstrual difficulties (including PMS), hormone disturbances, diverticulosis, anemia, circulatory diseases, weak immune system, hypertension, neuralgic conditions, gastrointestinal disorders, renal diseases, gout, obesity, myasthenia gravis and various skin diseases. Many of these ailments are not normally associated with nutrition. Section Two will present the science behind these seemingly outrageous claims.

It is very common, on a 90-100% raw diet, to be healed of supposedly "incurable" ailments and no longer need medications. I personally have met several people who had to take the drug Valtrex every day for many years for herpes. After going raw, they threw the drugs out and never had a breakout again. I have met people who no longer need medications for diabetes. I have also read of, and heard reports of, people with full-blown AIDS who became disease-free, sometimes the virus even disappearing from their blood and not showing up on blood tests. A number of the authors of raw food books cited in this book were healed of cancer or other serious diseases using raw diet alone.

The immune system is vastly enhanced on a living food diet. A clinic in Germany (*Klinik in der Stanggass*, Berchtesgaden) documented the influence of a raw diet on the immune system. They found effects that yielded antibiotic, antiallergenic, tumor-inhibiting, immunomodulatory and anti-inflammatory results. They recommend uncooked food as an adjunct to drugs in the treatment of allergic, rheumatic and infectious diseases.

Eskimos traditionally ate nothing cooked until very recently. They are the only Native American culture that has no history of a "medicine man" because they were extremely healthy until introduced to cooking.

Most people think of health as the absence of disease. Dr. Herbert M. Shelton was a renowned leader of the Natural Hygiene movement, a health reform movement that became prominent in the 1800s. He was quick to query, "Why must we accept as normal what we find in a race of sick and weakened beings?"

At his death, Shelton was writing a book to be called *Normal Man*, his vision of what *true* normal really is for our species. Perhaps we have yet to realize the full scope of our health potential.

Some people are motivated to get on the raw food bandwagon even though they were relatively healthy already. Some do it to prevent degenerative diseases. Much to their surprise, they soon encounter what can only be described as "ultra health" or "super health."

Gone is the need to sleep eight hours a day, and some even jump out of bed fully awake after three to six hours of sleep, with no desire for coffee or other stimulants. Excess fat melts off without any feeling of deprivation. The desire to overeat is diminished, as natural appetite control reestablishes itself.

Women find complete freedom from PMS, and for most, even their periods, which are a form of detoxification, dwindle down to one day. Birthing labor is sometimes painless and very brief. Women who have been eating raw diets for several years prior to the onset of menopause report having neither signs nor symptoms that indicate they are passing through menopause. The only way they discover that they have gone through the passage is via blood tests for hormone levels.

Temperature extremes are suddenly tolerated more easily. Body odors vanish or greatly diminish after a year or two of eating 100% raw. Skin becomes soft and smooth. Hair grows thick and wild. Bad breath becomes a thing of the past. Air travel does not entail jetlag.

Various other complaints, like athlete's foot, acne, allergies, colds, flus, dandruff, herpes or cold sores, vanish.

The physical senses sharpen. The person's psychic ability and feeling of being "in sync" or "in the flow of synchronicity" flourishes. The person finds himself more dynamic, radiant, charismatic and confident.

There is a feeling of lightness that everyone new to the raw diet comments on because far less energy is required for digestion. Digestive time is also reduced: While 48-100 hours are needed for cooked food, only 24-36 (or even less) may be needed for raw food.

Athletes eating raw food diets have found their athletic performance enhanced. Dr. Elmer in Germany and Dr. Douglas Graham in the USA both experimented with athletes they train by having them go on purely raw food diets. The athletes improved remarkably in strength, energy and stamina.

Jan Dries tells of a cancer patient on his raw diet regimen who was actually skiing better than before she fell ill (*The Dries Cancer Diet*, p. 67). Comedian Dick Gregory became a remarkable athlete on a diet of raw foods and juices and occasional fasting. He ran 900 miles on fruit juice alone in 1974.

Since the vast majority of your body cells are replaced every two years, after two years on a raw food diet, a whole new "you" will be formed. Only this will be the first time your body will be rebuilt with living food, full of nutrients.

A common thing people say when confronting dietary reform is, "Well, I have to die of something!" This feeling of resignation relieves them of all responsibility to watch their diets. Dr. Robert Young, a nationally known microbiologist and nutritionist, responded to this "common cultural myth ... I disagree with this because I feel that it's NATURAL TO DIE HEALTHY!" (*Sick and Tired*, p. 83).

If you have no interest in achieving abundant health, consider that most illnesses do not show symptoms until the eleventh hour. For example, most people don't know they have cancer until it is in very advanced stages, and the doctor gives them about a year and a half to live, despite the tumor's having been there for up to a decade or so already. For about 40% of the people who have heart disease, the first symptom they experience is death by heart attack! (Sorry, the living food diet cannot bring you back from the grave.)

Although living foods can help your body cure itself even in advanced stages of disease, it is not wise to wait until you are ill. In the Chinese medical classic, the *Nei Jing,* it is said, "To administer medicine after an illness begins is ... like digging a well after becoming thirsty or casting weapons after a battle has been engaged." Therefore, even if you are currently content with your state of health, consider this diet as a powerful way to *prevent future disease.*

2. Mental Ability and Mental Health

The concept "you are what you eat" applies not only to physical health, but also to the mind and mental health. Diet affects ideas, perceptions and even dreams.

Eating a raw food diet definitely gets rid of brain fog, makes the mind sharper, and gives one a "competitive edge" at work. One's short-term memory sharpens. Concentration and mental stamina improve. A raw fooder is also more alert, as excessive energy expenditure needed for digestion of cooked food is spared. The raw fooder doesn't fall asleep after eating dinner.

Raw food activist Viktoras Kulvinskas said, "When one eats a heavy meal, his energy goes from his head to his stomach." Digestion of cooked foods or unnatural foods consumes a great deal of energy.

The clean body of a raw fooder thus contributes to a pure mind.

Dr. Edward Howell, who studied the role played by food enzymes for over 50 years, found a connection between enzyme deficiency in diet, typical of cooked food diets, and a decrease in brain size and weight. He also found that the brain becomes smaller under the influence of obesity, and obesity vanishes with a raw food diet.

As you increase the fresh, raw food in your diet, you will notice an increase in positive thinking. This is partly because your body is being nourished properly, and the energy previously expended in digesting cooked food is now being used to cleanse your body of toxins. Especially if you do not overdo the phosphorus-containing, acidic foods (meat, nuts, seeds, grains, beans) and eat plenty of fresh, green, leafy vegetables, your body will alkalize, automatically creating the conditions for more positive thinking.

Visualization exercises, imagination and meditation will all happen much more easily. In time, your inherent psychic abilities may even blossom. Your natural intuition and instincts will sharpen. Decisions can be made with more clarity. Synchronicity will bring things into your life with ease and flow.

In his classic book *Mucusless Diet Healing System*, Professor Arnold Ehret wrote, "If your blood stock is formed from eating the foods I teach, your brain will function in a manner that will surprise you. Your former life will take on the appearance of a dream, and for the first time in your existence, your consciousness awakens to a real self-consciousness. ... Your mind, your thinking, your ideals, your aspirations and your philosophy changes fundamentally."

David Wolfe, prominent raw food author and publicist, says, "Raw food nutrition returns to you lost powers and abilities. I like to say that it bestows superhuman abilities — especially in physical endurance, clarity of thought and sixth sense perception." He sometimes works with corporations to teach them about this. He knew a man who was a raw food enthusiast for 37 years and became the number one insurance salesman for his company out of a field of 13,000 people. Nobody could compete with him.

Successful entrepreneur Steve Jobs is also a raw fooder, which is why he named his computer "Apple." The Macintosh computer is named after his favorite apple variety.

Creativity may also increase. Raw food guru Joe Alexander writes, "As an artist, when I ate cooked foods, I painted bleak, grotesque surrealist-type pictures with drab and dull, muddy colors ... but when I became a raw food eater, all of a sudden I began to paint instead vibrantly alive pictures with lush abundance of healthy shapes and brilliantly beautiful colors" (*Blatant Raw Foodist Propaganda!* p. 75). He created the painting depicted on the front cover of this book.

Valya Boutenko was in third grade and unable to concentrate on reading for longer than fifteen minutes at a time when her parents made her switch to a raw diet. Once her body became fully nourished with live food, she could read five hours at a time. "The biggest change I noticed from going on raw food is that I gained much mental clarity. I was amazed to discover that I can understand every subject. I'm sixteen and in college now. It's easy for me to write essays now for my writing class" (*Eating without Heating*, Sergei and Valya Boutenko, p. 13).

Leslie Kenton, health and beauty editor of the British periodical *Harpers & Queen*, and her daughter Susannah found that on a high-raw diet, they could write and research efficiently for seven or eight hours rather than just three or four as before (*Raw Energy*, p. 81).

Being a raw fooder somehow also makes people more open-minded. This is undoubtedly because the brain is clearer; however, I think it is also because taking such a radical leap makes a person begin to wonder if there are not other mental leaps to be taken and adventures to experience.

Joe Alexander declares that raw food eaters live in a more real world. "Their attitudes and opinions become transformed, energized by the reality of the Life-Force, whereas in most cooked food eaters, their attitudes and desires and opinions are programmed into their minds by parents, school, friends, clubs, organizations et al. and thus come from a very limited and superficial reality indeed, not from the deeper wisdom and reality of Nature at all" (*Blatant Raw Foodist Propaganda!* p. 59).

Mental health is tremendously enhanced. Many raw fooders find that they become freed from former addictions. For many, the desire to smoke cigarettes, drink alcohol or do drugs (prescription as well as recreational) falls away as the body becomes healthier, and one experiences a natural high. Furthermore, those who work with juvenile delinquents and former prisoners have found that abnormal nutrition alone can create a criminal mind. Children behave much better in school when on raw diets. Hyperactivity ceases, and brains fed with raw foods rich in omega-3 fatty acids (such as flaxseed) are able to focus better.

Part of the reason a raw food diet helps a person so much mentally is not only because live foods feed the brain, but also because unnatural foods are *eliminated* from the diet. (See Appendix A.) Working for several decades at the Hippocrates Health Institute, Brian Clement has seen mental problems like paranoia, depression, mania-depression and schizophrenia disappear on raw foods combined with psychological therapy. Over the years, he found out that mental illness is exacerbated by hormonal imbalances from eating meat pumped with hormones, pesticide poisoning from commercial produce and a high level of body acidity from eating animal and processed foods. Eating a raw, organic diet eliminates these problems.

3. Weight Loss and Beauty

Raw diet promotes beauty. To begin with, one reaches his or her ideal weight more readily and maintains it with much less effort than on a cooked diet. Many people lose 15 pounds in a month or two with no feeling of deprivation whatsoever. Obese people lose much more than that while eating raw fats all they want, including raw "ice cream," avocados, nuts and olives. Raw fats (from avocados, olives, nuts, seeds, coconut butter et al.) are actually needed by the body to maintain youthful skin, hair and glands. They are rich in the essential fatty acids linolenic acid and linoleic acid that are denatured by heat.

Raw food pioneer Dr. Ann Wigmore wrote, "The effectiveness of live foods and fresh juices, especially wheatgrass juice, has bankrupted many complex theories about why we become fat and how to reduce quickly ... Among our guests at the [Hippocrates Health] Institute, the average weight loss per week is between four and fifteen pounds" (*The Wheatgrass Book*, p. 59).

Studies have shown that raw food is less fattening than the same food cooked. According to Dr. Edward Howell, raw fats are not fattening and seem to belong in "a special pigeonhole in nutritional speculations" (*Enzyme Nutrition*, p.109). While cooked fats accumulate in the body and become very detrimental to our health, raw fats contain lipase (deficient in many obese people), the enzyme involved in metabolizing fat properly.

The word "Eskimo" means "raw eater," as the Eskimos traditionally ate nothing cooked but subsisted chiefly on raw meat and blubber. Dr. V. E. Levine examined 3,000 primitive Eskimos during three trips to the Arctic and found only one person who was overweight.

Cooked starches are also very fattening. Farmers have even learned that it is necessary to feed their animals cooked food to fatten them up for maximal profit. Hogs do not get fat on raw potatoes, but cooking the potatoes makes them gain weight.

In addition to reaching your body's ideal weight, many other beauty factors blossom on a raw diet. Cellulite, which is thought to result from eating heated fats, gradually disappears with the consumption of freshly squeezed grapefruit juice. On a raw diet, elimination of cellular waste and increased lymphatic drainage helps remove cellulite.

As the body's old cells are replaced with new, healthy cells through proper nutrition that only a raw diet provides, your hair grows in thicker and at times wilder. It may even regain color after having been gray, as did Ann Wigmore's. Your skin may become as soft and smooth as it was in your youth. Your nails will be strong, clear and shiny. Facial lines may fade or disappear; the face's pasty, white complexion becomes ruddy or rosy. People may remark on how much younger you look. Your eyes will sparkle.

The Hippocrates Health Institute, one of the places where people have gone to learn about the raw food diet, was once described by *Cosmopolitan* magazine as the "well-kept secret" of beauty and rejuvenation of various famous Hollywood movie stars and celebrities. Now the news media are letting the secret out.

When Demi Moore appeared in a bikini in the Charlie's Angels movie *Full Throttle* and looked every bit as great as the women younger than her, the word went out that the secret was her raw food diet. Other celebrities who have caught the wave include Alicia Silverstone and Woody Harrelson.

Model Carol Alt wrote in her book *Eating in the Raw* that the raw diet helps her stay beautiful, slim and young-looking. She attributes her current youthfulness and stamina to having eaten primarily raw food for eight years. She explains that in her thirties she had to starve herself and exercise a lot to stay trim. But as a raw fooder she is able to eat anything she wants, as long as it's raw, and she maintains her weight effortlessly, without ever feeling excess hunger. In addition, she claims she has better abdominal definition without exercising than she did as a cooked fooder who exercised regularly. She also has fewer wrinkles.

Health and beauty are intertwined. Dr. Herbert Shelton wrote, "The woman who maintains her health and youthfulness will retain her attractiveness. If she permits her health to slip away from her, if she values indulgences and frivolities more than she does health and impairs her health in the pursuit of false pleasure, she will lose her BEAUTY; and no art of the cosmetician and dressmaker will be able to preserve it for her."

Researcher Arnold De Vries writes, "In the final analysis, we must regard beauty, health and youth as intimately related. To the extent that you preserve one in your physical being, you also preserve the others. The uncooked fruit and vegetable diet, pure water, sleep and rest, sunshine, strong relationships, exercise, fresh air, fasting if necessary, and abstinence from drugs, vaccines, serums and other toxins are the prime requirements in your attempt to preserve your youth, health and beauty as long as you can" (*The Fountain of Youth*).

The face becomes more beautiful with a raw diet. "Skin loses its slackness and puffiness and clings to the bones better," write Susannah and Leslie Kenton (*Raw Energy*, p. 90). "The true shape of the face emerges where once it was obscured by excess water retention and poor circulation. Lines become softer. Eyes take on the clarity and brightness one usually associates with children or with super-fit athletes."

Nutritionist Natalia Rose, author of *The Raw Food Detox Diet*, profoundly praises the raw food diet as being the key to permanent weight loss. It's a lifestyle in which a woman can even attain her perfect shape without formal exercise or counting calories or grams of fat or carbohydrates and regardless of having had several children. The skin tone improves as cells become healthier and tighter. One dares to go out without make-up.

Tonya Zavasta describes her lifelong obsession with attaining beauty, which she finally discovered in her 40s through a 100% raw food diet. In her book *Your Right to Be Beautiful,* she explains how each of us can fulfill our full beauty potential, which is robbed by the toxic accumulation of cooked foods, dairy, wheat, salt and drugs. "Beauty lies latent under cushions of retained fluids, deposits of fat and sick tissues. Your beauty is buried alive" (p. 134).

She goes on to explain that on a diet of uncooked foods, "The landscape of the body will change. Fat that has accumulated in pockets under the eyes and at the jaw will melt away. The lumpy potato look of one's face will give way to sleek and smooth contours. The surface of the skin will become soft and smooth but still firm and supple. Visible pores will diminish. A sallow skin with a yellow pallor will turn into a porcelain-like complexion" (p. 137).

She furthermore describes the radiance and glow produced internally when there is "an abundance of clear, pink, almost transparent cells that light up the face," which is produced by superior blood circulation. Even the most beautiful supermodel would be enhanced by a raw food diet. She notes that the modern-day version of beauty is more in harmony with health than perhaps ever before, hence "the quest for beauty, instead of a narcissistic preoccupation, becomes a noble pursuit."

Tonya came across many women who would not eat a raw diet for their health, preferring just to take medications. However, they would go raw for beauty, as there is no pill for beauty. In her book *Beautiful on Raw,* ten women contributed their own experiences of how raw diets added to their beauty.

Various observations were that hair grew out with color instead of gray, sometimes with natural waves or curls, and fingernails grew strong, long and shapely. Cellulite vanished effortlessly. Puffiness in the body and face disappeared, and the skin cleared up. These women often get complimented on the "glow" of their faces. They feel confident without make-up. Their inner beauty and confidence also radiate. They look younger than ever and have no fear whatsoever of getting old. One of the women is 64 and still gets checked out by "the young whipper-snappers" when she is at the gym!

Interestingly, many of them, before eating raw, had never been called "beautiful" by anyone, even when they were much younger. One of the women wrote about suddenly becoming aware of the benefits of being attractive, benefits which one who had always been beautiful would take for granted. People were nicer to her, cops didn't give her tickets, and salespeople waited on her first.

The authors of *Raw Food/Real World* explain, "People who eat only raw, plant-based foods have an unmistakable shine, like a pregnant woman in her second trimester or someone newly in love. They have a radiant positive energy."

4.   Emotional Balance

The word "war" spelled backwards is "raw." On a raw diet, one loses the impulse to be at war with the world, feeling peace inside and out. The burden of digesting "dead" food, as well as all of the modern-day chemicals in food, can create quite a bit of stress on the brain as well as on the body. Dead, denatured food, with all of its toxins, pollutes the consciousness.

With the emotional balance that results from a natural diet of uncooked food, mood swings dampen. Mind chatter calms down. You now have the capacity to deal with stress, frustration and emotional pain like never before. You will feel less overwhelmed, as well as more grounded and capable. You no longer need antidepressant or anti-anxiety medications.

Emotionally, the raw food diet puts you at your peak. Your mind stops racing. You become more optimistic, even blissful, euphoric. You find joy where there used to be drudgery. You are at peace.

The Kentons explain how the raw diet affected their emotions (*Raw Energy*, pp. 119-121). "Instead of getting caught up in the emotional hassles when differences arise with other people, we can stand back and see what is happening. We no longer identify so much with what we think — we feel less threatened by someone who doesn't agree." They go on to say that life on the high-raw diet is "not the endless seesaw of minor ups and downs we once thought it."

They wonder, as I often have, if many of the negative feelings we get are not so much psychological in origin as physiological, "a sign that body chemistry is out of balance and toxins are building up." They read that Dr. Max Bircher-Benner discovered raw foods could not only cure his patients of illness, but also help them fulfill their potentials in every area of their lives.

15

Nutritionist Natalia Rose discusses how eating raw and therefore cleansing your body makes you more emotionally centered, with a clearer mentality. She has observed in her clients that internal cleansing gives one the desire to clear and cleanse one's living space and also create clear, honest communication with others. A sense of confidence develops, as well as respect for others.

5.   Spiritual Growth

People with low physical vitality have little energy available for spiritual focus. Therefore, a high-energy diet, i.e., an uncooked diet, can naturally enhance one's ability to commune with God, pray, meditate and perform whatever other spiritual practices one might do on one's path.

Entire books have been written about the spiritual benefits of a raw food diet. These include *Man's Higher Consciousness* by Hilton Hotema, *Why Christians Get Sick* by Baptist minister George Malkmus and *Raw Gorilla: The Principles of Regenerative Raw Diet Applied in True Spiritual Practice* by Da Free John.

Dr. Gabriel Cousens, MD, has written two books on the spiritual power of a raw diet: *Spiritual Nutrition and the Rainbow Diet* and another one published years later, *Spiritual Nutrition: Six Foundations for Spiritual Life and the Awakening of Kundalini.*

Victoria Boutenko, a famous raw food teacher, has also written a yet-to-be-published book about the spiritual power of raw food. In a lecture entitled, "The Spiritual Power of Raw Foods," Victoria explained that when we rely on indulgences, we burn ourselves out. As we eat more raw foods, we rely less and less on them because we become happier without artificial stimulation.

When we rely on stimulation and momentary pleasure, we drain our vitality. It physically exhausts our hormones and neurotransmitters. Stephen Cherniske explains it like this (*Caffeine Blues*, p. 111), "Have you ever felt a 'letdown' after an exciting event — even something really good? The intense stimulation subsides and is then replaced by a creeping sense of depression or languor. This happens because your dopamine receptors, the brain cells associated with excitement, have all been fired. What follows is a metabolic rebound that you must experience until your stores of dopamine are replenished."

Perhaps, as Victoria pointed out, that is why rich people who have funds for all kinds of gambling and other recreational highs do not derive lasting happiness from those events. With living food, we actually learn to find happiness from within.

The spiritual power of raw food is a concept that is even central to one religion. The Essenes are a religious group, dating back to the Hebrews, who are raw fooders and believe Jesus was an Essene and therefore a raw fooder.

Yogis of the Hindu tradition from India found that they could meditate better by eating only raw food. When less energy is needed for digestion, energy flows up to the body's higher chakras (energy centers) and enables one to experience higher states of consciousness. There is an ensuing "spiritual high" that makes one feel closer to the Source, whatever version of that one may believe in.

Renowned spiritual teacher Da Free John claims, "Anyone who engages the raw diet properly will more and more naturally discover this sattvic disposition" (p. 17, *Raw Gorilla*). A sattvic disposition is one that is spiritual and peaceful.

The Mormons were probably the first group in the USA to discover the spiritual power of the raw food diet. Joseph Smith and his core group ate a primarily live food diet after discovering that it enhanced their spiritual sensitivity.

Gabriel Cousens was looking for a diet to enable him to meditate better and to enhance his communion with the Divine when he found the raw food diet. He wrote *Spiritual Nutrition and the Rainbow Diet*, in which he outlines an ideal type of raw food diet to promote spiritual growth.

According to him, "Enzymes represent special high-energy vortex focal points for bringing Subtle Organizing Energy Fields into the physical plane for all general functions" (p. 101).

He recently claimed that, in his experience working with thousands of people turning toward live foods, the vast majority responded by becoming more open and moving toward a more spiritual life, whatever their particular religious tradition. Raw food, he says, opens one up to a lot of prana, the vital force that makes you feel high naturally.

"The light is switched on with raw food. You start seeing the Divine in everything," he stated at a lecture. He claims that a live food diet turns us into superconductors of both electrical energy and cosmic energy, enhancing our sensitivity to the Divine (*Spiritual Nutrition*, p. 305).

Christians have also discovered the power of a living foods diet in a big way. Reverend George Malkmus freed himself of cancer using a 100% raw diet and later got his Baptist congregation onto a vegetarian, primarily raw diet, citing Genesis 1:29 as biblical proof that this is the divine plan for our optimal health and spiritual well-being: "Behold, I have given you every herb yielding seed which is upon the face of all the earth, and every tree which bears fruit yielding seed; to you it shall be for food."

In his book *God's Way to Ultimate Health*, Malkmus quotes Tom Suiter, a Baptist pastor: "If we practice the laws of health, then we shall start a revolution in this nation that could shake us to our spiritual foundations."

Joe Alexander, author of *Blatant Raw Foodist Propaganda!* writes, "The raw fooder would enjoy a higher standard of living in a little hut than a junk food eater could in a palace. And raw foodism aids greatly in developing the spiritual maturity necessary for truly worthwhile achievements in life."

I once heard raw food activist David Wolfe say that he grew up as an atheist, but after being on raw food for some time, he *just knew* there was a spiritual realm! He experienced synchronicity and laughter for no reason. He has written in his book *The Sunfood Diet Success System* that a raw food diet also decalcifies the pineal gland, thought to be the source of the "third eye," or psychic center of the body.

Indeed, children who are raised on a 100% raw food diet have been known to be more psychic, as are animals in the wild. Wolfe has also made the comment, "The Bible says the body is the temple of the soul. Unfortunately, I used to treat mine like an amusement park." Many of us could say the same.

Raw food has also been called "sunfood" because it contains sun energy, which is absorbed into our cells. It can be thought of as "densified sunlight." Light affects our consciousness.

Dr. Rudolf Steiner, PhD, founder of the Waldorf schools and anthroposophical medicine, taught that outer light released into our bodies stimulates the release of inner light within us. The more light we absorb and assimilate, the more conscious we become. He felt that plant nutrition connects us to unrevealed cosmic forces, enabling us to go beyond the limitations of the mundane personality.

Many people report feeling an energy current flowing through their bodies after having eaten raw for some time. Professor Ehret wrote about this, "Your soul will shout for joy and triumph over all misery of life, leaving it all behind you. For the first time you will feel a vibration of vitality through your body (like a slight electric current) that shakes you delightfully" (*Rational Fasting*, p. 89).

Comedian-turned-raw-fooder Dick Gregory reported in *Dick Gregory's Natural Diet for Folks Who Eat*, "As my body was cleansed of years of accumulated impurities, my mind and spiritual awareness were lifted to a new level. I felt closer to Mother Nature and all her children. I felt more in tune with the universal order of existence." He also described, as a result of the cleansing his body went through, losing the "six basic fears": poverty, death, sickness, aging, being criticized and losing love.

Victoria Boutenko points out that Dr. Edward Howell's enzyme research indicates that a person typically has only 30% of his limited enzyme-generating capacity left by age 40. (See Section Two for more information on enzymes.) She says that while we can still walk, talk and think at this point, we have only 30% of our enzyme potential left, and these enzymes have to give about 75% of their energy to detoxify the body. "We become less sensitive to other people and to ourselves. We may survive physically but not spiritually" (*12 Steps to Raw Foods*, p. 5).

Many spiritual leaders teach that mankind is on the brink of a major shift in consciousness. Those who radically change the way they eat, switching to 100% raw food diets, may experience such a shift. If enough people discover the best kept secret of raw food diet, there could be revolutionary changes in mass consciousness and the patterns of mankind's thought-habits.

6.   Economy

On a raw food diet, you will save money on food. You will save on processed foods because, by the time you buy a processed food, it has gone through numerous steps and been passed through many hands between the farmer and you, and cost is added at every step. You will save on eating in restaurants unless you are fortunate enough to have several raw food restaurants where you live. You will save on junk food, eating simple fruit for snacks instead. You will also spend less on your grocery bill after eating raw for a year or so because, after your body rebuilds with raw materials, you will need less food. Consider that you will receive at least three times the nutrients from a raw fruit or vegetable than from a cooked one. In addition, you will save money on food immediately if you cut out meat.

Moreover, if you have been on a raw diet for a few years and have completely detoxified, you will no longer need to spend money on many personal-care products, such as perfume, mouthwash and deodorant. You will use less soap and laundry detergent because, since you will have far less toxic sweat, your clothes stay fresh longer.

Money spent on energy will also be saved. Since you may tolerate heat better, you might use the air conditioner less. You might even take up biking or walking to a lot of places you would have normally driven, thus saving on gasoline. You will save on the electric or gas bill because you will not use a stove or oven. Non-smokers get a fire insurance discount; since another major source of house fires is stove or oven use, raw fooders should also get a non-cooking discount!

You will save money on health care. You will also save money on doctors' bills and nutritional supplements. You may even decide, like some people have, to save money by eliminating or scaling down health insurance. You will feel in total control of your health, no longer afraid of being a helpless victim of disease. And even if you come down with an illness, your immune system will be strong enough to shake it off with a bit of fasting. After thoroughly educating yourself and becoming your own doctor, under no circumstances would you submit to toxic drug treatment; so why have costly health insurance? You might wish to purchase catastrophic insurance only, which is considerably cheaper and could be used in case of accidents.

Joe Alexander claims you will also save money on recreational drugs because the 100% raw food diet offers a better high than LSD, cocaine, speed and marijuana.

Sarma Malngailis (*Raw Food/Real World*) concurs, "Eating only raw plant foods ... can give you so much energy; it's like a natural version of Ecstasy, and you never crash."

In addition, many raw fooders lose interest in mass entertainment and take up new, less expensive activities, such as organic gardening, hiking and camping.

7.   Pleasure

It may be hard to imagine now, but after you have been eating raw for several months, food will begin to taste much better. You will derive more and more pleasure from the simplest foods, eaten in their whole, natural states. On occasion, eating will approach nirvana.

Cooked food loses so much of its taste that it has to be heavily spiced up with unhealthful additives such as monosodium glutamate (MSG) — a poisonous taste enhancer hidden in almost all canned and processed foods, disguised with many different misleading names. (See Appendix A.) In addition, cooked food is often "enhanced" with deadly table salt, as well as dressings and condiments. Once these are detoxified from your body, you will no longer crave them. Your tastebuds will open up to the ecstasy of whole, raw, natural foods.

When it comes to the sheer pleasure of eating raw food, perhaps no one puts it better than Juliano, the raw food chef genius, owner of a raw food restaurant in Los Angeles and author of *Raw: The Uncook Book*: "Why raw? Not because it guarantees me optimal health like the other 80 million species who eat only raw. Not because it's the last word in nutrition. Not for saving time or money, not for the endless energy it provides me, and not because it helps the planet because, instead of discarding packaging, which creates trash, I discard seeds, which give life. No, not any of these reasons. So, why raw? Taste and pleasure and only taste and pleasure."

In an interview with *Newsweek* (April 12, 2005), outspoken raw fooder David Wolfe was quoted as calling his "eating plan 'sensual nutrition' rather than restrictive. 'There's such an erotic and beauty side to these foods,' he says. 'They're alive, and the colors are bright and vibrant.'"

Wolfe also has astonishing news for chocolate lovers: *Raw chocolate is actually one of the most nutritious foods on the planet!* In his latest book *Naked Chocolate*, he documents the health benefits of chocolate, which include protection from heart disease, mood elevation, brain-boosting properties, appetite suppression and much more. Heating, processing and adding milk and sugar to raw cacao beans cause many of these benefits to be lost, but preparing the raw chocolate with raw agave sweetener and other raw ingredients masks the bitter flavor while retaining the super food benefits.

Natalia Rose explains that on a 95% raw diet she actually eats more calories than when she weighed 30 pounds more because what she eats exits the body quickly and is not stored as waste or fat (*The Raw Food Detox Diet*, p. 88).

Pleasure from eating on a raw diet increases, but the addictive aspect is gone. While one experiences more eating pleasure, it is balanced, and there is less attachment to it than with cooked food.

Sexual pleasure seems to work in the same fashion: While it may also become much more intense on a raw food diet, it is paradoxically less addictive and more balanced. The addiction, or strong compulsion, will diminish, but the enjoyment will be much greater because one is in far superior physical shape.

8.   Ecology

On a raw food diet, there is vastly less trash produced. There is a minimal amount of packaging to throw away. In fact, some raw fooders who grow their own food and compost their vegetative waste into their garden find that they have stopped producing trash altogether!

Furthermore, much forestation has been depleted in order to produce wood for cooking in areas where people are too poor to own a stove. For those who cannot afford wood to cook with, cattle dung is often used. I remember traveling in India and having to breathe in the polluted air as people burned water buffalo dung in order to cook.

When on a raw diet, you also don't destroy any of the nutrients; so you don't need as much food. People who have been on a 100% raw food diet for years need to eat even less food than the "newly raw," as they absorb so much more of the nutrients since digestion has become much more efficient.

Eating raw food saves the Earth. The conventional diet based on grains demands the plowing up of soil every year, which causes erosion, leading eventually to sterile deserts. The raising of cattle also creates serious erosion, with the legacy of destroyed land turning into desert. A raw food diet, on the other hand, encourages the growth of trees. Trees reach down deep into the ground and mineralize the earth's surface soil by pulling the minerals up to the stems, leaves and branches, which eventually fall to the topsoil.

The diet most Americans eat is rapidly destroying the planet for the next generation. Of prime concern is the fresh water used for cattle ranching. As Howard Lyman points out in his book *Mad Cowboy: Plain Truth from the Cattle Rancher Who Won't Eat Meat*, the water required to produce just ten pounds of steak equals the water consumption of the average household for an entire year! It took millions of years for the Ogallala Aquifer, the largest underground lake in the world, to form, and this vast water supply is in America. However, the meat industry is draining it dry very rapidly, and it will be nearly exhausted in half a century, as Lyman explains in his book.

John Robbins, vegan activist son of one of the founders of the Baskin-Robbins ice-cream franchise chain, estimates the date of depletion much sooner, at about the year 2020, in his video *Diet for a New America*. He cites a study from the University of California that explains that it takes 49 gallons of water to make a pound of apples, 24 gallons of water to create a pound of potatoes, but *5,000 gallons of water to make a pound of beef!* People who eat meat are almost always unaware of the true costs. When we eat meat, we are robbing from our children's most precious natural resource.

Water is also spared because people on raw diets don't need to drink as much since the food they eat doesn't have the water cooked out of it. On a diet of cooked food, the body also needs more water to suspend the pathogens and eliminate them from the body and to produce massive amounts of gastric juices to digest the cooked food.

Using our resources to produce fruits, vegetables, nuts and seeds, we could undoubtedly feed many more people. It is often reported by vegetarians that using the same land area to grow food for people instead of cattle, a vegetarian diet feeds many more people than a diet that includes meat. Yet a raw food diet feeds even more people, using the same land space, than a vegetarian one does. Of course, a raw food diet feeds many, many more people than the Standard American Diet (SAD) of meat and potatoes. According to Dr. Douglas Graham, "The Standard American Diet requires one hundred times the land of a raw food diet to produce the same amount of food. A vegan diet requires two and a half times as much land as does a raw food diet."

"We could feed forty people a pound of grain each, or one person a pound of beef," Graham asserts, "but nutritionists figured out long ago that we can feed 2½ times as many people from an acre of fruit than we can from an acre of grains" (*Grain Damage*, p. 35).

When asked about the issue of famine in the third world, raw fooder Guy-Claude Burger of the instinctive eating movement (see Appendix C) responded, "When you love the fruit, you love the tree as well. One plants and looks after one's orchard. Under the rule of cooked, starchy foods, fruit was demoted to the rank of snacks."

Raw food pioneer Dr. Ann Wigmore went to India and taught some beggars to sprout their grains and beans. The nutrient content of their diets increased so much from eating the food uncooked and sprouted that they were able to stop begging since they needed less food.

In addition to helping the ecology simply by being on raw diets, raw fooders report feeling closer to the Earth and all of its creation and more consciously take the effort to avoid polluting it. They frequently take up gardening, which reduces the need to consume scarce fossil fuels in transporting foods long distances.

9.   Free Time

No longer will you have to scrub the pots and pans of all that sticky, cooked food! You will no longer scrub endlessly at the greasy stains on the stove, oven and sink. Washing dishes and utensils used in raw food meals is simply a matter of rinsing. Sink drains will not clog up with grease.

During the six to twelve month transition stage, you may wish to experiment with many gourmet raw dishes that will take some preparation. But after a year or even less, you will become content to eat food in its most natural state. You will free up hours previously spent on food preparation and dishwashing. Eventually, you may also reduce your sleep time by a few hours a night. In a culture where time is more precious than money, this is perhaps one of the greatest gifts a raw diet has to offer.

10.   Longevity

Of the millions of animal species on earth, only humans habitually eat cooked food. There are the notable exceptions of farm and zoo animals, domesticated pets and wild animals foraging in our trashcans, and these also develop the degenerative diseases that humans get from eating cooked food diets.

Only humans deliberately heat what they eat, and only humans tend to die at or below half their potential life spans due to lifestyle related illness. Typically, an animal in an unpolluted environment will live seven times past its age of maturation. Humans, who reach physical maturity in their late teens or early twenties, should be living to at least 140 years, full of health and vigor up to the last few years.

The great historian Herodotus claimed that the Pelasgians, who ate a diet of raw fruits, vegetables, nuts and seeds, lived an average of 200 years. This would make them the longest living people in modern history.

On a raw food diet, you will not only have more time freed up from sleeping less, less food preparation and less time spent in dishwashing, but you will also likely add many years to your life. You may be one of the modern-day pioneers in pushing the boundaries of our life span. You could extend your "middle years," living in full vigor and health many years past 100.

Gabriel Cousens, MD, stated in a lecture that there are two types of genes: the genotype, which you are born with and never changes, and the phenotype, which is affected by environment, such as diet and lifestyle. Eighty percent of longevity is dependent on environmental factors, especially what we eat. Only 20% comes from the genotype. What you eat feeds your genes. When you eat the phytochemicals from raw foods, you can turn on the anti-stress, anti-aging, and anti-inflammatory genes. Resveratrol, a phytochemical found in red fruits and vegetables, is especially effective in turning on the anti-aging genes.

An important factor in the ability of raw foods to prolong our years is their enzymes. (See Chapter 7.) One is known as the "anti-aging enzyme," superoxide dismutase (SOD), because it discourages the formation of chemicals known as free radicals that do serious damage to the body.

The media tell us that we are living longer than ever before. This is misinformation because the statistics showing that the average current life expectancy is longer than the average life expectancy was, for example, 100 years ago factor in all of the infant mortality of those years. Currently, due to better hygiene, fewer babies die, which adds many years when calculating average life expectancy. Go visit a cemetery from the 1800s and early 1900s. You will marvel at all the gravestones for babies! So a big part of why the statistics tell us that we can expect to live longer is simply that fewer infants die.

According to the United States Department of Health and Human Services, the USA ranks 21st in life expectancy among all industrialized nations. People in modern America are not only *not living longer*, they are generally *getting sick much younger*. With the increase in cooked foods (sometimes a food is heated three times before it is eaten!) as well as processed and refined foods, we as a people are actually living shorter lives than our great-grandparents did, at least the ones who made it past 50.

Cancer, for example, hit only 1 in 8,000 people in 1900, according to Dr. William Donald Kelley, an expert on treating cancer. Now 1 in 2½, about 40% of us, can expect to get it. If such diseases as cancer were primarily caused by genetics, one would expect the rate of disease to remain somewhat stable, or even diminish (since many with the cancer gene would die before being able to reproduce). Instead, most diseases are on the rise because they are *environmentally caused*, having our unhealthful lifestyles and polluted civilization at their roots.

Much of the talk of our alleged increased length of life is due to medications and life support devices that prolong the agony of a sick body for a few years more while vastly draining one's financial resources. Yes, we are living longer in hospitals and nursing homes. But what quality of life is this? Would it not instead be better to prolong the *healthy years*, maintaining an agile, active body until the very end?

Eating a raw food diet will extend your youth and middle years, barring an early death from an unnatural cause like an accident. But even if someone eating raw gets killed in an accident before living out his maximal life span, the raw food diet still will not have been in vain. As David Wolfe says, "It's not about adding *years* to your *life*, but adding *life* to your *years*."

Now that we have explored ten reasons to eat raw, let's look at the amazing results obtained by a few real-life converts to this transformational diet.

2
Rah, Rah, Raw!
Raw Diet Testimony

Health is a state of complete physical, mental and social
well-being and not merely the absence of disease or infirmity.
—Constitution of the World Health Organization

In this chapter, I present testimonials from people who have
been consuming at least 80% of their dietary calories in the
form of raw food. Some of them were not writers; so I interviewed those people and prepared summaries of their stories.

"Raquel": No more cancer, diabetes, asthma, infertility, eczema and obesity!

"Raquel" (not her real name) is probably one of the most astounding cases I have personally encountered that demonstrate
the power of raw food. She'd had several miscarriages when a
doctor told her she could never have children due to "some
hormonal thing," as she put it. She'd had cervical cancer and
was told she needed another laser surgery shortly before she
switched to a raw diet. She had had asthma, eczema and Type
II (adult onset) diabetes for many years before going raw. She
was also overweight enough to qualify as "obese."

At the time of this writing, Raquel is 26 and free from all of
those maladies. She converted to a raw diet at the age of 20
under the influence of Paul Nison. (See Chapter 9.) Before that
she had been a self-proclaimed "junk food vegetarian," like
many people not eating meat but living on unhealthful meat-
free food. She'd had tonsillitis. She suffered eczema all over her
body. She'd had asthma her whole life and diabetes since the
age of seventeen, as well as cervical cancer since the age of thir-
teen. She'd also had frequent bladder infections, migraines and
insomnia.

After reading about the raw food diet, Raquel made the commitment to eat this way *within one day.* Within five months, her allergy to animals and asthma disappeared. She went to visit her mother on the Fourth of July and was able to be around her mother's dogs with no allergic reaction. In October, she experienced a brief bout of asthma, which she rode out without an inhaler, and it quickly went away. She thought it might have been a detoxification crisis.

Without counting calories or using any deprivation diet, she also lost 85 pounds!

In fifteen months, Raquel became pregnant and was able to carry the pregnancy through to term. She ate a diet of 95% raw food during her pregnancy and gained only 30 pounds, which was unusual because everyone else in her family had gained at least 60 pounds during pregnancy.

Raquel explains that her raw diet freed her from painful menstrual cramps, and she reasoned that the diet would also free her from pain in childbirth. This belief inspired her to deliver her baby at a birthing center.

Her research indicated that the use of epidurals had several negative effects, including an increased likelihood of the baby's becoming hooked on amphetamines as an adult. She became convinced that birthing was not the "emergency" that hospitals viewed it to be and that it could in fact be a sensual, wondrous experience. She proceeded to have a *pain-free delivery* lasting six hours and gave birth to a very healthy, beautiful, baby boy weighing seven pounds seven ounces.

Raquel's son, whom she fed a diet of about 80% raw food, was in perfect health his first three and a half years, never suffering from the usual childhood illnesses such as earaches, fever or even colds. Then, when he spent three months with his grandmother and was fed a cooked food diet, *he came down with ten colds!* It was one continuous illness lasting the duration of his visit.

In addition to total physical healing, Raquel experienced a sharper mental awareness, as most raw fooders report. She used to have "brain fog," feeling she was "in the clouds." Now she is down-to-earth, working full-time and going to school to become a dietician while caring for her son as a single mother.

Later, Raquel went from eating 95-100% raw to eating only 80% raw. While her illnesses never came back, she did gain back 30 of the 85 pounds. This motivated her to resume the 95-100% raw diet.

"I'm Cuban," she notes, "and we Latinos are more sensitive to cooked food than people of many other ethnicities."

Jessica: Her baby made her eat raw!

Jessica had never heard of the raw food diet. You could say that her body was her teacher — *or maybe even her unborn baby!* It was through a pregnancy plagued by morning sickness that she was forced to go raw. Her baby daughter, now three months old, was her raw food instructor. A month or two into the pregnancy she developed a strong aversion to anything cooked. It made her nauseous. Through trial and error, she began to realize that the same food eaten in its raw, natural state did not make her sick, whereas eating it cooked provoked nausea.

Prior to this pregnancy, Jessica had been on the typical American diet. Now she had to rethink her whole way of eating. She went online and discovered that there was a whole niche of society that was eating this way! Through intense research, she grew satisfied that she could obtain the essential nutrients for her baby and herself by eating a raw diet without meat or even many eggs.

This pregnancy proceeded much more smoothly than a prior one, and she had all the "happy hormones," as she put it. When she had been pregnant with her son, she had craved pizza, ice cream and Cajun chicken. With her daughter, she craved raw broccoli, bananas and kale. While she would prepare herself a smoothie, she pictured a happy little vegan girl inside of her.

She felt happy, with almost no mood swings, due to the raw diet. There was one week in which she ate cooked food and became crabby, but after resuming the raw diet, she felt fine again. Once in a while she craved eggs, which she ate cooked, and as long as she craved them, she did not get sick. If she ate them without the cravings, the nausea would return.

When pregnant with her son, Jessica had gained three times the recommended weight for pregnant women, whereas with her primarily raw pregnancy, she stayed within the recommended weight gain limits. The delivery was by Caesarian section with her son, whereas it was by unassisted homebirth with her daughter and with everything going smoothly. She had researched unassisted, at-home deliveries very well and also lived within a two-minute drive to a hospital just in case.

Jessica's daughter was born at nine pounds ten ounces. After that, Jessica would binge once in a while on cooked meat. She noticed that when this happened, her breast-fed baby would get colicky. When she ceased eating the cooked meat, the colic went away, and the baby felt great. The doctor, upon examining Jessica's baby, told her to keep on doing whatever she was doing, as the child was a "textbook case" of a healthy baby.

"I feel so happy when eating raw," says Jessica. "I used to have severe depression and took antidepressants with such bad side effects that I got even more depressed. But now I am really happy. I also have more energy." Jessica additionally credits the raw diet with her loss of weight and absence of migraines and colds.

Marie Tadič: "I've got energy for sale!"

Marie Tadič is from Croatia and has a very strong character. I met her nearly four years ago when I first went raw and took colonics (see Chapter 3), as she was my colonic therapist. Like most people, she never ate a diet of primarily raw food until health challenges arose. Her major health problems began in 1984 when she had a hysterectomy during which the doctor removed part of her colon after finding a lesion there. It never healed, and for years she struggled with a chronic infection.

In 1990, she knew she had to do something drastic when she became totally constipated for ten days, followed by bloody diarrhea. She consulted an MD who gave Marie three choices: She could take medicine for her problem; she could get reconstructive surgery every two years; or she could find a diet that would correct the condition.

She did some research and came across Herbert Shelton's book *Fasting Can Save Your Life*. When she told the doctor she was choosing this route, he warned her that she would not get enough vitamins and would lose muscle, sternly suggesting that she not practice fasting. But after she spent ten days taking in nothing but water, he checked her blood and told her that everything looked great.

She then went on to consume nothing but freshly squeezed juices for six months. She learned at the Gerson Institute in Mexico how to heal herself with raw juices and coffee enemas to cleanse the liver.

During this time, she had more energy than ever before in her life, working fourteen hours a day. Gone were her yeast infections, constipation, diarrhea and leakage from a breast. Through consuming only raw, fresh juices, she even got rid of a stubborn frozen shoulder that acupuncture, chiropractic medicine and homeopathy had not helped. She broke her six-month juice cleanse on nothing but organic grapes for six weeks.

Now that it was time to resume solid foods, Marie went to a doctor who told her to eat for her metabolic type, which required the inclusion of meat and dairy. Constipation came right back, as well as arthritis. After she got off that diet and began eating about 80% raw, these ailments quickly vanished. But because of that, she got interested in colon cleansing and, after taking a course and buying a colonic machine, started a colon-cleansing business.

She continued to eat about 80% raw for several years, but in January of 2005, she attended a lecture by Victoria and Igor Boutenko. (See Chapter 9 for more on them.) She was so impressed with Igor's strength and vigor that she committed to eating 100% raw, which she has done for some months now. She feels a huge difference between 80% raw and 100% raw. She sleeps better; her blood pressure is better than ever; and she is one "happy camper."

Having known her before, I can say *she looks younger now* eating 100% raw than she did *nearly four years ago* when I first met her (when she was eating about 80% raw), especially since she has lost inches around the waist and has more youthful skin and an even younger-looking face. She says, "I feel my body is healing the rest of the stuff that it couldn't do with a diet that was only 80% raw. I am so happy I don't have to fast and cleanse with this diet since everything I eat is good."

She also remarked that a big advantage to being 100% raw is that cooked food no longer tempts her. She doesn't salivate when smelling or seeing it; it no longer looks appealing.

Marie just turned 60, and she is working every day from 7 AM until 9 PM, both as a colonic therapist and also in two dental labs. She is fond of saying, "I have so much energy it is crazy. You want energy? I can sell it to you!" I asked her if she was like that before going raw, and she said, "No way! I was tired all the time!"

Marie also remarked on many other changes since taking the leap to 100% raw. For instance, her memory has improved. She used to be very forgetful and "in a fog." She also has more common sense and finds that when giving advice to a client, knowledge just pours out of her effortlessly. She experiences more synchronicity, earning more money because "everything just falls into place." She has also lost an allergy to metals and showed me that she was wearing a metal watch, something that formerly would have irritated her skin, making it bubble.

Spiritual changes have also occurred. "My emotions are cleansing. Emotions come up. I also get vivid dreams, and I see who needs help but doesn't ask for it, like my sister in Germany, whom I had been out of touch with. I learned she needed money, and she sent me a message in my dream. My consciousness is much higher. My consciousness is on love, sharing, service. My life is changing because I'm changing my attitude with the food I'm eating. I'm more pleasant and compassionate. I receive wisdom that was blocked before. My mind is much clearer."

Jenny Smith pre-raw in 1999 in Fiji.

Jenny Smith: Cure for twenty years of sleepwalking and obesity

Beginning in October 2000, I began a health journey, not knowing how much my life would permanently change. I was eating the typical SAD, weighing 215 pounds when I attended a health fair and learned about "fake" foods. I discovered how bad the SAD was for our bodies.

I was used to eating a diet rich in fat and refined carbohydrates and low in fiber. I learned that the answer wasn't to be found in eliminating carbs, but in dramatically reducing and/or eliminating refined, processed carbs. Thus began my journey towards health via nutrition.

In November 2000, I learned about the four deadly whites: white flour, white sugar, salt and dairy, as well as the dangers of meat. It was much too hard to give up all at once; so I started by just giving up salt. These five foods cause or contribute to over 90% of all physical problems experienced by most Americans today. I also began the popular blood type diet.

In December 2000, I eliminated white flour and used only grains acceptable for Blood Type A.

In January 2001, I eliminated sugar. In February, I switched to the Atkins diet and ate only 15-20 grams of carbs per meal, eating more eggs than chicken and fish.

In March 2001, I became a vegetarian. I also stopped eating dairy and grains, learning that these are unfit for human consumption. I had achieved a 25-pound weight loss by then.

By April 2001, with my on-going nutrition research, I became vegan, giving up all flesh and animal products. Author Erik Marcus (*Vegan: The New Ethics of Eating*) estimates that one 20-year old going vegan saves about 2,000 animals from enduring the suffering of factory farming and slaughter.

The rewards of becoming vegan included an enormous burst of self-awareness and lightness. I started drinking distilled water with added lemons. I have since discontinued this practice, as I have very little thirst eating raw foods. I soon realized that for optimal health I would need to go raw.

In May 2001, I went onto the Hallelujah Diet (85% raw/15% cooked). By this time, I had lost 42 pounds. And a most surprising thing occurred: I conceived on June 11, 2001. I was 44 with two grown children and two grandbabies! I had felt that I was infertile and had even gone two years with no prevention.

In addition, a doctor's test revealed that my HDL had risen to 48 (anything above 35 is healthy), even though it had been a mere 19 two months earlier!

By July 2001, I had lost 47 pounds. By that time, I realized I had made many choices which had led me away from the mainstream: no deodorant, toothpaste, vaccinations, drugs, television, hydrogenated oils, white flour, sugar, soda pop or processed, packaged foods. I was proud to be following a new path and wanted to convey the importance of being different to family and friends.

In March 2002, I gave birth (gaining only 10 pounds!) to a healthy baby boy. It was an 85% raw vegan pregnancy! I gave birth at home with no problems. I called the midwife an hour and fifteen minutes before the delivery of my son, using no interventions or drugs. The cord was cut two hours and 30 minutes later, which allows ample time for the baby's blood to flow back to his own body.

In January 2003, I read *Raw Eating* by A. T. Hovannessian, which finally inspired me to commit to 100% raw. What steeled my discipline was education — I kept reading books on the topic. I hosted the Boutenkos (raw food teachers) in my home in March 2004.

I have not been 100% raw 100% of the time but usually am because I do not crave cooked foods. Family food events have no hold on me. I bring my own food, and everyone leaves me alone. It is a non-issue now. My husband and son are both on board and very adapted to eating the new standard four "food groups": raw fruits, vegetables, nuts and seeds. I follow Doug Graham's protocol of 80/10/10 — 80% carbohydrates, 10% proteins and 10% fats. It works beautifully for me.

Dr. John Baby, PhD, of Calcutta University advises that any disease can be cured if proper nourishment is given to the body. He advises a raw food diet for 41 days, whereupon almost all diseases disappear. Only pure water is to be taken; all animal proteins are prohibited; and no tea, coffee or medicines are allowed.

As of July 2005, I have continued extended breastfeeding although only at night. I have plenty of milk due to healthful eating habits. It has been documented that vegan mothers have the healthiest breast milk.

To summarize the health benefits I experienced, I started at 215 pounds (Nov 2000), eventually losing a sum total of 95 pounds, dropping to 123 lbs (Nov 2003). Then I stabilized at

140 lbs (early 2004). My cholesterol tested 155 (mid-2004). My blood pressure is 125/64, and my pulse is 63 (July 2005).

In addition, 20 years of sleepwalking ended. It ceased after I eliminated animal products from my diet. I learned it was the toxic overload that caused it.

Moreover, I have enjoyed higher levels of awareness for the first time. I do not crave junk foods now, nor am I a slave to appetite. I am free of all food addictions.

Research shows that menstrual bleeding is not normal. The cleaner you become, the less likely you are to have monthly bleeding. I have not had bleeding for three or four months but am still very fertile (white mucus discharge). I will be 48 in a few weeks.

On my journey with living foods, I experienced great opposition. I was hounded by extended family most of the time: They missed their comfort foods that I used to make; they missed the holiday foods and my homemade rolls. My husband had several severe meltdowns, thinking he was going to waste away.

When my son was 19 months old, due to an anonymous report that my son's only source of "milk" was from a coconut, Child Protective Services (CPS) visited me on two separate occasions. They closed the case after his height and weight were found to be within their government chart guidelines. It seemed CPS was more concerned about the non-vaccination issue than our food habits.

I never said the family was eating raw, only that we consumed unprocessed whole foods, fruits and vegetables. I let them assume what they wanted. It left me shell-shocked and stunned. Months later, when I told a producer of the COX-TV station the story, she called and taped CPS saying they would not remove any child being fed any diet, so long as they were growing and looked healthy. It was a load off my mind. Still, there have been several cases of children being taken from vegan parents.

My son is all raw, and it is total freedom, as he never hollers like other children to eat candy or junk food. In fact, at my grandbaby's birthday party, after a piñata was broken, the kids were diving wildly for candy. My son was picking up the foreign matter and throwing it back to them. It was such a joy to see. We explained from the get-go that there would be fake food there, which should not be eaten. He never doubted our word.

Nutritional surveys have found that one in five children eat no fruit in a week, and of those who do, the average is just two portions a day rather than the recommended five. So it makes one wonder: Who should be accused of having malnourished children, SAD or raw vegan parents?

My church also became a source of frustration. I was labeled a fanatic; most women stayed away from me. One woman kept telling my husband he was too skinny; another told me I was putting my son in danger by not eating meat. These days, I keep my mouth shut. I do not feel I need to justify my diet to anyone. Besides, health advice seems not to be welcomed. We have stopped going to socials where it's centered on sugary desserts.

Most of my SAD friends left; I really cannot blame them. Most social life is centered on food. Most of my friends are on Internet chat groups or from raw support potlucks, although on occasion, I do attend raw food social gatherings.

It takes enormous power to reverse social tides. At first, I resolved to make waves, to erode ignorance. But I soon learned that it takes too much energy, and the majority do not want to leave the "herd." With more knowledge and experience, I gained confidence and pride in my lifestyle. This removed the weight from my shoulders and allowed me to act as a role model rather than a "food police cop" that family and friends grew to resent.

Those on the unconventional path are on a road less traveled. I have become quite used to it and have lately become very excited to see more and more people jump on board. I hope this information proves helpful to those coming up behind me on the path. Your health is well worth the effort.

I initially started this path when my husband asked for assistance to cure his hemorrhoids. It began many hours of nutritional study. I never resisted any part of the journey. It has been an absolute joy. I relish all that I have experienced — the good, bad and the ugly. Oh, and by the way, my husband's hemorrhoids are long gone! He joined my food regimens after his own learning curve was exhausted and only after many, many food wars. Because of my acquired knowledge, I was persistently constant, firm and unswayable — never desiring to return to the old ways.

My health journey hasn't stopped at food; I now enjoy sungazing as well, using Hira Ratan Manek's method.

Rich Smith pre-raw in 1999 in Fiji

Rich Smith:
High blood pressure reversed

Here is what Jenny's husband has to say:

For 35 years, I had very high blood pressure, sometimes as high as 200/110. The only cure I knew of was prescribed medication, which never did bring the numbers low enough. Doctors said I would need to take pills for the rest of my life. I learned medicine is a leading cause of injury and death; in fact, it's the *third leading cause of death in the US*. My wife mentioned (in the year 2000) that I could reverse my blood pressure by changing my diet and lifestyle and cure myself.

The change of belief began slowly. In October 2003, I began toying with the vegan diet, although I would periodically sneak out and eat fish. I decided to give raw food a chance in early 2005 but did not officially commit until May 2005. I realized at that point that to get rid of the pills I would need to commit 100%; so I went gung-ho on raw food. I had nothing to lose.

The results were phenomenal. In three months, I tested myself again. I would miss a day of pills, then two, then three days ... and behold, to my utter surprise, I didn't need the pills to keep blood pressure low! The raw food allowed my body to fix itself. My blood pressure is 134/76 (August 2005) and still dropping each day.

The changes did not come easily. I resisted the thought of any change. It was the hardest thing in my life to believe that I could better my health by eating different food. There were so many people eating cooked foods who seemed healthy. After I decided to participate, it was an on/off thing — raw, cooked, raw, cooked. Finally, I discovered raw food could taste "cooked," but better. My tastebuds changed, and it seemed a natural way to go. My weight was a constant worry too. I dropped down to 130 pounds but am now steady at 140 pounds. It was a big help having my wife's constant, unwavering influence. My wife's repetition was absolutely necessary for my reprogramming. The following ancient Ayurvedic proverb sums it up: "When diet is wrong, medicine is of no use. When diet is correct, medicine is of no need."

**Jenny and Rich Smith at the airport in July 2005 with
Indian sungazing guru Hira Ratan Manek**

Cherrie and Buddy pre-raw

Buddy and Cherrie B.:
A new life of living foods

In February 2002, Buddy and his wife Cherrie went to Sedona, Arizona. They had been SAD eaters all their lives. There was something about their last meal there, the chicken, that suddenly made them want to become vegetarians. When they returned to San Diego the next day, they ran into a friend. He told them he had been eating a raw vegan diet for a couple of months. They noted how radiant he looked and decided to go for this radical switch.

"Little did we know that our decision to become (raw) vegetarians would lead to vibrant health that we could have only dreamt about," writes Buddy in a page of the workbook of the workshop they now give:

> During the first four months, Cherrie lost fifty pounds, and I lost sixty pounds. Along with that, we both had what seemed like lifelong health issues disappear. Cherrie had chronic headaches, high cholesterol, poor circulation, walked with a limp because of a pinched sciatic nerve, had constant backaches, couldn't eat anything without getting sick to the stomach, had high blood pressure and much more. For me, I had high blood pressure, an irregular heartbeat, high cholesterol and a high sugar count. My body hurt so much that I couldn't even tie my shoes without pain, due to a pinched sciatic nerve.
>
> *All of these symptoms disappeared like magic without the help of any medication!* It's just like Cherrie and I started a brand new life at the age of 55! We both feel incredible and are still amazed with our results. We were living with aches and pains that felt normal, or rather, a part of life. Once we became committed to eating living foods, we soon felt the blessing of living with healthy, ache-free bodies. From our experiences, we feel certain that we have found the fountain of youth, and we'd like to share our experiences and knowledge with you.

When I met Buddy and Cherrie for lunch, they went into more detail. Cherrie had had to take 10-12 aspirins a day for headaches before going raw. She'd had such poor circulation that her feet were purple! All this went away in a matter of weeks. They showed me the amazing "before" and "after" photos. The weight loss was incredible. They both are now slender, have a raw glow and exhibit radiant skin. Best of all, they are bubbling with energy and enthusiasm.

They explained in more detail their raw journey. The first six months they went 100% raw. Then they switched to about 90% raw and went back and forth between 100% and 90% three or four times. I asked them to describe the difference they experienced between being 90% and 100% raw. They said it was a huge difference. Although the 10% of cooked food they ate would have been considered healthful by most people (baked potatoes, garbanzo beans, Asian salad with noodles, pasteurized salad dressings), they would notice the aches and pains coming back, though not as severe. It would be harder to get up and go to work. More sleep was needed to detoxify that bit of cooked food. Cherrie would find herself getting up at night with stomachaches. Worst of all, perhaps, *they lost "the raw glow."*

"When I would look at myself in the mirror, I would see an old man!" exclaimed Buddy.

They both agreed that staying 100% raw was easier than being 90-95% raw. The temptation to eat cooked food is now gone since their determination to remain 100% raw as of January 1, 2005. Now they can watch their children prepare and eat a lavish cooked Easter dinner and not be tempted. "Giving up cooked food is easier than giving up cigarettes," said Buddy, a former smoker who quit years before going raw. Cherrie even has to prepare cooked food as part of her work but is not tempted to eat even a bite.

One of the best things about being 100% raw, they both agreed, was that the whole food addiction was gone from their psyche. When eating cooked food, they would often ponder about what they were going to eat, where they were going to eat and so forth. Now they just eat very simply and barely even think about food. They desire less and less food and eat very little, occasionally dining at the local raw restaurant for some fancy gourmet variety.

"You get really free when you flop over to 100% raw," remarked Buddy. And they both need very little sleep: Cherrie sleeps only six hours a night, and Buddy sleeps only four to five hours a night!

Like many raw converts, they want to tell the world because they feel so fantastic at the age of 58. They devote much of their free time to giving workshops, teaching others why and how to make the switch to living foods. People affectionately call them "Rawdaddy" and "Rawmomma." Recently when I ran into the couple at the local food co-op, I noticed that Cherrie's hair had grown out dark, the gray having disappeared.

Cherrie and Buddy raw

Allen: Live food for bodybuilding and higher consciousness

Allen is my husband, who was at first reluctant to eat a raw diet. He had to, by default, because I was the only one who would prepare food. Within weeks, he was absolutely astounded by the results. I didn't have to do any convincing. The experience of the raw diet spoke for itself. Although he has always taken good care of himself, he looks more youthful than ever with the "raw glow." In fact, people often mistake him for mid-30s although he is 54. Here is his story in his own words:

My experience is that cooked food stresses out the immune system. It takes a lot of energy that can be used for consciousness. I am interested in higher consciousness, and I've noticed that cooked food lowers my consciousness level. I've noticed that living food makes it so easy to absorb nutrients that energy can go to the higher centers of awareness so I can experience bliss. I feel blissful, especially when I am 100% raw.

I am also a bodybuilder. I've noticed that on the raw diet I'm actually stronger than when I was spending hundreds of dollars a month on strength-enhancing nutrients. Now that I'm off cooked foods, I'm actually stronger than when I spent more than a car payment a month on bodybuilding supplements.

Initially I was afraid of weight loss, and with good reason, because I lost thirty pounds in just six weeks. Also, I was originally afraid that I would not get enough protein, and it was hard for me to give up my protein powders, which I drank several times a day. When I replaced them with a dehydrated, but still living, green grass powder, I was amazed that I actually got stronger and could lift heavier weights than when I ate [processed] whey protein! After some time, I regained ten of the thirty pounds I lost. I never regained the other 20 pounds of muscle because I don't work out that much anymore. Yet, even though I rarely work out these days, I am still stronger than when I took protein supplements — whey protein — and worked out four times a week! I have heard that this is because the muscles grow back with better building blocks and, though they may not be as bulky, they are superior.

Mentally, I am less forgetful. I used to have a very bad memory. It has also greatly reduced my dyslexia. It is much easier to read now.

Emotionally, I experience more peace. I think that raw food is conducive to recognizing our true, original, natural state of consciousness, which is blissful, harmonious and loving. Eating live food is simply allowing us to experience our true nature. It isn't giving us any more than who we are; it simply allows us to experience more readily who we are because there are fewer detoxifying processes involved than with cooked food.

The main thing about this diet is that I feel better. Even when I am going through a detox, I have more energy than I used to when eating cooked food.

Whenever I backslide by eating cooked food, even one meal, I get constipated. I feel tired. But when I stick to the raw diet, I feel happier, more vital, more energetic, more life force flowing through me, more creative and more youthful. This gives me the inspiration to discipline my mind and say no to dead, life-force-draining food and eat only live food.

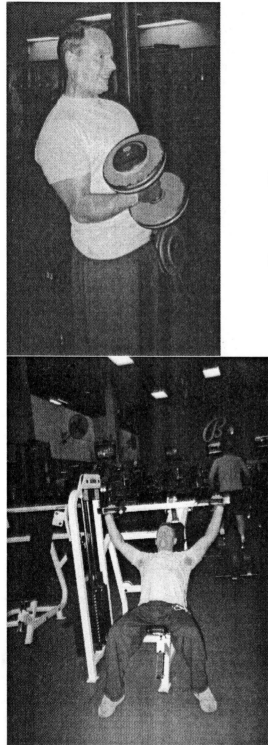

Allen at the gym in 2005 after more than three years on raw foods performs his biceps curls (left) and presses 280 pounds (below), something he couldn't do on a cooked food diet.

Dana Pettaway in Detroit at 160 pounds pre-raw in 2002

Dana Pettaway: Increased awareness and freedom from vices

Dana Pettaway just turned 36; yet if she had told me she was 25, I would have believed it. Before entering the world of raw food, she had been vegan for a couple of years, and the second year she decided to cut back on her food, losing 30 pounds. She was wondering how she would keep it off when, a year ago, she saw model Carol Alt on a TV show teaching the benefits of a live food diet. Dana began her journey into raw foods at that time, the initial motive being vanity. Little did she realize that she was about to embark on a diet that would also change her very personality!

She wisely felt the need to educate herself, attending seminars and raw food preparation classes and beginning to realize there was a whole lot more to food than she had thought. As she dug deeper into the rabbit hole of nutrition and health issues, she became increasingly aware of fasting, cleansing, tinctures and food politics, such as the controversies surrounding organic and genetically modified food, the ethics of eating honey, as well as issues relating to the environment.

She realized that cleansing the inner environment wasn't enough: The outer environment also had to be clean if we are to be healthy. She began to recycle for the first time in her life. She became much more discriminating about the people she hung out with, realizing that negative people influenced her for the worse. "The more raw I've become, the more I realize I can choose to omit those negative forces from my life."

She began to hold herself accountable for violating what she now felt to be wrong, such as throwing out plastics or eating honey that had been taken away from bees that were forced to eat sugar water instead of the honey they produced.

"I changed my whole attitude and consciousness. I decided to be as pure and raw as I can be — to be *conscious, humane and not just healthy*." She started to connect with like-minded people in the local raw food community in San Diego.

Dana quickly became 100% raw and felt that anything less was not enough. Not only did she find the weight very easy to keep off, but also, to her amazement, the craving for cigarettes disappeared in a matter of weeks. She explained that while she had stopped smoking a few years prior to that, she had still craved cigarettes, especially if someone nearby was smoking. She would even have dreams that she was smoking and would wake up in sweats over the anxiety of this recurring temptation.

"Now," she says, with a look of great relief, "the idea of smoking disgusts me."

Other vices left her consciousness. She used to partake of organic wine, thinking, "Well, this is raw, after all." But even after just one glass, she woke up with puffy skin and a slight hangover. "Why am I doing this?" she thought. She quickly stopped.

Dana, like many others, found coffee harder to give up than cooked food; so she decided to at least use agave nectar (a sweetener from cactus) instead of sugar and nut milk instead of cream. But after six months of eating raw, even this desire stopped, and she is no longer tempted by coffee. She also experienced no withdrawal symptoms!

In addition to the ease of keeping trim, Dana found a multitude of other health benefits to live food. "I felt after a month that I had found the Holy Grail."

Her long struggle with acne vanished, as did severe hemorrhoids. She acquired tons of energy, as well as the light feeling everyone who goes 100% raw gets. She also got more clarity of mind. "I became more aware of my surroundings and more clear as to my focus and life path."

She also got her son to eat raw food. "He eats a lot of the foods the other kids eat, but raw. He doesn't even know it!"

Her four-year-old is about 70% raw, eating tofu and vegan "meat" as part of his cooked food.

Her mother was a tougher convert, often calling Dana a "raw Nazi." But Dana lovingly prepared her mom some raw dishes and fresh juice from time to time, perhaps replacing only three of her mom's meals per week with raw goodies. To her mother's surprise, she lost 21 pounds in one year *only because of this*! Most amazingly, her mom also stopped drinking coffee.

When I first met her at a raw potluck, she announced her intention to go at least 80% raw after completing a cleansing fast she was on. When I later saw her again at the monthly potlucks, she had gone 100% raw.

Like many raw fooders, Dana wants to help spread the word about this marvelous lifestyle, although she no longer considers herself a "raw Nazi." Like others, she has learned not to be as pushy as she was initially.

"Now I think it's more about spreading awareness. If people want to own that, it's fine. Some are just not ready."

Dana is actively involved in organizing a monthly local raw food potluck. She is also writing a local raw food guide with some of the recipes and pointers she has learned, such as getting kids to eat raw food. In addition, she has started her own business selling gourmet raw food. (You can find her web site at www.theraway.com.)

"I want to become a better person and surround myself with more positive people."

Dana Pettaway, after 1 year raw, enters the pool with son Kyu, age 4, in October 2005

Tim: An awakening
of the mind and creativity

Tim has been a 100% live food vegan for about five years. Before that, he ate the SAD "to the max." As a young, single, working man, he fit the standard profile of the fast-food junkie, even a connoisseur, stopping at MacDonald's since they had the best fries and then popping over to Wendy's to get the best burgers. He claims he was in "fast-food heaven." But fast-food heaven soon turned into "health hell."

His health began a rapid decline after the stresses of being exposed to PVC pipe glue at work and also having to survive on canned foods during a three-month electricity outage following Hurricane Andrew in 1992. The toxic overload incurred by the hurricane experience led to chronic sinus infections, exacerbated by cheese and wheat allergies.

In 1998, at the age of only 34, he was at "death's door," suffering from chronic fatigue, listlessness, and ear, kidney and sinus infections that had grown worse and worse. He was 55 pounds overweight.

Once he had an ear infection that was so bad that his eardrums burst, oozing pus. Experiencing the worst pain of his life, he went to a hospital emergency room.

The doctors struggled to find an antibiotic that was strong enough: It took four tries and 1½ months to quell the infection. In the meantime, his liver and kidneys went into overload trying to detoxify all the debris from the infection, coupled with other toxins he had accumulated, including residues of the antibiotics themselves. His healthful bacteria having been killed by the antibiotics, his chronic fatigue worsened.

Since his serum cholesterol was 285, he was put on Lipitor, a cholesterol-lowering drug. A friend who worked at the hospital said that since his liver was shot, he could die from taking this medication. Tim was so disturbed that his doctor hadn't even tested his liver before prescribing the drug that he became afraid of drug therapy. He looked everywhere for a naturopathic physician, but because the practice was not legal in Florida, he had to ask around discreetly.

Finally, a friend referred Tim to her teacher at a massage therapy school. He spoke with her for just two hours, but the encounter changed his life. She empowered him with total responsibility for his own health. Under her guidance, he did a liver cleanse (see Glossary) and a two-week fast, cut out red meat and sugar, and took herbs.

He gradually got better as he looked for a health-conscious girlfriend. He got involved with a vegan woman who encouraged him to get off all animal products. But as he read *Nature's First Law: The Raw Food Diet*, he felt that they should be not only vegans, but also raw. After two weeks on the diet, they both became totally convinced.

Tim lost the last 25 pounds that he couldn't lose on the cooked diet. With a gradual, full detox, he even slimmed down to 127 pounds. People were now concerned that he was too skinny. Although he "looked like hell" for three or four months, *he felt fantastic*, better than he had ever felt before in his life! Most of the weight came back with healthy, rebuilt tissue, leveling off at a comfortable 145 pounds.

"My creativity skyrocketed," said Tim. He started writing songs about raw food. As he describes it, "I felt I wasn't even writing but was just a vessel. I was tapping into a higher source. I woke up with songs in my head." A former band member, he had had creative flows before but *nothing like this*.

Tim even experimented with starting a raw food restaurant but later decided not to work so many hours after so recently regaining his health. Moreover, the community's consciousness didn't seem ready to support a raw food restaurant at the time.

Tim's mental clarity also went through the roof. Before, he hadn't read much at all. After reading a few pages, he would struggle to comprehend the material, even having to reread it. So he would put the book down and watch TV instead.

After going raw, he *couldn't stop* reading! His thirst for knowledge compelled him to devour books cover-to-cover; thus he absorbed knowledge on all manner of subjects.

He now owns a car powered by used restaurant vegetable oil as a result of information gleaned from one of his books. He has become a self-taught expert on composting after reading *The Humanure Handbook*, as well as on solar and wind power.

He also learned the importance of re-mineralizing plants and soil by reading *Sea Energy Agriculture* by Maynard Murray. He got his dying citrus trees to produce wonderful fruit once again by employing methods taught in that book.

Annette Larkins: Super health at 63

Just get onto the Internet and click on www.annette larkins.com to see more photos of what being raw for decades can do for a woman! Annette's health journey, as told in her booklets *Journey to Health I & II*, began when she was 21.

Annette was born in 1942 to a family of omnivores. As an African American reared in the South, she grew up on "soul food," consisting of lots of big, greasy, Sunday dinners. She was raised on chitlings, fatback, fried chicken and the like.

She very abruptly diverted from this path one day in 1963 while she was taking some pork chops out of the freezer. She intuitively felt, "If I eat these, I will throw up." At that moment, what she called a metamorphosis took place inside of her, and she never again wanted to consume animal flesh of any kind.

Later, when she announced to her husband, who at that time owned a butcher shop, that she had not eaten any animal flesh in two weeks, he looked at her perplexedly and asked, "What's wrong, honey? Do you need to see a doctor?"

Her rationale for becoming vegetarian had nothing to do with health but rather inner transformation. Being unaware of the health implications, she continued fixing meat dishes for her husband and two sons while preparing vegetarian dishes for herself.

The next juncture of her journey took place as a result of being a self-described bibliophile. She has a personal library of 5,000 books in all sorts of genres! She discovered that refined sugar and flour deplete the body of micronutrients, so she gave them up. Later on, she also gave up dairy after learning that it creates phlegm.

Still further on, she read books by Ann Wigmore and Viktoras Kulvinskas about raw food. It took some time for her to make the switch because she grew tired of eating salads. She said to herself, "Girl, you have got to put some *zeal* into this raw *deal!*" This led her to experiment and devise creative recipes reminiscent of the Southern soul food she'd been raised on, foods like okra, fried green tomatoes, cornbread and collard greens.

As she became 100% raw at the age of 42, Annette noticed gradual changes. Having been vegetarian for 21 years, she had commenced the raw diet with pretty good health already so her health did not change radically. But she observed that what had already been *good* became *great*. For example, her weight became balanced, with no more yoyo-ing. Her small waistline got smaller. Her memory became remarkable, and her awareness heightened. Her mental focus increased, and her thoughts became clearer.

When eating cooked food, she would get painful cramps the first day of her period, so bad that she would have to stay in bed for a day. These went away on the raw diet. Five or six years after going raw, she noted that she had missed her period for three months and hoped she was not pregnant. She found that instead she was going through menopause. She had absolutely none of the typical symptoms: no weight gain, emotional distress, insomnia, night sweats or memory loss. She has absolutely no idea what a hot flash feels like!

At family gatherings, her family members would make fun of her for refusing to partake of their traditional food. She never minded the teasing but stuck to what she knew was best. Sadly, she now sees who had "the last laugh," so to speak, as many of these people are quite ill with heart attacks, strokes, hypertension and diabetes. Annette, however, remains youthful and without a single health complaint! She is in super health despite inheriting what many would consider "bad genes": Her mom died of breast cancer at the age of 47, and her grandmother also died of breast cancer at the age of 36.

Many people would not have liked to continue living with a spouse who remained on the omnivorous path. During her first 18 years as a strict vegetarian, Annette continued making meat dishes for her husband despite loathing the smell of cooked flesh. When he finally announced his intention to become vegetarian, she proclaimed, "Okay, but if you go back to eating meat, you must cook your own food."

He did end up going back to eating meat and took charge of his own food at that time. When, three years later, Annette decided to eat her food raw, at least she no longer had to cook for him.

Annette compared the differences to being in a marriage with political differences. "There is much more to my husband than what he eats." They will soon celebrate their 47th year of marriage, and she feels very fortunate to have him as her husband, as he still treats her like a queen.

Now, however, her husband fervently wishes he had switched to her diet because his health is deteriorating, whereas hers is not. "Sadly," she said of her beloved husband, "he's *hooked on cooked.*"

Annette recently was given a free blood analysis by a nutritionist who was curious to see the blood of a live fooder. The nutritionist announced to everyone at the health fair that this was the most perfect blood she had ever seen! There were no clumps whatsoever, and all cells were perfectly formed. Her blood pressure was also "like that of a child."

Annette's energy, enthusiasm and curiosity are also like those of a child! Perhaps because her health is so great, she has absolutely no fatigue, aches or pains that could slow her down. If you go to the biography section of her web site, you will be amazed at how much energy the woman has. She said to me, "If I could bottle my energy and sell it, I would be a millionaire."

She is engaged in reading, lecturing on raw food, assembling her own computers, creating her own greeting cards, sewing her own clothes, growing her own garden food and publishing her own booklets on raw eating. Recently she published a DVD entitled, "Annette's Raw Kitchen," in which she shows how she prepares her own comfort foods, including raw versions of some of the Southern soul foods she grew up on. She unpretentiously proclaims, "I'm not a chef. You won't see me throwing around any knives. If I can do this, so can you!"

She also produced a twelve-series show on a local cable TV station called, "Health Alternatives with Living Foods," which she based her DVD upon. (Her booklets and DVD are for sale on her web site.)

Annette sees herself as someone who introduces the raw diet to others. If they want to know more about the science behind it, they can read a different book. But her booklets, which include recipes, are enough to get people started.

She says the African American diet is heavily laden with fat and grease because the slaves were given only table scraps from their masters. Now it is time for them to enter the "kingdom of living foods." Her message to the African American community is, "We no longer have shackles on wrists and ankles. Now we need to let go of the *shackles of the mind.*"

A
N
N
E
T
T
E

L
A
R
K
I
N
S

A
T

6
3

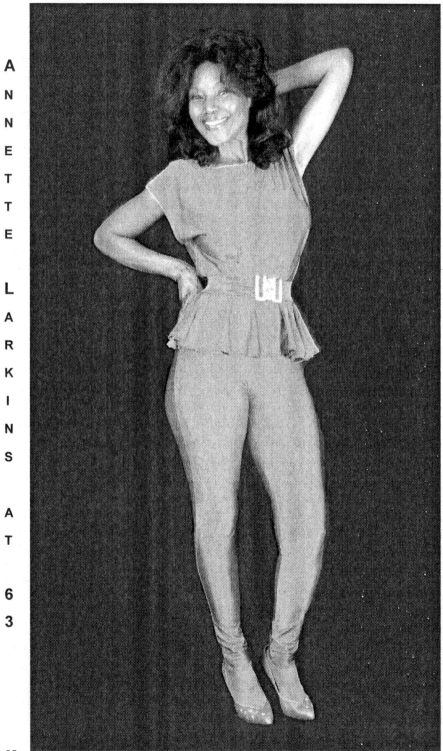

Mike McCright: Raw for life

I am Mike McCright. I am 47 and have been raw for about 3½ years. I remember reading an old *Organic Gardening* magazine about 25 years ago and seeing a picture of a guy in his garden; he looked about 19 — tall, lanky and healthy-looking. The caption read that he ate all of his food raw. It kept him fit and young-looking. He was 30 years old! That simmered in my mental file for a couple of decades.

I was having lunch at a gardening seminar in October 2001. I sat across from a vibrantly healthy man in his mid-60s. He was very energetic, more than any other man his age I had ever seen. He attributed his health to eating only raw foods. He had a girlfriend of about 60 who had gone raw soon after meeting him several months before. She had been on over a dozen prescription drugs for over three years. During the first six months of being raw, she dropped them all, as they were no longer needed. She dropped 40 pounds to boot!

I felt that it was time for change in my life. I was trying to eat more healthfully to keep my temple clean. Being reminded about that vibrant increase in health tipped the scale. I went raw after that meal.

I thought it wise to have a transition period; mine lasted two weeks. I could not then, nor now, mix cooked and raw. Cooked food is too addictive. I am currently over 95% raw, usually falling down in annual family events like Christmas and Thanksgiving.

I started out eating almost exclusively fruit. I thought, "This is great, dessert for all meals!" I noticed after about three weeks that my odors became less. I previously had bad breath almost constantly. My bad breath disappeared; my foot odor disappeared; my normal body odor largely went away; even bathroom odors were greatly diminished. I had loads of energy, no afternoon lull. I felt strong and vibrant. I ate lots of food, twice as much as before. While eating all the food I wanted, I was losing five pounds a week.

I went home to my mom's house for Christmas and found that I had little willpower around my family. I ate what everyone else was eating after the first day and got very sick; I felt awful!

I had introduced all those food toxins into my body after purifying it and let down my intestinal defenses. I also put on 15 pounds over the few days I was home. Eating cooked food then and now causes me to put on weight extremely fast.

I came back from my mom's house, went raw again, and quickly lost the 15 pounds and a few more. My body settled on a 25-pound loss — 190 pounds after three months mainly raw. Over the next few months, I drifted down another 10 pounds. My weight has gone up and down all my life but is stable at around 180 pounds so long as I remain 100% raw.

After a couple of months of eating only fruit, I began to notice that my mouth felt different. By the third month, it was noticeably different, like my teeth were getting looser. I met other raw fooders and asked a guy who had been raw for three years about my mouth and teeth.

He explained to me that I needed greens to get the minerals I needed; fruit alone was not cutting it. I started with supplements for a boost, bought a nice juicer and started juicing greens. I also learned of the variety of wild greens in my yard and began juicing them too. Drinking a quart or more of wild green juice was like taking a power pill. I could not believe that the weeds I was composting were so good for you!

When I first began to eat greens, I didn't like them or desire them. I asked my new roommate who had been raw for five years about that. He explained that the salt I was using in my food was satisfying my need for sodium, which greens are high in. I stopped using salt and soon began to desire greens.

I have learned that my body needs plenty of greens and some fruit. If I eat too much fruit, I will have created an acidic environment in my mouth where gum disease can flourish. If I eat plenty of greens, that acidic environment will turn alkaline, and any gum disease will stop entirely.

Now when I floss, I never get any blood. The bacteria that caused my gums to bleed when flossing and slowly recede moved out and don't live there anymore! I had gum disease for almost 30 years. Now it is gone.

Salads are great, but I have plenty of non-sweet fruit in them like tomatoes, peppers, squash and cucumber. They are fruit, not *greens*.

To get my quota of greens, I make a green drink every morning, usually of dried herbs and sometimes of wild greens as well. I also eat a salad in the afternoon and a small amount of fruit (like an apple lately) and a handful of nuts in the morning.

Early on, I ate large volumes of food to get the nutrition I needed. My body is much more efficient now, and I eat much less than the average person. If I eat more, I get fat. If I eat cooked foods more than an occasional small portion, I get sick and fat in a hurry.

I am raw for life. There is no reason to return to cooked foods. I am much healthier now than I was three years ago. Being raw was and is part of a whole new turn in my life. I am much healthier now and more outdoorsy. I get more sun and am much more active, more intuitive and much more spiritual.

I wish you well on your path. I am glad *mine* changed.

Mike McCright in June 2004 after 2½ years 95% raw

Amy Schrift: Total life makeover

Amy Schrift converted to a 100% raw diet at the age of 37 a couple of years ago. Within one year, she noticed that her skin became clear and clean of blemishes, and she no longer wore any make-up. There was no longer bloating, gas and discomfort after meals. She no longer had colds, congestion or clogged nasal passages.

She stopped wearing the contact lenses that she had worn for twenty years, and her eyes have improved substantially, from -4.75 to -2.00 in less than two years. Her eliminations improved to the point of effortlessness. She stopped having menstrual bleeding, which is not uncommon among serious raw fooders and is actually a sign of health in a well-nourished female. She experienced greater clarity of mind, peace, calm and feelings of joy and lightness of being. She is the only one of five siblings, all close in age, who is pain-free.

Perhaps most of all, however, was the complete change of lifestyle she underwent. Eating raw brought her a sense of yearning to be closer to nature, and she simplified her life to focus on what was really meaningful and important to her.

Amy had lived in New York City, working as a musician performing a lot of gigs in restaurants that reciprocated by giving her free meals. She had begun to observe how she felt after eating various foods and stopped eating bread and pasta, noting the ill effects of wheat.

After reading a magazine article on the raw food diet, she realized this was the way to go and started attending support groups. Initially she ate the raw gourmet dishes for that full "cooked" feeling, but eventually she began to eat lighter and lighter "mono-meals" consisting of eating one food at a time and then perhaps a second food later.

She now eats fruit during the day, picked fresh from trees that she forages from when possible, and eats greens and occasional seeds in the evening. "I am basically hydrating myself with my food choices and spend as much time outdoors in the sun and fresh air as possible, which may be our most important sources of nutrition."

"Being raw has made me super aware of my environment, aware of the mind-body-spirit connection. When I eat something, I try to feel the sensations it brings me on all levels."

Many changes took place after Amy switched to a raw diet. She educated herself on how to safely select wild greens, which are high in minerals, and began foraging for wild greens in New York City parks. She noticed that body odor from toxic cooked food was gone and felt the need to shower less frequently. She started sleeping on the floor, finding it more healthful for the circulation than a mattress. She brushes her teeth without toothpaste.

She began doing yoga, meditation and sungazing for the first three hours of every morning. Formerly an avid swimmer, she stopped swimming due to the toxic chlorine. She eagerly devoured spiritual books. Despite being a musician, she stopped listening to recorded music so that she could experience deeper levels of silence and the sounds of nature to "tune in rather than tune out."

After her body cleansed, Amy realized that New York was too toxic, and she is currently moving to Costa Rica, where she will build her own nontoxic home on some land she bought. There she intends to live a simple life right in the midst of nature.

Amy points out, "I am healthy, not because of what I eat, but in spite of what I eat." She is convinced that eating cooked food and nonfoods is a major cause of illness, and even on a diet solely of raw foods, less is more.

She canceled her health insurance policy. "My health insurance is what I put into my mouth every day. What's yours?" she will ask others. She points out that people will even take a job they do not like just for the health insurance benefits, not realizing that they can take full responsibility for their own health!

Amy's enthusiasm for raw food is quite contagious. She converted several members of her extended family and has had a positive influence on her young nieces and nephews, who love to tell her how many fruits and vegetables they are eating.

"I'm definitely passionate about extolling the virtues of a healthy, living foods lifestyle. It's not just about the food; it's about rediscovering our earth connection, communing with nature, moving our bodies and getting to the essence of who we really are."

Amy Schrift in Costa Rica in 2005

Sandra Schrift: Young at 68

Amy's mother Sandra caught on within months. Sandra, who is 68, went raw about 1½ years ago. After she made the switch to 100% raw, she lost 17 pounds, and her stomach flattened. Her osteoarthritis of the knee and hip is greatly reduced. People who hadn't seen her in a while asked what she had been doing; was there a new love in her life? Where did the sparkle and glow come from? She also got the courage to stop wearing make-up. She experienced more energy and a need for less sleep.

As a speaker's coach, Sandra often has to eat out. She has found a simple way to make it work. She calls the chef in advance and asks him to have a dish of uncooked salad and vegetables ready.

In her words, "I have been 95% raw since July 2004. I have more energy, need less sleep, and have healthier looking skin. People say I have a glow in my face and eyes. This is a great way to diet. I lost 15 pounds and holding — no more bloat or gas. And mostly, I think I have a way of life that permeates everything I do and how I think about my environment and my community — more gentle and caring."

Photo by Joe Peiri

Sandra Schrift in October 2005

**Jackie Nash pre-raw in 2003 at age 68
with 10-years-raw Bob Avery at age 56**

Jackie Nash: Lost 45 pounds and became active at 69

Prior to giving up cooked food, I was starting to feel my nearly 69 years: My cholesterol was high enough that I was urged to take statins; I could barely climb one flight of stairs without frequent rests; and running for a bus for more than a few yards left me red in the face and fighting for breath.

I was working approximately 30 hours a week, and after a day's work, I could not stay awake past 7 PM. My life consisted mostly of working and sleeping. The heat and humidity of Philadelphia, and then of Toledo, kept me dreading summertime when my energy would drain away in the effort to cool myself.

I started eating raw at the end of April 2004. I weighed in at that time at 165 pounds. Now, a year later, eating as much as I wish, I weigh in at *a steady 120 pounds*! My dress size is a 6/8 (formerly 16/18), depending on the vendor. My cholesterol is acceptable to my demanding doctor; climbing stairs is a whole lot easier; and I am able to run for a bus for a considerable distance without any noticeable effect.

Most of the time I have plenty of energy left at the end of the day and am able to engage in whatever activities I wish, even until midnight when I make myself go to bed in preparation for an early morning start.

There have been two problem areas in this transitional period. For several months in the beginning, I was unwell for days at a time from the detoxification to which my body was subjecting me. I survived these periods without resorting to my old dietary habits because I felt so marvelous in between these bouts of misery.

The other downside is that my excess weight fell off me so quickly that my body decided I didn't need all the bone density that had been previously needed to support all the extra toxic tissue. Had I known this in advance, I would have engaged in weight-bearing exercises at the beginning of my raw-food adventure.

I am currently attending a gym, under my doctor's orders, and spending an hour four times a week working on the treadmill and also building up my atrophied muscles, their true condition being visible now that there is no fat tissue to hide them, so that they will, in turn, pull on and strengthen the bones they are attached to. I go early in the morning before work and find that the combination of diet and exercise is a powerful source of increased daily energy.

Twenty-five minutes of my gym time is devoted to the treadmill. With all of its wonderful dials before me, I find I am spending most of that time at a fast walk of 4.3 miles per hour and am even starting to jog — half a mile at a time, so far — and am improving rapidly. This is remarkable to me because my bronchial tubes were severely damaged by a serious illness in my late teens, contributing in large part to my lifelong short-ness of breath.

It was while pushing myself to jog, alternating in the begin-ning with 10 steps of jogging to 60 steps of walking, that I felt something deep in my chest give way, and all of a sudden I could take a full breath, something I had not experienced for over 50 years! Sometimes I stop whatever I am doing and inhale deeply, just for the sheer pleasure it gives me to be able to do it. This development, I assure you, would not have occurred had I not been a raw fooder for the previous nine months that led up to it.

Since I did not have any serious or life-threatening physical conditions before April 2004, it is possible that none of the above seems very dramatic. However, the quality of my life has increased immeasurably, even to such a minor effect as not be-ing bothered nearly as much by heat and humidity. Oh, I forgot to say that my persistent minor allergies are either gone or are much improved. I feel mentally much healthier and positive.

For all the reasons above and also because my tastebuds have come back to life, I love my new raw food lifestyle.

Jackie Nash in the summer of 2005, after 1 year raw, enjoying the flowers at the Toledo Botanical Garden

Paula Wood pre-raw in June 2003

Paula Wood: Thyroid removal no longer needed

On September 11, 2003, I was diagnosed with cancerous tumors on my thyroid. My naturopath said I needed to have my thyroid removed immediately, possibly followed up with radio-active iodine. I had a surgery scheduled for mid-October.

Finally, about two weeks before the surgery, I told my parents and sister. You see, I didn't want to cause worry until I knew which road I was going to take, as my mother had been diagnosed with breast cancer 6 weeks before my own diagnosis.

As each day passed, and I drew closer to surgery, I became more and more distressed. After spending three days straight crying, I woke the morning of the surgery. I called at 9 AM (1½ hours before surgery, mind you) and canceled. I knew that surgery and a lifetime dependency on hormone medication was not the answer for me. At the time I was aware of no alternatives.

I ended up scheduling a second surgery, which I canceled about one week before the date. The tumor was about the size of a ping-pong ball and very visible to the human eye. I was scared to death.

Finally, I met my health coach (and now very dear friend), Arnoux Goran. Arnoux was a friend of a friend. I knew he taught about raw food. I went to a holiday/New Year's party and, after talking to him, made the decision to do my first cleanse. He agreed to coach me through it.

I began eating 100% raw food and cleansing on January 19, 2004. My first commitment was to eat raw food for the duration of the cleanse and a few weeks afterward.

I did a lot of reading, as suggested by my coach, and had many long talks about nutrients and the way my body should be working. After two weeks, I had committed to six months on raw food. I was *totally loving it*! At the end of the cleanse, I knew I could easily commit to one year of 100% raw food.

I extended the cleanse 9 days; so it was 39 days total. I lost 51 pounds, and the tumor was no longer visible to the naked eye — unless I tilted my head back; then you could see a little knob.

It was so awesome! I have an ultrasound done every three months to measure the progress. I believe that once I purge the underlying emotions that created the dis-ease within my body, the tumor will go away completely!

I am still 100% raw vegan. At this point, I am committed for the rest of my life. It's hard to fathom what I used to put into my body, and I have no desire ever to do that again!

My eleven-year-old son still eats the SAD. I am troubled about this and hope that one day he will see the light, so to speak, and stop being so stubborn. (He gets it from his mom!)

I have started a business with three colleagues, and my web site is www.iamhealthyinc.com.

Paula Wood raw in March 2004

Samara Christy pre-raw

Samara Christy: Lost weight, yet no surgery needed for loose skin

My name is Samara Christy; I am age 57, and I have been, like many others, overweight for most of my life. As I got older, my inability to lose weight got increasingly worse. I would try diet after diet with my friends; they would lose 30-40 pounds, and I would lose about ten. Then, in a few months, I would return to my original weight, and then, over a period of about six months, I would gain an additional ten to twenty pounds.

What made matters worse was that I had been a health care practitioner for more than 25 years, and I was truly embarrassed and humiliated by my inability to lose weight. My heart would break when my clients, all meaning to be helpful, would hand me yet another diet to try. In retaliation, I threatened to wear to the healing center my super size tee shirt over my 200-lb-plus body that said, "I fought anorexia and won."

I often made jokes about my weight in an attempt to cover up my pain. When my fiancé, now husband, Ken and I were first dating, he took me on a wonderful vacation to Puerto Vallarta. We had a wonderful time as we sat on the beach and sipped margaritas as we watched the sun set so magnificently, as only Puerto Vallarta is famous for. I was in love. As my fiancé and I looked dreamily into each other's eyes while we ate our sumptuous dinners, I shared my concerns that what we were eating was more than I usually ate and that I would probably gain weight on this trip. Ken looked at me incredulously and blurted out, "That's impossible!"

You see, to support me in losing weight, we would order one lunch or one dinner and ask for another plate so that we could split our meal. In fact, we would split all our meals on that trip. Because I did not speak the language, and Ken spoke enough Spanish, we agreed that he would carry all the cash and pay for everything. So my fiancé knew everything that I ate because he was the only one with the money to buy anything.

When we returned from our vacation, we both weighed in on our first morning home. He had lost eight pounds, and my worst fears had been realized; I had gained five. My fiancé apologized to me, saying that he had a confession to make — that all those nights that we were dating and that we had been splitting our meals, he had just assumed that I must have been eating when I went home from our dates.

Ouch! That really hurt! Don't get me wrong, my fiancé truly loved me in spite of my weight, but as you know, unless you have lived it, you don't fully understand it.

Finally, I just gave up (see photo) and resigned myself that this was going to be my fate. I still continued to pray, "God, you have had an answer for everything else in my life, why not the weight? There just has got to be an answer — somewhere!"

Soon, a group of clients started coming to me, many of them, like me, over fifty and overweight. This group was in a ten-week program, and they all lost about 25–30 lbs in three months. Well, that really got my attention, and I wanted to meet this guy who taught that class. His name is Arnoux. He may be contacted at www.iamhealthyinc.com.

He was 27 years old at the time and looked about nineteen. I began having second thoughts. What could this kid teach me? Then I remembered my wonderfully thin clients. I immediately arranged to meet with him.

Arnoux shared with me the amazing story of how he had come to embrace this program. It was hard to imagine that this handsome, articulate man/boy was born to deaf parents who were drug addicts. As a result of their drug addition, Arnoux's health was seriously compromised. Though he was never over-weight, he shared with me that his doctors didn't give him long to live.

As Arnoux went from doctor to doctor, desperately looking for help, he finally discovered the raw food program and went on to heal every single one of his many ailments. Then he went on to teach what he knew to help others by creating the "How God Eats" course and to make himself available as a raw food coach. His clients began to get radiantly healthy, and his hopelessly overweight and over-fifty women began to lose weight and to keep it off.

Arnoux asked me to trust him; so I decided to give his program a try. After all, what did I have to lose? — about eighty pounds to be exact. So I plunged headlong into the world of raw foods, and to my shock, I too lost ten pounds the very first month.

What happened next was even more amazing. My energy level just shot through the roof! My food before, though healthy, had left me feeling tired all the time. I know that experts preach that exercise is key, but how do you exercise when you barely have enough energy to get though your day?

After a month on raw foods, I had energy to burn, and I began going to Curves, where at first I could only get halfway around their circuit. Six months into raw foods, the Curves owner offered me a job there, telling me that people were asking when I worked out because they found me supportive and inspiring, and they wanted to work out with me.

To my delight, the raw foods program worked. I lost 50 lbs in the first 5½ months, and I am still losing. I am 5'4", and I weighed 213 lbs. I weighed 163 lbs when the "after" picture was taken. Not only did I lose the weight, but I am also in glowing health. To my amazement, the loose skin that many women who have lost a lot of weight have to have surgically removed didn't happen to me or to any of the other raw fooders that I met. We are all living proof that all the enzymes in raw foods completely change your skin to yummy.

Arnoux also has several techniques designed to handle the emotional reasons people can't lose weight, and these techniques are contained in the complete package, "The Total Health and Weight Loss Package."

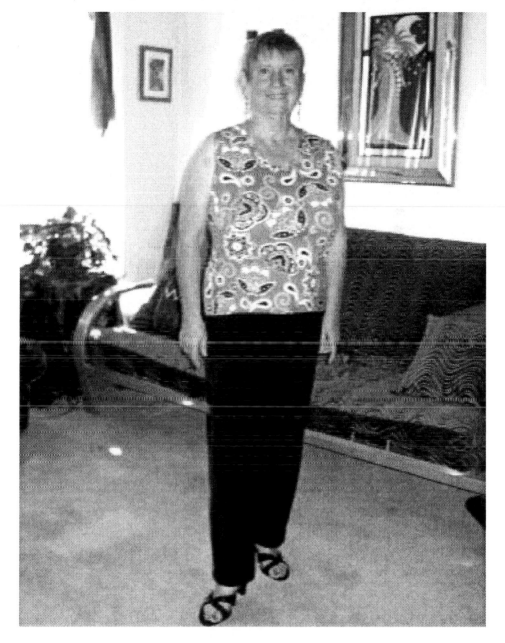

Samara Christy raw

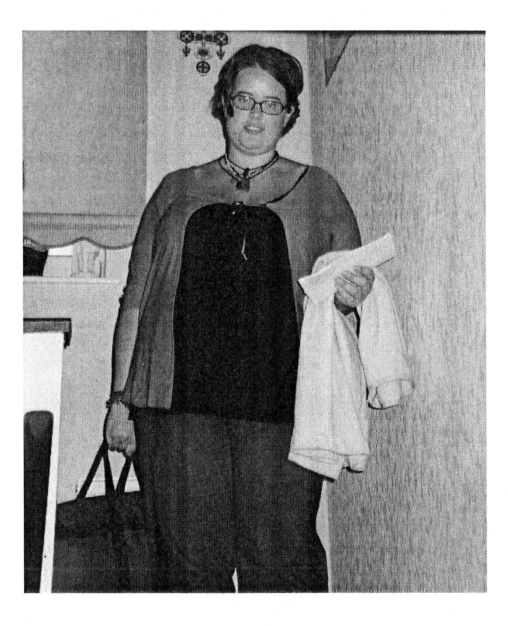

Angela Stokes in August 2001

Angela Stokes: From morbid obesity to a new life with raw foods

Just a few years ago, I weighed 294 lbs (21 stone/133 kg) and was depressed, lonely and constantly ill. These days, after moving over to a mainly raw vegan diet since May 2002, I weigh in at a healthy and happy 135 lbs (9 stone 9 lbs/62 kg) for my 5'7" frame, and my life has been completely transformed.

I have lost more than half of my body weight over the last 3½ years, but my transformation has been remarkable on more than just the physical level. At the emotional and spiritual levels too, my recovery on this path has been extraordinary.

I frequently feel as if I am "talking about a different person" when I reflect on my life as a morbidly obese person. Things have changed in so many ways, from the little details like being able to see and feel my rib bones again to the freedom this lifestyle has brought me from isolation and living in serious denial of how much I was damaging myself.

I was not always overweight. I was a very active child and the fastest runner in my school at the age of ten. My problems began when, at the age of 11, I developed an underactive thyroid and began to gain weight. The weight gain escalated with uncontrolled overeating such that a decade later, at the age of 21, I found myself weighing in at nearly 300 lbs.

I lived in a bubble of total denial about my weight. I would not discuss the issue with anyone and showed no interest in diets or weight loss. My pre-raw diet consisted of enormous quantities of chocolate, fried foods, stodgy carbohydrates and greasy fats.

Everything changed the night a friend lent me a book on raw foods, and since then I have never looked back. I realized immediately that this was the answer I had always been waiting for and went 100% raw overnight. During the first year alone, I lost over 100 lbs of excess fat.

In January 2004, I set up my popular testimonial web site www.rawreform.com to share my message of hope with others. The response ever since has been phenomenally heart-warming, as others are inspired to lose weight naturally too and reclaim their own health on this path.

I have recently finished a book about weight loss on raw foods, which will be published soon. I also offer consultations for those who would like personal support to lose weight naturally and simply with raw foods.

Furthermore, I provide a free e-newsletter to subscribers, and my web site hosts a forum where a growing community of like-minded individuals share experiences and build networks.

I "walk my talk," and my "before" and "after" photos speak for themselves. I am a living example of the healing power of raw foods and am uniquely qualified to carry this message of health to others who currently struggle with obesity and over-eating.

I sum up my transformation on raw foods in the following way: I may now be half the person physically that I was before going raw, but I am so much more myself in every other way.

I am delighted to share my experience and hope with others.

Photo by Karen Kessi-Williams

Angela Stokes in August 2005

More testimony...

There are many great books with more testimonials by raw fooders. Paul Nison's books *The Raw Life: Becoming Natural in an Unnatural World; Raw Knowledge: Enhance the Powers of Your Mind, Body and Soul; and Raw Knowledge II: Interviews with Health Achievers* are filled with extensive interviews with raw fooders, many of them long-term, and many with "before" and "after" photos.

Other books attesting to the power of live food diets include *The Living Foods Lifestyle* by Brenda Cobb and *Perfect Body* by Roe Gallo.

There are also a number of web sites sporting testimonials and before/after photos. Currently, some of these include:

> **www.shazzie.com/raw/transformation**
> **www.rawandjuicy.com/photoalbum.html**
> **www.thegardendiet.com/testimonials.html**
> **www.rawfamily.com/testimonials.htm**
> **www.rawfood.com/testimonialsgen.html**

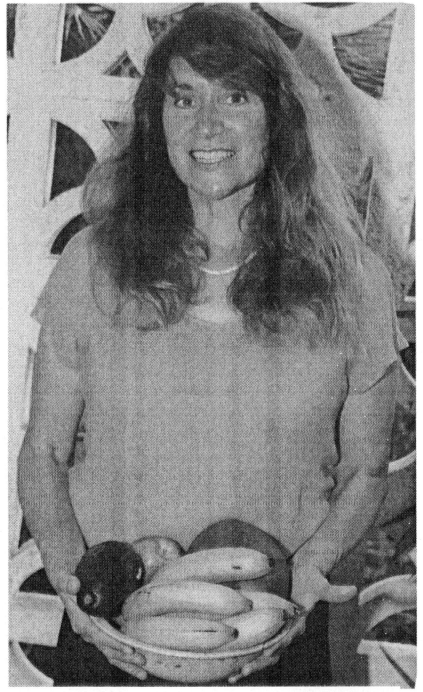

Photo by Joe Peiri

**The author at 3½ years raw
one month before her 50th birthday**

3
Radically Raw: My Story

The best retirement plan is to be so healthy
that you never *need* to retire. —Susan Schenck (1956—)

Like most Americans, I was raised with constant reminders of the importance of food and the seemingly contradictory value of being trim. My parents were always on some diet, constantly struggling to abstain from the abundance of available food. Food was a minor obsession for my parents, and I am sure that this impacted my consciousness and influenced me to become determined to master the art and science of eating.

Growing up in the 1960s, I was always told to clean my plate because of the starving children in China. Later, as an adult, I always wanted to go to China, clasp my hands around my fat tummy, and say to the people, "See? Look at what I did for you all!"

I came from the first generation that was raised on processed food. I remember eating Campbell's soup for lunch, half the bowl filled with soaked saltine crackers. I recall that one day in particular, when I was about five years old, I tried to form a mental "time warp" into the future. I thought to myself, "On the day I get married, I will remember this moment, sitting here, eating Campbell's soup." Well, I didn't remember the incident on *any* of my wedding days, but for some reason I have often recalled that moment since.

Processed food was just becoming commonplace when I grew up in the '60s: Pop-Tarts for breakfast, Twinkies for lunch, Oreo cookies, graham crackers or ice cream after school and TV dinners for supper. When I reflect, I think I may have had an average of one fresh food item a day: an apple, a banana, a carrot or the occasional salad smothered in pasteurized, sugary dressing.

After my parents divorced when I was 14, I moved from a small town in Indiana to a larger city. Convinced that I would be more successfully popular if I lost the fat around my waist, I went on my first diet and lost ten pounds in a couple of weeks.

In spite of the fact that this did not add anything to my popularity or confidence, I was so proud of myself that I kept strict tabs on my eating. I memorized the entire calorie book and counted calories every meal, every snack, every day, diligent never to allow myself to go over 1,600 calories a day.

I slowly slipped into anorexia nervosa, the golden cage of needing a figure like that of Twiggy (a fashion model of the late '60s who made it stylish to be skinny), but at the same time being obsessed with forbidden foods. When I restricted my intake to 1,300 calories a day, I slimmed down to 96 pounds at the age of 16 at 5'4".

My diet consisted of things like sugar-free sodas, sugar-free diet gelatin, sugar-free gum, low-fat cheese, lettuce, sugar-free Kool-Aid, canned tuna, canned green beans and dry air popcorn. I thought it was a glorious time that we lived in; technology had enabled man (and best of all, me!) to defy the law of calories by eating all these delicious, synthetic, "foods."

My diet was so full of chemicals and so nutrient-deficient that it was no wonder I came down with asthma, allergies and hypoglycemia. My blood sugar became so unbalanced that I sometimes fainted. I spent nearly a week in the hospital for tests, as my parents were quite concerned about my sudden illness.

The asthma and allergies got so bad that sometimes I would gasp for air, unable to sleep; so the doctor had me take asthma medication. I quickly became addicted to over-the-counter asthma pills, which were a mild form of speed (amphetamines). This went on for about a decade as I battled an addiction to stimulants that kept my nervous system very hyperactive.

At that time, few doctors knew about anorexia. This was nearly a decade before pop singer Karen Carpenter's death made the public aware. Like many anorexics, I had elaborate food rituals. For example, I would spend eight hours creating gourmet Christmas cookies and then eat only one.

After I'd been anorexic for about three years, suppressing my desires to eat and dreaming every night about food, the dam suddenly burst. I became bulimic and gained about 60 pounds within months. This was very depressing, as I had always had full control of myself until then. In fact, my willpower had made me feel superior to everyone I knew. Losing my willpower and my figure shattered my self-image.

86

Then bulimia, or binge/purge syndrome, kicked in and lasted for seven years. It was seven years of hell that completely changed my life.

On a positive note, it made me a much more compassionate person. Within months, I transformed from the most judgmental person I have ever met to a non-judgmental person with insight into why people do the most insane things. I developed the insight *to seek to understand* the reason behind the actions or words I disagreed with *rather than condemn* the doer or speaker.

But I hated this disease. Worst of all, perhaps, I believed that I was alone, that no one in the world was sharing my illness. When I confessed my compulsive behavior to a doctor, counselor or psychologist, no one had any idea what was going on with me. I even took eight psychology classes at the university, hoping to find some insight that would lead me to a cure. I knew that I couldn't wait for some doctor to treat me or for someone to find the cure or magic pill. *I had to heal myself as soon as possible.* I couldn't wait for medical science to figure things out.

One day I picked up a copy of the magazine *New Woman* and read an article explaining that B vitamins from brewer's yeast reduce stress. I started reading about nutrition and trying out various high energy and high mineral foods, such as bee pollen and brewer's yeast. Several months before that, I had also begun to exercise regularly.

Gradually, I freed myself. I no longer felt the mood swings, stress and compulsive behavior to binge and purge. After seven years of hell, I was free! (Well, relatively free, at least.) *From that time on, I knew that nutrition played a key role in mental, emotional, spiritual and physical health.*

In retrospect, I realize another reason I was able to rid myself of eating disorders was that I was living in Mexico that year. I wasn't exposed to most of the food additives and chemicals found in American food. (See Appendix A.)

About a year later, Karen Carpenter suddenly died from complications of her own eating disorder, and the topic of eating disorders suddenly sprouted in all the media. Books were written about it. Treatment centers started advertising to help women with this disease. It was interesting to me, but it didn't really matter because I had been freed. I was on to other things, like traveling around the world.

In my mid-twenties, I was still somewhat addicted to stimulants of the legal variety, such as asthma pills. To unwind at night from the stimulants, I had to drink beer. I also smoked. My vices got to be so habitual that I thought I had better clean myself out. For years I had longed to go to the exotic Middle East; so I went to a place where alcohol was even illegal: Saudi Arabia. After a year of teaching English in Arabia, I still indulged on occasion after returning to the USA, but the addictive compulsion was gone.

After tiring of traveling the world, I returned to the United States and got a master's degree in traditional Oriental medicine. I had an acupuncture and herbal clinic for a while but felt frustrated because I knew that this alone wasn't getting people well enough fast enough. Those with chronic pain would have to spend a lot of money and come for months, even years, and that was something that few could really afford.

I gave up the clinic but continued working from my home or doing house calls while searching for more of the missing pieces to the health puzzle. I realized that my calling was not so much to be a healer, but rather an educator. I've always been a teacher at heart, and I hope to empower others to heal themselves.

Meanwhile, now in my mid-thirties, I was struggling to keep slim. I never reverted to the eating disorders but retained a very typical female concern for keeping my figure. My weight fluctuated within a 15-pound range, yo-yoing between 130 and 145 or so pounds. I tried low-calorie diets, low-fat diets and low-carbohydrate diets. I exercised by running, lifting weights and walking. Once a year I would take a one- or two-week juice diet. While others indulged in Oktoberfest, I experienced my annual "Octoberfast."

Whenever I went to Canada to visit relatives, I observed how much older they got, year after year. I listened as my grandmother would talk endlessly about her helplessly aging friends and relatives, mostly people I didn't even know. Their organs were falling apart; they were incontinent; they needed operations. Life as an old person was pretty miserable. My grandmother lived to be 95 but had a pacemaker, had two hips replaced, and was very fragile during the last decade or two.

As I pondered how everyone around me was aging, I vowed that this would not happen to me. Whatever it took, I would not age like this. I would grow old, but I would never lose my strength, fitness and health.

Exercise grew into a part-time job, as I incorporated yoga for flexibility, weightlifting for strength and muscles, and walking. I was constantly reading books about health, preventive medicine and nutrition. My monthly purchase of supplements slowly grew to hundreds of dollars, often more than a car payment. I drove my ten-year-old car around Southern California, where nearly everyone has the latest luxury auto. But I preferred to spend that money on my body, the most precious of vehicles.

Throughout my adult life, I was constantly on the lookout for the fountain of youth, as well as the elixir of ecstasy. You name the herb, drug, pill or potion, and I probably experimented with it.

Convinced that I had attention deficit disorder after reading the book *Driven to Distraction* (Hallowell and Ratey), I even took Prozac for a year. At first I thought it was splendid, but later it gave me anxiety attacks and a weight gain of 30 pounds. A key ingredient, I learned later, was fluoride, an extremely toxic substance. Read *The Fluoride Deception* by Christopher Bryson or *Fluoride the Aging Factor: How to Recognize and Avoid the Devastating Effects of Fluoride* by John Yiamouyiannis for more information on that.

Fortunately, I stopped taking it before some of the other effects could manifest: thyroid damage, loss of calcium in the hipbones, brain damage and more.

A number of my closest friends also experimented with these selective serotonin reuptake inhibitor (SSRI) antidepressants that year. We all had bad results after the initial mild euphoria. Yet these drugs remain frighteningly easy to obtain from just about any doctor. Incidentally, after going raw, I discovered that my "spacey" feeling and short attention span were not due to "attention deficit disorder," but rather to wheat sensitivity.

Some people may think I was obsessed with health due to fear of death. Oddly, I have never been able to relate to that fear very much. I was born with an innate knowing that we are immortal spiritual beings here on a journey. I may have wanted to prolong my health and life span a bit, but death per se has never given me any angst. My spiritual life was always more important to me than my health. In fact, one of the reasons for my health quest is that I found, like so many others who know about the body-mind-spirit connection, that I feel a higher spiritual vibration when I feel healthy.

Another part of the reason for my obsession with health, I confess, is that I was a total wimp when it came to pain. Even a minor ache or infection would throw me out of my comfort zone. I had completely outlawed headaches from my body. I wanted to be sure that I never, ever experienced pain and had no need for pain medications.

Another reason for my health quest, though, was that I noticed early on that how I felt had almost nothing to do with outer circumstances and almost everything to do with how my inner biochemistry was. In other words, my happiness quotient depended primarily on my level of health.

I could have won the lottery, and yet if I had a bad case of PMS, I would feel miserable. On the other hand, I could lose my job or go through a bad relationship breakup and feel great as long as my health was up. I was therefore determined to discover the greatest health secrets to controlling the high states of well-being and felt it was my mission to teach this to others.

Nutrition was always one of my passions, and I experimented with several diets throughout the years. I tried out vegetarianism for several years, as well as the trendy low-fat diet. How fortunate, I thought, to live in a time when technology can create zero-fat "butter" out of chemicals, zero-calorie spray for frying, and Olestra zero-fat chips. But to compensate for the low fat, I would eat lots of carbohydrates and fall asleep after eating zero-fat pasta.

Then I read *The Zone* by Dr. Barry Sears. This led me to a new diet, low in carbohydrates. Again, thanks to technology, I was able to eat protein powders and protein bars that fit perfectly into the 40% carbohydrates, 30% fat and 30% protein of the "zone" diet. I devoured seven of Dr. Sears' books.

Although my energy soared as a result of having low insulin levels, I noticed a dull headache and even fatigue as I ate the protein bars, which, unbeknownst to me, were loaded with excitotoxins — MSG and aspartame.

My mother discovered she had kidney cancer at the age of 73. I knew she was not going to make it to 100 with her eating habits, but it was really shocking that this would happen in her early 70s. A year and a half later, she died of a stroke when the cancer metastasized to her brain. It was such an amazing thing to see her last breath. I even wrote (though didn't publish) a book, *Losing a Parent: The Ultimate Wake-Up Call.*

As I mentioned, I was never really afraid of dying myself. For one thing, I knew the afterlife was much better than this one. Secondly, I felt I was always two steps ahead of disease through exercising, abstaining from red meat, drinking plenty of water and taking enough supplements to feed a family of ten.

Then, in my 40s, I was suddenly diagnosed with hepatitis C. During a routine exam, my liver enzymes were found to be very high, and some doctor thought I should be tested to see if I had the virus. Well, I did.

At that time, I knew zilch about hepatitis C, and it scared me. I felt vulnerable for the first time in my life. I felt mortal. Even I, despite my complete focus on health, was capable of illness. It was reminiscent of the unforgettable scene in the movie *Philadelphia* when the character played by Tom Hanks realizes he has AIDS and is listening to the sad opera music.

Since I was not really afraid of death, it was bittersweet. I observed the drama of it all with a bit of detachment. If I died, okay. But if I lived, *I simply had to have good health.* Life without excellent health, I held, was not worth living.

Within a month or so, I brought the liver enzymes down to very healthy levels simply by abstaining from alcohol and consuming ample quantities of the herb milk thistle. When the medical doctor saw that my enzyme levels were to be envied by anyone, he thought maybe the test result had been faulty so he retested me. However, the test had been accurate: I had hepatitis C.

The doctor convinced me to take interferon for six months. I felt fine, I argued. He frightened me by saying that as long as the virus was there, it could suddenly cause cirrhosis of the liver or even lead to liver cancer.

I finally relented, but since the drug had only a 30% chance of knocking out the virus, I decided to cover all bases and take vast quantities of herbs and liver supplements.

Along with the interferon, I took ribavirin, a viral suppressant, to increase the effect. The interferon made me so depressed that I had to take an antidepressant. A side effect of the antidepressant was insomnia; so I had to take a heavy-duty sleeping pill.

I was inundated with various drugs and their side effects. Six months later, the virus was apparently gone. But so were half my hair, my energy, my life spirit and my healthy complexion. The interferon weakened and aged me. My face was white and pasty. My hair was turning gray.

Had I known about raw foods, I never would have gone the drug route. It was so unnecessary because my liver was just fine before the drugs so long as I ate well and avoided alcohol.

Though warned I had only a one-out-of-three chance, I won the battle against the virus. Then the doctor threw me for a loop when he told me that although the drug had succeeded in combating the hepatitis, yearly checks were needed because it could come back — after everything I had been through!

How could that be? I thought the drug was supposed to *cure* me. I knew then that I had to change my lifestyle. *Something radical had to be done.*

On an Internet chat room, I met someone who told people everything about the raw food diet. I prided myself in knowing a lot about nutrition. I had read dozens of nutrition books and was convinced that a raw food diet would be too low in protein.

But this person was one of the few who knew more than I did about nutrition. It took about three months of debate before I decided to give it a try. Although I was most skeptical and a "hard sell," one week of the diet was enough to convince me. No amount of reading about the diet could equal the experience of trying it myself.

In April 2002, I did something I hadn't done in a decade: I fasted on only water and juice for two weeks, consuming nothing but fresh juice and water. I also took a series of colonics, which are much stronger than enemas for cleaning out the colon.

To my amazement, pounds of phlegm came out. And when I did the liver cleanse, hundreds of gallstones poured out of me. This made me realize how unnecessary gallbladder removals are, with the difficulty in digesting fats that comes as a result.

I felt so light and euphoric I didn't even want to break the fast. Finally I did. I wanted to keep that light feeling. I wondered if going raw would do the trick so decided to give it a try.

Within a month of going raw, I lost about fifteen pounds. But much more than that, things I never expected I would ever be free from disappeared completely. Athlete's foot that I'd had for a decade, and nothing would rid me of, vanished, as well as the fungus on my big toenails.

I had had PMS that was getting worse every year to the point that I had been depressed three weeks out of every month. After going raw, I didn't even feel the usual depression and irritability the day before my period; thus, it was always a surprise when my period came. Whereas before, the PMS had become progressively worse the closer it got to my period. My period, a form of detox, went from three days to one.

On the raw diet, I felt lighter, more mentally clear than ever, more energetic, more alive, more joyful. My skin was as soft as when I was a teenager. Hypoglycemia was gone. Cellulite vanished. Brain fog and sluggishness became a thing of the past. My energy, previously scattered, became focused. My face, which had been whitened by the interferon, grew rosy again. I had my youthful rosy cheeks back. Most surprisingly to me was that I regained the bounce and energy of my pre-adolescence.

I sensed that this was the fountain of youth I had been looking for. I gave away about eight grocery bags of dead food from my cabinets. After buying several raw food recipe books, I experimented with new food creations and invited friends over to try these delightful new taste treats. By making food that tasted so much better than cooked food, I knew I would not be tempted to go back to old eating habits.

Most exciting was that I found an ecstasy from having an alkaline body (See Chapter 12 for more on that.) I felt joy, peace, a natural high. My energy became smooth, balanced and stable. My addictive tendencies melted effortlessly.

Although I cannot brag that the raw food diet cured me of cancer, as it has several of the people I have met since going raw, I nonetheless have my own testimony. I now have the vigor and energy of my youth. I look younger, feel younger, sleep less, and feel freer than ever. I am able to sing much better since the phlegm is gone. A chronic upper back and neck pain is gone. When I travel, I no longer get jetlag! I can also endure humid weather like never before.

Before going raw, I thought I was "regular" because I eliminated once a day; now I realize I was, like most people, chronically constipated. I now go to the bathroom two to three times a day, effortlessly and quickly.

My addictive personality is growing dimmer and dimmer. When I stick to a 100% raw diet, my weight is effortlessly stabilized. There is no longer a need to periodically go on a weight-loss diet; yet I am free to eat delicious foods such as olives, avocados and nuts that formerly would have been off limits due to their high calorie and fat content.

I no longer feel throbbing pain with minor injuries. After I'd been 95% raw for a few years, people began remarking about how shiny my eyes were. Best of all, my mood swings are gone, and I feel much happier than when I ate the SAD. I am not so overwhelmed by "the things I have to get done," and most of the time I feel that life is a joy. Most amazingly, I no longer have the remotest fear of disease. I feel totally in control of my health.

As a child, I used to pray, right before going to bed, "Now I lay me down to sleep, I pray the Lord my soul to keep. If I should die before I wake, I pray the Lord my soul to take." Having experienced the death of several childhood friends, I was convinced that I too could die *any day*. I was often conscious that I had to experience life fully and also get certain things done because I could die any day from meningitis, toxic shock syndrome, a brain aneurysm or something. Like most people, I felt powerless against a number of diseases that seemed to hit randomly and destroy people with no rhyme or reason.

Another interesting phenomenon that occurred after switching to a raw diet was that in my dreams I would find myself at a large buffet, happily selecting only the uncooked food. I couldn't help but compare this to the years of self-deprivation as an anorexic in which I would always gorge myself on doughnuts, ice cream and all sorts of other "goodies" in my dreams. Dreams give us a way to peak into our unconscious, and this confirmed to me that even unconsciously I was not feeling deprived.

People in the raw movement are prone to ask each other two questions: "How long have you been raw?" and "What percentage raw are you?" I have found that at some times it is easier to be 100% raw. At other times, however, I allow myself the occasional "cheat" of a cooked potato once a week or so and even popcorn a few times a year, as I have found no adequate raw substitutes for these two favorite indulgences.

However, I have developed a healthy respect for the addictiveness of cooked food. Cooked food can be so addictive, especially if you are living under constant psychological stress, that I have learned it is simply easier to stay out of that addictive zone altogether and remain 100% raw. It removes one more source of stress from my life.

When I am 100% raw, it is incredibly easy to decline the most elaborate of cooked smorgasbords. When I indulge in the occasional cheat, it evolves into a constant internal battle not to "treat" myself to cooked food almost daily.

Recently, I have begun to experiment with Victoria's green smoothie diet. (See Appendix C.) I feel this is the next step forward and have noted dramatic improvements in my health.

One regret I have is that I did not find the raw diet sooner. Although I had come across a few people in California who told me about it — including a housemate! — it didn't register because I didn't know the science behind it. So I just assumed I could take a vitamin pill and a few enzyme pills to compensate for the nutrition lost from heating.

I never realized how much more complex eating cooked food was. Furthermore, these raw fooders didn't hit me over the head with missionary zeal. Perhaps that is why I can often be zealous to the point of being obnoxious. And that is also why I put so much science into this book, so that the diet would make sense to the left-brained people like me.

Take heed, those of you who want to put this off until you are older or sicker: *I wish I had started sooner!* I am told that people who start young maintain their youth well into middle age. Furthermore, my mom would still be alive today if I had discovered this diet just a year or two earlier.

Another reason I didn't know about it is that almost all the books on the raw food diet are self-published and are therefore not found in bookstores, where I would peruse and purchase any books I wanted to read on health. All of my adult life I used to go to bookstores every week, looking for new avenues to research to satisfy my curiosity about health, spirituality and other subjects; yet I never encountered a raw food book.

The only way I could research this topic was by ordering books from the Internet, obscure titles that no one has ever heard of. As Victoria Boutenko points out, people are so hungry for health that they begin seeking answers, not waiting for scientific research to catch up. "We witness hundreds, if not thousands, of books on nutrition written by average people ... sometimes without the necessary background" (*Green for Life*, p. 5).

During my first year of going raw, I bought every raw food book I could find. I read about 70 books on the raw food diet and related nutritional subjects, all of which I reference here in the Bibliography and Other Resources section. I voraciously read all but a dozen or so of the books you will find there. Within a year and a half, I had also read literally hundreds of health and raw food diet articles on the Internet.

Although it is not necessary to study the diet as extensively as I did, I know that educating myself about it helped tremendously with the ability to stick with it. Every week or so I would search the Net for books on the raw diet, consumed with passion to learn as much as I could because the topic was so fascinating for me.

People who enjoy life would like to live forever, or at least a long time, in order to synthesize and share all they have learned. Some people like to think they achieve immortality or regain their youth by having children. Others like to marry people young enough to be their children. Some achieve immortality by changing a law or inventing something or writing a book.

As Woody Allen said, "*I prefer to achieve immortality by not dying.*" Since that is highly unlikely, I can least live a long, healthy life on a raw diet.

This is why I researched the raw food diet with a zeal found only in those who have discovered the secret of immortality. Many people uncovering this secret also have the same zeal, almost a missionary passion. Actor Woody Harrelson made a documentary, *Go Further*, in which one of his traveling partners got turned on to the raw diet and was shouting on the streets to people something like, "You've been lied to! No more corn dogs! You've been lied to!"

If you count my two master's degrees, as well as my continuing education, I have eleven years of university/college education. But the truth is that, for many people, most of our learning occurs when we *study on our own*. What I learned in my years of college and university was *how to do research*.

As I explained in the preface, I felt compelled to write this book. I had discovered the secret of a lifetime. I couldn't sleep at night unless I shared it with others! The results of years of my research reading, talking to people, attending lectures and workshops, experimenting on my own, and coaching others on the raw diet are summarized in this book.

As for the title of this chapter, the word *radical* is defined as "arising from or going to a root or source," as in "a radical solution." This certainly applies to the raw food revolution we are witnessing today and how it goes to the root or source of illness, unlike orthodox treatment. *Radical* is also defined as "departing markedly from the usual or customary; extreme," which also applies to the raw diet. A third definition is "favoring or effecting fundamental or revolutionary changes in current practices, conditions, or institutions." What could be more radical than changing the fundamental institutions of medicine and cooked food? The final definition of *radical* is slang: "excellent, wonderful." Indeed, it is!

I will have to say, along with Dr. Herbert Shelton, one of the early 20th century raw food proponents, "If the views presented herein seem radical to my readers, if they seem revolutionary, I shall be happy; for I strive always to be 'radical' in the true meaning of this much abused term, to be revolutionary in a world that is reeking with decay."

The truth is not only radical, but also often too *simple* for people to accept. As Albert Einstein said, "If at first the idea is not absurd, then there is no hope for it."

So there is great hope for this diet and its power to heal body, mind and soul. And there is also my favorite Einstein quote, "Condemnation without investigation is the height of ignorance."

So I invite you, dear reader not only to *read* what I have written, but also to *investigate* for yourself to see if it is not true. Do some research on your own body. See if it does not thrive most wholeheartedly on a raw food diet, and read some of the books I quote throughout this one. But most of all, try the diet! See if your body, brain and spirit do not love you for feeding them what they truly need!

We shall deal next with the science showing how and why the raw food diet is one of the most, if not *the* most, potent keys to optimal health.

If you are eager to begin implementing this diet right away, you may wish to proceed to Section IV first, which shows you how to get started, coming back to the science later. Just be sure not to skip Section II entirely, especially Chapters 4 and 5, as the science behind the raw diet is sure to leave a deep impression, reminding you why you should never revert to your old eating habits.

This is not just another fad diet, weight-loss program or disease-specific diet. This is the diet *you were genetically designed to eat* for optimal, overall well-being. Reading through the science section, even if you are not keen on studying science, will explain why this is so.

**At age 49, right after a 2-week green juice cleanse,
your author works out at the local gym.**

Section Two

Raw

Proof:

The Science

4

A Paradigm Shift in Our View of Disease and Its Treatment

All truth goes through three stages. Truth will first be ridiculed,
then violently opposed and finally accepted as self-evident.
—Arthur Schopenhauer (1788-1860)

A paradigm shift is a dramatic change in one's belief system, a fundamental change in underlying assumptions. If a scientist works from the wrong theories or from misconceptions based on wrong assumptions, he will ask the wrong questions and design and carry out irrelevant experiments. As Dr. Lorraine Day has said, modern medicine isn't getting great results in treating disease because its scientists are looking in the wrong direction, wasting time and money on incorrect theories.

Beliefs are the hardest addictions to break. We are so addicted to our convictions that we don't want anything to disrupt the cozy little belief-world that we feel safe in. Our preconceptions become like a religion for us. We are so attached to our ways of thinking that, even when presented with strong evidence that would indicate that a painful or fear-inducing belief is untrue, that the truth is infinitely better, and that the universe is far more benevolent than we suspected, human nature makes us shrug off the evidence and meld back into the "comfort" zone of negative, although familiar and therefore comfortable, beliefs.

To confess, even to our own selves, that we may need some belief or paradigm adjustments, that we have been wrong and even blinded to the truth, takes not only humility but courage and a willingness to shift into initially frightening, although ultimately freeing, modes of seeing reality. Beliefs are so ingrained within us that we are willing to die for them or enlist others to die for these cherished ideas about what is right and wrong, true and false.

Some people would even prefer to have their children die at war or from chemotherapy than question their beliefs and their trust in "the system."

A paradigm shift occurs when people begin, slowly perhaps, to view something from a radically different viewpoint. It is a shift, not in a mere theory, but in an entire perspective. Sometimes it is mind-blowing. People often become amazed at how funny it is to have believed the previous way.

One example is the formerly popular belief that the world was flat until Christopher Columbus proved it otherwise by sailing to the New World without falling off the edge.

Another is Galileo Galilei's (1564-1642) early adoption of Nicolaus Copernicus' (1473-1543) new theory, radical for its time, that the earth orbited the sun and was not a stationary center around which the whole universe rotated. He was branded a heretic by the Catholic Church, arrested, and publicly humiliated. It was only in 1992 that the Vatican reversed its earlier position that the earth was the center of the universe!

People arrogantly cling to old theories. Imagine having dedicated the focus of your *entire life* to a theory and then watching as some radical upstart comes along and pulls the rug out from under it! Most would react with a staunch egoistic desire to protect their theories, especially when a lot of money has been invested in them, as is the case with our trillion-dollar-a-year medical system.

To quote Dr. Gabriel Cousens, "Paradigm-shifting breakthroughs often hit cul-de-sac dead-ends in societal acceptance due to the vagaries of vested economic interest, political intrigue and pride of the ego" (*Rainbow Green Live-Food Cuisine*, p. xv).

Eventually, though, the truth emerges. Those who are heavily invested in the earlier paradigm eventually die. Then the younger scientists, unattached to old theories, become free to test new theories without scorn from older scientists. Hence, it is said that science changes one funeral at a time.

We have already seen the many benefits a raw food diet confers. Chapter 1 gave us ten reasons to go raw, but only one of those reasons is powerful enough to motivate most people.

The one main reason that people will sacrifice their french fries, convenience foods and even social life is *health.*

Eating raw food is not difficult. But giving up cooked food *is.* Let's face it: How many of you will give up that mouth-watering dish of twice-baked potatoes just so your skin will soften? How many will quit making lasagna just to save 15 minutes of scrubbing the melted cheese off the pan? How many will sacrifice sampling all the goodies at a potluck just so you could feel more spiritual? Who among you will give up the convenience of packaged, processed foods just to spare the landfill of paper and plastic wrapping?

On the other hand, if you were faced with a life-threatening illness, you might take a closer look at this diet Nature has bequeathed us. If you were losing your mind or mental capacity, you might also consider this diet. If you were emotionally depressed, this diet might be worth learning.

If you wish to have extra energy to commune with God at a higher spiritual level, this diet could be for you. Let's face it: *Health is one of the most important things in this life — mental, spiritual, emotional and physical health.* People want to feel good, as the title of this book suggests, in body, in mind and in spirit.

If you are interested in improving any of these areas of your well-being — and they are all intertwined, each affecting the other — you might want to educate yourself and see why it works. The first thing we need to do is to unlearn some of the false ideas we have been indoctrinated with throughout our whole lives.

Most raw fooders no longer accept the orthodox model of disease origin and its treatment via drugs, radiation and surgery. That model believes it is natural to become sick with age, genetic predisposition or unfortunate encounters with viruses and bacteria.

One Disease, One Cure?

There are several models. or theories, of how disease originates. One is the genetic model, which blames disease on the destiny stored within our genes. While it is true that there are some diseases that are genetically determined and thus not preventable, such conditions are rare.

About 80% of our health status is determined by diet, lifestyle choices and other environmental factors. This is why identical twins can grow up with one staying very youthful and healthy well into old age and the other, who smokes, drinks, eats dead food, and doesn't exercise, experiencing disease and debility relatively early in life.

This is why, in the most comprehensive study on nutrition ever conducted, genes were found to be irrelevant compared to diet (*The China Study*, T. Colin Campbell, p. 71).

As Gabriel Cousens, MD, points out, genes themselves don't cause disease, but rather lifestyle and diet change gene expression in such a way that disease occurs. What we eat and the toxins we expose ourselves to affect our genes.

Gerontologists now believe that 75% of a person's health after the age of 40 depends not on his genes, but on what that person has done to keep his genes healthy.

Even the Human Genome Project researchers are stating that genes are only a part of the story. The book *Genetic Nutritioneering: How You Can Modify Inherited Traits and Live a Longer, Healthier Life* by Jeffrey S. Bland, PhD, shows that scientists now have a huge amount of evidence that many diseases previously attributed to "bad genes" are now known to be caused by a bad diet that "feeds the genes," affecting them for the worse.

Another model of disease origin is the germ theory. As we shall see later in this chapter, this model is largely based on misleading information.

There is a third model of disease origin based on accumulations of internal toxicity. The treatment prescribed according to this model is the only one that gets dramatic results.

When people are sick, they really don't care about the theories involved in disease. They simply want to get well. They want results.

Fasting, detoxifying one's environment, and staying on a clean, healthful diet gets results in at least 90% of the cases, as shown by adherents to this model. This 90% cure rate, unheard of with the treatment methods based on the other disease models, has been proven in tens of thousands of cases, as in clinics run by Dr. Edmond Szekely, Dr. Herbert Shelton and Rev. George Malkmus. (See more about them in Section Three.)

Note: If a person's immune system has been weakened by toxic drug therapy, such as chemotherapy, the cure rate is much lower. Unfortunately, most people go with drug treatment first and try natural methods of detoxification as last resorts after the immune system is too weakened to recover.

The vast majority of diseases are *preventable* and *curable* because they are due to one simple cause: toxic accumulation. This can be demonstrated by the following example: One hundred years ago, cancer struck only 1 in 2,500 (by some accounts, only 1 in 8,000). Now 1 in 2½ will get cancer. Soon cancer will overtake heart disease, which affects 1 in 2 people, as our number one killer disease. How could this be if disease were purely genetic? Some argue that the cancer rate is on the rise because we live longer, but then how would that explain that cancer is increasing at an alarming rate among young children?

If we do the research, it becomes clear that the cancer increase parallels the increased pollution in our environment. We are being bombarded by toxicity in our food, water and air. For many of us, our work environment and homes are polluted. Even our clothes, rugs and dry-cleaning chemicals bombard us with toxins. According to National Institutes of Health directors Donald Frederickson and Arthur Upton, *most of the toxins that cause cancer are from food* (*The Cancer Industry: The Classic Exposé on the Cancer Establishment*, Ralph Moss, p. 231). For this reason, the diet connection to health is most important.

Nutritionist Natalia Rose concurs that glowing health doesn't arise only from what we put into our bodies today, but also from "the removal of waste matter — built up from years of improper eating" (*The Raw Food Detox Diet*, p. 10). She explains that most diets don't work for permanent weight loss because they don't address the issue of removal of those toxins that cause sluggish metabolic, digestive and circulatory systems.

The body simply does not know what to do with processed, unnatural foods and cannot break them down fully; so they get stuck in various parts of the body, especially the colon. She compares this toxic overload with an overloaded hospital emergency room in which, at the end of the day, only half the patients have been attended to. So it is with our overloaded body, and "the worst offender of this system happens to be your diet" (p. 227).

Thus, in the new paradigm, most ailments fall into the category of *only one disease* — toxic accumulation — and for that *there is only one cure* — removal of toxins. This model is elaborated in detail in the writings of Drs. John Tilden, Herbert Shelton and other leaders of the Natural Hygiene movement.

Dr. Shelton also noted that some diseases arise from malnutrition: deficiency diseases like scurvy (Vitamin C deficiency), beriberi (Vitamin B_1 deficiency), pernicious anemia (Vitamin B_{12} deficiency) and so forth. However, the vast majority of diseases that we see in the affluent Western world are diseases of excess, and excess leads to toxicity.

Note: Deficiency diseases may be on the rise even in the West due to increasing mineral deficiencies in our soils, as explained later in this book.

Furthermore, since fasting, the ultimate detoxification process, has been known to heal even these deficiency cases, perhaps toxicity is sometimes at the root. This is explained by lack of absorption, perhaps due to toxic interference. An example given by Albert Mosseri, author of *Mangez Nature Santé Nature*, is that anemia has been regressed not by ingestion of iron, but rather by fasting.

Arnold Ehret observed the idea of one disease when he wrote, "Nature, alone ... heals through one thing — fasting — every disease that it is possible to heal. This, alone, is proof that Nature recognizes but one disease, and that in every body the largest factors are always waste, foreign matter and mucus [phlegm]" (*The Mucusless Diet Healing System*).

Even Florence Nightingale, the famous Civil War nurse, observed this: "There are no specific diseases, only specific disease conditions."

When asked if he could make specific dietary recommendations according to the disease, Dr. T. Colin Campbell, author of the recently published landmark book *The China Study: Startling Implications for Diet, Weight Loss and Long-Term Health*, based on the largest nutritional study ever, replied that he has come to see, through decades of research, that diseases all have impressive commonalities and that the same good nutrition that can prevent or heal *one* disease works for all of them.

According to the theories of Natural Hygiene, poisons that accumulate in the body may originate in either the inner or the outer environment. Those from within include metabolic waste (toxic byproducts at the cellular level) and stresses of the emotional, mental and physical sorts. Those from the outer environment include unnatural food, such as table salt, wheat (see Appendix A), chemical additives, and so on; natural food spoiled by cooking, refining or processing; all drugs, including medical, both prescribed and over-the-counter, and non-medical/recreational, both legal and illegal; and environmental pollution, especially of air and water.

This toxic overload causes poisonous waste accumulation because the body, being burdened by poisonous byproducts of cooked food on a daily basis, rarely has the energy to excrete all of it. Thus the body, in its wisdom, stores the toxins wherever they will do the least harm: in connective, fatty and subcutaneous tissues. This toxic buildup accumulates in joints, fat, arteries, tumors and cysts.

Toxins accumulate most in the weakest organ, which eventually falls into an abnormal behavior pattern in its efforts to detoxify. Note that the weakest organ may be determined genetically; yet it is not the genes, but rather the toxins, that actually harm the organ.

The symptom pattern that results from the body's efforts to eliminate toxins causes the disease to be named accordingly. For example, if a woman's weakest area is her breast tissue, perhaps due to genetics, she may build up toxins in that part of her body that lead to malignant tumors. This pattern will be called breast cancer. A woman with the same genes who leads a cleaner lifestyle, however, will likely remain cancer-free.

Or perhaps a foreign virus will enter the body. If the body is clean inside, the virus will not get far with a healthy immune system. If the body is toxic, the virus will trigger a cleansing response as it "feeds" on the toxic debris.

An allopathic (see Glossary) doctor who sees the symptom patterns will attempt to diagnose the disease pattern, giving it a name. He will undoubtedly blame the germ if one is involved and may blame the patient's genes if a germ is not involved. He will prescribe specific drugs accordingly. By not treating the initial cause, he will not cure the underlying disease.

Drugs do not cure, but rather attack the symptoms, relieving some pain and perhaps even extending life, but not really solving the problem and healing the patient. Disease symptoms are expressions of the body's ingenious ways of removing toxins. Symptoms are evidence of the body's healing processes in action. Drugs stop the body's elimination of toxins, thus giving rather quick relief from the detoxifying symptoms.

However, there is a huge, hidden price to pay for mere symptomatic relief. Since drugs contain inorganic substances that are toxic to the living organism, they will add additional toxins to the already overloaded, toxic body. After some time, the symptoms will again flare up when the body finally accumulates enough energy to undertake another cleansing episode. By opting for "quick fix" drug therapy to get relief from annoying symptoms, you are only pouring more and more toxins into your body.

Note that since the original problem remains unaddressed, the damaged organ or tissue that was experiencing symptoms continues to deteriorate. Thus ever-increasing doses of drugs are needed to mask the symptoms until finally the drugs stop "working." You are not only postponing recovery, but also making your health much worse in the long run. Your body will now have to work so hard at eliminating the drugs that it won't have any energy left to deal with the problem you were treating in the first place.

Sometimes, as with chemotherapy, the side effects of the drug kill the patient before the disease gets to. Or the drugs so greatly sicken the patient that there is little quality of life. As Bruno Comby so puts it in his book *Maximize Immunity*, "How can we hope to heal sick and weakened patients by giving them medication which engenders side effects that would make a *healthy* person ill?"

The Simplicity of Disease Origin and Cure

Let's review. In the new model, *there is only one disease*: toxic accumulation called "toxemia," and there is *only one treatment* that is effective in helping the body to heal itself: "toxin removal." It is that simple. There is a scientific principle known as Occam's razor, which states that the best explanation is always the simplest one. What could be simpler?

We are dazzled by all the gadgets, machines and knowledge that the last century has brought to medicine. As an acupuncture student in pathology class, I was in awe at all of the diseases discovered and labeled. But where has all that gotten us?

For example, after decades of fighting the "war on cancer," cancer is a $120,000,000,000 per year industry! Before you submit to chemotherapy, I suggest you look at its recovery rates versus negative side effects. (See more in Appendix B.)

There is a great deal of waste involved in the obsession with labeling diseases. Think of the hundreds of drugs that medical students have to memorize, along with their indications and contraindications. Think of all the diseases and symptoms that have to be memorized. Think of all the diagnostic tests and all the expense involved in that. Yet many times doctors do not even agree among themselves on a diagnosis.

The same holds for Oriental medicine. To pass my classes and the boards to get my license, I had to memorize all sorts of ailments — Oriental diagnoses and Western ones — as well as hundreds of herbs and acupuncture points with their indications and contraindications. Yet most Oriental doctors do not agree on exact diagnoses and treatments either.

Dr. Herbert Shelton liked to talk about all the -itises and how arbitrary the classifications were. If you had inflammation in your rectum, it was labeled proctitis, but if it was a quarter inch farther up the colon, it was sigmoiditis, which was a completely different disease according to the medical establishment. Yet inflammation is simply one of the seven stages of the disease process that any cell or tissue can go through, and it's no different just because it happens to be located in a different spot on the body.

Natural Hygiene holds that the seven stages of disease are enervation (fatigue), toxicosis, irritation, inflammation, ulceration, induration (hardening) and cancer.

Furthermore, think of the anxiety the patients go through when doctors cannot label or agree upon their disease or ailment. Finally, when it is labeled, they breathe a sigh of relief, as if labeling it will somehow make it better.

The conventional disease model has as its root assumption that the body is fundamentally flawed and subject to invasion or attack by enemy germs or just random breakdown through aging or genetic defects — hence the perceived need to declare "wars" on germs, cancer, AIDS, SARS and whatever the latest and newest disease is. We are told we must wait for chemists to concoct a new drug that will ease its symptoms. We wait for someone to invent vaccinations that will prevent the disease, although their toxic contents lead to autism, Alzheimer's, Parkinson's and more.

Through aging and wear and tear, organs and body parts are thought to require replacement or removal, such as hip and knee replacement, gallbladder removal, colostomies, organ or bone marrow transplants, stents, heart bypass surgery, removal of tonsils or appendix and other mutilations.

As Victoria Boutenko points out, a baby's runny nose is not an indication of a "nose drop deficiency." I would add to that: Is a headache really an aspirin deficiency? Is a tumor a chemotherapy or radiation deficiency? Is constipation a laxative deficiency? Is indigestion an antacid deficiency? Is pain a pain medication deficiency?

All of these medications are toxic. Chemotherapy kills incredible numbers of healthy cells for each cancer cell it destroys. As Aajonus Vonderplanitz remarks, administering chemo to kill cancer is akin to killing everyone on the entire planet in order to get to a few that you want dead. (See Appendix B.)

Would Nature or God be so cruel as not to provide the ingredients we need for radiant health? Is health really dependent upon alchemists experimenting in a lab, searching for the Holy Grail of medicine, that elusive combination of chemicals needed to formulate the "miracle drug"?

Look at animals in the wild: They are healthy, able to thrive and frolic in weather extremes and enjoy long life spans, comparatively speaking. In fact, wild African monkeys infected with HIV are perfectly healthy, but the same virus is lethal for infected ones in captivity. Wild animals do not cook their food. We are the only species that does that. *We have suffered greatly for this aspect of our creativity.*

The new model of disease and health is actually quite ancient knowledge that once was forgotten and has since been rediscovered. It holds that the body is genetically designed to heal itself. Once polluted, it must detoxify and then rebuild with the correct building blocks.

So how does one go about cleansing the body? For thousands of years, the power of fasting has been known. And now the power of the 100% raw food diet to cleanse and maintain health is becoming known. The body must minimize the incoming toxins in order to have energy to remove the toxins that caused the disease. For most people, cooked food is the main source of toxins that stress their bodies (see Chapter 6). By eating raw, one spares the body of additional toxins while providing essential building blocks that would otherwise be destroyed by heat. It is really that simple.

For doctors trained in the allopathic model, dietary remedies seem too simplistic, even naïve. Their training has been along the lines of different pills for different diseases. They think it insignificant that in order for such miracle pills to be patented, they cannot be entirely natural. Therefore, they are toxic because anything not natural to the body is toxic to the body. Even some plants are toxic. Since plants cannot be patented unless genetically modified, drug companies will not research and promote foods or herbs, although they result in more healing with less toxicity than drugs. There is simply no profit in natural healing.

Yet diet is most certainly the key when all the research is examined. In *The China Study*, Dr. Campbell reached the conclusion that "nutrition [is] far more important in controlling cancer promotion than the dose of the initiating carcinogen" (p. 66). In other words, a person's diet is far more important than how much exposure to a dangerous chemical one has had!

He also writes, "More people die because of the way they eat than by tobacco use, accidents or any other lifestyle or environmental factor" (p. 305).

In France, scientist Bruno Comby has studied the raw, instinctive diet and its ability to treat AIDS. In his book *Maximize Immunity*, he reports, "Scientifically, the dietary theory of immunity, which at first glance appears bizarre in the extreme, turns out to be unshakable, something that cannot be said for other forms of natural or holistic therapy" (p. 101).

He has found the evidence to be inescapable that a 100% natural diet permits the development of immunity. "Observation of more than 15,000 individuals who have followed this natural diet over the past 25 years demonstrates that almost any immune disease follows a different course in people who exclusively eat foods that are natural and have not been denatured." He has witnessed full-blown AIDS go into a 100% remission and remain so.

Diet, cleansing and lifestyle change do not constitute an instantaneous "miracle cure." But by persisting in these disciplines, one allows the body to detoxify slowly and heal itself as it eliminates toxemia and accumulates energy for regeneration and repair. You did not get sick overnight, and you cannot expect to heal overnight.

Cleansing is not a complicated process if you educate yourself by reading about fasting and the raw food diet. You may wish to consult a naturopathic or holistic doctor if you are very sick; otherwise, a simple three-day fast does not usually require supervision.

One might not be inclined to undertake a water fast, perhaps because the detoxifying symptoms, such as headache, might prove too intense, which can be particularly annoying if one must go to work. If so, several days of taking only freshly squeezed juice can work wonders. Eating nothing but organic fruit for a number of days can also help propel the body into cleansing.

Animals fast when sick. Humans also lose their appetites and are inclined not to eat when ill. Nature provides a natural, gentle way for the body to heal itself. Nature is gentle, not harsh.

Bacteria & Viruses: Not Guilty as Charged!

In the new model, *microorganisms are our friends.* Provided that we cleanse internally, we no longer have to fret about visiting sick friends, fearing that we too will get ill. We no longer fear people sneezing on us, passing on viruses by shaking hands with us, or breathing germs on us during airplane flights. We no longer have to worry about bio-warfare! Germs, come and get us — *we no longer fear you!*

Remember hearing about the black plague that supposedly killed about a third of the population in Europe? What about the two-thirds who didn't die? They were mostly exposed to the same germs; some of those people even buried the victims. Maybe it is time to study healthy people instead of the sick.

To discover where our germ-phobia began, let us go back about 150 years. Louis Pasteur, after whom the process called pasteurization is named, was the man who promoted the alleged primary role of germs in the causation of disease. He popularized the notion that one germ causes one disease. To get rid of the disease, one must rid himself of that germ.

At the same time, a man named Antoine Béchamp, who remains unrenowned to this day, discovered microzymas, which are smaller than cells. They are the smallest living unit in our bodies and in other living organisms. Béchamp found that microzymas are in all living things and that their forms vary according to the general health of the cells they inhabit. When the body chemistry is in balance through a clean lifestyle, the microzymas develop into benign bacteria. When the state of health is bad, as from malnutrition, stress or toxicity, the microzymas are transformed into harmful germs.

Later, Dr. Enderlein, through 60 years of observing human blood, proved Béchamp's theory of pleomorphism, which states that microzymas, or protits, change form according to conditions in the blood. He concluded, "The most powerful diet for bringing a diseased biological terrain back to normal is live foods."

In his book *Sick and Tired? Reclaim Your Inner Terrain*, Robert Young, PhD, DSc, explains that a healthy or diseased body is determined by four things: pH balance (acid/alkaline), electromagnetic charge (positive/negative), levels of toxic accumulation and nutritional status (p. 21). He claims that an unhealthy blood cell can morph into a bacterium, which can later change into a yeast or fungus, which will become a mold in an advanced state of bad health. He states that the growth of bacteria and fungi in a drop of fresh blood is one of the most dramatic things he has seen in his career.

Thus there arose two conflicting theories about what is to blame for disease: the pathogen versus the biological terrain. Pasteur's theory stated that the germ was an enemy; Béchamp's theory stated that germs cohabit with us but do not proliferate when we are healthy and are taking care of our inner terrain.

Pasteur's theory won out because the establishment found it much more profitable to convince people that they had to fight a battle against germs than to teach people that they had to take good care of themselves.

Great profits for food processors resulted from pasteurization, the process of destroying germs by heating food, especially dairy. Millions of dollars also came from attacking germs with various drugs. Today, the "war on germs" is a multi-billion dollar a year industry in the United States alone. Think of all the waste! If we taught people to eat right, they would not succumb to these microscopic creatures. But, hey, what profit is there in that?

There is an oft-quoted comparison of germs with mosquitoes originally made by the father of pathology, Rudolph Virchow: "If I could live my life over again, I would devote it to proving that germs seek their natural habitat — diseased tissue — rather than being the cause of the diseased tissue; e.g., mosquitoes seek the stagnant water but do not cause the pool to become stagnant."

In other words, germs are opportunists who feed on diseased tissue but do not *create* disease. The "critter," be it a bacterium, fungus, virus or parasite, has nothing to feed on in a *pure* body.

Arthur M. Baker writes in *Awakening Our Self-Healing Body: A Solution to the Health Care Crisis*, "Virulent bacteria find soil in dead food substances only and cannot exist on living cells. Cooked food spoils rapidly, both inside and outside our body, whereas living foods are slow to lose their vital qualities and do not as readily become soil for bacterial decay."

Incidentally, even Pasteur himself caught on to the fact that he was not correct and that the body's terrain, not the germs, was to blame for ill health. He confessed this to his assistants on his deathbed.

Meanwhile, as Dr. Young points out (*Sick and Tired*, p. 25), "The American Medical Association, pharmaceutical companies and others wish us to plan our health care around this scientific error."

Raw food experts go a step beyond viewing germs as harmless: These experts claim that they *do us a service by helping us clean ourselves out.* If you saw a gathering of rodents and flies eating trash, you wouldn't likely blame them for creating the trash. More likely, you would be glad they are helping to get rid of it. The same is true with bacteria. They cannot be blamed as the cause of your toxic body; they are merely the scavengers that eat the toxic buildup. Think of all the dead bodies of animals there would be cluttering up the earth if bacteria did not decompose them! Could it be that the bacteria are helping you get rid of the dead waste from cooked food and other toxins in your body?

I remember that when I used to get a cold or the flu, I would feel really great when it was finally over. I would feel a wonderful taste in my mouth and nose. Though others I talked to agreed that they also experienced this, it didn't fit our paradigm, so no one knew why this happened. I realize now it was the "alkaline high" from having some of my body's acidic waste cleaned out. See Chapter 12 for more on alkalinity.

In *Maximize Immunity*, Bruno Comby states, "Conventional medical theory regards illness as resulting from chance or from microbes or from a genetic predisposition. This view does not square with the fact that the manifestation of illness is diminished or non-existent in animals and humans whose lifestyle and diet are more natural" (p. 103).

His "dietary theory of immunity" includes a sub-theory called "useful virus theory," in which he proposes, based on his research data, that *a virus can actually offer to the cell useful genetic information to assist the cell in carrying out its positive job of detoxification.* He proposes, from years of study, that viruses, bacteria and other microbes are not harmful in themselves. They present harm only if the immune system is greatly disturbed by a toxic diet, drugs or stress.

These microbes, including seemingly dangerous ones such as HIV, are not harmful in the context of a 100% raw food diet. If someone is reasonably healthy, microbes can actually be *beneficial* by triggering the elimination of abnormal substances accumulated in the body. Thus, they can actually fulfill a natural and useful biological function. If the person is so clean that there is nothing, no toxic debris left to eliminate, then the microbes will cause no reaction and will not proliferate.

On several occasions, Comby and his colleagues witnessed tapeworms, which had resisted conventional treatment, be eliminated spontaneously on raw food diets.

So, with this good news, why do we cling so defensively to the Old Model?

For many people, including myself, it has taken a lot of time to switch models. The reasons vary for our clinging, almost desperately and defensively, to the old paradigm. For one thing, the mind is initially shocked and needs time to digest the new ideas and verify that they are correct.

For another thing, we love our doctors and cannot imagine they might not know absolutely everything. We put them on a pedestal and want them to be infallible. My father was a general medical practitioner and surgeon in a small town. I was always so proud because everyone I met knew and admired him.

Doctors are only doing what they learned in medical school. Most doctors, having spent so many years in medical school and having seen patients' symptoms relieved by their treatments, feel they are on the right track. For people who do not take good care of themselves, some drugs, such as antibiotics and painkillers, appear quite helpful because they mask symptoms. Doctors believe that most people are simply going to get sick sooner or later. They have been taught, as we all have, that sickness is normal and natural.

Yet the root cause of illness is never tackled by drugs. Taking drugs to cure an illness is like cleaning your kitchen with dirt. Many doctors get frustrated at their inability to cure their patients permanently. A few medical doctors manage to break the mold by thinking outside the box. But those who do are at risk of being branded "quacks" and losing their licenses, not to mention being sued for not following standard procedures.

As David Hawkins, MD, PhD points out, "The fact that many opinions are held by great masses of people is hypnotic. Few minds can escape the appeal of the authority of mass agreement ... Few can resist the propaganda of the news media" (*The Eye of the I*, p. 182).

We have been erroneously led to trust the media and their reporting on scientific studies. In the book *Trust Us, We're Experts! How Industry Manipulates Science and Gambles with Your Future* by Sheldon Rampton and John Stauber, we get a behind-the-scenes view on that. We have been conditioned to worship the men in white laboratory coats for reasons of control so that we will buy pharmaceutical remedies, for one thing. For more information on how we have been hoodwinked by the pharmaceutical companies, see Appendix B.

Public relations expert Edward Bernays confessed to having been hired to promote the health benefits of bananas, bacon and Crisco cooking oil. In his book *Propaganda*, he explains how people are made to depend psychologically on what physicians and other opinion leaders say. "Those who manipulate this unseen mechanism of society constitute an invisible government which is the true ruling power of our country. ... Our minds are molded, our tastes formed, our ideas suggested, largely by men we have never heard of."

When you come to realize that the pharmaceutical corporations and government agencies like the Food and Drug Administration (FDA) care more about money than they do about your health, *it is a bit like discovering that your mother has Munchausen syndrome*, a mental disorder in which a mother poisons her own children. It is quite a shocking revelation to learn that those you trusted to protect your health are actually poisoning you with their vaccinations and drug treatments.

Another reason we cling to the old model is that *people prefer to make someone else*, the doctor or the pharmaceutical company, *responsible for their health.* In the short run, it is vastly easier to take a pill or injection than to change dietary habits or lifestyle. The results, though limited, are instantaneous symptomatic relief, unlike the much slower process of natural recovery.

It is so much easier to take drugs than to revamp one's entire lifestyle by exercising regularly, eating a raw food diet, abandoning cigarettes and educating oneself about true health. It is easier to swallow a pill and, if that doesn't work, to feel like a helpless victim, ranting and raving about how bad it is to grow old and how the medicine didn't work and had bad side effects. At least it's not *your* fault!

It is easier to have someone else do the research and reasoning concerning your bodily needs. Yet, as Victoria Boutenko writes, "When we let others observe and reason for us, in a sense we consciously choose to stay blind and deaf" (*Green for Life*, p. 3).

Most people will cling to the old model because they are lazy and want the quick fix, even if it doesn't cure in the long run. Dr. Joel Fuhrman, author of *Fasting and Eating for Health: A Medical Doctor's Program for Conquering Disease*, once wrote that the time might come when doctors would be accused of malpractice for not prescribing the substantially more effective nutritional approach to their patients.

In an interview with Shelly Keck-Borsits in her book *Dying to Get Well*, however, Dr. Fuhrman was quoted as saying, "The masses will continue to seek instant gratification via dangerous nutritional habits and drug-seeking." Most people don't want to put much effort into their health.

People also don't want to invest much money in their bodies. If health insurance won't cover the alternative doctor or fasting clinic, they won't go. They spend more money on upkeep of their cars' bodies than on *their* bodies. They take more pride in luxury vehicles than in the *vehicles of their souls*!

Another reason many cling to the old model is financial. The new approach would put many people out of jobs. Most medical professionals, food companies, restaurant owners, pharmacists, drug salespeople, people employed by the American Cancer Society and other such organizations searching for cures via drugs, companies that produce toxic pesticides and even veterinarians, as well as some alternative healers, would have to change or radically revamp their careers. *Toxicity is big business in this country!*

The good news about the new paradigm is that *we are no longer victims*, fearing that at any time our genes or some pathogen from without or cancer from within could wreak havoc on our health. We no longer feel fear and trepidation every time we get a cancer screen, which some of us no longer even bother with. We are now in near total control of our health! Good dietary habits, exercise, breathing clean air and drinking clean water will make us *masters of excellent health*.

Another pleasant surprise about this paradigm shift is that it doesn't cost anything. Some people with advanced stages of disease may want to spend initially on colonics or fasting clinics, but for the most part, this new paradigm in health care is free. There is no need to pay costly medical bills for doctors, tests, surgery, drugs, vitamins and so forth.

Your body is its own healer and doesn't charge you a penny. For those of us who are used to thinking that health care and even preventive medicine should be expensive, this can come as quite a relief.

The bad news about the new paradigm is that we have to do a whole lot more than swallow magic pills to stay healthy. We have to learn to accept responsibility. We have to learn what is poisonous, detoxify our environment, and maybe even quit our jobs if they are too stressful or the workplace environment is too lethal.

We resist the idea that diet is so intimately connected to health. We have been so conditioned to hand over responsibility for our health to some authority that we often separate diet and health in our minds. When an animal is sick, we inquire as to what it has eaten. When a person is sick, we just take him to the doctor. When there is an advertisement for pet food, it will emphasize the nutritional value. When there is an ad for human food, it emphasizes the taste and convenience *or even sex appeal.*

Veterinarians and farmers both know that an animal's health depends principally on diet and that artificial foods will fatten their bodies and destroy their health. Raw food diets for pets are all the rage. More and more people are putting their dogs and cats on raw meat instead of the more convenient canned, bagged or boxed food that has been heated and processed for extended shelf life. Yet few people consider that such a diet of uncooked food may also be healthier for *them.*

Perhaps most challenging of all, we have to relinquish some of our favorite toxic foods and switch to health-building diets. Indeed, reluctance to give up our favorite foods in exchange for health may be the biggest mental stumbling block to making the needed paradigm shift. *Too much of our identity revolves around food.*

The idea that we might have to radically change our diets to obtain health is for some a fate worse than the diseases they would cure. Some people would sooner change their religions or even let themselves die than change their eating habits. Our entire social structure revolves around food.

As Devivo and Spors point out (*Genefit Nutrition*, p. 181), food is "linked with love, sex, agreement, admiration, obedience, control, belonging, reward, indulgence and self-destruction. Our very identity of who we are contains food likes, dislikes, events, recipes and restaurants. To be outside of that paradigm can be very unsettling."

"Let food be thy medicine."
—Hippocrates, founder of modern medicine

Eventually a person may become disillusioned enough with the old system to try something radical, such as a raw food diet. After a few weeks of eating a 100% raw food diet, the person is sold: Nature has proved to be the best medicine. Hippocrates was right. Food can be thy medicine.

And it all seems so fantastical, so strange. You feel like Alice in Wonderland; everything is upside down. Suddenly the real pharmacopoeia becomes the "farm-acopoeia"! Attributed to Meryl Streep is the statement, "It is bizarre that the produce manager is more important to my children's health than the pediatrician."

You start to realize that cooked food destroys life. My parents took a photo of me on my first birthday. I was dazzled by the flame of the single candle, touched it, and cried. Fire can be seductive, as it gives warmth, a secure feeling. It looks dazzling, and it adds aroma to cooked food. But don't be fooled: It kills. Plant an uncooked seed in the ground and watch it sprout; watch it grow. Plant a roasted seed and watch it rot!

Unheated food is true "medicine." The body heals itself, cures itself of disease, when properly nourished and not overwhelmed with toxins. It needs the proper building blocks found in natural food. Raw foods are alive. Processed, cooked, denatured foods are dead.

Look at a juicy organic apple. *If you eat it, its life force will become yours!* That is not so with the cooked apple. *Instead, the cooked apple's toxic byproducts will add to your burden!* If you want more out of life, eat living foods. If you want to die in pain and misery, eat dead food. Raw food is full of rejuvenating properties: enzymes, biophotons and stored energy from the sun and soil.

The proof is in the raw pudding: Try the diet yourself. Chances are, no matter how healthy you are now, you will be amazed at how much healthier you become!

5
Cooked vs. Raw Diet Experiments

The strongest arguments prove nothing so long as the conclusions are not verified by experience. Experimental science is the queen of sciences and the goal of all speculation.
—Roger Bacon (1220-1292)

There have been quite a few experiments done comparing the raw food diet with the cooked. I have listed numerous such studies here, many performed on people and others on animals.

Since some of the studies, those done by the same people or those with similar topics, are grouped together under one heading, this comprises over 30 scientific studies. Combined with those described in Appendix D, there are well *over 50 studies illustrating the dangers of cooked food.*

Unfortunately, no one stands to make much of a financial profit from selling anything related to the uncooked diet. Selling raw, unprocessed, organic produce is not a highly profitable venture. The entire pharmaceutical and processed-food industries would stand to lose if this diet caught on. Furthermore, think of all the restaurant chains that would lose profits, not to mention those making and selling cooking appliances and apparatus.

Therefore, little funding has been allocated for research in this area because those with the deep pockets simply don't want it. As a result, most of these studies have been done by individuals so driven by curiosity and humanitarian concerns that they were motivated enough to fund their own research.

If you would like to research these articles for yourself, start by going to www.ncbi.nlm.nih.gov/entrez/query.fcgi. You will see a web site called "PubMed," which contains the National Library of Medicine. It enables you to search for articles by ID number, subject, title and such. There you will find article abstracts and links to the journals that published them. For your convenience, I have included the PubMed ID numbers, when available, of the research papers cited here.

There is also an article "Raw Food Diets Living Food — Review of Scientific Literature Journals," which summarizes some of the findings from studies into raw food diet research located at www.living-foods.com/articles/scientificliterature.html. As the author points out, the vast majority of research into the raw, or living, diet has been done in Europe.

I compiled in this chapter every raw food experiment I came across in all the different books I read. I thought it would be useful to have all of these experiments assembled in one book so that people could show anyone who is skeptical. I was inspired to do this by several events.

My doctor, when I told him of my new raw diet, scoffed, declaring that no research had been done. There was, in his tone of voice, an insinuation that I was hopelessly naïve! I have heard of numerous other raw fooders and aspiring raw fooders receiving the same treatment from their medical doctors.

Well, I handed him what little bit of research I had managed to gather at that point, but shortly after beginning my raw journey, I realized it was hopeless to work with someone so entrenched in the drug therapy paradigm and never went back to him.

I also had a dear friend, a medical doctor, who died of an inoperable brain tumor. When I suggested the raw diet, he had replied, "People get healed by that diet only because of their beliefs."

Certainly, the power of the mind to influence healing has been proven. The scientific name for that is the "placebo effect." There is a definite body/mind connection. However, raw food diets work with animals that have not been indoctrinated in a belief system.

Perhaps if I had already had this collection of experiments, I could have convinced him. Since I hadn't yet compiled the evidence, he died, having tried only a few fruitless treatments, including chemotherapy.

Admittedly, there may be a dearth of scientific studies showing that people on raw foods can heal of advanced stages of AIDS or eleventh-hour cancer. Who has the financial incentive to fund such studies? Certainly not the pharmaceutical companies! But what makes me laugh is people not only denying the healing power of natural foods, but also going so far as to think that eating a 100% raw food diet could be *dangerous*.

How do you think man's ancestors survived for literally millions of years prior to the invention of cooking?

I admit it would be nice to have still more research performed verifying the healing power of the body when it is fed a diet of natural, living foods. Personally, I do not need it, as I am totally convinced from the experiments I have done on myself and the results observed in others. But maybe more research would convince the skeptics and doctors.

Perhaps, as enough of us begin to compile research on ourselves, people will eventually view with amazement how utterly naïve we were to have ever believed that drugs could heal us better than Nature. Maybe then, finally, all the medical doctors will wake up and smell the fruit!

1.   Pottenger's Cats

Probably the most well-known study on the effects of cooked versus raw food was performed by Francis Pottenger, MD. He was raising cats for a scientific study on adrenal glands. He ran out of the raw food he had been feeding them; so, to economize, he gave some of them leftover, cooked table scraps.

He noticed health degeneration in the latter group, and so he decided to do an additional controlled experiment on the effects of raw versus cooked food. Over a ten-year period, he raised about 900 cats. Half were fed a diet of cooked meat, whereas the other half were fed raw meat. Both groups were given supplementary milk and cod liver oil.

These groups were kept in separate pens so there could be no eating from the other group's food. Pottenger was very careful to use scientifically controlled methods and even used the same male cat for breeding with both groups to minimize genetic factors. He kept such meticulous records that his study was published in the *American Journal of Orthodontics and Oral Surgery*.

The first generation of deficient cats began its cooked food diet only as adults. Their kittens were called second-generation deficient cats, and their "grand-kittens" were called third-generation deficient cats.

Pottenger noticed health declines with each generation. Gingivitis and gum tenderness worsened. Skulls got progressively smaller. Teeth did not grow in straight, and there was a narrowing and foreshortening of the dental arches. The calcium content of the bones worsened progressively until, by the third generation, the deficient cats had bones like sponge rubber with "spontaneous fractures on the slightest provocation."

Note: Cooked food often creates acidity in the body, and acidity causes calcium and other alkaline minerals to be leached from the bones in order to neutralize it.

In the second generation of deficient cats, 83% of the males were sterile, as were 53% of the females. The third generation cats were not even able to produce kittens and, in fact, died prematurely at about six months, the period corresponding to childhood in humans.

Symptoms displayed by the deficient cats were: incomplete development of the skull and bones, bowed legs, rickets, curvature of the spine, paralysis of the legs, convulsive seizure, thyroid abscesses, cyanosis of liver and kidneys, enlarged colon and degeneration of the motor nerve ganglion cells throughout the spinal cord and brain stem, with some cells affected in the cerebellum and cerebral cortex. The raw-food-fed cats suffered none of the above.

Behavioral differences were also documented. Cooked fooders were more irritable. A role reversal occurred, with male cats becoming submissive and females becoming more aggressive.

Furthermore, it was found that by returning kittens to the optimal diet of raw food, a gradual regeneration could occur. Yet from the second-generation deficient cats, it took *three generations* of kittens to get a litter that returned to the optimal health of the original cats! In the *second generation of cats returned to raw food*, deformities and allergies were still present due to *their parents'* having eaten cooked food! It was only *their* kittens that could achieve optimal health.

Pottenger made the following comments: "Man is rarely restricted in his dietary to a totally cooked food ration. It must be remembered that these cats do receive raw milk of market grade and that this is not sufficient to overcome the effects of cooked meat. Man seems to be more like a rat, having greater vitality than the cat, and he can apparently respond to deficient conditions in a better manner. Nevertheless, the changes found in cats are comparable to many of those that we see in human beings. Moreover, we are being told today by the anthropologists that civilized man is physically steadily on the downgrade. May not the heat processing to which we are subjecting a great portion of our foods be a factor in this downward trend?"

He goes on to remark that his colleague, Dr. Weston Price, dramatically documented the same downhill spiral of civilized man in his book *Nutrition and Physical Degeneration: A Comparison of Primitive and Modern Diets and Their Effects*. Although humans, rats and hogs are the most versatile animal species on the planet, they still suffer when eating cooked food, as has been borne out by many experiments.

There was even an experiment within this experiment. At some point, various types of milk were tested: raw, pasteurized, evaporated and sweetened, condensed milk. Plants that sprang up in the various pens were observed. Those that had been fertilized with the urine and feces of the cats fed raw food were vigorous and healthy. Plants fertilized with the excreta of pasteurized milk cats were less healthy. The growth was very poor with evaporated milk, and almost no growth occurred with the sweetened, condensed milk. The implications of using fertilizer from cooked-food animal excrement are staggering!

For more information on this experiment, read *Pottenger's Cats: A Study in Nutrition.*

2. Dr. Edmond Szekely's 33-Year Study

One of the greatest human experiments on the raw food diet was conducted by Dr. Edmond Szekely, who guided more than 123,600 people over a 33-year period (1937-1970) on a raw diet. Seventeen percent of these patients had been diagnosed "incurable." His treatment method was published in his book *The Chemistry of Youth*. He achieved amazing results in increasing people's health status in comparison to the control groups by using raw foods. Over 90% of the 123,600 patients regained their health.

Dr. Szekely was inspired to undertake this project by a trip he took to visit the Hunzas in Central Asia in the 1920s. These people lived long, productive lives (100-120 years) without the customary infirmities of aging.

Their undiminished vitality he attributed to their high consumption of sprouted seeds. "We may have learned how to extend the life span through the conquest of epidemics and contagious disease; but until we can achieve that level of vitality, well-being and complete freedom from degenerative disease known by the Hunzas at extremely advanced ages, we will not even have begun to penetrate the real secrets of longevity" (*The Chemistry of Youth*, p. 31).

It was at his center at Rancho La Puerta, Mexico that Szekely claims to have pioneered organic gardening, long before the term became popular. From his observations in what Dr. Szekely called his "Great Experiment," he classified foods into four groups. The first he called "biogenic" food, the most life-generating and cell-renewing group. These high-energy foods include all sprouts: soaked and germinated nuts, seeds, grains, legumes and grasses such as wheatgrass.

According to Dr. Edward Howell (*Food Enzymes for Health and Longevity*), sprouting increases enzyme content by 6-20 times. Vitamin and mineral content is also greatly increased. For example, according to Ann Wigmore (*The Hippocrates Diet and Health Program*), Vitamin B_6 can be increased up to 500%, B_2 up to 1300% and folic acid by 600%. These biogenic foods are the most capable of healing and regenerating the body; so Szekely felt they should make up 25% of a healthy person's diet, perhaps more if the person were seriously ill.

The second category he called "bioactive," which were raw fruits and vegetables, unheated and untreated. These foods are capable of maintaining and slightly enhancing an already healthy body. Dr. Szekely felt these foods should make up about half of a healthy person's diet.

The third category he termed "biostatic," referring to foods that stabilize or actually slightly diminish the body's functioning and slowly age a person. These include cooked foods and even raw foods that are not fresh. Dr. Szekely allowed for these foods to be 10-25% of a healthy person's diet, not because they are needed or healthful, but because he felt most people could not stick with a diet so limited as to exclude cooked foods.

The fourth category, "bioacidic," he considered to be so life-destructive that he felt we should eliminate these altogether, even if we presently feel healthy. These are processed and/or refined foods full of additives, preservatives and/or pesticide residues. They rapidly tear down and age the body.

3.   Lewis Cook and Junko Yasui's Rats

Described in their book *Goldot*, Cook and Yasui studied three groups of rats. The first group was fed a raw diet from birth. They suffered no diseases, remained very healthy and full of energy, and were never fat. They mated with enthusiasm, producing healthy offspring. These rats were gentle, playful and affectionate, living in perfect harmony with each other.

They were killed and their bodies examined when they reached the equivalent of 80 human years and found to be in perfect health with no sign of aging, degeneration or disease.

The second group was fed from birth a diet consisting of cooked food: bread, milk, salt, junk food, soft drinks, candies, vitamins and medications — in other words, the SAD. They grew fat. They developed the same degenerative conditions that humans on such a diet do: heart disease, cancer, diabetes, arthritis, obesity, colds, bouts of the flu and so on.

Their behavior was also affected, and they became nervous, mean, self-destructive and violent toward each other. They even had to be kept apart to prevent them from killing each other. Their offspring were the same. Many died prematurely.

Autopsies showed great degeneration throughout their organs. All of the organs, glands, tissues, skin, hair, blood and nervous systems were negatively affected by the diet.

The third group was fed the SAD too and also exhibited poor health. They were just as mean and vicious as the second group and had to be kept separated. But when they reached middle age, the equivalent of 40 human years, they were fasted strictly on water. Then they were given the raw, healthful diet of the first group of rats. This was alternated with periodic fasting in order to gradually detoxify the residual toxins remaining from the SAD.

They gradually became as healthy, playful and affectionate with each other as the rats in the first group. They could co-exist in harmony and displayed no illnesses.

Upon reaching the same age as the other rats, they were put to death and autopsied. They were shown to be just as healthy as the first group.

The implications of this are astounding: A raw diet and fasting were found to have reversed aging and degeneration! The lesson we learn is that although we have polluted our bodies, we can reverse much of the destruction with raw food diets. Fasting helps speed up the detoxification process.

The authors state, "The same principles apply to human life as there is only one truth! Thus it may be concluded that sick people may be restored to health simply by choosing the proper diet, fasting and observing the other rules of health. There is no mystery. There is no external force that will help — all healing [is] being accomplished within the body by the body in accordance with the laws of organic life and health."

4. Numerous Studies at the University of Kuopio, Finland

Quite a few controlled studies of the raw food diet's effects were performed at the University of Kuopio in Finland. One study conducted by the department of physiology found that the raw vegan diet had beneficial effects on fibromyalgia.

Fifteen control patients continued their omnivorous diet while 18 ate the raw diet for three months. Those eating the raw diet experienced significant improvement compared to the control group. Their pain lessened, joint stiffness improved, sleep improved, and general health improved. Serum cholesterol and urine sodium were lowered, and the majority of the patients, having been overweight to begin with, lost weight.

Results were published in an article called, "Vegan diet alleviates fibromyalgia symptoms," which appeared in the *Scandinavian Journal of Rheumatology* (2000, Vol. 29, Issue 5, pp. 308-313, PubMed ID 11093597).

The department of physiology also published a paper called, "Shifting from a conventional diet to an uncooked vegan diet reversibly alters fecal hydrolytic activities in humans" in *The Journal of Nutrition* (1992, Vol. 122, Issue 4, pp. 924-930, PubMed ID 552366).

The test group adopted a raw vegan diet for one month and then resumed a conventional diet for a second month, while the control group consumed a conventional diet throughout the study. Blood levels of the chemicals phenol and p-cresol, daily urine output and fecal enzyme activities were measured.

Within one week of commencing the raw vegan diet, fecal urease had decreased by 66%, cholylglycine hydrolase by 55%, beta-glucuronidase by 33% and beta-glucosidase by 40%. These values remained lowered throughout the diet. Within two weeks of resuming the conventional diet, however, the fecal enzyme activities returned to normal values.

In plain English, these results suggested that the raw vegan diet caused a decrease in bacterial enzymes and certain toxic products that have been implicated in colon cancer risk.

The same department also performed a study that found that a raw food, vegan diet benefited patients with rheumatoid arthritis. In this study, the benefits were found to be both subjective and objective. Subjectively, the patients felt better. Objectively, joint stiffness was reduced, and significant increases of antioxidants (protective chemicals) were found in the blood of the raw fooders. This study was published in the *British Journal of Rheumatology* (March, 1998, Vol. 37, Issue 3, pp. 274-281, PubMed ID 9566667). The article is entitled, "Uncooked, lacto-bacilli-rich, vegan food and rheumatoid arthritis."

They also published a study entitled, "Effects of eating an uncooked vegetable diet for 1 week" (*Appetite*, Vol. 19, pp. 243-254, PubMed ID 1482162). That study concluded that such a vegetable diet may be of some benefit in the short term, but any longer-term use requires further evaluation.

Yet another study conducted by this university entitled, "Antioxidants in vegan diet and rheumatic disorders" was published in *Toxicology* (November 30, 2000, Vol. 155, Issues 1-3, pp. 45-53, PubMed ID 11154796).

A living food diet of uncooked berries, vegetables, roots, nuts, germinated seeds and sprouts was fed to one group, whereas the control group ate the typical omnivorous diet.

The raw food eaters experienced decreased joint stiffness and pain, as well as improvement in their self-experienced health. They also experienced improvement in objective health measures.

An article called, "Vegan diet in physiological health promotion" appeared in *Acta Physiologica Hungarica* (1999, Vol. 86, Issues 3-4, pp. 171-80, PubMed ID 10943644). It was written by members of the department of physiology at the University of Kuopio.

It was found that eating a diet of raw vegan food increased levels of carotenoids and Vitamins C and E. It also lowered cholesterol concentrations, as well as urinary phenol and p-cresol. Several fecal enzyme levels that are considered harmful were also lowered. The patients that had arthritis reported a lessening of pain, stiffness and swelling of joints. Those with fibromyalgia lost weight. Upon resuming their normal diet, these all got worse.

The same university's department of clinical nutrition performed a study in which they found that the living food diet "provides significantly more dietary antioxidants than does the cooked, omnivorous diet and that the long-term adherents to this diet have a better antioxidant status than do omnivorous control subjects." This was published in *The American Journal of Clinical Nutrition* (December 1995, Vol. 62, Issue 6, pp. 1221-1227, PubMed ID 7491884). The article is called, "Antioxidant status in long-term adherents to a strict uncooked vegan diet."

The department of clinical nutrition also wrote an article entitled, "Effect of a strict vegan diet on energy and nutrient intakes by Finnish rheumatoid patients." It was published in the *European Journal of Clinical Nutrition* (October 1993, Vol. 47, Issue 10, pp. 747-749, PubMed ID 8269890).

Forty-three Finnish rheumatoid arthritis patients were divided into two groups. The experiment lasted three months. The experimental group of 21 patients ate uncooked vegan food and had tutoring by a living-food expert. The control group of 22 ate their usual diets and had no tutoring.

It was found that shifting to an uncooked vegan diet significantly increased the intake of energy and many nutrients. The raw vegan dieters also lost 9% of their body weight.

5. Studies at Hallelujah Acres on the Effect of a Raw Diet on Fibromyalgia and Nutrient Intake

A study was done at Hallelujah Acres, a center founded by Rev. George Malkmus, who advocates an 85-100% raw food diet. The study is entitled, "Fibromyalgia syndrome improved using a mostly raw vegetarian diet: an observational study," published in *BMC Complementary Alternative Medicine* (2001, Vol. 1, Issue 1, p. 7, PubMed ID 11602026).

Fibromyalgia patients generally suffer from chronic pain, fatigue, poor quality sleep and depression. Thirty patients were put on a mostly raw, vegan diet. After several months, 19 of the patients experienced significant improvement as measured by tests like shoulder pain at rest and after motion, abduction range of motion of shoulder, flexibility, a chair test and a six-minute walk.

Michael Donaldson, Director of Research at Hallelujah Acres, published another study, "Food and nutrient intake of Hallelujah vegetarians." It was published in *Nutrition and Food Science* (2001, Vol. 31, Issue 6, pp. 293-303).

For 28 months, 141 followers of the Hallelujah diet, which is 100% vegan and at least 85% raw, kept dietary journals. Members reported significant improvement in health and quality of life after adopting the diet. Mean daily consumption of fruits and vegetables was 6.6 servings and 11.4 servings, respectively. The mean energy intake was 1,460 calories for women and 1,830 calories for men. It was found that, with some modification, this diet pattern allows people to adopt a low-calorie diet sufficient in most nutrients.

Donaldson published another study in *Annals of Nutrition & Metabolism* (2000, Vol. 44, pp. 229-234, PubMed ID 11146329) entitled, "Metabolic vitamin B_{12} status on a mostly raw vegan diet with follow-up using tablets, nutritional yeast, or probiotic supplements."

It was concluded that people following the Hallelujah diet or other raw vegan diets should take cobalamin (Vitamin B_{12}) supplements. (See Chapter 12 for more on the B_{12} issue.)

6. John MacDonald's Mice

Ann Wigmore describes the following experience in her book *Be Your Own Doctor: A Positive Guide to Natural Living*. A friend of hers, John MacDonald, had a pet shop that specialized in white mice, selling them by the thousands all over the world. In the enclosure for the mice would be their "apartment complex" made of a large bale of hay. There they led happy, peaceful, playful, harmonious lives.

When John became concerned about the rising cost of grain to feed his mice, a neighbor with a boardinghouse offered to supply him with leftover table scraps. John saw this as a way to increase his profits, but when the mice began eating the same food that humans ate, quarrels broke out, and battles raged through the corridors of the baled-hay cooperative mouse house. Within a week, there were many dead mice, having been killed by other mice. Parent mice ate their young. Weaker mice were killed for no reason.

Finally John went back to feeding them grain, refusing the table scraps. Once again, peace reigned, and the mice returned to sound mental health.

7. South African Studies of a Mainly Fruit Diet

Inspired by a 45-year-old woman he met who was in excellent health despite having eaten a fruitarian diet for 12 years, Professor B. J. Meyer of the University of Pretoria in South Africa performed an experiment. He fed a control group of 50 people fruits (mostly raw, though some canned or stewed) and nuts alone for six months.

They became sickness-free, with greatly improved health and weight. Many claimed that their stamina increased, along with their ability to undertake serious physical tasks and compete in sports. The pH of their urine changed from acid to alkaline. The four subjects who were originally hypertensive had decreased blood pressures.

The February 20, 1971 issue of the *South African Medical Journal* published the results in an article called, "Some physiological effects of a mainly fruit diet in man" (Vol. 45, Issue 8, pp. 191-195, PubMed ID 4928686).

In the next issue, March 6, he published a sequel article, "Some biochemical effects of a mainly fruit diet in man." The effect of the nut-supplemented fruit diet on glucose tolerance, secretions, plasma proteins and plasma lipids was investigated. It was found to be not merely adequate with respect to those measures, but even commendable.

8.   Raw Diet Increases Intelligence

Renowned raw food teacher Victoria Boutenko performed a raw food study herself. A university professor conducted the experiment. There was a control group that did not eat raw food. The experimental group ate raw food for only two days. (She wanted them to do it for a week, but no one thought he could!) They were given an intelligence test before eating raw and after.

Although many people still believe that IQ is something static, her amazing findings were that after eating raw for only two days, the average IQ was raised by 40%! Victoria discussed her findings at a workshop she gave. She may be contacted through her web site at www.rawfamily.com.

9.   Dr. Jean Seignalet's Study

Dr. Jean Seignalet of the hospital St. Eloi in Montpellier, France undertook a large-scale experiment with a diet he prescribed to hundreds of patients. The diet consisted of as much raw food as possible and excluded all dairy and wheat products. Success rates were defined as remission and a 50% reduction in disease or ailment symptoms. He tested people with dozens of different diseases and syndromes.

Success rates for all ranged from 75% to 100%. Patients enjoying a 100% success rate included those with systemic lupus, scleroderma, juvenile diabetes, Crohn's disease, acne, atopic eczema, hay fever, rhinitis, allergic conjunctivitis, edema and more. Patients enjoying a 92-98% success rate included those with fibromyalgia, ankylosing spondylitis, psoriatic arthritis, multiple sclerosis (MS), depression, spasmophilia, irritable bowel syndrome, urticaria and asthma. (See *L'Alimentation ou la Troisième Médecine* [*Nutrition or the Third Medicine*], Dr. Jean Seignalet, Édition François-Xavier de Guilbert, Paris.)

10. Dr. Israel Brekhman's Study

Dr. Israel Brekhman of the former Soviet Union performed a simple experiment with telling results. He fed mice cooked food and live, raw food at different times. When these mice ate only the raw food, they had *three times more energy and endurance* than when eating cooked food. Dr. Gabriel Cousens writes about this in *Rainbow Green Live-Food Cuisine* (p. 117).

11. Dr. Otto Louis Moritz Abramowski and His Hospital Patients

Dr. Abramowski was an Australian medical doctor who was cured of hardening of the arteries, loss of vigor and inability to work by means of a raw, vegetarian diet in his middle years. After turning to raw foods, he felt better than he had felt even as a young man. So enthusiastic was he that he decided to conduct an experiment at his hospital.

As told in his booklet *Fruitarian Diet and Physical Rejuvenation*, he divided over a hundred patients into two groups: The first was kept on standard hospital food and drug therapy, and the second was taken off all drugs and given only fresh fruit, three pounds a day.

Several weeks into the experiment, it was abruptly terminated when the head nurse objected to the inhumanity of the experiment. She felt it would be immoral to continue giving drugs and cooked food to the first group because, she said, it was clearly killing them!

12.   The Prisoner of War Diet

Prisoners of war in Japan during WW II were fed a scanty diet of brown rice, vegetables and fruit, totaling only 729-826 calories per 154 pounds of body weight. In 1950, Dr. Masanore Kuratsune, head of the Medical Department of the University of Kyushu in Japan, thought that this diet might be a remarkable way to validate previous studies comparing raw and cooked food. He and his wife decided to be the guinea pigs. Both followed the raw version of the same diet for three periods: 120 days in winter, 32 days in summer and 81 days in spring. Mrs. Kuratsune was breastfeeding a baby during this time. Both continued to do their usual work. Remarkably, they both continued to enjoy good health. Mrs. Kuratsune even found that breastfeeding was less of a strain than before eating this raw diet.

Next, they both switched to the same prisoner diet in cooked form. They became as hungry and diseased as the prisoners of war. They quickly came down with edema, vitamin deficiencies and collapse. It became so bad that they were forced to stop the experiment.

This study was recounted in a 1967 monograph written by Dr. Ralph Bircher-Benner of Zurich entitled, *Dr. Bircher-Benner's Way to Positive Health and Vitality, 1867-1967.*

13.   Dr. Werner Kollath's Animal Study

Just before World War II, Professor Kollath at the University of Rostock in Germany raised animals on processed food that had neither vitamins nor minerals except for thiamine, potassium, sulfate and zinc.

Despite the depleted diet, the animals initially appeared healthy, showing no signs of deficiency. But when they reached adulthood, they displayed degenerative signs much like those of humans living in the Western world: osteoporosis, intestinal toxemia, dental cavities and damaged organs.

He then gave them vitamin supplements to see if that would reverse their conditions. No improvement was noted. The only thing that reversed the chronic degeneration was a diet of fresh, living, raw food composed of many vegetables.

A control group raised on raw food all along that was never fed the processed food did not acquire the degenerative disease conditions. He labeled these differences "meso-health" and "super-health."

Researchers in Sweden and Germany later confirmed Dr. Kollath's findings. Research scientists studying raw food diet and its use in treating illness believe that great numbers of people in industrialized societies are living in states of "meso-health" due to their highly processed and devitalized food.

14. Raw Diet's Effect on Athletes

Professor Karl Eimer, director of the Medical Clinic at the University of Vienna, had athletes eat their usual cooked diet for two weeks of highly intensive training. He monitored and evaluated their athletic performance. Next, they were put on a 100% raw food diet and continued with the same training.

Every one of the athletes improved in reflex speed, flexibility and stamina. Eimer and his colleague Professor Hans Eppinger concluded that raw foods increase cellular respiration and efficiency. His article, "Klinik Schwenkenbecher," is written in German and was published in the July 1933 edition of *Zeitschrift für Ernährung*.

15. Sir Robert McCarrison's Monkeys

In India, Sir Robert McCarrison fed monkeys their usual diet, but in a cooked form. The monkeys all developed colitis. Autopsies revealed that they also had gastric and intestinal ulcers. The book *Raw Energy* describes this study on page 37.

16. O. Stiner's Guinea Pigs

In Switzerland, O. Stiner put some guinea pigs on their usual diet, but cooked. The animals quickly succumbed to anemia, scurvy, goiter, dental cavities and degeneration of the salivary glands. When 10 cc of pasteurized milk was added to the diet, they got arthritis as well. The book *Nature's First Law* refers to this study, as do several web sites. It is also mentioned in *Raw Energy*, page 37.

17. Dr. John Douglass and His Addiction, Hypertension and Obesity Studies

Dr. John Douglass, MD, PhD, of Kaiser-Permanente Medical Center in Los Angeles, California, prescribed raw foods to his patients and noticed that common addictions, such as to alcohol and nicotine, lose their addictive power on raw food diets.

Experimenting with specific foods, he found that sunflower seeds in particular were especially effective at fighting the cravings of addictions. He found that raw foods make the body more sensitive to what is good for it and what is bad for it.

He discussed some of his findings in an article called, "Nutrition, nonthermally-prepared food, and Nature's message to man," which was published in the *Journal of the International Academy of Preventive Medicine*, Vol. VII, Issue 2, July 1982.

Douglass went on to publish another article with five other researchers entitled, "Effects of a raw food diet on hypertension and obesity," which was published in the *Southern Medical Journal*, July 1985, Volume 78, Issue 7, pp. 841-844, PubMed ID 4012382.

They examined responses to cooked and uncooked food in 32 people with hypertension, 28 of which were also overweight. Patients acted as their own controls.

After a mean duration of 6.7 months, average food intake of uncooked food comprised 62% of the calories ingested. The mean weight loss was 3.8 kg (about 8.3 pounds!), and mean diastolic pressure reduction was 17.8 mm Hg, both statistically significant. Most interestingly, perhaps, was that *80% of those who drank alcohol or smoked abstained spontaneously.*

18. Dr. Robinson's Living Foods Cancer Treatment

As President and Research Director of the Linus Pauling Institute of Science and Medicine, Dr. Arthur Robinson studied the effects of live foods, including wheatgrass, as opposed to synthetic Vitamin C, on cancer in laboratory mice.

He used various groups of mice, giving them skin cancer with ultraviolet radiation and then feeding them on differing diets that included supplementary Vitamin E and varying amounts of Vitamin C. The control group got "standard" mouse feed only. Some of the groups got raw foods similar to those recommended by Dr. Ann Wigmore.

It is important to point out that although Dr. Robinson was aware of a low-calorie, raw food diet's power to *totally reverse* cancer, this experiment was designed merely to test the ability of the raw food diet to *slow down* cancer growth.

The living foods alone were found to decrease cancer incidence by about 75%. This could be duplicated with vitamin C supplementation only by giving doses so massive as to be nearly lethal for the mice and far beyond any reasonable range for humans to consume.

However, when high protein, high fat foods were added to the diet, even raw ones like nuts and seeds, cancer suppression stopped. It seemed that only raw fruits and vegetables, which are lower in calories, worked.

In other words, if these rodent results translate to humans, a diet considered healthful and ample for a healthy person could be deadly to a person with cancer, who really needs calorie restriction in addition to a raw produce diet to starve the cancer.

"The effect is so large that, in my opinion," states Robinson, "if diet restriction were practiced by all cancer patients in the United States, the resulting life extension might equal or surpass that resulting from the combined efforts of the entire current medical oncology effort."

Interestingly, Robinson also found that Vitamin C supplementation at less massive megadoses of from 1 to 5 grams daily would actually *accelerate* cancer growth. Only near-lethal doses of about 100 grams could give the same effect as the raw fruit and vegetable diet.

This discovery was so disturbing to Linus Pauling that Robinson and Pauling terminated their 16-year professional collaboration! Dr. Pauling was not willing to accept the fact that artificial Vitamin C supplementation in moderate megadoses accelerates cancer growth.

Robinson's study, "Suppression of squamous cell carcinoma in hairless mice by dietary nutrient variation," *Mechanisms of Ageing and Development*, July 1994, pp. 201-214, is described in an article entitled, "Living Foods and Cancer" that can be found at www.nutritionandcancer.org.

19. Effects of a Diet High in Vegetables, Fruit and Nuts on Serum Lipids

A study entitled, "Effect of a diet high in vegetables, fruit and nuts on serum lipids" was published in *Metabolism* (May 1997, Vol. 46, Issue 5, pp. 530-537, PubMed ID 9160820). The effects of a diet high in leafy, green vegetables, fruit and nuts on serum lipid risk factors for cardiovascular disease were assessed. Ten healthy volunteers consumed their habitual diet for two weeks and then for another two weeks ate a diet largely consisting of vegetables, fruits and nuts.

After two weeks on the plant diet, the lipid risk factors for cardiovascular disease were significantly reduced in comparison with the control diet. The reduction in total serum cholesterol was 34% to 49% greater than would be predicted by differences in dietary fat and cholesterol.

The researchers concluded: "A diet consisting largely of low-calorie vegetables and fruit and nuts markedly reduced lipid risk factors for cardiovascular disease. Several aspects of such diets, which may have been consumed early in human evolution, have implications for cardiovascular disease prevention."

The same team of researchers published another study entitled, "Effect of a very-high-fiber vegetable, fruit, and nut diet on serum lipids and colonic function" (*Metabolism*, 2001 Apr; 50[4]: pp. 494-503, PubMed ID 11288049). That study demonstrated that a very high vegetable fiber intake reduces risk of cardiovascular disease and colon cancer.

20. Cooked Milk Bad for Calves

The *British Medical Journal* published a study entitled, "The effect of heat treatment on the nutritive value of milk for the young calf: the effect of ultra-high temperature treatment and of pasteurization" (Vol. 14, Issue 10, 1960).

Calves were fed their mothers' milk after it had been pasteurized. The calves died before maturity in nine out of ten cases, proving the harmful effects of cooked milk, *even for creatures designed to drink cow's milk.*

21. Research in Germany

An article entitled, "Raw food and immunity," published in *Fortschr Med* (June 10, 1990, Vol. 108, Issue 17, pp. 338-340, PubMed ID 2198207), summarizes research on the raw diet. "Uncooked food is an integral component of human nutrition and is a necessary precondition for an intact immune system. Its therapeutic effect is complex, and a variety of influences of raw food and its constituents on the immune system have been documented. Such effects include antibiotic, antiallergic, tumor-protective, immunomodulatory and anti-inflammatory actions. In view of this, uncooked food can be seen as a useful adjunct to drugs in the treatment of allergic, rheumatic and infectious diseases."

22. A Summary of 30 Years of Clinical Experimentation on Diet Therapy and Advanced Cancer

Dr. Max Gerson, MD, wrote an article entitled, "The cure of advanced cancer by diet therapy: a summary of 30 years of clinical experimentation," which was published in *Physiol Chem Phys* (1978, Vol. 10, Issue 5, pp. 449-464, PubMed ID 751079). The study concluded that *even advanced stages of cancer* respond to the treatment of raw fruits, vegetables and raw-liver-derived active, oxidizing enzymes (which facilitate rehabilitation of the liver), with no fats, oils or animal proteins. Iodine and niacin supplements were also given, along with coffee enemas.

23. The Effects of Raw Diet on Weight Loss and Amenorrhea

Published in the *Annals of Nutrition and Metabolism* (1999, Vol. 43, Issue 2, pp. 69-79, PubMed ID 10436305), this study was called, "Consequences of a long-term raw food diet on body weight and menstruation: results of a questionnaire survey." This study was performed at the Institute of Nutritional Science at Justus Liebig University of Giessen, Germany.

The study involved 216 men and 297 women who ate raw diets varying from 70% to 100% raw for 3.7 years. An average weight loss of 22 pounds (9.9 kg) for men and 26 pounds (12 kg) for women was observed. About 30% of the women under 45 years of age experienced partial to complete amenorrhea (loss of menstrual bleeding). Those who ate a large percentage of raw foods (over 90%) were affected more than moderate raw food eaters.

The study concluded that raw diets are associated with a high loss of body weight and amenorrhea. The writers of the article stated, "Since many raw food dieters exhibited underweight and amenorrhea, a very strict raw food diet cannot be recommended on a long-term basis."

This statement displays the cultural bias ingrained in our belief systems that being underweight is not healthy when, in fact, it has been shown to extend life, along with the idea that menstrual bleeding is healthy when, in fact, apes in the wild in their natural habitats do not experience it. Some modern-day apes do bleed slightly, perhaps due to environmental pollution and zoo diets that are not always 100% raw.

In humans, menstrual bleeding is thought by raw food experts to be a sign of toxicity and/or Vitamin C deficiency. It would be nonsensical to state that people should not be on a raw food diet for a long-term basis when that is how we, as all animal species, evolved over millions of years!

24. Height and Weight Effects of the Live Food Diet on Pre-adolescent Children

Dr. Gabriel Cousens of the Tree of Life nonprofit foundation felt that research needed to be published on the effects of live food diets on children since so many raw food parents get harassed by the authorities for "child abuse."

His preliminary results as of June 2004 show that the heights of 74% of the children were above the lowest 25th percentile and the weights of 68% of the children were above the lowest 25th percentile. All children were above the 10th percentile. The heights of 37% of the children were above the 75% percentile. Over 60% of the children were above average for both weight and height as measured by the National Center for Chronic Disease Prevention and Health Promotion.

Dr. Cousens notes that these children are also not under the influence of the stimulating effects of growth hormones to which the majority of non-vegan children are exposed since the vegans do not consume meat and dairy, which are full of hormones. He also notes, "The preliminary conclusion of our data is that a live food diet has no major positive or negative effect on height and weight. None of the children in the study have a score above the top 90th percentile or below the lowest 10th percentile. Therefore, the children fall into the middle 80% of normal height and weight."

This study has not been published, as it is not yet finished. The preliminary results were written in a handout passed out at the 2004 annual Raw Food Festival in Portland, Oregon.

Note: Dr. Cousens is very aware of one risk for children on a raw vegan diet: the potential lack of Vitamin B_{12}. He is very careful to monitor the children for this, which all responsible parents of raw vegan children should do. (See Chapter 12.)

25. Bone Mass in Long-Term Raw Fooders

Led by Dr. Luigi Fontana, MD, a study was published entitled, "Low bone mass in subjects on a long-term raw vegetarian diet" in the *Archives of Internal Medicine* (Vol. 165, Issue 6, March 28, 2005, pp. 684-689, PubMed ID 15795346).

This was a cross-sectional study of 18 volunteers aged 18-85 who had been eating a raw vegan diet for a mean of 3.6 years. They were compared with people of their own age who ate a conventional diet. Both groups were measured for body mass index, bone mass, bone mineral density, markers of bone turnover, levels of Vitamin D and inflammatory markers, such as C-reactive protein and insulin-like growth factors.

The raw vegans were found to have less inflammation, indicated by low levels of C-reactive protein, which is made by the liver in response to inflammation in the body, inflammation being a sign of disease progression and aging. They also had lower levels of IGF-1, which meant lower risk of breast and prostate cancer. Their bone turnover rates were normal. They had higher levels of Vitamin D, which Fontana initially thought was going to be a problem area since vegans don't consume dairy fortified with Vitamin D. He attributed their high Vitamin D levels to their being conscientious enough to expose themselves to sufficient sunlight. Those on the raw diet also had lower body mass indices and lower body fat percentages.

Interestingly, the raw fooders also had low levels of the hormone leptin, which is associated with high bone density. They exhibited lower bone mass in significant places, such as the hips and spine, which theoretically could lead to osteoporosis and fracture risk. However, they didn't have the negative biological markers that typically accompany osteoporosis.

Fontana proposed that, despite having lower bone mass, those on the raw diet actually may have good, healthy bone quality. He hypothesized that since their bone turnover markers were normal, their Vitamin D levels above normal, and their inflammation levels low, it was possible that the raw fooders didn't have increased risk of fracture. Perhaps, he said, their bone mass is related to the fact that they weigh less because they take in fewer calories.

26. Raw Vegetables Protective Against Cancer

The *Journal of the American Dietetic Association,* October 1996, Issue 10, pp. 1027-1039, PubMed ID 8841165, published an article entitled, "Vegetables, fruit and cancer prevention: a review." A review of 206 human epidemiologic studies and 22 animal studies on the relationship between fruits and vegetables and cancer risk found that raw vegetables are the number one protective food against cancer.

27. Other Studies Linking Raw Vegetable Consumption to Reduced Cancer Risk

In 2005, a study done at the University of New Mexico showed that women migrating from Poland to the USA tripled their risk of breast cancer. This resulted because they no longer consumed at least three servings a week of raw cabbage and sauerkraut, which were found to contain glucosinolates that help protect against cancer. Brussels sprouts, broccoli and kale also contain glucosinolates.

Another study published in the *Japanese Journal of Cancer Research* (June 1993, PubMed ID 8340248) showed that raw vegetable and fruit consumption reduces the odds of incurring lung cancer among smokers and former smokers. The study was entitled, "Protective effects of raw vegetables and fruit against lung cancer among smokers and ex-smokers: a case-control study in the Tokai area of Japan."

A study published by the Kaunas University of Medicine in Lithuania (2005) found that higher consumption of raw vegetables, such as cabbage, carrots, garlic and broccoli may decrease the risk of stomach cancer.

28. Long-Term Raw Diet Associated with Favorable Serum LDL Cholesterol and Triglycerides

An article published in the October 2005 edition of *The Journal of Nutrition* (135, Issue 10, pp. 2372-2378, PubMed ID 16177198) is entitled, "Long-term consumption of a raw food diet is associated with favorable serum LDL cholesterol and triglycerides but also with elevated plasma homocysteine and low serum HDL cholesterol in humans."

On the positive side, the raw diet reduces some of the causes of cardiovascular disease. However, raw fooders must make certain to take Vitamin B_{12} supplements, or they may accumulate excess homocysteine, a risk factor in heart disease and a marker for B_{12} deficiency. (See Chapter 12.) Additionally, some raw fooders in the experiment had lower amounts of HDL, known as "the good cholesterol."

The study makes mention that there was high consumption of raw fruits and vegetables, but perhaps the participants were not eating sufficient nuts. Almonds, for example, were found to increase the "good" cholesterol, HDL, in a study published in *Circulation, Journal of the American Heart Association* (2002). A study published in *The Journal of Nutrition* (2003) found macademia nuts did the same. Additional studies have found that pistachios and walnuts improve the ratio of HDL to LDL.

29. The Roseburg Study

Victoria Boutenko and Paul Fieber, MD executed this study on the effects of raw, green smoothies on patients who had low levels of hydrochloric acid (HCl). Twenty-seven participants drank a quart of green smoothies prepared by Victoria's husband every day for 30 days, adding it to their normal diet. Three participants dropped out; of the 24 remaining, 66.7% showed vast improvement in their HCl levels. The doctor did not expect to see such dramatic results in such a short period of time. The participants reported many other beneficial effects, such as improved sex life — one man even saying it was like being 15 years younger! — reduced cravings for bad foods, better sleep and elimination and much more. For further details on this study, read *Green for Life* by Victoria Boutenko. See Appendix C for more on her revolutionary, green smoothie raw diet.

The Most Important and Convincing Experiment of All

Additional experiments reported in scientific journals are summarized briefly in Appendix D. Finally, if not one of these experiments convinces you, it is time to try the most important experiment of all, the one on yourself! The living food diet speaks for itself.

About two weeks of a 100% raw food diet changes the most skeptical and cynical of people, who need no "scientific proof" at that point that it really works. Experience is sufficient to satisfy them.

The next few chapters explain the scientific theory behind the raw food diet so that you will understand how important it is to eat raw and how toxic it is to eat cooked.

But if you can't wait to get started, skip ahead to Section Four, and come back to the rest of Section Two later.

6
Man's Fatal Chemistry Lab: The Great Cooked Food Experiment

> We cannot escape from being entangled in the
> conclusion that intractable disease is as old as cookery.
> —Dr. Edward Howell (1898-1987)

Even if you are not a "science person," I encourage you to read this. Reread it if you backslide into cooked foods or are tempted to. Even if you don't understand some of the terms, you will get the gist of it, and it will become ingrained into your mind that "cooked food is poison." You may not understand what the chemical byproducts mean. You may not even be able to pronounce the terms. But you should be aware that you do not want these chemicals in your body!

A couple of terms used in this chapter include "carcinogenic," which means "cancer-causing," and "mutagenic," which means "causing mutations in the DNA sequence of a gene or chromosome." Mutations are often precursors to cancer, and so the two are related.

As stated in *Diet, Nutrition and Cancer* (p. 277), "Initiation of the carcinogenic process may involve an alteration in the genetic material of a cell. Therefore, it is reasonable to suppose that chemicals that alter DNA (i.e., cause mutations) will have a high probability of being initiators of carcinogenesis."

People have asked me, "But why focus on the negative?"

I feel that both the positive aspects of a raw diet and the negative aspects of a cooked one are important to recognize. It is too easy to backslide into the world of cooked food if you do not understand the rationale behind avoiding it.

It is not simply a matter, as the American Cancer Society would say, of eating a certain number of fruit and vegetable servings per day. The implication here is that once you finish your quota of the good stuff, you can eat pretty much whatever you want. This is clearly not the case. *What you refuse to eat is as much a health factor as what you do eat*, especially in a world in which cooked food is everywhere.

I know some people who merely pop a few pills of dehydrated fruits and vegetables and think they can get away with eating whatever they like after that. They are sadly mistaken.

Cooking and organic chemistry operate primarily in the temperature range between 68° F and 572° F (20° C and 300° C). When you were in chemistry lab at school, you no doubt learned that heating things changed their chemical structures. Why would heating food be immune to this process?

Think of a kitchen as a chemical laboratory, producing a multitude of new chemical substances that do not normally occur in a natural setting. And think of modern man as unknowingly being immersed in a grand chemistry experiment by eating cooked and denatured food.

When various foods are commingled and cooked, thousands of new molecules are created. Serious researchers do not believe the human body has adapted to these numerous complex molecules that we have been ingesting for only a few thousand years. In fact, so many new chemicals are created that it would take millions of years of evolution even to make a dent in adapting to them all.

Is Cooked Food Toxic?

In Chapter 4, we explained that it is the body's environment, not the germ or gene, that is most responsible for our state of health. One of the keys to maintaining a healthy biological terrain is staying free of toxic accumulations. As we shall see, cooking food makes it toxic.

Are we playing with fire when we cook our food? Man is the only creature on earth that cooks its food. Animals in the wild do not cook. When these creatures die of old age, they remain free of the degenerative diseases of civilization, such as cancer, diabetes, arthritis and heart disease, so long as they haven't been subjected to heavily polluted water or air.

In the 1930s, research done in Switzerland showed that leukocytes (white blood cells) increased in people after eating cooked food. This leukocytosis was otherwise known to happen in a person only after being exposed to toxic substances, trauma or infection. Because cooking is so deeply ingrained in all cultures, when "digestive leukocytosis" was first observed, it was assumed to be normal, and it occurred to no one that the cooked food was toxic.

Then Dr. Paul Kouchakoff discovered that eating raw food or food heated at very low temperatures, under 118° F (48° C) provoked no digestive leukocytosis. He also found that refined, homogenized, pasteurized, preserved or otherwise denatured foods greatly increased the white blood cell count.

Since then, Dr. Howard Loomis has repeated Dr. Kouchakoff's results with hundreds of patients in his clinical work. He found that over-stimulating the immune system three to four times a day by eating cooked food is very stressful to the human body.

Cooking and processing food destroys nutrients by changing their shape, size and chemical structure. The ensuing biochemical chaos results in the accumulation of indigestible and harmful substances, residue and debris. Moreover, cooked food is prepared in utensils that emit toxic metal, plastic or paint particles.

After cooking, look at what sticks to the pots and pans: grease, sticky starches, gooey cheese! This is a reflection of what sticks to your intestines. On the other hand, raw foods cling neither to the pots nor to your intestines. In addition, look at the clogged sink drains common among those who prepare cooked foods. Raw fooders' drains don't clog up with grease and don't need to be roto-rooted. Nor do their arteries clog up and need stents, angioplasty or bypass surgery!

Cooking has been proven to produce millions of different "Maillard molecules," sugar and protein combinations. In 1916, the chemist Louis Maillard proved that brown pigments and polymers that occur in pyrolysis (i.e., chemical breakdown caused by heat alone — in other words, cooking) are formed after the reaction of an amino acid group of a protein with the carbonyl group of a sugar.

The substances generated are endless chains of new molecules that are variously toxic, aromatic, peroxidizing, antioxidizing, mutagenic and carcinogenic. For example, in a broiled potato alone, Maillard identified 450 novel chemicals and tested them one by one for toxicity. Every one of the first 50 he tested was proven to be carcinogenic to laboratory animals. At that point, his employer terminated that line of research and gave him something else to work on before he could test the others.

This remarkable proliferation of biologically incompatible chemicals resulted just from cooking a potato all by itself. Try to imagine, if you can, what chemical mayhem occurs in most kitchens when that potato is cooked together with butter, vegetable oils, sour cream, herbs, spices, condiments and various other food items. And this represents only one small side dish of a typical cooked meal! It is believed by some that the chemical byproducts of cooking food are *so chaotic and unpredictable that our biochemistry will never, ever fully adapt to them.*

Maillard's research was swept under the rug. It would have been devastating to the food processing industry had it become widely known. But it was later published in 1982 in a French journal (*Cahiers de diététique et de nutrition*, Vol. 17, pp. 39-45). The name of the article, translated into English, was "Pyrolysis and risks of toxicity."

Marilyn Willison of the Hippocrates Health Institute writes, "We should not cook our food. During the apparently harmless process, vital enzymes are destroyed; proteins are coagulated, making them difficult to assimilate; vitamins are mostly destroyed, with the remainder changing into forms that are difficult for the body to utilize; pesticides are restructured into even more toxic compounds; valuable oxygen is lost; and free radicals are produced."

One researcher who found out how chemicalized foods are made even more toxic with heat was Dr. William Newsome of Canada's Department of Health and Welfare Food Research Division, Bureau of Chemical Safety. He discovered that cooked, fungicided tomatoes had 10-90 times more ETU, a mutagen and carcinogen, than raw tomatoes from the same garden.

Dr. Bernarr Zovluck, a holistic doctor who has been eating a raw diet for over 50 years, writes, "Cooking causes the inorganic elements to enter the blood, circulate through the system, settle in the arteries and veins, and deaden the nerves. After cooking, the body loses its flexibility; arteries lose their pliability; nerves lose their ability to conduct electrical signals; the spinal cord becomes hardened; the tissues throughout the body contract; and the human being becomes prematurely old. In many cases, this matter is deposited in the various joints of the body, causing joint disease. In other cases, it accumulates as concretions in one or more of the internal organs, finally accumulating around the heart valves." See his article, "Why Raw?" on his web site at www.healself.org.

Moreover, cooked food is bad for the teeth. Harmful bacteria thrive only on dead, cooked food, and this encourages plaque buildup, cavities and gum recession. Cooked foods are highly acidic; so the body has to dissolve calcium and other alkaline minerals from the teeth and bones to neutralize that acidity. Decreased dental exercise from the softness of the cooked food also leads to dental abnormalities, such as crooked teeth.

Cooked food causes obesity. Because you do not get fed the nutrients you need on a cooked diet, your body will often remain hungry even when it is calorically overfed, causing you to overeat. Since the toxic residues of all this cooked food leave an abundance of particles in your body that are not properly metabolized, the weight piles on as toxins are stored in fat cells and tissues. As the toxins build up, so does disease potential.

Dr. Gabriel Cousens sums up the hazards of eating cooked food: "Cooking coagulates the bioactive mineral and protein complexes and therefore disrupts mineral absorption, including calcium absorption. Cooking also disrupts RNA and DNA structure, which minimizes the amount of complex protein that our bodies are able to take in. It destroys most of the nutritive fats and creates carcinogenic and mutagenic ... structures in the fats, as well as producing free radicals" (*Rainbow Green Live-Food Cuisine*, p. 109).

I once saw a cookbook entitled *Healthy Cooking*. This is an oxymoron because no cooking is healthful! No doubt about it, cooked food is toxic.

Food destruction by pyrolysis is a function of both time and temperature. The longer something is cooked and the higher the heat applied to it, the more toxic it becomes. If meat is seared for a few seconds, it will be vastly less toxic than meat that is well-done. Also, the higher the temperature at which something is cooked, the more toxic it becomes. Steaming vegetables would produce less toxicity than baking them.

Microwaving may be the most destructive form of cooking because of the extreme violence with which it rips apart food molecules. (See Chapter 14, p. 319.)

The cause/effect relationship between eating cooked food and physical degeneration usually goes unnoticed for two reasons:

First, the time lag between eating and serious illness is great, as it is a cumulative effect, slowly accreting over decades. As Bruno Comby says, when we eat cooked food, we are "committing suicide on the installment plan." Because of this gradual, cumulative, toxic effect, illness is thought to be a part of the normal aging process.

Second, there is no modern-day society free of cooked food that we can hold up as a comparison. The cooking habit is deeply ingrained in the human psyche. Maybe our minds have adapted to it, but our bodies certainly have not.

What Happens to the Macronutrients in Cooked Food?

Proteins, carbohydrates and fats are known as macronutrients. All are greatly denatured by heat, becoming toxic to us.

Cooked fats have been known to be toxic for some time. Fats heated above 96° F (36° C) create lipid peroxides, which are oily, oxidizing compounds, proven carcinogens. Heating unsaturated fats, those liquid at room temperature, at high heat produces trans fatty acids, which create toxic free radicals in the body that cause cancer, aging and liver toxicity.

Heated fats lower the blood's capacity to carry oxygen and also block capillaries with fat globules. Fatty deposits then accumulate on the vascular walls and contribute to atherosclerosis and other forms of heart disease. Heart disease is currently the number one killer of Americans, with cancer coming in a close second.

Heated oils come loaded with mycotoxins, toxic byproducts of the microzymas discovered by Béchamp. (See Chapter 4.)

Processed foods usually contain hydrogenated or partially hydrogenated oils. Just read the labels. They are often found even in "health food stores." This type of cooked fat is solid or semi-solid at room temperature and was created by food oil refiners to create products like margarine to compete with saturated animal fat products like butter and lard.

The trans fatty acids they contain raise the "bad" cholesterol (LDL) levels while lowering the "good" cholesterol (HDL) levels, thus increasing heart disease risk. In fact, they have proven to be even more atherogenic than the saturated animal fats they compete against in the marketplace. Those who think they are making a healthy choice by buying margarine instead of butter are gravely mistaken.

David and Annie Jubb write, "All cooked fat, and pig fat especially, is unable to combine with water, causing it to separate out and be stored in the body. Cooked fats are not miscible with water, so they travel separately making blood sluggish, eventually being stored" (*Secrets of an Alkaline Body*, p. 25).

Cooked carbohydrates are also toxic. In the spring of 2002, Swedish officials were so alarmed by recent research findings that they decided to inform the public immediately rather than wait for them to be published in a scientific journal. Shortly afterwards, the World Health Organization held a three-week emergency meeting to evaluate the Swedish scientists' recent discovery. They learned that starchy foods, such as potato chips, french fries, baked potatoes, biscuits and bread, contain very high levels of acrylamides, chemicals that have been shown to cause genetic mutations leading to a range of cancers in rats.

Acrylamides are 1,000 times more dangerous than the majority of cancer-causing agents found in food. They have been found to cause benign and malignant stomach tumors, as well as damage to the central and peripheral nervous system. The US Environmental Protection Agency considers acrylamides so dangerous that it has fixed the safe level for human consumption of them at nearly zero, allowing for very little in public water systems. Yet the amounts found in an ordinary bag of potato chips is 500 times the amounts allowed in a single glass of water by the World Health Organization.

Until very recently, there was a law in force in California requiring potato chip manufacturers to put cancer warnings on their packages! Most did not comply with the law. There were also supposed to be cancer warning labels on the food most ordered at American restaurants: french fries! Would parents who fed their children fries and chips have been charged with child abuse?

Unfortunately, this law was superseded by national legislation that prohibits states from enacting food contamination standards and warning labels that are stricter than federal requirements. Lobbyists from food companies succeeded in getting Congress to pass this bill.

In addition, cooked carbohydrates contain glycotoxins, one of which is an "advanced glycation end product" (AGE). AGEs contaminate the body, making it vulnerable to cancer and molds, such as *Candida albicans* and other yeast infections.

The May 2003 edition of *Life Extension* magazine discusses AGEs, referring to a new study published in the *Proceedings of the National Academy of Sciences.* Eating food cooked at high temperatures was proven to cause the formation of AGEs, which accelerate aging. AGEs also cause chronic inflammation, which can lead to devastating, even lethal, effects directly involved with diseases like diabetes, cancer, atherosclerosis, congestive heart failure, aortic valve stenosis, Alzheimer's and kidney impairment.

The article declares, "Cooking and aging have similar biological properties. The process that turns a broiled chicken brown illustrates what happens to our body's proteins as we age. As the proteins react with sugars, they turn brown and lose elasticity; they cross-link to form insoluble masses that generate free radicals (which contribute to aging). The resulting AGEs accumulate in our collagen, skin, cornea of the eye, brain, nervous system, vital organs and arteries as we age. Normal aging can also be regarded as a slow cooking process."

The glycation reaction cross-links the body's proteins, making them barely functional. Their accumulation causes cells to emit signals that produce dangerous inflammation.

Several studies of diabetics who ate cooked foods producing AGEs confirmed that the AGEs definitely showed up in their blood and urine.

The book *Diet, Nutrition and Cancer* also cites studies in which the frying of potatoes and toasting of bread formed mutagenic activity. The authors explain, "The browning of food results from the reaction of amines with sugars." They cite studies that show that "the increase in mutagenic activity with time paralleled the increase in browning" (p. 285).

Cooking meat changes the molecular structure of some of its proteins, rendering them unusable by the body and making cellular healing, reproduction and regeneration difficult. The protein molecules become bound, making them harder to digest. Up to 50% of cooked proteins that one eats will coagulate and cross-link.

Cross-linking of proteins is associated with Alzheimer's disease, as shown in the first study presented in Appendix D.

Because of coagulation, the protein is 50% less assimilable, as research showed at the Max Planck Institute for National Research in Germany. This means that a person needs to eat twice as much protein if it is cooked as opposed to raw.

Even meat cooked at low temperatures produces mutagens. The book *Diet, Nutrition and Cancer* explains that mutagens in beef stock have been found in temperatures as low as 154° F (68° C). Frying fish with heat as low as 374° F (190° C) also produces mutagens, as does broiling hamburgers at 266° F (130° C).

Cooking protein above 104° F (40° C) begins to produce toxins. Higher temperatures create even more dangerous toxins, such as heterocyclic amines (HCAs), which are caustic compounds that have proven to cause cancer in laboratory animals. Some HCAs are so toxic to the neurotransmitters and their receptors in the brain that they eventually cause brain diseases, such as Alzheimer's, Parkinson's and schizophrenia.

Grilling is one of the worst ways to cook meat. The high temperatures of charcoal broiling and grilling create polycyclic aromatic hydrocarbons (PAHs). PAHs have also been found in smoked meats and roasted coffee.

According to T. S. Wiley, author of *Lights Out: Sleep, Sugar and Survival*, "The average serving of barbecued or burnt meat imparts to you an amount of cancer-causing particles equivalent to what you would get from smoking 250 cigarettes" (p. 176). The next time you have your barbecued ribs, just remember you may as well be smoking 12 packs of cigarettes!

Among the novel substances produced by cooking proteins are beta-carbolines. While the body produces its own beta-carbolines, the ones that result from cooked protein are toxic and imbalance the body much like taking foreign hormones imbalances the body, although the body produces its own hormones. Also, 99% of the exogenous (foreign) beta-carbolines are different from the natural ones and influence the brain in unpredictable and chaotic ways. This results in attention deficit hyperactivity disorder (ADHD) in children, as well as stress, apathy, aggression and distorted sexual behavior in adults. The web site www.13.waisays.com/adhd.htm is devoted to thorough documentation of studies confirming these findings.

It has long often been observed by vegetarians that meat eaters are more aggressive, angry and violent than vegetarians. Perhaps this "warrior consciousness" is not due to increased testosterone levels produced by meat or some ethereal density of consciousness but rather to exogenous beta-carbolines from heated meat. One way to test this would be to compare the behavior of raw meat eaters with that of cooked meat eaters.

When you think about how toxic cooked food is, it is really a wonder that we are still alive and that mankind has survived for so many generations. This is only because humans, along with rats and pigs, are some of the most versatile and genetically hardy of species. However, I wonder how long we will be able to survive as new toxic chemicals are introduced into our diet at faster and faster paces. (See Appendix A.)

Appendix D summarizes a number of informative studies published in professional scientific journals that demonstrate the toxicity of cooked food and support the claims made above in this section.

Toxic Cookware

As if the poisonous byproducts of cooked food were not enough, there is ample evidence that cooking pot materials create additional toxicity. Iron skillets are not recommended for people who have too much blood iron. Aluminum pots and pans may contribute to Alzheimer's disease.

The news program "20/20" once did an exposé on Teflon, which is so toxic that it often kills pet birds that breathe its fumes. Teflon also causes flu-like symptoms in people when the pan gets overheated, creating fumes. Some women who worked at the DuPont plant mixing the chemicals to make Teflon gave birth to babies with birth defects. Almost all Americans now have some detectable amounts of Teflon in their blood, and it is getting close to the level that harms lab animals. Pending review, the Environmental Protection Agency is now advising consumers to stop using Teflon products.

Is Cooked Food Addictive?

We know that fermenting food sugars into alcohol makes it addictive for many people. Would heating food do the same thing?

Raw fooders are convinced that cooked food is addictive. They base this conviction on empirical (observational) evidence, including their own experiences. Raw fooders very rarely become addicted to a favorite raw food; they may develop temporary cravings but know that this is simply the body calling out for certain nutrients it needs.

However, the longer you have been 100% raw, the more you don't eat unless you experience true hunger. Eating for social, emotional or pleasurable reasons gradually fades for the raw food eater.

Studies have shown that proteins heated by any cooking method contain harmful beta-carbolines that make a person want to eat more. The more protein in the food, the more beta-carbolines are produced. High protein foods include meat, eggs, nuts, seeds, fish, dairy, soy and beans.

Guy-Claude Burger states, "Cooking induces an intoxification that sets off a feeling of bogus hunger that impels us to eat even more. ... Cooking has made men into compulsive eaters."

He says that an instinctive raw fooder (Appendix C) might indulge in a bit of cooked food and find that his instincts go out the window. The person then finds himself completely over-taken by cooked food, which jams the instincts and makes initial foods (unaltered foods we are genetically designed to eat) seem less appealing. The person then goes on to compensate by eating even more cooked food, and it becomes an addictive cycle. When returning to 100% initial foods, one can require a rather long time before fully regaining the pleasure of eating them.

Dr. Robert Sniadach explains in his Essential Natural Hygiene course that cooked food eaters get hangovers from eating cooked food. They also experience withdrawal symptoms when giving up cooked food, just as addicts of drugs, alcohol or tobacco do.

On the Internet, I once read a posting by a man who had been a heroin addict. He credited a 100% raw food diet as a major factor in his healing. Some time later, he decided to eat only 80% raw, 20% cooked. This went on for a while until he decided to go back to eating 100% raw. As he compared cooked food to heroin, his words were telling: "Cooked food is the *addictive tincture* of food in its natural form."

Victoria Boutenko worked with many people, teaching them to eat raw. Yet those who would not commit to a 100% raw diet would often backslide. For example, a friend of hers chose to eat 95% raw at the same time Victoria and her family switched to 100% raw food. Victoria and her family suffered cooked food cravings for only two months; her friend was still struggling *eight years later* with cooked food temptations!

For years, Victoria observed many people and wondered why they backslid. Some had even been completely healed of cancer and went back to cooked foods, only to die after the cooked diet brought back the cancer. She wondered what the factor was until one day she attended an Alcoholics Anonymous meeting with a friend and realized that cooked food was addictive in much the same way that alcohol is.

Thus she began a 12-step support program to get people off cooked food, which worked wonderfully for nearly all her students. Her complete program is found in the book *12 Steps to Raw Foods: How to End your Addiction to Cooked Food*. (Note: Most of the steps do not correspond to the ones found in the typical 12-step programs, like Alcoholics Anonymous.)

Boutenko emphasizes the need to go on a 100% raw food diet. That 1% of cooked food leaves the door open to temptation. She met many people who ate 99% raw and returned completely to cooked food months later. She urges people to commit to two months of 100% raw, avoiding temptation zones — restaurants, parties and potlucks where cooked food is served. Then the physical cravings will disappear.

Before setting up the raw food 12 steps, Boutenko studied dozens of books on drug addition. She learned that the earlier in life that the addictive substance is taken, the harder it is to stop. Since all of us began eating cooked foods as infants, this might explain why Boutenko noticed that only one person in 1,000 could stay 100% raw without support. She met only two or three people who remained successfully raw for one year by sheer will power alone.

People tend to use cooked food like a drug to numb the feelings when feeling bad. She found that cooked food was an addiction more difficult to overcome than even drugs because it is legal everywhere in our environment and socially acceptable, indeed strongly encouraged. People do not become ostracized when getting off drugs but may become social pariahs when getting off cooked foods.

In her book *The Raw Food Detox Diet*, nutritionist Natalia Rose declares that foods from mainstream supermarkets are especially addictive. "You must take the first step in healing your body by admitting that you are addicted to these unquestionably habit-forming substances that may currently rule your tastes and food impulses" (p. 14). MSG is one ingredient sly food companies add to their products to create addiction. (See Appendix A.)

Morgan Spurlock, creator and director of the renowned documentary film *Super Size Me*, found that he became seriously addicted to the food at McDonald's. He would even suffer depression until he got his "fix" of fries and burgers!

One reason people on cooked diets experience so many cravings is not only addiction but also malnutrition. They simply are not getting enough nutrients, and so they are constantly hungry. Obese people are often the most undernourished people in the world, which is why they are always hungry and always eating.

When I was eating only about 90-95% raw, I personally noticed just how addictive wheat and dairy are. If I ate just a bit of either, I would crave it strongly the next day. Food manufacturers know this, and this is why they manage to slip some hidden form of these in processed foods.

My body was so sensitive from eating mostly raw foods that when I ate wheat, I noticed that I would feel a mild stupor, somewhat like a drug-induced state in which I lost all alertness. If I had much of it, like a few pieces of bread or cake, I would fall asleep. For more information on the addictive nature of wheat and dairy, see the web site www.13.waisays.com/zombie.htm. (Also see Appendix A.)

The web site www.13.waisays.com contains much more information on the effects of food on health, all documented with scientific journal references. The writer even compares the toxicity of cooked food to that of cigarettes (see www.13.waisays.com/cigarettes).

Now that we've discovered what's wrong with cooked food, let's next take a look at what's right about raw food.

7
The Raw Ingredients

So many people spend their health gaining wealth
and then have to spend their wealth to regain their health.
—A. J. Reb Materi, *Our Family*

It was once believed that the only concern with food was getting sufficient calories. The calorie paradigm, originated in 1789, is completely outdated, although nutritional science is still influenced by it. Calories are the body's fuel supply, and they are not destroyed that much by cooking. But thinking that simply getting enough calories is enough would be like thinking that gasoline is the only thing you need to put into your car. How long would your car run if the only thing you fed it was fuel, but neglected to add oil, brake fluid, radiator coolant, spark plugs and so on?

Raw food contains numerous essential nutrients that are either damaged or destroyed by heat. Most of them have been discovered only within the last century or a little more. This makes one wonder how many other components might yet remain undiscovered in food that may also be destroyed by fire.

Vitamins & Minerals

Ann Wigmore, founder of the Hippocrates Health Institute, determined that 83% of a raw food's nutrients are lost in the process of cooking. Each vitamin has a different ability to withstand heat: For example, about 50% of B vitamins are lost in cooked foods and 70-80% of Vitamin C. Overall, nutrient destruction is thought to be 83-85%. Think of all the waste!

Jan Dries, who worked extensively healing cancer patients using raw food, explains that cooking renders minerals inactive. "The electromagnetic field that is very important to minerals (because it makes their catalytic action possible) disappears when you heat them. Inactive memories of a mineral have a very disturbing effect on the kidney filters, which have to make sure they are removed" (*The Dries Cancer Diet*, p. 100).

In addition, some of the minerals may actually become toxic after cooking. Inorganic minerals are naturally combined in raw foods with molecules containing carbon, making them organic.

According to Dr. Vivian V. Vetrano, "These [organic minerals] are the useful mineral compounds, and they are in the proper balance for human nutrition. When food is cooked, the minerals are separated by the heat from this organic combination, returning to inorganic molecules which recombine as toxic inorganic salts, such as sodium chloride, causing many health problems, such as arterial plaque, arthritis and Alzheimer's disease."

Don't fool yourself into thinking that taking vitamins and minerals in supplements will compensate for their loss in cooked food! Such supplements are usually minerals extracted from rocks rather than from food sources (because it's cheaper) and are not easily absorbable. The vitamin or mineral in a pill is rejected by the body and becomes more toxic pollution. On the other hand, if one can find a food supplement that is living, such as low-temperature dehydrated greens, this could be more successfully absorbed and utilized.

Review Professor Kollath's experiment described in Chapter 5. He was unable to get his mice to achieve good health using supplements. Only a raw food diet worked.

Furthermore, there could be numerous nutrients yet to be discovered, making any multi-vitamin and mineral supplement incomplete. In fact, in April 2003, Japanese scientists discovered the first new vitamin since 1948: pyrroloquinoline quinone, which plays a role in fertility. If someone had depended purely on supplements for vitamins, she may have found herself infertile without knowing why.

In addition, nature has everything combined synergistically such that all constituents work together in ways we do not understand. Professor Dr. Peter Schauder of the University of Göttingen in Germany says, "The various macro- and micro-nutrients influence each other and are able to strengthen or weaken each other during bio-chemical processes."

Dr. T. Colin Campbell, PhD, claims, "The whole is greater than the sum of its parts. Unlike supplements, fruit and vegetables contain a variety of nutrients which cannot be extracted."

For more arguments against using supplements as opposed to raw foods, see Chapters 12 and 14.

Enzymes

Enzymes are protein molecules that act in specific ways, working in a "lock and key" manner with other molecules to facilitate chemical reactions in the body. They play very specific roles in the body, helping it digest food, build protein in skin and bones, and aid in detoxification. They are catalysts that facilitate chemical reactions. Enzymes are what enable fruit to ripen and a seed to sprout and grow into a plant. Without enzymes, earthly life would be impossible.

Enzymes are the catalysts of life. Mason Dwinell, LAc, even compares enzymes to "miniature suns." Perhaps this is why people who eat raw foods, full of enzymes, report feeling "switched on," as if a key has turned on the light and energy. But when they backslide into cooked foods, it's "power down."

We use three kinds of enzymes: metabolic enzymes to run our bodies, digestive enzymes to digest food, and food enzymes in raw foods that enable the food to partially self-digest, thus conserving our bodies' limited enzyme-producing capacities.

Food enzymes are active, or "alive," in uncooked food. Once a food is heated, they chemically degrade, or "die." By conservative estimates, enzymes may begin dying at temperatures as low as 105° F; within 30 minutes at 119°-129° F, all are dead. Cooking alters an enzyme's "lock and key" configuration so that it can no longer perform its intended function. The protein molecule is still present, but its life force is gone, much like a battery that has lost its power.

Dr. James B. Sumner, a Nobel Prize winner in 1946, claimed that the easily-fatigued feeling of being middle-aged or older is due to diminished enzymes as you add years to your life.

Dr. Edward Howell was the 20th century's foremost researcher on food enzymes and their significance to human nutrition. He discovered that food heated above 118° F for any extended period of time is devoid of active food enzymes.

If we eat cooked food, we force our pancreases to crank out more digestive enzymes than they were designed to. By age 40, the average person has only 30% of his digestive enzyme production potential left. This is a major reason for increasing tiredness with age. According to Dr. Howell, "The length of life is inversely proportional to the rate of exhaustion of the enzyme potential of an organism."

In other words, the more cooked food you eat, the sooner you exhaust your limited digestive enzyme potential, and the sooner you begin to disintegrate and die.

It is believed that there is no way to replenish this enzyme potential, and so the best strategy is not to overuse it, but to eat solely raw food instead.

Some raw fooders even take enzyme supplements along with their 100% raw diet. Brian Clement of the Hippocrates Health Institute recommends doing so. Lou Corona does as well. Dr. Cousens also suggests that enzyme supplements, even on a live food diet, can be useful for increasing our enzyme content and energy.

Declining enzyme reserves are associated with aging. People who are 25 have about 30 times more amylase in their saliva than people in their 80s for example. Each child is born with an inherited amount of enzyme potential. When it is used up, he will die of some degenerative disease that will correlate with his weakest organ. If he is a raw fooder, eating primarily or only raw, unheated food, he will more likely reach his optimal life span free of degenerative diseases. The more cooked food he eats, the shorter and/or more diseased will be his life.

It was formerly believed, with the "theory of parallel secretion," that enzymes were expendable, unimportant because the body could create them without limit and could waste them without concern. Later the "law of adaptive secretion of digestive enzymes" was shown to be true. This law states that the more digestion that is accomplished by food enzymes, enzymes inherent in raw food, the fewer digestive enzymes must be pumped out by the pancreas and intestine.

The body "knows" it has a limited amount of enzyme potential and secretes only the particular enzymes it needs at any given meal. It is as though the body has a limited bank account, a limited savings it can draw upon. Most researchers believe there is no way to make a "deposit," or to add to that limited enzyme-generating potential. We can only refuse to dive into our "savings" by eating raw food exclusively and no more of it than the body needs.

It was also formerly believed that eating cooked food was irrelevant to the enzyme question because enzymes were destroyed in the digestive process. Digestion begins in the mouth with salivary enzymes, but many of the enzymes lost in cooking are those that help further digestion in the "food enzyme," or cardiac, stomach (its upper section) for the first 30-60 minutes of the digestive cycle, before the hydrochloric acid and protein-digesting enzymes secreted by the lower stomach could destroy them.

Moreover, numerous meticulous studies on humans and animals have proved that some enzymes survive digestion and are reused. Some of them escape gastric breakdown and reactivate in the small intestines where they continue to facilitate further digestive processes. Extensive European studies (see *Raw Energy*, p. 57) have confirmed the durability of most of the enzymes throughout the digestive process.

Dr. Howell's research revealed that the pancreas, being the main producer of digestive enzymes, grows larger when it is habitually overtaxed. The typical human pancreas is relatively large compared to those of wild animals when adjusted for body size. This hypertrophy indicates the pancreas is being overworked.

Dr. Howell also found that animals on cooked food diets had enlarged pancreases. For example, laboratory rats eating cooked foods had pancreases three times as big as those of the raw food eaters. When their bodies were dissected, "An astonishing array of typically human degenerative diseases was revealed" (*Enzyme Nutrition*, Dr. Howell, p. 84).

In her video "Drugs Never Cure Disease!" Dr. Lorraine Day, MD, claims, "It takes the same amount of energy to make the enzymes for three meals a day of cooked food as it does *eight hours of hard labor.* Is it any wonder people are suffering from fatigue?"

Dr. Nicholas Gonzalez, who uses enzyme therapy, was influenced by the research of Howell, Pottenger and also Dr. John Beard, who first suggested that the pancreatic proteolytic enzyme trypsin could treat cancer. Gonzalez explains, "Our immune cells, our neutrophils and lymphocytes, use enzymes to attack and kill bacteria, viruses and fungi, as well as dangerous cancer cells that some scientists believe form every day in all of us" (*Eating in the Raw*, p. 10). He regrets that enzymes never get the press coverage they deserve and explains that without enzymes, DNA, which is always in the news, could do nothing.

Because eating raw food spares unnecessary depletion of the body's limited enzyme potential, the body is free to perform other vital, enzyme-mediated, health functions. Enzymes enhance our vitality, body detoxification, tissue regeneration, metabolic function, scar tissue dissolution, excess fatty tissue digestion and dissolution of crystallized deposits in the tissues. In other words, our body has much greater capacity for house-cleaning and self-repair if we ingest only fresh, raw, foods.

Dr. Rudolf Steiner, PhD, who wrote on anthroposophy, or spiritual science, referred to enzymes as "the bridge between the physical and the spiritual worlds." Perhaps this is because when eating foods rich in enzymes, one spares considerable energy that can be used for the body's more exalted energy centers.

Phytochemicals

Phytochemicals are substances recently discovered in plant foods that differ from other nutrients in that they are not assimilated by the cells nor used for fuel. They stimulate the immune system, serve as antioxidants, block carcinogenic substances from the cells, quiet and calm the nervous system, and reduce cholesterol levels. They also help protect us from pollution, radiation and disease, along with performing many other functions. Scientists are trying to genetically modify them so that they can be patented and thus be profitably sold in the form of "nutraceuticals," the food counterpart of pharmaceuticals. Of course, it is much more healthful to eat Nature's versions than man's.

Phytochemicals include resveratrol, which will switch on our anti-aging genes, as mentioned in Chapter 1. Red fruits and vegetables tend to contain resveratrol. Rich sources include grapes, grape juice and red wine. According to Dr. James Howenstine, author of *A Physician's Guide to Natural Health Products That Work*, 20 mg of resveratrol daily provides maximal health benefits. Red wine has 0.2 mg per glass.

Phytochemicals also include flavonoids, lycopene and quercetin. To get the full spectrum of phytochemicals, you should eat from each of the colors of fruits and vegetables: green, yellow, red, orange, white and purple.

Biophotons: Light Energy from the Sun

In 1982, German physicist and Nobel Prize winner in physics Dr. Fritz Popp and his colleagues proved the presence of biophotons, biologically produced units of light, in vegetables.

One of the colleagues proved that these biophotons are stored in the DNA. Dr. Popp developed an instrument, the biophoton meter, to measure biophoton emission. Dr. Popp was able to demonstrate on a screen the luminosity of a fresh plant, contrasting that with the greatly reduced luminosity of a withered plant.

Biophotons can be thought of as a kind of biological laser light with a very high degree of coherence, capable of transmitting information, which ordinary incoherent light cannot achieve.

Dr. Popp's research went on to prove that the quality of a food is mainly dependent on the number of biophotons it contains. Cooking, adding chemicals to, processing, preserving and irradiating all endanger the biophotons of a food. Fresh, sun-ripened, organic food eaten straight from the vine contains the greatest number of biophotons.

We know that sunlight is essential to life. It is now known that the more light stored in food, the more nutritious that food is. Stored sun energy is transferred from the food into our body's cells in the form of biophotons, containing bio-information that has the power to regulate all metabolic processes in the body, elevating the body's functioning to a higher order. Consequently, biophotons counteract the chaotic loss of structure in an aging body due to the force of entropy.

Dr. Popp found that healthy cells store light longer and radiate coherent light, whereas unhealthy cells radiate chaotic light. The biophoton energy of healthy people was observed to be much greater than that of people in poor health.

Wild foods were found to emit two times as many biophotons as cultivated organic foods. Organic foods emit five times as many biophotons as commercially grown foods. *Cooked or irradiated foods contain almost no biophotons.* Thus, it follows that uncooked food is absolutely essential to good health, and wild food is best. Dr. Gabriel Cousens has even coined the term "malillumination," the counterpart to the word "malnutrition," to denote people lacking in the essential nutrient of sunlight. "We are human photocells whose ultimate biological nutrient is light." (*Conscious Eating*, Dr. Cousens, p. 587).

Fruits are also very rich in biophotons. Fruits originate from flowers or blossoms. Because of their suitable structure, they are capable of accumulating vast numbers of biophotons.

Electrons

German scientist Dr. Johanna Budwig found that live (raw) foods are rich in electrons that act as high-powered electron donors and solar resonance fields in the body to attract, store, and conduct the sun's energy. Her research led her to believe that the sunlight's photons are attracted by sun-like electrons, termed pi-electrons, resonating in our bodies. Our bodies' pi-electrons attract and activate the sun photons, giving us an anti-entropy, or anti-aging, edge.

She found that live foods, especially flaxseeds, were a particularly good source of electrons. The more we can take in solar electrons by eating live foods, the better we can attract and absorb solar electrons in direct resonance from the sun, thus enhancing our health and even our consciousness. Perhaps this is where we get the term "sunny disposition."

Dr. Hans Eppinger found that all cells are essentially batteries that seem to be charged up when people are healthy. Sick people's cells exist in a discharged state, and only uncooked foods are able to maximize the cell battery potential.

Dr. John Douglass theorizes that live foods have a "higher energy ability to awaken relatively inert molecules in our systems by either taking an electron or giving them one. This high-energy electron transfer ability is described as the 'high redox potential' of a particular molecule" (*Conscious Eating*, p. 575).

Dr. Douglass feels that the high redox potential of living foods, which is destroyed by heat, is an important factor in their healing power. Another raw food researcher, Dr. Chiu-Nan Lai, agrees that this high redox potential is a major reason for the healing power of raw foods (*Raw Energy*, pp. 46-47).

A free radical is a molecule that is missing an electron, and since it wants to rebalance its electrical charge, it will try to steal an electron from wherever it can: molecules of fat, protein, DNA, etc. When DNA is altered, it can lead to cell mutation, possibly leading to cancer. Therefore, it is good to have spare electrons to give to these free radicals, so that they don't wreak havoc.

A healthy, vital body contains lots of spare electrons. According to David and Annie Jubb, people who radiate, appearing to glow with light, are those with abundant spare electrons.

Foods rich in electrons are raw fruits, vegetables, nuts, seeds and sprouted or soaked grains. Spirulina and flaxseed (also flaxseed oil) are especially high in the capacity to absorb solar electrons.

Bioelectricity

Our bodies have a bioelectric potential. Human tissues and cells are electrically charged, working much like an alkaline battery. Brian Clement explains, "Just as an alkaline battery has a positive and a negative pole, a cell has a nucleus and cytoplasm. ... The nucleus and cytoplasm of a cell attract opposite charges; the nucleus is the positive 'pole,' and the cytoplasm is the negative 'pole'" (*Living Foods for Optimum Health*, p. 35). A drop in this bioelectric potential is the first step of the disease process; hence many people do not feel good even though their lab tests show no signs of disease. On a cellular level, they are unable to properly dispose of toxins and absorb nutrients.

Kirlian photography has been able to visibly display the difference between the bioelectric field of a person eating dead food and that of a person eating live food. Kirlian photographers Harry Oldfield and Roger Coghill show such photos in their book *The Dark Side of the Brain*.

They also illustrate differences between the fields of cooked and raw plants. Their research indicated that the electroluminescence, the radiance seen in Kirlian photographs, is a measure of life force, and hence health, in the plants' cells.

The painting depicted on the front cover of this book shows an artist's rendition of the appearance of a fresh pineapple's Kirlian force field, or aura — its live food factor.

European nutritionist Jan Dries researched along these lines beginning in the early 1980s. He found there is a bioenergetic value (BEV) of each food and that this value depended on the number of biophotons and also the luminous intensity of light energy. He found that particular foods could be identified by their individual frequencies. A high reading indicated a high BEV.

Readings allowed for a determination of the medicinal properties of foods and herbs, linking specific foods to certain diseases. He found that certain people had what he called "cancer resistance," which differed from cancer immunity, and that certain foods had the same "cancer resistance" frequency. It was discovered that people ingesting these foods could develop cancer resistance.

He has been very successful in treating cancer patients with this diet. It is outlined in the book *The Dries Cancer Diet: A Practical Guide to the Use of Fresh Fruit and Raw Vegetables in the Treatment of Cancer*. The majority of the diet consists of tropical fruits, as they have the cancer resistance frequency. Hence, people with cancer on his diet will eat primarily oranges, bananas, pineapples, avocados, melons, kiwi, persimmons, apricots, papayas and mangoes, among other foods. His diet stimulates the body's healing by increasing the bio-energy and electrical potentials of cells, which leads to a depolarization of cancer cells.

Dr. Gabriel Cousens discusses the bioelectricity of live foods in *Rainbow Green Live-Food Cuisine* (p. 117). He claims that live foods increase the electrical potential in cells, between cells and at cellular interfaces. The electrical potentials of our tissues and cells directly result from our cells' aliveness, which is enhanced by live foods. In *Spiritual Nutrition* (p. 294), he explains that given proper microelectrical potential, cells are better able to expel toxins; assimilate appropriate micronutrients, oxygen and hydrogen into cell nuclei; and feed the mitochondria. This enables cells to maintain, repair and activate their DNA molecules.

Dr. Hans Eppinger of the University of Vienna found that a live-food diet raised microelectrical potentials throughout the whole body. He found that, in addition to improving the intra- and extra-cellular excretion of toxins and the absorption of nutrients, live foods were the only types of foods that could restore the microelectrical potential of tissues after their electrical potentials and consequent cellular degeneration had begun.

It is believed that living foods get their electrical charges from the highly charged electrons sent to us by the sun.

Hormones

The Pottenger cat study was one study that showed that hormones are destroyed in cooked foods. Meat is a valuable source of hormones. This study indicated that hormones, such as the adrenal cortical hormone and insulin, among others, were definitely thermolabile, that is, destroyed by fire. They were even destroyed at the moderate temperatures of pasteurization. When given adrenal cortical hormone, the cats' adrenal glands were restored to normal function.

Curious to know why wheatgrass (in addition to a raw diet) had been so powerful in healing Eydie Mae Hunsberger, author of *How I Conquered Cancer Naturally,* of breast cancer, her doctor discovered that wheatgrass contained a plant hormone called abscisic acid. He found, doing tests on laboratory animals, that even small amounts of abscisic acid proved to be deadly to any form of cancer.

Water

Water is necessary to dilute and flush out toxins, transport water-soluble nutrients, and perform a whole host of other functions. A young body is more than 80% water, but with age this can decrease to 60%. Water found in fresh food is superior to drinking water. Plants purify water by filtering it through their roots. Water from living plants is electrified. The best water is found in fruit. If one eats enough juicy fruits, one doesn't need to drink nearly as much water.

Cooking eliminates some of the water and lowers the quality of the remaining water found in fresh foods.

Essential Fatty Acids

The essential fatty acids (EFAs) linolenic acid and linoleic acid are necessary for healthy heart, brain, skin, glands and hair. Most people are deficient in essential fatty acids because cooking destroys much of them. Foods rich in EFAs are flaxseeds, raw fish, avocados, nuts and seeds.

Friendly Bacteria

People often think it is necessary to cook foods in order to destroy harmful bacteria, not realizing they are also destroying the necessary "friendly" bacteria that our intestines need for balance. A lack of good bacteria can create yeast infections, a weakened immune system and other symptoms. Eating cooked food, especially cooked meat, causes the natural population of beneficial intestinal flora to become dominated by putrefactive bacteria. This causes colon dysfunction and allows for the absorption of toxins from the bowel. This disease state is called dysbiosis, or dysbacteria.

According to Dr. Gabriel Cousens, some factors in raw foods stimulate production of healthy bacterial flora (*Conscious Eating*, p. 565).

Oxygen

According to William Richardson, MD, "Heat processing reduces the oxygen found in fresh food — oxygen we need to resist disease." Cancer and AIDS-causing viruses thrive in blood low in oxygen. Raw foods contain small amounts of hydrogen peroxide, which provides oxygen to kill these particular viruses.

Chlorophyll is what gives plants their green color. It has been likened to the "blood" of the plant. The chlorophyll molecule is almost identical to the hemoglobin molecule, which is the oxygen carrier in human blood. Therefore, when you eat plants in their living, non-heated state, the chlorophyll actually feeds oxygen to your body. Cooked food does not contain this organic type of oxygen. This is why, when you eat lots of greens or drink wheatgrass juice, you immediately feel a surge of energy. Wheatgrass is an especially good source of oxygen.

Oxygen stimulates digestion, promotes better circulation in the body, promotes clearer thinking, protects against anaerobic bacteria, and nourishes every cell in the body. Without sufficient oxygen in the blood, the metabolism, energy and digestion become sluggish. The body becomes ripe for disease.

In addition to eating live plant food, other factors contribute to our oxygen supply: breathing clean, fresh air and exercising aerobically for at least 20 minutes, three to five times a week. It is also beneficial to have green plants in your environment.

Breathing exercises also help increase internal oxygen. According to Dr. Cousens, although 90% of metabolic energy comes from breathing, most people use only 10% of their breathing capacities.

Increasing our oxygen supply is especially necessary nowadays because, unfortunately, our air, especially the air in cities, where most people live, now contains less oxygen than it used to due to pollution. Since there is far less oxygen inside a building than outside, the Boutenkos even sleep outdoors in a gazebo.

Suggested Reading

Some of the best books to read in order to learn about these gems of wisdom pertaining to raw food diets are the books by Dr. Edward Howell and Dr. Gabriel Cousens' *Conscious Eating* and *Spiritual Nutrition.*

Coming Up...

People often wonder, "If this diet is so great, why did it take so long for us to realize it?"

Section III will show you that various niches of societies have actually known about this diet for thousands of years. There we shall discover the history of the raw food movement and introduce its modern-day leaders, who relate their powerful personal testimonies, having miraculously healed themselves of "incurable" diseases by means of this diet alone.

If you are already eager to start your new diet, you may choose to proceed to Section IV and return to Section III later, but I do encourage you to return to it at some point.

Section Three

Raw

Pioneers:

History & Leaders

"At your age, good health is pretty much a thing
of the past. My advice is, find an illness you enjoy."

8

A Brief History of the Raw Food Movement

The disadvantage of men not knowing the
past is that they do not know the present.
—G. K. Chesterton (1874-1936), British author

This chapter presents a *very* brief sketch, by no means exhaustive, of the history of the raw food movement and its teachers, illustrating how passionate people are about the power of a raw food diet.

The modern raw food movement is essentially a grassroots movement, receiving very little if any assistance from the media, medical establishment and government agencies. As mentioned earlier, part of the reason for its obscurity is that nearly all the books on the subject have been self-published and therefore not reviewed in magazines nor typically sold in chain bookstores. This is starting to change, however, due both to the diet's widening popularity and to its Internet presence.

For millions of years, mankind and his ancestors were raw fooders, as are all other animals currently on earth. Fire is thought to have been discovered some 400,000 years ago and put into widespread use for cooking around 10,000-20,000 years ago.

Thus, man became the first and only animal species to experiment with chemically altering his food. No one knows why this came to be, although one theory is that a forest fire destroyed much of the food, and people were forced to eat some of the cooked food on the outskirts of the fire.

Another theory is that people found that cooking destroyed visible parasites in spoiling meat. Further speculation is that people discovered that accidentally burnt food had an alluring aroma, thus leading them to start doing it on purpose.

In my opinion, the most credible explanation for the onset of cooking is one held by some anthropologists: As man migrated to colder climates, the only way he could eat frozen food he stumbled upon or food left over from a kill was to heat it. Perhaps ice covered the meat and fire thawed it out.

Any or all of these theories may be true. Once the practice of cooking began, however, the cooked food seemed to become addictive in a way similar to the addictive quality of alcoholic beverages, produced by the fermentation of food.

Despite the many social pressures to partake of cooked food preparations, certain groups of people throughout history have rediscovered the power of eating pure, unheated food.

One of the earliest known documents advocating a raw food diet may be the *Essene Gospel of Peace*. It is alleged to have been written over 2,000 years ago and indicates that Jesus was a member of the Jewish Essene sect, a group who advocated such a diet.

In the *Essene Gospel of Peace*, Book One, it is written, "And Jesus continued: 'God commanded your forefathers: *Thou shalt not kill.* I say to you: Kill neither men, nor beast, nor yet the food which goes into your mouth. For if you eat living food, the same will quicken you, but if you kill your food, the dead food will kill you also. For life only comes from life, and death always comes from death. For everything which kills your food kills your bodies also. And everything which kills your bodies kills your souls also. Therefore, eat not anything which fire or frost or water has destroyed. For burned, frozen and rotted foods will burn, freeze, and rot your body also. Be not like the foolish husbandman who sowed in his ground cooked, frozen and rotted seeds. And the autumn came, and his fields bore nothing. And great was his distress.'"

The Essenes felt that the secret was to eat not only raw food, but also food as fresh from the vine as possible. Modern science has since proven that these two secrets were correct.

The Essenes established communities two to three hundred years before Jesus was born and were reported by historians to have lived an average of 120 years.

The Greeks also discovered the raw food diet. The Pelasgians, a group of people thought by Classical Greek writers to have inhabited ancient Greece, ate only raw fruits, nuts and seeds. They lived on average to 200 years, according to Herodotus, the "father of history."

Pythagoras, who lived in Greece around 580-500 BC, was a famous Greek philosopher and mathematician, one of the earliest men in the Western world to formulate philosophical and mathematical theories.

According to his biography, Pythagoras studied with the Essenes on Mount Carmel. There he learned about live foods and took this knowledge back to Greece. He became a fruitarian and established a school of followers who also became fruitarians. He used raw food to cure people with poor digestion. This knowledge was later passed down to Socrates and Plato.

In India, there have always been yogis and seekers of high spiritual development (enlightenment) who ate only raw food. One of these was Shivapuri Baba, who at the age of 50 went on a 35-year world walking tour. He even spent four years with Queen Victoria in England. Born in 1826, he died at the age of 137. He remained very vital until the last few years, when he aged rapidly due to eating the cooked food offered him by his hosts.

Paramhansa Yogananda, author of *Autobiography of a Yogi*, spoke admiringly of meeting a yogi who had been on a raw food diet for nine years.

In 1897, the Bircher-Benner Clinic of Zurich, Switzerland became one of the first modern clinics using the raw food treatment approach. Founder Max Bircher-Benner, MD, discovered the writings of Pythagoras and began experimenting with live foods. He healed himself of jaundice with raw food and thereby learned of its power. He discovered that live food treatment worked for a wide range of ailments, no matter how serious the disease.

In the USA in the 1920s, the Mormons, who numbered Joseph Smith and 25 of his followers, ate mostly raw foods because they knew that it increased spiritual awareness.

In the early 1900s, Max Gerson, MD, worked with raw foods, first healing himself of migraines and then proceeding to treat various patient ailments, including lupus.

One of his patients was the famous doctor Albert Schweitzer, who was healed of diabetes with raw food, enabling him to stop taking insulin. Albert's wife was healed of tuberculosis.

Gerson used raw food to treat cancer and wrote *A Cancer Therapy: Results of Fifty Cases*, which he published in 1958.

There are several Gerson institutes in Europe and Mexico today. The Mexican clinic used to be in the USA but was chased out by our draconian laws persecuting anyone using alternative treatments for disease. (See Appendix B for more detail.)

Also early in the 20th century, Professor Arnold Ehret of Germany was dying of Bright's disease, a kidney problem. All treatments failed him, including mainstream medicine and alternative approaches.

Remarkably, Ehret discovered hidden secrets about health quite by accident. Attempting to recover in a resort area by the ocean by means of rest and fresh air, he ran out of money while still quite ill. Discouraged, depressed and broke, he decided to commit suicide by starving himself to death.

Somewhere around the tenth or eleventh day, the depression and fatigue lifted, and he suddenly felt healthy and energetic, regaining his will to live. He decided to take control of his health, researching on his own what to do. After fasting and taking on a fruitarian diet, not only did his kidneys clear up, but he also obtained a level of vitality and mental health so superior that he termed it "Paradise Health."

He found that ill health is caused by the accumulation of toxins and "mucus" (phlegm) in the body and wrote several books and pamphlets, including *Rational Fasting* and *Mucusless Diet Healing System*. In the 1920s, he moved to Los Angeles, California, where he gave health lectures.

In addition to Ehret, Germany's heritage of raw fooders who influenced the California raw food movement was significant enough to warrant an entire book: *Children of the Sun,* a pictorial anthology edited by Gordon Kennedy. Many of these raw food leaders were actually forerunners of both the natural healing and the hippie movements. These include Bill Pester, who influenced author Hermann Hesse, as well as Louis Kuhne and Adolph Just, who had a profound affect on Mahatma Gandhi.

Additional Germans made quite an impact on California's early raw food history. John and Vera Richter operated three live-food cafeterias in Los Angeles from 1917 until the late 1940's and published *Mrs. Richter's Cook-Less Book* (1925). Hermann Sexauer opened a natural foods shop in Santa Barbara. Maximilian Sikinger published a concise little booklet about live foods, meditation and sunshine, *Classical Nutrition,* in the Santa Monica Mountains (1943).

Iran has had a long history of raw foodism. One of the more recent promoters of the diet was Arshavir Ter Hovannessian, who wrote *Raw Eating* in 1967 and founded a "Raw Vegetarian Society."

He had been a sickly, middle-aged man, only able to work a few hours a day. After switching to a raw diet, he professed more energy than in his youth, able to run up mountains and work all day and late into the night.

He raised one daughter from birth on raw food and claims that it is easier to raise 100 children on raw food than one on cooked. His previous children, who were raised on conventional cooked food, were frequently sick, noisy and messy, with emotional tantrums, while the raw child was never sick and remained quiet and happy.

Arshavir also mentions in his book that in certain Asian countries, condemned prisoners were executed by giving them nothing to eat except cooked meat! They usually died within 30 days.

Ann Wigmore (1909-1993) founded the Hippocrates Health Institute in Boston in 1958 together with Viktoras Kulvinskas, who is still active in the raw food movement. Dr. Ann was a pioneer in the development of raw gourmet cuisine, inventing such recipes as "energy soup," flax crackers and seed cheese.

Chased out of Boston by persecution from the authorities, she set up a clinic in Puerto Rico, where she successfully treated AIDS patients prior to her untimely death in a house fire. She was 84 at the time of her death and in such great health that she needed only two hours of sleep a day and had no gray hair. Laboratory tests proved her hair was not dyed.

Kulvinskas went on to author *Survival into the 21st Century* and *Life in the 21st Century*, both raw food classics. Since then, Brian Clement has assumed the leading role at the Hippocrates Health Institute at their center in West Palm Beach, Florida. One of the happy clients of the Hippocrates Health Institute, Eydie Mae Hunsberger, wrote the book *How I Conquered Cancer Naturally* after recovering from breast cancer on a live food diet.

Perhaps the most influential and well-educated leader of the 20th century health revolution was Dr. Herbert M. Shelton (1895-1985). Herbert Shelton became the most prominent leader of the Natural Hygiene movement, which advocates a primarily raw food diet, while also emphasizing a complete program of healthful lifestyle practices, including obtaining adequate sunshine, clean air, exercise, sleep and fasting, not to mention avoiding all drugs, vaccinations and supplements.

He became a doctor of chiropractic medicine in order to legally practice in the health field, although he never practiced that specialty, believing Natural Hygiene to be superior.

He helped about fifty thousand people regain health at his fasting clinic. Only three people out of those thousands died, even though many of the patients who came to see him had already been pronounced terminal by the medical profession! (To compare such a death rate with that of drug treatment, see Appendix B.) When one of those who later died came to the clinic, he came at a very late stage in his disease. After the patient's death, his wife sued the center for $890,000 and won, which bankrupted Shelton.

Dr. Shelton dedicated his entire life to promoting the truth about health. Not only did he run a fasting clinic full time, but he also researched, authored, and published a monthly health newsletter for 30-some years. He traveled and gave health lectures, founded and established the American Natural Hygiene Society (now the National Health Association), and wrote 39 books on the subject of human health and its philosophy.

He was often persecuted by the medical "authorities" and was in and out of courtrooms and periodic incarcerations. He once spent 30 days in jail for "practicing medicine without a license" despite telling the judge, "I wouldn't practice medicine if I *had* a license!" During this time he preferred to fast rather than eat the poor prison diet, using his energy and time to write one of his books while in jail.

Shelton was such a busy man that he did not have time to sleep or rest much, although obtaining adequate sleep was one of the health precepts that he taught. By skimping on sleep, he sacrificed his own health in order to get the word out about Natural Hygiene. Sleep is necessary for rejuvenation, especially of the brain and nervous system.

Consequently, in 1985 he died at age 89 of Parkinson's disease. Though he worked himself to death and exhausted himself from the stress of constant battles with the authorities, he outlived all but three of his dozen siblings despite being the oldest child.

One of his former patients, T. C. Fry, then became a very active leader in the Natural Hygiene movement. A gifted writer, he was one of the most enthusiastic promoters of raw foods during the '70s, '80s and first half of the '90s. He wrote books and magazines, lectured all over, and developed a 1500-page correspondence course that awarded health counseling certification diplomas upon completion.

Two of his students were Harvey and Marilyn Diamond, who went on to write the bestsellers *Fit for Life* and *Fit for Life II: Living Health.* Fry encouraged his other students to become health counselors, proclaiming, "The health field is wide open — there's nobody in it!" meaning that all of the conventional and "alternative" doctors were not preaching true health practices.

Early leaders of the Natural Hygiene movement, which sprang up in the mid-19th century, were Dr. Russell Trall, Dr. Sylvester Graham, inventor of the graham cracker, Dr. Mary Gove, Dr. John Tilden and Bernarr Macfadden, who was Dr. Shelton's mentor.

Bernarr Macfadden (1868-1955) was a major force in the first half of the 20th century. Besides converting Dr. Shelton to Natural Hygiene, he may have also influenced Paul Bragg and Jack LaLanne. He was a bodybuilder and an astute businessman, building a small health and fitness publishing empire. Always after publicity, he parachuted out of an airplane to celebrate his 80th birthday.

Among Natural Hygiene's most prominent leaders today are Dr. Vivian V. Vetrano, Dr. Shelton's protégé, and Dr. Bernarr Zovluck, both of whom also suffered persecution at the hands of the authorities. Dr. Zovluck was forced to close his all too successful New York City clinic in the late '60s and now practices only by telephone consultations and his Internet presence.

Another 20th century figure, Dr. Norman Walker (1876-1985), became known for promoting raw juices and wrote several books on the topic. He invented the Norwalk hydraulic press, one of the premier juicers on the market today and the best of its day. He lived to be 109.

Naturopathic doctor Paul Bragg (1881-1976) was crippled by tuberculosis as a teenager and developed his own version of the raw food diet, advocating 80% raw, and an exercise program. He went on to become a health guru to many, including famous people, like Jack LaLanne, Dr. Scholl, Conrad Hilton, J. C. Penney and others. He wrote 20 books, including the classic *The Miracle of Fasting.* He remained very active and healthy until suffering a severe blow to his head *while surfboarding* at the age of 94 that culminated in his death a year later.

Dr. Edmond Bordeaux Szekely (1905-1979) claimed to have treated 123,600 people over a period of 33 years at his clinic in Mexico, many of whom came to him with "incurable" diseases.

They had more than a 90% success rate using live foods. Unfortunately, Dr. Szekely himself didn't practice what he preached.

Other 20th century raw food advocates have included Dr. Bernard Jensen, Dr. Paavo Airola, comedian Dick Gregory and numerous others.

For more information on notable raw fooders, read *Blatant Raw Foodist Propaganda!* by Joe Alexander, one of the most inspiring books I read while transitioning to the raw diet.

The people mentioned in this chapter laid down the foundation, started institutions and set the wheels in motion for the live food movement of today. The next chapter discusses some of the foremost modern-day leaders.

9
Modern-Day Leaders of the Raw Food Movement

To be a leader of men, one must turn one's back on men.
—Havelock Ellis (1859-1939), British psychologist

The raw food movement is now growing by leaps and bounds, especially since the flowering of the Internet-based information explosion. It would be an unending task for me to profile all of the movers and shakers in this grassroots movement; so I have included only those whose workshops I have attended plus Rev. Malkmus, Roe Gallo and Dr. Vetrano, who I feel deserve special mention. I was most impressed with all of those I met — their high energy levels and radiant, "raw glow." Most of them have also written books that I have quoted throughout this text.

Elizabeth Baker:
Active and Consulting in Her 90s

Elizabeth Baker wrote some of the very first books on the living foods diet, such as *The Uncook Book, The Unmedical Book, Does the Bible Teach Nutrition?* and *The UnDiet Book.* I saw her speak and lecture at the 2004 Raw Food Festival in Oregon, at which point she was 91 years old and still quite active! She said that her consultations kept her very busy. Her husband was also on the diet but died eight years previously after sustaining major injuries in a car accident.

The Boutenko Family: Healed of Four "Incurable" Diseases

Victoria Boutenko writes that she and her family became raw after she was faced with a life-threatening illness. The whole family gained superior health: Her husband became free of hyperthyroidism, her daughter of asthma and her son of juvenile diabetes. Victoria was healed of heart arrhythmia and also lost 120 pounds. The book *Raw Family: A True Story of Awakening* goes into much more detail.

Victoria went on to teach classes in raw foods, as well as to cater raw food. She noticed, however, that her students would very frequently backslide. In fact, although she personally met hundreds who were healed of cancer by raw diet, she knew of 132 who reverted to cooked foods, got cancer again, and died. It appeared that they actually preferred death to a raw food diet.

She kept wondering why this was happening; yet her own family seemed immune to the temptation to backslide. Finally, she figured out that cooked food is addictive, and unless one is eating 100% raw, as opposed to even 99%, one will be tempted to eat more and more cooked food. Victoria observed that it takes about two months of 100% raw eating to break the addiction. She explains all of this and much more in *12 Steps to Raw Foods*.

More than any other teacher I have read about or heard lecture, Victoria encourages a 100% raw food diet. She has witnessed in her clients the power of cooked food to pull one back.

Her children, Sergei and Valya, also went raw perforce and improved in schoolwork in addition to their physical health. But being children, they would fantasize about how, on their 18th birthdays, they would celebrate their independence by going out to eat pizza, nachos and corndogs, which they were not allowed to do until then.

Gradually, such desires faded, and their love for raw food and its life-changing effects grew. They learned how to create raw dishes and published their own recipe book, *Eating without Heating: Favorite Recipes from Teens Who Love Raw Food*. In this book, they also discuss how their health became superior. Sergei even regrew some teeth, and his wisdom teeth grew in perfectly straight.

Most amazing was the improvement in the children's academic performance. Formerly below average in school, the two kids, after eating 100% raw, were able to complete two school years in one year. Then school became boring, and so they went on to college.

When I attended one of the Boutenkos' workshops, Victoria said that Valya was taking 27 units in one semester — which for many would be a double load! — while also working 20 hours a week.

Recently, the Boutenkos were tested extensively for a scientific study being conducted in a university in Missouri on raw fooders. (See Chapter 5, experiment 25.) They were found to be in extraordinary health. Victoria's heart was like "that of a baby," and her bone density was like that of a 17-year-old. The MDs performing the study were extremely enthusiastic about their health findings, asked them many questions, and gave them additional tests beyond what was required of the study.

Victoria's latest book, *Green for Life*, is sparking a new revolution among raw fooders who have reached a plateau, as well as among people who have never eaten a raw diet. See Appendix C for more information about this radical, yet wonderful, way of eating raw.

Brian Clement and the
Hippocrates Health Institute

For the past 27 years, Brian Clement has worked as director of the Hippocrates Health Institute founded by Ann Wigmore and Viktoras Kulvinskas. This is a 70-person in-residence health facility. Clement does blood tests to see what residents need. I heard him lecture once and was especially impressed with his experimentation with wheatgrass. He found four ounces a day was the optimal amount for the average person. Any more than that did not seem to make a difference. His book *Living Foods for Optimum Health* was acclaimed by Coretta Scott King as a "landmark guide to the essentials of healthy living."

Lou Corona

I have heard Lou Corona speak several times. He is radiant and dynamic. At the age of 53, he could pass for a 30-year-old. This is because he began the 100% raw vegan diet about 31 years ago! He was very sick: badly constipated, plagued by severe acne and a tumor on his head, but he didn't want to have surgery because he knew of someone who died from that. He prayed for guidance, and a white light presence told him to eat living foods, no animal products. He was told that he would receive a mentor, whom he later met: a man who looked *decades younger* than his chronological age. He immediately adopted the diet, and the tumor completely disappeared within six months, along with the acne and constipation. Lou gives workshops and is currently writing a book.

Dr. Gabriel Cousens, MD: Seeking the Optimal Diet for Spiritual Growth

Dr. Gabriel Cousens, MD, is probably the foremost medical doctor promoting the raw vegan diet. He has done a great deal to verify its validity and usefulness through research. Because he has so much knowledge, Gabriel seems to have a hard time writing a book under 600 pages. But each page is packed with useful and interesting information.

Dr. Cousens was not satisfied with the results he obtained from the use of allopathic medicine. He began exploring various diets to find the right way to eat to enhance one's spiritual life.

After an amazing spiritual awakening experience, he was eager to find a diet that would reinforce that state. Eventually, he discovered the raw food diet and wrote about it in *Spiritual Nutrition and the Rainbow Diet* and again in *Conscious Eating*.

He established the Tree of Life Rejuvenation Center, a live food retreat located in Patagonia, Arizona. He now offers a university master's degree course in the study of live foods.

Gabriel wrote *Rainbow Green Live-Food Cuisine*, which explains how he has modified his raw food diet even more, eliminating foods that push the "composting button," which means that they cause disease-promoting fermentation of the digestive system. The book starts with a scientific overview but is mostly a low-sweet (hence not raising the blood sugar), live-food, non-acidic, book of delicious recipes.

Finally, Cousens has come out with a second book on the effect of diet on spiritual life: *Spiritual Nutrition*. In this book, he mentions that, although in his 60s, he has the same weight he had in high school. On his 60th birthday he did 600 consecutive push-ups, whereas at the age of 21 he was able to do only 70.

Also at the age of 60, he competed in the Native American Sundancing cycle. He completed three Sundance cycles of four days in the desert without food and water when no one else in the group of 52 people, which included dancers 40 years younger than he, was able to do so. He attributes this entirely to his live-food lifestyle.

According to Dr. Cousens, "The optimal diet is an individualized, live, organic, locally grown, vegan, highly mineralized, low-glycemic, well-hydrated diet of whole food prepared with love and eaten with consciousness and gratitude" (*Spiritual Nutrition*, p. 304).

Roe Gallo: Allergic to the 20th Century

Roe Gallo's childhood was plagued by illness. She was likely one of those people who are "allergic to the 20th [now 21st] century" — hypersensitive to all the thousands of chemicals in our environment that have been synthesized only within the last hundred years or so.

She suffered asthma, constant colds and several bouts of pneumonia. One day she experienced a severe allergic response after eating pancakes. She was taken to an emergency room and reacted so badly to the medication, aminophylline, they gave her that her heart stopped. She ended up spending several weeks in the hospital growing weaker and weaker. Later she learned the doctors were recommending that she take a smaller dose of the aminophylline, though it had stopped her heart, because it was the best medication for her condition.

Intuition told her that taking this drug would only lead to a slow death as opposed to a fast one. While still in the hospital, she stopped taking it, substituted certain visualization exercises, flushed out the drug residues with a lot of water, began eating only fresh fruits and vegetables her friends brought her, and slowly recovered, not telling the medical staff what she was doing. Within a week, she had the physical strength to sign herself out and walk away against the doctors' wishes.

Later she again resorted to a drug: cortisone for pain, which relieved the pain only for a few days. Then the pain would return along with difficulty breathing, and the doctor would simply increase the dosage. After reading up on it in the *Physician's Desk Reference* manual, she discovered it was addictive and that it too would eventually kill her. When she confronted the doctor about her suspicion that the drug would shorten her life span, he warned her that she would die without it.

That's when Roe decided to take personal control of her health. She threw out the pills although, as she put it, "That was the most frightening thing I have ever done. I had always listened to doctors. I grew up on medications." She fasted on water alone for two weeks, after which she felt better than she had ever felt in her 25 years of life. In her book *Perfect Body: The Raw Truth*, she describes how she attained super health on a fruitarian diet and exercise. She passed through menopause with virtually no symptoms! Her book includes testimonials of others she has helped with this diet.

Dr. Douglas Graham and Training Athletes

Dr. Doug Graham is a chiropractor who focuses on raw food counseling and writing. A lifelong athlete himself, he especially loves to counsel athletes on the raw diet, most notably tennis star Martina Navratilova and Ronnie Grandison of the NBA. Olympic athletes from Aruba, Australia, Mexico, the USA, Canada and Norway have also sought his counsel. His books include *The High Energy Diet Recipe Guide* and *Grain Damage*.

Dr. Graham has been a pioneer in making raw fooders aware that they are typically eating way too much fat. He has done histories on over 5,000 raw fooders and found that on average they consume 65% of their calories from fat! (The usual American diet contains about 40% fat.) He works with people to get this down to 10%. Fat is very difficult to digest, he explains, and also prevents absorption of many nutrients. Read more about Dr. Graham and his controversial 80% carbohydrate, raw vegan diet in Chapter 12.

David Jubb, PhD: Living on Little Food

David and Annie Jubb (no longer married) have written several books on the raw diet, including *LifeFood Recipe Book: Living on Life Force* and *Secrets of an Alkaline Body: The New Science of Colloidal Biology*. Annie Jubb has owned and managed raw, organic, vegan restaurants in San Francisco and Hawaii and is currently providing health readings, overseeing fasts, running corporate workshops, writing, filming, and conducting health research.

David Jubb, originally from Tasmania, a southern Australian island grouping, gives health readings, writes, and lectures both in the USA and abroad. He was the scientific advisor to live foods pioneer Ann Wigmore. (See Chapter 8.) David has recently written the book *Jubb's Cell Rejuvenation: Colloidal Biology: A Symbiosis.*

While I have never met Annie, I have seen David several times when he has lectured in San Diego.

Live foods form the basis of the Jubb diet, foods full of life force as demonstrated by Kirlian photography, a kind of photography in which an image is obtained by application of a high-frequency electric field to an object so that it radiates a characteristic pattern of luminescence that is recorded on photographic film.

David defines live food as meeting three criteria: containing life force (not cooked or irradiated), prepared in a way that is easy to digest, and some semblance of it continuing to grow wild in nature.

Hybridized foods having no wild counterparts are omitted because they are very low in life force and tend to increase the body's release of insulin, which promotes hypoglycemia (a precursor to diabetes), causes fatigue, and is believed to speed up aging and weight gain. These hybridized foods include commercial bananas, dates, corn, rice, legumes, wheat and tuberous vegetables like carrots, potatoes and beets. Wild plants, such as burdock root, kale, bok choy, heirloom tomatoes, squash and dandelion are preferred. Oddly, this diet also includes raw, organic cheese, preferably goat cheese, which is easier to digest.

Using live blood cell analysis, David has seen how the blood turns bad when we eat hybrid food, even when it is raw.

I once asked David what he ate, and he said he almost never eats. He does drink, however, the drinks listed in his recipe book, such as sun teas and lemonade. Although he is primarily a liquidarian, consuming minimal calories, he is of medium build and not at all emaciated. He is quite full of energy and enthusiasm.

I spent three evenings in a row with him when he was here giving lectures, a sweat lodge event and a raw food potluck. I did not see him eat anything. Others have concurred that they don't see him eat. Apparently, he continues being a gourmet chef and just takes minimal nibbles to make sure that his food tastes excellent.

There are people who have cleaned out their bodies to such an extent that their food intake needs are very minimal, and he has eaten a pure, raw diet for over 30 years. Nutrient absorption increases with a clean system, and metabolism slows down when one fasts extensively. Moreover, cells do not die and need replacing as often.

David Klein and *Living Nutrition Magazine*

It was ulcerative colitis that prompted David Klein's interest in the raw food diet. His physicians had tried prednisone and Azulfidine drug treatments, which helped with the symptoms but ruined his health and had a "devastating effect" on his mental abilities.

He discovered and studied T. C. Fry's Natural Hygiene course, adopted the diet, and was restored to robust health within a few years. He now publishes *Living Nutrition Magazine* and, along with Dr. Douglas Graham, sponsors an annual raw food seminar called "Rawstock." In collaboration with T. C. Fry, Klein wrote the book *Your Natural Diet: Alive Raw Foods.*

Rev. George Malkmus:
Why Christians Get Sick

A Baptist preacher, Rev. George Malkmus was diagnosed with colon cancer, "a tumor the size of a baseball," at the age of 42. Having already lost his mother to the recommended chemotherapy, he was determined to find something else that would cure him. So in 1976, he began researching health, nutrition and how lifestyle relates to health.

Another minister friend told him about the raw food diet, and it just seemed "too simplistic," but he decided to try it. After going on a raw food diet, he found that not only did his cancer go away, but also every minor complaint he'd had for years vanished. Gone were his hemorrhoids, hypoglycemia, allergies, sinus problems, high blood pressure, fatigue, pimples, colds, bouts with the flu, body odors and even dandruff.

Rev. Malkmus had always wondered why so many of the prayers for people's healings didn't seem to make a difference. He observed that the same percentage of Christians as non-Christians died of every disease. He began to believe that God had established certain universal laws that are perfect, eternal and unchangeable. When people violate these laws, they suffer the consequences. For example, if one jumps off a building, gravity will cause him to fall. If one eats denatured, dead or toxic food, she will slowly poison herself.

Malkmus came to realize that according to the Bible, mankind did not get sick after the fall from grace. No, man was quite healthy, living on uncooked fruits and vegetables and living an average of 912 years. It was only after the Flood that man began eating meat and cooked food. The life spans recorded in the Bible were greatly reduced from that time on.

He proceeded to write *Why Christians Get Sick* and later *God's Way to Ultimate Health*. He also founded Hallelujah Acres, a healing and educational center. He found that eating just 85% raw would maintain most people in good health. He now eats that way himself, an 85% raw, vegan diet and has remained cancer-free since 1976. Pastors who have convinced their church members to adopt this diet claim they never have to pray for people's illnesses anymore!

George claims that in six months or less, over 90% of the diseases at his center are healed. In just three to five days, the person experiences increased energy. Only about 10% of the people suffer intense detoxification symptoms. On his staff are numerous medical doctors, registered nurses and other medical professionals who help supervise patients.

People from *all* spiritual paths can learn a lesson from this. Various highly spiritual or highly conscious people teach that we can avoid illness through prayer, meditation, visualization, hypnosis, positive thinking, intention and other spiritual practices. Yet many of these teachers themselves suffer heart attacks, strokes and cancer.

Perhaps using the mind and spirit is not enough. We must heed God's, or Nature's, laws set up for the physical body. Eating uncooked food certainly appears to be one of them. Just as we would not attempt to avoid the harm in jumping off a cliff by using prayer or meditation, we must also not think we can escape harm in tampering with Mother Nature's food.

Nature's First Law: David Wolfe, Stephen Arlin and Fouad Dini

David Wolfe, his cousin Fouad Dini and his close friend Stephen Arlin collaborated on *Nature's First Law: The Raw Food Diet*. The interesting thing about this trio is that they began a 100% raw diet while still in their early twenties and already quite healthy, except for Fouad, who was obese.

They found that with raw diet they were propelled into a state of superior health and vitality. Fouad lost 156 pounds. The fact that they started so young shows us that you can obtain vastly greater levels of health by going on a raw diet even if you are already relatively healthy.

Stephen Arlin is much more muscular than the average raw food person. In fact, he is bigger than the average bodybuilder. People often cannot believe that he doesn't take steroids or at least meat. When people ask how he gets his muscular physique, he replies, "The same way a gorilla does!"

He wrote the book *Raw Power! Building Strength & Muscle Naturally* to show how he is able to maintain such a muscular body on a 100% raw, plant food diet. He has repeatedly said, "A raw fooder is not something you become; it is something that you already are."

David Wolfe once said in an interview that his goal is to be the world's foremost promoter of the raw food diet, and he has worked diligently toward that goal, traveling and giving lectures full-time and also authoring three books: *The Sunfood Diet Success System*, *Eating for Beauty* and *Naked Chocolate*.

The notoriety of being a naturalist earned him spots on a reality TV show ("Mad, Mad House" on the Sci-Fi Channel), the Rosie O'Donnell show and the Howard Stern show. My favorite David Wolfe quote is, "We are tired of eating pesticide, herbicide, fungicide, larvicide, suicide, pasteurized, homogenized, cooked, boiled, glow-in-the-dark, pus-filled food."

David and Stephen established a raw food grocery called Nature's First Law, which can be found online at www.rawfood. com. Nature's First Law also runs Eden Hot Springs near Tucson, Arizona, where they hold retreats that include raw food classes, yoga, hiking, hot-spring bathing, wild-food walks and, of course, 100% raw, organic meals.

Paul Nison: Healing Crohn's Disease

Paul Nison ate the SAD until age 19, when he was diagnosed with ulcerative colitis, a later stage of inflammatory bowel disease (IBD) and an earlier stage of Crohn's disease. He suffered colitis flare-ups about six times a year that included ulcerations, sometimes bleeding, and spasmodic and frequent bowel movements. Although his doctor told him that food had nothing to do with his condition, his symptoms improved when he eliminated dairy, eggs, meat and sugar.

When Paul was 23, he moved to West Palm Beach, Florida. By coincidence, he was living near the Hippocrates Health Institute, where he learned about the health benefits of eating raw foods. He improved further after switching to an 80% raw food diet, but again his physician warned that raw foods would only worsen his condition.

Later, after meeting a number of raw fooders and hearing their success stories, he progressed to a 100% raw food, vegetarian diet. It was only then that he completely overcame the ulcerative colitis.

He has since written *The Raw Life* and *Raw Knowledge*. Both books include interviews and photos of long-term raw fooders.

Paul also has his own web site and online raw food store at www.rawlife.com.

Dr. Vivian Vetrano and Natural Hygiene

Dr. Vivian V. Vetrano, DC, hMD, worked as manager and doctor at Dr. Shelton's Health School; guiding people through long fasts; teaching the principles of Natural Hygiene; editing, writing for, and producing *Dr. Shelton's Hygienic Review*; and saving lives. Being fluent in French helped make her an international promoter of raw diet and the other health principles of Natural Hygiene.

Although she has been involved in numerous projects with Natural Hygiene, one stands out. In the early 1980s, when T. C. Fry was in South Korea buying persimmon trees, he boasted at the Tubercular Sanitarium near Seoul that he could have all their tubercular patients well within one month.

When the Koreans took him up on the offer, he had Dr. Vetrano put in charge of the project. She started out with 50 patients as hundreds more called to see if they could be admitted to the project. Many became completely well within one month, while many of the others were well on their way to complete recovery by the time Dr. Vetrano left Korea. Both T. C. Fry and Dr. Vetrano were presented with awards and invited to come back and take charge of the entire sanitarium.

Dr. Vetrano was once president of the American Natural Hygiene Society for two terms and served on its board of directors for several years. She continues to counsel patients by telephone to this day.

Many Others

As I mentioned before, this list is by no means complete, but includes some of the teachers who have made a major impact, although there are more and more appearing every year as this grassroots movement gains momentum.

Author and comedian Tonya Zavasta is carving her own niche in the raw food community by teaching how to stay beautiful on raw food. Author Frédéric Patenaude is reaching many aspiring raw fooders with his free online newsletter, "Pure Health and Nutrition," as is health educator Roger Haeske.

Numerous people have web sites and offer coaching in raw eating, some of whom are listed in the Bibliography and Other Resources section at the back of this book, which also lists restaurant owners and chefs who have contributed a lot. Many of these other fine raw food renegades and their stories can be found in *The Complete Book of Raw Food*, which is also a compilation of their favorite recipes.

Additionally, there are also two controversial, *really radical* branches of the raw food movement that are so vastly different that they are not well accepted by the raw food mainstream, although they eat 100% raw foods. See Appendix C for more information.

Let's Go!

It is now time for you, dear reader, to embark upon your own personal raw diet evolution or revolution. The next section of this book will show you how to get started and answer any remaining questions or lurking doubts you may still harbor.

Get ready for the most rewarding and exciting personal growth experience of your life!

Section Four

Raw

Passage:

Your Journey to Raw Life

"Snow White was poisoned by an apple,
Jack found a giant in his beanstalk, and look
what happened to Alice when she ate the mushroom!
And you wonder why I won't eat fruits and vegetables!?"

10
Getting Started

Now is the time to begin the work of restoring good health —
not next week, next summer or next year.
> —Dr. Herbert Shelton (1895-1985)

Do not wait; the time will never be 'just right.' Start where you
stand, and work with whatever tools you may have at your
command, and better tools will be found as you go along.
> —Napoleon Hill (1883-1970)

It has been said, "It is easier to get a man to change his religion than his diet." The switch to a raw food diet may be one of the most significant things you can do in your life, opening up levels of energy and health you never dreamed possible. But it does not happen overnight. It takes commitment, planning and education. Those who learn from the mistakes of others and those who take time to inform themselves about the reasons the raw diet is superior and what to expect during the transition period are the ones who tend to stick to the diet.

The Decision

"A journey of a thousand miles must begin with a single step" is a famous saying from *The Way of Lao Tzu*. The first step to going raw is to make up your mind to do it. For some, it may be easier to commit to a brief "experiment." A sudden decision never to eat another cooked food in your life may be too disturbing to the ego. So some have simply resolved, "I will experiment and go 100% raw for a one-month period."

I know of one man who decided to commit to a one-year trial period. After each year, he would "renew the experiment." So far he has gone over ten years of eating 100% raw!

Do not say, "Oh, I want to go raw, but I am going to wait until all my canned, packaged, frozen and boxed food is finished." That could take weeks, or even months, by which time you may have lost most of the inspiration to go raw.

Do it now! Give all your food to a hungry neighbor or friend. Or donate the non-perishables to the Salvation Army, and get a tax write-off. Or keep some of it, the foods you know won't tempt you, for guests who want processed food.

Remember, it is not eating the raw foods that is usually the mental barrier; most people find that changing the emotional and social associations with cooked food to be the biggest block. One must reprogram one's thinking and view food as medicine and nourishment rather than as an object for emotional comfort, love, entertainment or social activity.

For all of the importance we give food, eating is nothing more than a few brief moments of savoring something that we chew and swallow, never to taste again. The "pleasure" of cooked food items is momentary and fleeting, but the negative effects linger on and on.

What the protesting cooked food addict never seems to understand is that once you have been raw long enough, the raw foods give *much* more pleasure in the eating than the cooked foods ever did. *Then, it's not a matter of deprivation anymore!*

What we ingest ultimately makes us feel alive or moribund. The next time you are tempted to eat something you know is not good for you, ask yourself, "Is it worth being overweight, fatigued and poisoned for those fleeting moments of pleasure?"

Methods of Transitioning

The easiest way for many people is to commit to a 100% raw diet without a period of dietary transition. The big danger in a slower transition is that you may lose your initial enthusiasm and inspiration, perhaps even forgetting the reasons you decided to go raw. How many of us have bought supplements that we stopped taking because we forgot why we started them in the first place?

The benefits also may not come fast enough for you to see the superiority of a 100% raw food diet. For some people, a slow transition results in backsliding into a diet of mainly cooked foods because of their addictive qualities.

Nonetheless, some people do find it psychologically easier and physically less disruptive to transition gradually into a raw diet. There are several ways in which this can be done.

Transitioning One Meal at a Time

One way to transition is by changing one meal at a time. You can work out a plan in which you eat only raw breakfasts for a month. The second phase will consist of raw breakfasts and lunches. The third phase will have everything raw.

For some, this process may be too slow, and the results will not be dramatic enough to sustain positive feedback. They may wish to move on to the next phase weekly instead of monthly.

Soon enough, after just transitioning two meals, you will be 60-70% raw. Most people eat more for dinner than the other meals. So if you eat just half of your dinner cooked, you will be eating about 75% to 85% of your diet raw. Many people feel so great eating this way that they stick with that plan as a way of life. That way they need not feel deprived of their favorite cooked dishes.

If you decide to eat 80-85% of your calories raw, I recommend saving the cooked foods for dinner. There are several reasons for this.

The first is well-being: You'll have energy all day, and the cooked food won't slow you down. At night, it's usually okay to wind down, but not at work.

The second is social: Dinner is the one meal most people share with others, and the other people may be eating cooked food.

The third is pleasure: For many people, cravings for cooked food, or any food for that matter, arise more strongly in the early evening. In my case, for example, I feel my tastebuds "open up" for more variety in the evenings. When I have eaten 90-95% raw, it has only been in the evenings that I have been tempted to eat something cooked.

Food Elimination Transition

Another way to transition is to give up certain kinds of "bad foods" first. For example, one week cut out all sugar and table salt. The next week maintain the sugar and salt elimination while also cutting out pasteurized dairy. Next, omit cooked meat, then grains and later processed foods until everything cooked is substituted with raw dishes.

Again, for many, this process will prove too slow. Nonetheless, for those who have not determined to go 100% raw, numerous benefits may be derived from simply eliminating the "white evils" flour (wheat), table salt, sugar and dairy. (See Appendix A.)

Indeed, some people are so pleased with the health improvements obtained just by cutting out these four deadly whites that they never do make full transitions to raw diets.

Reduced Temperature and Heating Time Transition

A third way to transition is to cook your foods at lower temperatures for less time. For example, if you typically eat your vegetables fried, steam them instead for five minutes, then three, then two.

This really only applies to vegetables, though, because few people cook their fruits, and people who eat cooked nuts usually buy them that way. It is actually rather difficult to find truly raw nuts, especially because of companies' fear of salmonella poisoning or mold growth, but you can find stores that sell them in the Bibliography and Other Resources guide in the back of this book.

So this method should be used in conjunction with another method. For example, you could go "cold turkey" into raw foods but eat your broccoli and other vegetables steamed for a while. This has worked for a lot of people.

Instantaneous (Cold Turkey) Transition

Many have found that cooked food is so addictive, however, that it is simply better to take the plunge into 100% raw food to get the cravings and withdrawal symptoms over with as soon as possible.

One way to do this that will not frighten the ego so much is to think of it as an experiment. You might commit to only one month of 100% raw foods at first, renewable after that.

This is the most sure-fire way to guarantee you will become hooked on a 100% raw food diet. After an entire month of eating 100% raw, organic food, the vast majority of people notice such profound health improvements that they find it impossible to return to old eating patterns. If you want to see dramatic results, stick with it for six months.

A huge advantage of jumping into a 100% raw diet is that you will not battle temptations as much as a part-timer does. After having gone "cold turkey" for a few months, you will no longer be seriously tempted by cooked foods. Even the aromas of coffee and cooking will not disturb you. I have heard a number of long-term raw fooders say that, for them, cooked food looks like "plastic" or "pretty decorations" or smells like flower bouquets, but is not something they would desire to eat.

Most people who are battling serious illnesses are wise to commit to 100% raw diets immediately, as this may be the only way to detoxify at a rapid enough pace to recover. When your life is in danger, you do not have time to waste.

Kristine Nolfi, MD, who healed herself of cancer with a raw diet, said, "The day I discovered I had cancer and had to face death — a painful death within about two years — it was not difficult for me to switch over to a raw food diet. I was grateful that something as simple as that could help me."

In her book *Raw Food Treatment of Cancer,* she explains her choice of this healing method over conventional drug treatment.

Fasting Followed by Instantaneous Transition

For many, including myself, a brief fast or a diet of only freshly squeezed juice just before beginning an all-raw diet has proved very useful. I went two weeks on raw juice, during which time I lost my cravings for salt, coffee and sugar. This made it much easier for me to stick with the raw food diet thereafter. After two weeks of not eating solid food, I was *thrilled* with just some salad and avocados!

When it comes to fasting for more than a week, you may want to consult with your holistic or naturopathic physician or at least read some books on fasting so you'll know what to expect and how best to break the fast safely. If you have been taking drugs (recreational, prescription, or over the counter — your body doesn't know the difference), you will go into a more intense detoxification than would happen on the raw diet alone.

Many of these drugs are addictive and might be more comfortably tapered off gradually if you decide to stop them. Cold turkey withdrawal symptoms can sometimes be most unpleasant. In that case, you should eat a raw diet rather than fast while weaning yourself off the drugs, if you make the decision to do so, under the guidance of a doctor who understands what you are doing. Refer to the Bibliography and Other Resources section in the back of the book for a directory of doctors experienced in supervising fasts.

No drugs, not even insulin, should be taken while fasting, as drugs are even more harmful to a fasting body than to an eating one. Taking insulin while fasting is likely to send you into a diabetic coma.

Legally, an MD is the only health professional who can tell you to stop or reduce your drugs. Holistic physicians, such as chiropractors, acupuncturists, homeopaths and naturopaths know how bad these drugs are but won't tell you to cease taking them for fear of going to jail. See Appendix B for more on how the medical system works.

Therefore, I can't advise you to stop your prescription medications either, but I can tell you that other people have very successfully gone cold turkey on various prescription drugs, including insulin, while fasting.

Fasting should be a physiological state of rest for the entire body: rest from food, drugs, emotional stress and all strenuous physical activity. It's even best to stay in bed sleeping or with eyes closed 24/7, or as close to that as you can manage, for the duration of the fast. This permits the body to focus as much of its attention on healing as is possible.

Dr. Gabriel Cousens stated in an interview that fasting is like rebooting your computer. Often when your computer acts up, a simple reboot is all you need to get rid of the problem.

It is debatable among raw fooders about whether one should take enemas or colonics during the fasting period. Some say it is not natural to have a gadget up your colon that takes out toxins with water, coffee and/or wheatgrass and may upset the body's electrolyte balance.

My personal feeling is that we have done so many unnatural things to clog up our colons, one of our major organs of elimination, that we may as well take advantage of technology to unclog it. Therefore, it may be useful during the initial stages of detoxification to take enemas or colonics. Just be sure to replace the lost electrolytes and healthful bacteria. Getting colonics will inspire you, as you will be able to see through the glass all of the gray, white or black toxic debris and phlegm leaving your body.

A colonic that works with gravity, as opposed to one that depends on electricity to push the water in by hydraulic pressure, poses no risk of a ruptured bowel, no more so than an enema. A colonic is neither a stimulant nor an irritant like a laxative, and it works with the body's natural peristalsis (bowel motion) to rid the body of waste that may have been stuck there for years and even decades.

According to nutritionist Natalia Rose, *no one passes even 60% of the average American diet*! Obviously, she is referring to tiny, toxic and indigestible bits and particles that over the years, however, can add up. This means that a great deal of our *waist* is actually *waste*! She claims that if your intestines are clean, and you suck in your stomach before eating breakfast, "your belly button should be almost kissing your spine" (*The Raw Food Detox Diet*, p. 237). She warns that being skinny does not mean you don't have a lot of junk stuck in the colon. In fact, the skinny person often dies of cancer before the obese one because her toxins are stored in the organs rather than in fat tissue.

In addition, there are special formulas designed for liver or gallbladder detoxification. While using one of these formulas combined with a colonic, I saw through the colonic glass hundreds of small, pca-sized, green gallstones fleeing my body. I marveled as I wondered, "How many people could be spared gallbladder removal by this simple procedure?"

I had merely ingested a mixture of half a cup of unheated olive oil, a cup of raw apple juice, a tablespoon of garlic, a tablespoon of raw apple cider vinegar and a tablespoon of ginger without having eaten anything all day, taken within five minutes of lying down to sleep. It doesn't work if you don't lie down on your right side afterwards. This was followed by a colonic the next day.

Invariably, I felt incredible ecstasy and energy following these releases.

Green Smoothie Transition

Victoria Boutenko, in her Roseburg Experiment (See Chapter 5 and Appendix C), found that when participants simply added a quart of her green smoothies to their daily diets, their cravings for cooked foods, including meat, sweets, alcohol and processed chocolate, disappeared! They began to crave raw food. By gradually replacing meals with her green smoothies, many people would experience smooth transitions to raw diets. For more information, see her book *Green for Life*.

Just Get Started!

Only you can determine which is the best transition method for you. I've always been one who gets impatient for results, but some like to take things slowly.

Carol Alt (*Eating in the Raw*) says that her athletic, hockey player boyfriend transitioned overnight, but she agrees that this way is not for everyone. She says you can start with baby steps, such as adding olive oil to the pasta or other cooked dish after it is cooked instead of before. Sauté in water instead of oil. Make your own salad dressings instead of buying the pasteurized ones in the store. Buy Ezekiel bread, which is sprouted and baked at low temperatures, though not truly raw, instead of regular bread. For some people, adding a few of these differences every week can build up momentum toward a mostly raw, or 100% raw, diet.

For those of you who are not in a great hurry, an excellent book on transitioning to a raw diet slowly is *The Raw Food Detox Diet* by Natalia Rose. Using her methods, you can transition over a period of years while still achieving many benefits and staying on track.

Invest Time in Food Preparation during the First Months

People often remark that I have fantastic willpower to stick to a raw food diet. I tell them that I don't at all, but I eat such delicious raw food dishes that are so tasty that I actually prefer them to cooked food. Taking time to create wonderful dishes will definitely assist you on the road to raw.

You will not feel deprived.

During the transition phase, you will want to take the time to prepare some elaborate dishes to satisfy your tastebuds. Just remember that these recipes, initially time-consuming until you get the hang of them, will only be necessary for three to twelve months. Your tastebuds are used to dead foods that have been "enlivened" with intense spices, table salt and other additives, many of which are toxic. After some time, your tastebuds will become normalized, and live foods, without any sauces or complex chopping and blending, will satisfy you.

At that time, you will probably spend less time in food preparation than you did as a cooked fooder.

Whatever plan you work out, write it down, commit, and stick to it! Give it a chance to see how the experiment works on you.

(Un)Cookbooks

Although you can find many raw food recipes on the Internet, it is always nice to have several raw food cookbooks. There are well over 20 raw recipe books at the time of this writing. I have 19 of them myself. Even if I get only one recipe that becomes a staple in my diet from a particular book, it was worth the investment. I find the books with color photos most inspiring. After a few months of food preparation, you may find yourself creatively coming up with your own raw recipes.

Your tastebuds take time to revert to normal. You have spent decades tantalizing them with spices, MSG — which by law does not have to be listed if it is mixed in with other spices (see Appendix A) — sugar and many other refined and unnatural "foods" or food additives. Once you have cleansed your body of those toxins, you will derive great pleasure from Nature's food, our original diet. Then you will feel quite content to munch on olives, nuts or cucumbers. You may not even think in terms of "meals" but simply eat when hungry.

Until the time when you can eat as Nature intended, however, you may want to take the time to prepare scrumptious food combinations from raw food recipes. This will keep you from backsliding, as you will find raw food recipe counterparts for nearly every cooked food you once enjoyed. For example, there are raw food recipes for hummus, pizza, spaghetti, Thai stir "fry," mock meatloaf, burgers, "mashed potatoes," corn chips, soups, tabbouleh and many more.

If you need photographs to inspire you, there are several books with plenty of color photos of raw dishes. Juliano Brotman's *Raw — The Uncook Book* contains some of my favorites. He owns a raw food restaurant in Hollywood and is also chef to some of the stars, such as Demi Moore. Some of the recipes are time-consuming, as they entail making two or three recipes in one. But the results are well worth it — truly gourmet eating.

Roxanne Klein and Charlie Trotter's *Raw* is also heavy-duty gourmet. I used to think Juliano's recipes were complicated until I saw this book. The recipes look intimidating, but once you get started, they are worth it. Each recipe has a color photo.

A book with simpler and faster-to-make recipes and plenty of color photos is Nomi Shannon's *The Raw Gourmet: Simple Recipes for Living Well.*

A more recent book with plenty of inspirational color photos is *Raw Food/Real World: 100 Recipes to Get the Glow* by Kenney and Malngailis.

A book with simple and fast recipes that kids would love is *Eating without Heating* by Sergei and Valya Boutenko. I recommend this to people who have kids since many of the recipes and color photos are of raw cakes, burgers and healthful raw versions of "junk foods" that kids love. It also has the teenage authors' story about how eating raw changed their lives and made them much smarter.

A couple of other books that specialize in quick recipes are *Raw Foods for Busy People: Simple and Machine Free Recipes for Every Day* by Jordan Maerin and *Raw in Ten Minutes* by Bryan Au.

One of my favorite raw recipe books is *The Complete Book of Raw Food*, edited by Lori Baird. Although there are no photos, it is worth purchasing because it is a compilation of over 350 recipes from the world's top raw food chefs — often their favorites — so every recipe is a winner.

Three books that go into detailed information about each type of raw food and its value, i.e. each specific kind of fruit, vegetable, nut and seed, are: *The Sunfood Cuisine* by Frédéric Patenaude; *Rawsome! Maximizing Health, Energy and Culinary Delight with the Raw Foods Diet* by Brigitte Mars; and *Living Cuisine: The Art and Spirit of Raw Foods* by Renée Loux Underkoffler. One thing I liked about *Rawsome!* is that it contains recipes for raw Indian cuisine, a cuisine that I really missed after giving up cooked foods. It also contains many other "ethnic" recipes as well as other gourmet raw dishes.

A recipe book that specializes in low-fat raw dishes is Frédéric Patenaude's *Instant Raw Sensations: The Easiest, Simplest, Most Delicious Raw Food Recipes Ever!*

Gabriel Cousens' *Rainbow Green Live-Food Cuisine* provides 159 pages of scientific and other information about the diet and about 300 pages of recipes.

Don't buy Vonderplanitz' *The Recipe for Living without Disease* unless you are interested in raw animal foods, which make up the bulk of his recipes. (See Appendix C.) He has a lot of interesting scientific information before the recipe section, however.

There are many other wonderful recipe books that contain useful information or other educational material in addition to the recipes. See the recipe book bibliography for more recipe books.

There are also quite a number of videos that show how to make raw food dishes, but don't wait to get a recipe book or a video to get started! You can find dozens, if not hundreds, of raw recipes on the Internet. Simply search for "raw recipes" using your favorite search engine.

I have discovered many recipes on the Internet simply by inserting under Google (www.google.com) the words "raw recipe" along with the particular produce item I wanted to include or dish I wanted to mimic. You will also find many other free recipes at the web sites listed in the Bibliography and Other Resources section at the back of this book.

Educate Yourself

It cannot be emphasized enough how important it is to invest in books, especially recipe books, concerning the raw food diet to educate and inspire you. I suggest you read some of the books quoted or cited in this book, the ones that pique your interest. (See the Bibliography and Other Resources section.) Go to the web sites referenced in the bibliography also.

When you study the health benefits of the raw food diet, you will become less likely to eat cooked food. You will realize that chewing something for a few minutes in your mouth and deriving pleasure for a short period does not come close to compensating for the detrimental effects.

When I was in college, I had a poster that read, "Short on the lips, long on the hips." Since I always put weight on my waist instead of the hips, I added, "Short to taste, long on the waist."

I remember how much I loved to eat at Kentucky Fried Chicken. I used to say, "The saddest moments are when I eat the last bite of my KFC!" Now I realize the highly touted "secret ingredient" was the MSG (see Appendix A). The pleasure of cooked food ends with the last bite and is often followed by painful indigestion, whereas the pleasure of radiant health continues throughout the day.

Reading, attending workshops and talking to other raw fooders will reinforce your knowledge and belief system, making you stronger in your convictions when you are tempted to give in.

For example, some people quit prematurely because they don't know that detoxification symptoms happen only at the beginning of the diet and are actually a good thing, a sign of cleansing.

Some quit because they don't know that eating too many raw nuts or vegetables can result in indigestion, and they think the diet is bad for them.

Others quit in despair because they spend so much time in food preparation. They don't know that after a few months, they will be happy without complicated recipes.

Those who educate themselves on the raw food diet tend to be the ones who stick with it long term.

Always Focus on the Positive!

It is much easier to take on a new, pleasurable habit than to stop practicing an old, somewhat pleasurable, but destructive, habit. So don't think of yourself as being deprived, having to stop eating the old way. Instead, view this as an adventure!

You will be substituting new, brand new, raw food dishes for every cooked dish you eliminate. *Think of all the exciting new dishes you will be tasting!* Take time to prepare raw gourmet dishes from recipe books or from the numerous raw recipes online.

Take time to hunt for ripe, mouthwatering, luscious fruit. There are thousands of different kinds of fruit. Although you may not have access to many varieties where you live, it is possible to mail order others from the Internet. Think of all the new foods you have never even tasted!

This is not a diet of deprivation. Many women who have been accustomed to limiting their fat find that they can eat all the raw fat they desire and still lose or maintain their weight! Raw fat is wonderful, useful for the brain and nerves and required for beautiful skin. Raw fat also helps digest body fat by bringing lipase to it, the enzyme for fat digestion.

Get excited about how wonderful you will soon feel and how great the food you eat will be for perhaps the first time in your life! Inspire yourself by reading testimonials from raw fooders online or in books such as *The Raw Life* and *Raw Knowledge* by Paul Nison. Educate yourself for months reading about the benefits of the raw food diet. Join a raw food support group. If there is not one in your city, join an online one (see the list of chat groups in the Bibliography and Other Resources section), or get one started in your area by posting notices at your health food store.

Kitchen Gadgets

If you prepare raw food that looks and tastes similar to cooked food, it will lead to an easier transition. The food will be so delicious that you will minimize any temptation to go back to cooked foods.

However, you will have to invest in a few gadgets if you don't already have them. Some are more important than others. For the budget conscious, I suggest getting the top brand of only a few, perhaps one at a time, such as the Cuisinart food processor and the Vita-Mix heavy-duty blender, or a slightly less expensive, but equally fine brand, the K-Tec machine. I have learned that buying the top quality brands saves money in the long run. You can also find them used in your local classi fieds or online at Ebay (www.ebay.com).

If money is not an issue, you may even consider an "extreme kitchen makeover." Some people, for example, get rid of the stove altogether to create more kitchen space for the gadgets or for an additional refrigerator.

In preparing gourmet raw food recipes, there are two indispensable kitchen tools: a food processor and a temperature-controlled dehydrator. The food processor will blend the food into a much creamier consistency than a simple blender will, and every week it will save you hours of chopping, grating or stirring.

If you can afford it, get the Excalibur dehydrator. It dehydrates evenly throughout all the trays and makes it possible to remove some trays so you can put a pan or bowl in it, thus making raw pies or warming up soup.

Whatever dehydrator you get must have a temperature control, or chances are it will heat up to 140° F or so, which is well beyond the point of enzyme destruction. You should generally not heat things above 105° F for maximal enzyme protection. I learned to tape the control down, as several times I accidentally bumped the temperature control button, and everything got heated up to 140° F. I had to give the food to a neighbor.

When first transitioning to a raw diet, you will love the foods from the dehydrator the most because they will be slightly warm and crunchy or chewy, more like what you are used to. When first going raw, I found myself eating "garden burgers" or mock pizza straight from the dehydrator so they would not lose any heat!

Another item of great utility is a juicer. I recommend the Omega brand masticating juicer. Nowadays, juicers can be found for very reasonable prices that do much more than juice. They may also blend soft-serve dishes like frozen fruits, make nut butter, grind seeds and nuts, and even make nut milk.

For most raw fooders, either the K-Tec or Vita-Mix is indispensable. This is a blender-like machine that has such a powerful motor that it can make cream out of celery in seconds. The motor goes 240 miles per hour, like a hurricane! The K-Tec machine is more powerful and a little less expensive than the Vita-Mix but carries a shorter warranty.

The advantage of these machines is that you can make wonderful, creamy soups. Using them, you can also make juice and nut or seed milk if you then apply a strainer.

The money is a lifetime investment in your health. If you use the cheap blenders instead, you will never be able to make the creamy, green smoothies (Appendix C) that tear down the cellulose walls of the greens, releasing all of the nutrients.

Be careful not to blend things too long in these machines, as the food can actually become somewhat cooked if over-blended. Some people add ice cubes to keep from overheating the food if it must be blended a long time. However, I have not found this to be necessary in the vast majority of cases.

If your juicer doesn't make nut milk, you can purchase a SoyaJoy, which has a non-heating option for making nut milk. Nut milk is great for getting calcium and for kids who are used to dairy milk. Milk from unhulled sesame seeds is also high in calcium. Be sure to use the calcium-rich cream skimmed off in another recipe, such as a soup. These milks look like cow's milk and taste great. You may add a few dates, a bit of agave nectar or unheated honey to sweeten it a bit.

For just a few dollars you can get a sprouting jar, usually found at your local organic produce store. This is a jar with a wire mesh lid so that you can conveniently rinse the sprouts at least twice a day. In particularly hot, humid climates, the sprouts may need three rinses per day. Missing even one rinse, especially in hotter weather, can cause mold to grow on the sprouts. I once got a headache from eating moldy sprouts. After that, I never forgot to rinse them! Another way to avoid mold is to rinse the sprout seeds with a solution of 0.3% hydrogen peroxide, which would be about one ounce of 35% food grade H_2O_2 per gallon of water.

A coffee grinder is useful for grinding nuts and seeds if your juicer can't do that. Be aware that ground nuts and seeds go rancid after three days and should be kept refrigerated even during those few days. The fresher they are when eaten, the better.

Many people like to grind flaxseed to sprinkle over their soups or salads. The "omega-3" fat that flaxseeds contain is great for the brain, and since it may be difficult to find raw flax oil, this is the best way it can be absorbed. A coffee grinder is also handy for grinding raw cacao beans into a powder. (See the Raw Chocolate recipe on page 346.)

The Saladacco, also known as a "spiralizer," is a useful tool for making "spaghetti" strips from zucchinis, carrots, beets, spaghetti squash and yams. The texture of spaghetti is often missed more than the taste; so this makes a great transition food. It also makes flower-like strips for garnishing, which truly adds beauty and color to a dish.

A citrus juicer will save you a lot of time when you want to squeeze the juice from an orange or lemon and don't want to clean the juicer or take time to peel the fruit. You can get a plastic one very inexpensively or spend a bit more for an electric one. The electric one might be a better investment in the long run, as you will tend to extract even more of the juice.

Be aware, however, that juicing fruits throws away a lot of valuable nutrients. For example, oranges are naturally high in calcium, but orange juice has very little because the calcium is in the pulp. The soluble fiber is beneficial too.

Ice cream lovers may wish to purchase an ice-cream maker so that they can make raw ice cream. Even if you are a vegan, you can enjoy wonderful, delicious "ice cream" by using the cream left over from making nut or seed milk. (See the recipe in Chapter 15.) Coconut cream and milk mixed with a sweetener also make great ice cream.

You will also be able to use many of the same things you used for cooking: a spatula, a set of sharp knives, mixing bowls, measuring cups, a vegetable peeler, a cutting board, a strainer, cheesecloth and a salad shooter.

As for your old pots and pans, you may wish to donate them to a favorite charity or give them away. Keep a few for guests. Unplug your stove and cover it with a large board to give you more kitchen space. Throw your microwave out, as studies have shown that food from it is very toxic.

Hang on to your coffee maker. If you get involved in fasting, it is useful for making coffee enemas to aid in detoxification. This is part of the famous cancer cure at the Gerson Institute. Some people go through a mild coffee withdrawal after the cleanse, however. Yet coffee seems to be a powerful way to detoxify the liver. But some people, wanting to kick the coffee habit, may not be able to endure the temptation to make beverage coffee with this gadget hanging around.

Meal and Snack Planning

If you have been eating the SAD, you may be used to little or no meal preparation. You may have been eating out of cans, bags, microwave prepared dishes, restaurants and such. You may have gone to the grocery as infrequently as once in two weeks!

Going raw after spending so little time on food preparation can at first appear overwhelming. Suddenly you realize you cannot depend on the freezer or cupboard to stash "dead" food that seems to have no expiration date. Suddenly, you realize you cannot eat from vending machines or count on corner fast-food restaurants in times of emergency.

You will have to spend time planning meals, but *your health is worth it*. You may want to join a food co-op if one is conveniently located, as this will save on your grocery bill when you buy high quality organic produce.

You could also join a Community Supported Agriculture (CSA) farm and frequent farmers' markets for fresher produce — the fresher, the more nutrients — than you will usually find at your grocery store.

You may wish to visit U-pick farms and rural roadside food stands; learn to grow your own food, even if from the balcony of your apartment; and purchase sun-dried fruits and truly raw, organic nuts by mail order or online at some of the stores listed in the back of this book.

You can also save money by ordering produce by the case from the local organic supermarket. For information about where to find local farmer's markets, CSAs and food co-ops, visit www.greenpeople.com or www.localharvest.com.

You will need to pore through recipe books, planning which dishes to make for the week. Make a list of all the produce you will need, along with the corresponding dishes you will prepare. Make a list of all the snacks or lunch meals you will need. Then prepare enough food so that you will have leftovers the next day and not necessarily have to prepare food each day, although if you have the time, fresh is always better in taste and nutrients.

You will need to pack lunches and snacks for work or school. Do this the night before to be sure that you will have them no matter how rushed you are in the morning.

Although going raw will temporarily mean more time for food prep, eventually you will become satisfied to eat more simply. A plain avocado will have its own symphony of flavors. A burst of flavor will spring forth from a bite full of raw walnuts.

There are now a vast number of good, prepared, raw snacks available online or in stores. They may appear somewhat expensive when you are used to buying cheap junk food like crackers or chips, but remember that this is fresh food with a shelf life of weeks, not years, and that it is all organic produce. _You are worth it_. Moreover, you will find that you will not need to eat as much since the food is so nutritious and satisfying.

As this diet catches on, more companies will produce more goodies because consumers will vote with their money and demand it. _In the meantime, don't let society's preferences set standards for you!_

Stand Firm in Your Commitment!

If you decide to go 100% raw, you may want to inform all of your friends, or you may decide to wait until you've passed your first one-month hurdle so you don't look like a fool if you give up after three days or something.

Victoria Boutenko suggests that you decline all dinner invitations, potlucks or any social activities with cooked food for the first two months. Putting yourself in a "temptation-free zone" for two months will give you time to detoxify until most of your cooked food cravings are gone.

Why needlessly suffer by being around cooked food that you want but won't allow yourself to eat? After a few months, such food may not even be tempting. The physical cravings will be gone, at least. Some of the psychological cravings may take longer. For example, the smell of freshly baked cookies may remind you of your mother's love for you. But once you are free of addiction, the memory won't compel you to eat them.

Foods to Stockpile

There are six basic kinds of raw plant foods: fruits, vegetables, nuts, seeds, sprouts and fermented foods. Sprouts include sprouted seeds, grains and legumes. Fermented foods include miso, tempeh, vinegar, sauerkraut and even wine. Although some of these are not technically raw, having been cooked prior to fermentation, the fermentation process imparts enzymes and makes them acceptable to many raw fooders when eaten occasionally. From this palette of raw foods, a huge variety of soups, salads, salad dressings, crackers, breads, desserts, smoothies, pâtés and entrées can be prepared.

Some of the foods mentioned in this section may be hard to find, even at your local health food store. For this reason, some raw food stores that accept orders by phone or e-mail are listed in the Bibliography and Other Resources section.

You will want most of your food to be as fresh as possible. However, there are certain things you can store in your cupboard. Just make sure they are really raw, as the word "raw" means different things for different people. (See Chapter 13.)

Throw out your table salt, which is very toxic. (See Appendix A.) In its place, invest in Celtic sea salt. Another great salt is Himalayan crystal salt, discussed in *Water & Salt: The Essence of Life* by Dr. Barbara Hendel.

Although many raw fooders claim that *any salt is bad*, I have found that a bit of these natural salts works for me. If you feel that they are toxic for you, use celery salt or dulse flakes.

Since you will not be using iodized table salt, you will need to make sure you get sufficient iodine. This is important in keeping the thyroid in good health. Low thyroid function is often a cause of fatigue and weight gain. Great sources of iodine include the following sea vegetables: dulse, kelp, arame, nori, wakame, hijiki and spirulina algae. I get liquid dulse and put some drops in my green juice. I sometimes sprinkle sea vegetables in with my salad.

Keep raw olive oil on hand for making salad dressings. Just mix it with raw apple cider vinegar and possibly unheated honey or raw agave nectar if you don't have time for a more elaborate recipe. The vinegar should be refrigerated once opened. Some feel that the oil needs to be refrigerated as well, whereas others, such as Aajonus Vonderplanitz, feel that refrigeration destroys too many of its nutrients.

Another oil to keep on hand is raw coconut butter or oil. This is used in a lot of desserts and takes the place of dairy butter. I found out the hard way that it shouldn't be used in salad dressings because when you refrigerate it, it congeals like butter. However, you could use it in a dressing if it's oily at room temperature and eaten right away.

I suggest having several jars of raw, organic olives in the refrigerator. These make great snack foods and garnishes. Frédéric Patenaude suggests soaking olives that contain salt in pure water for 24 hours to release the harmful salt.

Nuts and seeds are items you can stock up on to a degree. If you buy them in a health food shop, and they have been sitting in bins for a long time, they may not be very fresh. You can purchase them from an organic food distributor, such as The Living Tree Community or Sunorganic Farm, both in California, and they will be shipped in thick, plastic bags, which keep them very fresh. (See the Bibliography and Other Resources section for contact information.)

You can store some in the freezer for up to six months. Freezing does destroy some enzymes, but not so much with nuts or other low water content foods. If you plan to use them soon, you may keep them in tightly enclosed containers or sealed, thick bags. It is better to keep them in the refrigerator or freezer if they will not be eaten within a month or so.

Keep a few cups of flaxseeds around for making crackers. Sunflower seeds should be kept handy, as they are often found in raw recipes and are also good for sprouting, trail mix, and sprinkling on salads.

Brazil nuts should be around your kitchen at all times. They are rich in selenium, an essential mineral depleted in much of our soils.

Keep a stock of pumpkin seeds, as they are high in zinc and tryptophan, an amino acid that aids in depression and insomnia. If you wish to be a raw vegan, selenium and zinc are difficult to obtain in sufficient quantities without Brazil nuts and pumpkin seeds.

Before eating nuts and seeds, make sure you soak them overnight and thoroughly rinse them to get rid of enzyme inhibitors. Before doing that, however, it is good to soak them in a solution of $11/12$ water and $1/12$ food grade hydrogen peroxide in order to rid them of molds. Note that hydrogen peroxide purchased at drug stores, which is not food grade, contains toxic preservative chemicals.

According to Elizabeth Baker, this step is necessary because, as the oxygen is becoming more and more depleted in our environment, molds are increasing. Soak them for just eight to ten minutes, then drain the solution and rinse them very well. After that, soak them six to twelve hours in distilled or spring water. In a pinch for time, you can soak them two to three hours.

Nuts and seeds nearly double in volume after being soaked. Soaked nuts and seeds not used right away should be kept in the refrigerator. Dehydrate them if you like them crunchy.

As explained in Appendix A, "Killer 'Foods' to Avoid," dairy is not the great source of calcium that it has been hyped up to be. You need to have a stock of seeds and nuts for calcium. Unhulled sesame seeds are the best. Almonds are also high in calcium.

Nut and seed butters are great to have on hand. They are used in quite a few recipes and are also handy to spread on a cabbage leaf or flaxseed crackers. Once opened, the jars should be kept refrigerated.

Organic seeds for sprouting should also be kept on hand; they have a shelf life of ten years. They should be kept in tightly closed containers or bags.

Dehydrated or dried fruit is great to have around. If the label says "sun-dried," you know it is raw; if not, you must call the company to find out at what temperature it was dehydrated because it is typically over 118° F. Dehydrated fruit, such as sun-dried mangoes, apricots, apples, figs, prunes and raisins, can be kept on the shelf in tightly closed containers but should really be kept refrigerated unless eaten within a few weeks, as they often tend to ferment. These dried fruits can be used during the winter when fresh fruits are out of season. They can also be combined with nuts to make trail mix.

Make sure dehydrated fruits are organic and unsulfured. Sulfur nitrate and nitrite are chemicals used for preservation and color. For example, while orange-colored dried apricots may look more appealing to the eye than brown ones, the orange ones are sulfured.

Dr. Harvey Wiley, former chief chemist of the United States Department of Agriculture (USDA), claimed that adding sulfurous acid to food is harmful. It destroys vitamins in the fruit, degenerates the kidneys, and retards the formation of red blood corpuscles. If the label does not indicate unsulfured, assume that it is sulfured.

Garlic, ginger, parsley, cilantro, onions, unpasteurized miso and lemons may always be kept in stock, as they are used as seasonings in many raw recipes. Avocados and raw olive oil are commonly used as well.

Raw, unheated honey is a great food to have in your cupboard. It will last forever! Unprocessed honey has been known to last literally thousands of years. Honey is also very rich in enzymes. Unheated honey can be found at farmers' markets or from local beekeepers, but honey is not considered vegan.

Stevia extract is best if you are hypoglycemic. Even when it is not raw, you need only a tiny bit since it is 200 times sweeter than sugar. You can also grow your own in flowerpots.

If you do not like its aftertaste, use agave nectar, which is low in its glycemic effect on the body and is plant-based. Agave is a sweet liquid that comes from the cactus plant. If it is dark, it is not raw, but the light-brown-colored one is raw if so labeled.

Keep a tray of wheatgrass if you have a juicer that juices wheatgrass. Dr. Ann Wigmore, founder of the Hippocrates Health Institute, experimented with feeding animals grasses and found that they instinctively preferred wheatgrass. She encouraged city dwellers to take two ounces a day to protect themselves from air pollution and people with degenerative disease to take two ounces three times a day. I prefer to save time by keeping dehydrated wheatgrass on hand. If you do that, check with the company that processes it to be sure it has been dehydrated at less than 118° F.

Always have mixed, green, leafy vegetables in the refrigerator. Putting them in the refrigerator inside a large plastic container with an unbleached paper towel on the bottom will make them last longer, as much of the moisture will be absorbed by the towel. You can also buy special green, plastic produce storage bags at a Whole Foods supermarket that supposedly keep produce fresher longer.

By the way, don't toss the leaves from carrot, turnip or beet bunches. *The leaves are actually higher in minerals than are the root vegetables themselves.*

Always have a variety of fruits on hand. Fruits are foods that come from a flower and are the ripened ovary of the female flower. They typically contain seeds.

There are many different categories of fruits.

Sweet fruit is what we usually think of when hearing the word "fruit." These include apricots, bananas, blackberries, dates, persimmons, grapes and so many more.

Acid fruits are sour. These include oranges, lemons, limes, sour grapes, raspberries, cranberries, grapefruit, sour apples and more.

Sub-acid fruits are less sour and include apples, figs, cherimoyas, most berries, papayas, peaches, pears, mangoes, plums and more.

Very few fruits have significant fat content. Those that do are *fatty fruits* and include avocados, olives and durians.

Non-sweet fruits are commonly mistaken for vegetables but are really fruits, as they bear seeds. These include tomatoes, cucumbers, okra, eggplants, bell peppers, zucchini and squash.

Melons include cantaloupe, casaba, crenshaw, honeydew, muskmelon and watermelon.

A common beginner mistake is to eat fruits before they have fully ripened. For example, bananas should have brown spots or streaks on the skins when they are ready to be eaten. Mangoes, persimmons, kiwis and various others should be soft with wrinkly skin. Papayas should have an orange, not green, skin. Eating unripe fruit can be a rather unpleasant experience. When in doubt, look for a tempting aroma to emanate from it before digging in.

11
What to Expect

There is no love sincerer than the love for food.
—George Bernard Shaw (1856-1950)

Detoxification

Now that you are going raw, your body will conserve a lot of the energy that it would have otherwise expended to make digestive enzymes necessary for digesting cooked food. Your body will now have that energy free for other health-enhancing purposes. It will begin to detoxify, and the detoxification will occur in cycles. Tiny particles of cooked food residues and chemicals from processed foods have built up and are circulating in your lymph system. During detoxification, these toxins enter the bloodstream and exit the body through its organs of elimination: the skin, intestines, bladder and lungs.

Food residues and ingested or inhaled chemical pollutants will usually detoxify in reverse order of consumption. In other words, you will probably detoxify from the hamburger you ate yesterday before the grilled steak you ate last July.

Detoxification proceeds rapidly on a 100% raw food diet but much more slowly even when you are eating merely 5% cooked food. So if you stay 100% raw, you may eventually get to rid your body of toxins accumulated ever since childhood. This process could take years. By some estimates, you need about a month to detoxify for every year of eating cooked food.

You may encounter some challenges during this transition period. Detoxification symptoms may include: colds or flus, fever, headache, irritability, foul breath and body odor, cold sores, weakness, shakiness, skin rashes, insomnia, temporary weight loss, sensitivity to cold, shivering, diarrhea and more, depending on what toxins you are eliminating.

Do not try to suppress these symptoms with medications, as the drugs will usually completely halt the detoxification process while adding still more toxins to your body! A friend I counseled to juice diet for three days experienced shakiness and headache, for which she took a tranquilizer.

To do this is a mistake! However, if you are already on prescribed medications, it may be wise to wean yourself off them gradually under the guidance of an open-minded, holistic MD, as mentioned in Chapter 10.

As Chapter 10 also explains, a series of colonics may greatly ease detoxification discomforts.

At times, you may feel weak. Do not worry; you will regain your strength, even on a strictly raw vegan diet. Just rest when you are tired. Your body is under reconstruction, and much of its energy is needed for that purpose.

You may also experience loss of libido. It will come back, but not with an addictive quality. Many raw fooders report feeling freedom from the compulsion to have sex yet able to enjoy it even more. One theory is that when one's body is full of cooked food toxins, especially chemical-laden food residues, it feels a compulsion to reproduce since, in its wisdom, it knows its life span is in danger of being foreshortened.

Do not worry about weight loss. This is normal. If your body loses too much weight, this will be only temporary. It will rebound with new, healthier tissue within months — a year at the most. On the other hand, overweight people will be delighted to lose excess weight and keep it off easily with the raw food diet. This is one thing that distinguishes the raw food diet from other diets: Excess fat is much easier to keep off long term because this diet is a permanent one, a way of life. *This is the way your body was genetically designed to eat.*

Another sign that you are healing is feeling chills. Some people in transition may even wear a sweater in the summer. The chills are due to the body's sending its energy, blood, oxygen and nutrients inward to heal the vital organs and tissues. (Read Chapter 14 for more on this topic.)

If you experience detoxification symptoms, *be glad*, as this means you are cleansing! If you do not have any symptoms whatsoever after fasting a few days or going raw for a week or so, it may mean you are so weakened that you have no energy left for healing. So having no symptoms at all could be a warning sign of a very unhealthy body, while having at least some symptoms may be positive.

Prior drug use or abuse will intensify detoxification symptoms. It doesn't matter whether the drugs were legal or illegal, prescription or recreational. After all, drugs don't know anything about the law. They don't think, "I'm a prescribed drug; so I'd better not be toxic to these cells," or, "This person is breaking the law; so he deserves to get sick!" The truth is that our bodies have adapted to drugs even less than they have to cooked food.

Be patient during the detoxification period. It may be over in just a matter of days, after which you will feel much better than before you started. Then, it may recur cyclically days or weeks later when your body has stored up energy for another round of purification. The more cooked food you have eaten, the older you are, and the more drugs you have taken, the more toxins you have in you that need to be eliminated. Some relatively young and drug-free people may experience only very minor detoxification symptoms.

Remember that the most intense phases of detoxification will be over in a matter of months. If you find the detoxification process is too intense to bear, you can always slow it down with fats (avocados, nuts) or starches (bananas, root vegetables). Aajonus Vonderplanitz has counseled elderly people whose detoxification processes remained intense after three months to eat one cooked meal a week in order to slow them down.

Detoxification proceeds in gentler, much subtler, but deeper cycles after the initial purge. For example, Victoria Boutenko describes how, after being raw for a significant length of time, she finally eliminated residues of the DDT her father had sprayed when she was only three.

Vonderplanitz reports that after having eaten cleanly for *decades*, his body finally felt healthy enough to detoxify a substance a surgeon had used to glue his bone together when he broke his nose at age fifteen. When a rash broke out on his nose, he had the substance tested out of curiosity, and the laboratory test came back positive for aerospace/dental epoxy!

Some people also report that their stools smell like the food they are detoxifying. Suddenly, in the bathroom, they may smell food or drugs ingested previously, even years before.

It is controversial whether a person who is detoxifying should take enemas or colonics. Enemas are something one could do at home, filling the bottle with wheatgrass or coffee along with water. Colonics are "heavy-duty," with far more water and more pressure to push out the debris stuck deep within a colon subjected to decades of eating cooked food. These are performed by trained colonic therapists.

My personal opinion, as mentioned in Chapter 10, is that even though these gadgets are not natural, we have done some pretty unnatural things to our bodies; so why not take advantage of technology? Colonics can even be necessary in severe cases in which the change in diet and lifestyle don't have time to take effect.

As a cooked food eater, your body may accumulate a thick, mucoid, intestinal plaque, according to the observations of some colon therapists. The body tries to expel it, but may not be able to as long as you are dumping in new layers of toxic debris. This plaque is a thick, tar-like substance, the long-term result of undigested cooked food that could not be eliminated and has putrefied and congealed in the intestines.

Autopsies of dead people's colons have revealed that, in some cases, the mucoid plaque grew so thick that only a pencil-thickness in the center of the colon was empty! Of course, such a person was usually very constipated. Not only that, but the plaque has made the intestinal walls nearly impermeable to nutrient absorption; so such a person was also malnourished. The compaction also becomes a breeding ground for unhealthful microorganisms, hence the saying, "Death begins in the colon."

Autopsies have also revealed colons with pounds of toxins that look like black tar. Go for a colonic, and chances are your colonic therapist will be able to show you photos of this.

Actor John Wayne, a real "meat and potatoes man," was said to have had 35-40 pounds of fecal matter in his colon. While this may just be an urban legend, it is easy to believe because cooked fooders, especially of cooked meat, do indeed risk impacted colons.

A healthy colon weighs only about five pounds. It is because of this buildup that fasting and colonics are beneficial in the initial stages of cleansing. Some people on poor diets take colonics on a regular basis because they know they keep polluting their intestines.

The more plaque in one's colon, the less nutrition he can absorb from his food. This is why, as cooked fooders get older, they may feel hungrier as well as sicker and weaker from nutritional deficiencies.

Once the colon has been cleansed, and a person has been eating raw for a few years, nutrient absorption becomes so high that he may need very little food to sustain him.

Victoria Boutenko reports in her book *12 Steps to Raw Foods* that her family members can each get by on a salad a day. They simply do not crave food anymore, nor do they need it. Even her teenage son would go snowboarding for ten to twelve hours, and two oranges was all he wanted or needed. You may think, "But I want to eat more than that!" Yes, *now* you do. But after being 100% raw, or close to it, for a few years, you might not care. *This is freedom.*

Detoxifying Your Environment

As your body grows cleaner and purer, it will become more sensitive to environmental toxins. You will want to wear natural fabric, such as cotton, preferably organic if possible, hemp, silk and wool instead of polyester. You will want to use non-toxic cleansers, including dish soap, laundry detergent and household cleaners. You will want the most natural personal-care products and may eventually want to make your own shampoo out of natural ingredients. The rule of thumb is, never put *on* your body what you wouldn't want *in* it.

You will want to get the mercury out of your teeth. I know of one man who went on a 100% raw diet. His body finally had the energy to detoxify his teeth, and he had a lot of problems until he got the mercury all out. If you are on a tight budget, get it done at a dental college for 60-70% of normal rates. Make sure a dental dam is placed in your mouth during the procedure to prevent you from swallowing the mercury that is being removed.

You will become aware that you also don't like dry cleaning chemicals, the toxins from new carpets, plant mold, perfume and many other things that didn't bother you before when your body was polluted with cooked food. You will want to detoxify your environment and make it more natural.

Cravings for Cooked Foods

It has been empirically shown, through observation of numerous cases, that when one is detoxifying a particular food, one craves that food. So if, for example, you have eaten a great deal of ice cream over the years, the toxins of the indigestible bits of pasteurized cream will seep out of the lymph and into the bloodstream to be eliminated by the eliminative organs. You may unconsciously sense the food while it is leaving your body and get a sense of desire for it.

If you can get through this brief period without succumbing to that urge, you will never crave that food again unless more of it is detoxified later. Perhaps another layer of plaque in your digestive tract still has remnants of this food, and when it is detoxified down the road, you might get a very mild, whimsical craving for that food. But the most intense cravings are only at the initial stages of eating raw. After a period of eating 100% raw for weeks or months, you will find nearly all cravings for cooked food are gone.

You will find it easiest to get through the cravings by substituting raw versions of that type of cooked food. For example, if you crave candy, simply eat some raw "candy" of blended dates and nuts.

Aajonus Vonderplanitz once counseled an obese woman weighing 280 pounds who loved ice cream to eat raw food. She ate raw ice cream consisting of unheated honey, unpasteurized cream and raw eggs nearly every day, sometimes up to a gallon a day! Yet, in five months, she had lost 140 pounds.

The most common type of food people miss when going raw seems to be cooked starches, which we have become so accustomed to eating as "comfort foods," but many contain wheat, which contains addictive opioids. (See Appendix A.)

During the transition period, you may wish to use a dehydrator to make "Essene bread," bread made of sprouted grains, or raw pizza with a crust of sprouted grains. Grains are generally difficult to digest, but you may wish to experiment with them during the transition period. Many people can tolerate some of the ones that are easier to digest, such as quinoa.

It has even been observed by some raw fooders that eating a particular raw food helps detoxify that same food which was formerly eaten cooked. So if you have eaten a lot of roasted peanuts, for example, in order to detoxify from them, you may need to eat raw peanuts for a while.

How to Stay Raw in a Cooked World

Eating raw on a tropical island would be very easy. But, as the saying goes, no man is an island. So how do you remain on your raw food diet in a world so biased in favor of the culinary art of cooking? How do you stay on a raw food diet in a world of cooked food?

Social Situations

Undoubtedly, the most difficult thing about going raw is that it is virtually unheard of in every culture. Society simply does not make it convenient. You are going against the whole American culture when you cease to eat cooked food. Actually, no matter what country you live in, you are defying cultural norms. It is truly a cooked food world. You appear "radical" when you shift back to man's original, natural diet.

You therefore have to make arrangements in advance for social situations if you plan to stick to your diet. If someone invites you over for dinner, explain what you are doing and why. If you want to decrease the resistance, place the blame on your doctor. "My doctor has me on a special diet."

Offer to bring your own food, and insist that the host not take this personally. Insist that the hostess allow you to contribute a dish so that you know there will be at least one raw dish there. I often use this as an opportunity to share with people a mini-lesson on the virtues of a raw diet.

Just remember that you are not socializing with your friends just to partake of the same food. The real reason you are socializing is to exchange conversation and love, not food. Food is just an excuse to get together. True, "breaking bread" together is an ancient custom. But some customs, such as eating cooked food, need to be changed, at least for those who care about their health.

The worst situations may occur in the rare event of traveling to foreign cultures where diet is not associated with health at all, such as in Asia. In such cases, you may politely explain that you are "allergic" to cooked food or that your doctor has given you strict orders to eat uncooked food only. Just don't mention the fact that *you* are your own doctor!

When I first went raw and visited out-of-town family and friends, I brought my raw recipe books and made meals for everyone. This was my way of advertising that raw dishes are delicious, and it also gave me a gracious way to avoid eating their food. Sometimes they would joke that they couldn't wait for me to leave so they could have "real" food. I would point out the irony: What is "real food," food as it comes from Nature or food denatured by man?

When going to a cooked potluck meal, I suggest you eat beforehand and take a small bag of sun-dried fruit with nuts (trail mix) or sprouts in a little bag in case you get hungry so you won't be tempted to eat the cooked food. For your contribution, take along a raw food dish. Unless it is an ordinary salad, it will probably be the hit of the party; so you had better take the recipe along as well!

I have some dishes that are so tasty nearly everyone asks me for the recipes. (See Chapter 15.) So I have gotten into the habit of writing them on cards that I tape to the dishes. Your friends will appreciate your raw food dish, especially if it contains raw fat, which is very delicious. Most likely, it will be a novelty, especially if it is a gourmet or dehydrated raw dish.

Eventually, all your friends will understand and to some degree accept your raw food "fanaticism." They will be prepared for it and get used to it. Furthermore, you will, with time, make converts of the few who are open-minded or those physically sick enough to be desperate enough to go raw. These will be grateful to you forever!

If you live in a big enough city, you will eventually connect with other raw fooders through postings on the health food store bulletin board or the Internet, and you will join them in raw food potlucks and gatherings. In other words, the social situation will, with time, improve.

Find support by joining raw food Internet chat rooms. Go to www.yahoo.com and click on "groups." Under "search," type in "raw food" or "living food." To find a local group, add the name of your city and state. You will find numerous groups of people with whom you can share experiences, recipes and advice, even if they are not local. Many are listed in the Bibliography and Other Resources section at the back of this book.

The social life situation is often a major reason people refuse to go all raw, but as Dr. Doug Graham points out in an interview with Frédéric Patenaude, "I want to know how the person has a social life when they're sick. How does the person go out and have a good time when they don't feel well?"

He further points out that one's social life may also be impaired by lack of confidence owing to poor skin or overweight from a cooked diet.

He goes on to remark that the social life issue is especially a problem for young people who are single. He tells them, "It's cool to be different. It's cool to be healthy." He advises them to seek out others with similar values.

Eating Out

As you might suppose, eating out will not be as frequent on a raw food diet. After all, you pay restaurants to cook the food. Almost all restaurants are geared only towards cooked foods. Even the salads in a "cooked" restaurant will have added cooked cheese, chicken, or shrimp (which jack up the prices), as well as salad dressings with pasteurized oils.

Those of you who eat out for lunch breaks on a regular basis will need to begin packing lunches. One lunch that I always brought to work was a raw salad of mixed greens with dressing or avocado, along with a snack of dried fruit and raw nuts or raw olives. I also packed an emergency snack of fruit in case I got stuck in traffic on the way home.

So what about the times you are more or less forced to eat in a restaurant? This happens often in social and business situations. But it can be done; one can actually eat in a restaurant and remain totally raw. Victoria Boutenko manages this by handing the waiter/waitress a card stating that she is a raw-food-only-eater and suggesting a salad of various raw vegetables. She states that the chefs must derive great pleasure from the opportunity to exhibit their creativity because the resulting salad she receives is always remarkably beautiful.

Traveling

What about when one is on the road or flying to a destination? How can one remain raw while traveling? In such cases, it is necessary to plan ahead, as is the case always with the raw food diet.

You simply cannot count on restaurants, be it on the road or in the airport, to cater to raw fooders. Remember, you are paying them to cook the food, which is a service you no longer need. Therefore, you must be proactive and plan ahead so that you do not backslide due to hunger. Come armed with "fast-food" raw munchies in a bag. Such snacks include raw, home-made, trail mix; raw nut butter in a jar; raw flaxseed crackers; raw, homemade, "banana nut bread"; raw cookies; sun-dried fruit; raw nuts, and so on. See the recipe section (Chapter 15) for some of these dishes.

The point is to be prepared. The word is not out enough for the world to cater to raw fooders. Since we are not getting much help from the media, the movement is growing slowly, which means there is simply not yet a big enough market for food producers to commercialize raw food products. However, thanks to the Internet and a few celebrities who are openly raw, the word is starting to spread at a faster pace.

If you are lucky, there may be a fresh juice or smoothie stand for you to order a drink, even if it is not organic, but never count on it. Never leave the house without an emergency snack. In fact, you may wish to leave some dried fruit, raw nuts or flaxseed crackers in your car for such cases, rotating the unused ones every few weeks or so.

A Word about Backsliding and Enhanced Sensitivity to Cooked Foods

While in transition, try to avoid putting yourself in temptation zones: restaurants, parties, potlucks, dinner invitations and so on. When you are shopping and you see the free samples of food, don't give in to the lie that "one little bite won't hurt."

Anything you put into your mouth that doesn't add to your health will eventually rob you of your health.

Besides, an attitude of having "just one bite" is very habit-forming. Before you know it, every day you will be having many samples and bites, leading to a gradual return to old habits.

If you fall back into cooked food addiction, which is easier to do if you are eating only partially raw, don't worry. It is usually easy to get back on the program if you fast for a few days. Fasting will quickly detoxify the cooked food you ate, as well as lessen your cravings for it. It will quickly give you the light feeling that keeps you hooked on raw food.

However, do not get into the habit of bingeing on cooked food, thinking that it will be easy to get rid of the toxins later by fasting! This kind of thinking could set up the binge/purge syndrome characteristic of eating disorders. It could also greatly weaken your self-esteem and willpower if you yo-yo back and forth between the world of cooked food and a raw, healthful diet. It may become more difficult to muster up the determination to get back on a raw diet if you feel you have failed.

As Mark Twain said, "It is easy to stop smoking. I have done it hundreds of times!"

That is why it may be beneficial to start out committing to shorter periods, such as a month, rather than promising yourself you will never eat another cooked food for the rest of your life. After the month is up, you can renew your commitment for another three months.

In addition, you will notice that if you do fall back into cooked foods, you may feel so terrible that it will be easy to get back to the raw diet if you do so right away, before readjusting to the cooked food. This is because your body will have cultivated sensitivity to any unnatural or cooked foods, as it will have rid your body of them.

Someone who smokes his first cigarette will react with symptoms because his lungs are pure. After he has smoked a lot, his body "gives up" reacting strongly and adapts to the toxin, although he has not become immune to the damage smoking causes.

The body follows "the law of vital adjustment," which states that the body will do everything to protect itself and keep the species going, regardless of the obstacle. It will adapt itself as best it can to whatever influence it cannot destroy or control. Therefore, if your body is given a toxin, it will struggle to survive, building walls of plaque to protect it rather than give up and die. The walls of plaque will slow down absorption so that the poison will not be absorbed at a rate that could be deadly.

A clean body is more sensitive and more efficient at eliminating toxic invasions. A raw eater given novocaine may find that it has worn off during the middle of the dental procedure because the body so efficiently and swiftly eliminates it. This has happened to both my husband and me. Fortunately, the pain is much reduced when you're eating raw. There seems to be a higher tolerance for pain. Some raw fooders I know don't even accept novocaine during dental work, not wishing to add more toxins to their bodies.

Toxins that used to go unnoticed may suddenly cause strong reactions. As a former eater of processed foods, I often unknowingly consumed MSG. (See Appendix A.) After going raw, if I accidentally ate some, as I did when buying some guacamole with "spices" labeled in the ingredients, I would not be able to sleep until about 3 AM and would feel itchiness all over my skin. Sometimes I got migraine headaches.

If you decide to go 100% raw, people will tell you, "Oh, but you have to eat at least some cooked food," or "You are too fanatical, too obsessive, and this is not healthy." Just remember, if you do give in to that "one piece of bread," you will feel much worse than you did when your body had built up a tolerance to it.

As Frédéric Patenaude puts it, "You will be much more affected by small doses of poisons than most people. A cup of coffee could have the same effect on you as five cups on your neighbor" (*The Raw Secrets*, p. 54).

David Wolfe said in a workshop that his uncle would say to him, "Everything in moderation!" He would reply, "Yes, *especially moderation!*" What he means by that is that there is a time and a place *not to be moderate*, and certainly this applies when your health is at stake.

Herbert Shelton used to say that there is no such thing as moderation when it comes to poison, and he mocked the "in all things moderation" statement by saying, "Would such people advise moderation in adultery or moderation in murder?"

You might think, "Well, if my body is adapted to toxins and cooked foods, what's the big deal?" But it is important to know that the adaptation, while helping the body tolerate the toxins to a degree, does not totally cancel out their negative effects. As Herbert Shelton says in *Orthobionomics*, "Toleration to poisons is merely a slow method of dying."

Finally, if you do backslide into cooked foods, don't beat yourself up over it! Just re-inspire yourself by reading more about the benefits of raw food and pamper yourself with some great raw recipes or your favorite organic melons.

Use the Smart Recovery method, an addiction rehabilitation program. If you give in to the temptation to indulge in something that is negative to your health, observe it. See how you feel after that, including the next day. Take notes. Read the notes the next time you are tempted. Use the rational part of your brain to make the decision to abstain.

World Beyond Temptation

At last, after a few years of being on a 100% raw food diet, you will have entered into the world beyond temptation. Then, cooked food will appear to you as mere "plastic," "pretty decorations," or "fake pseudo-food," at which point you can sneer, "How in the world can they ever eat that?"

The smell of some cooked foods will be utterly repulsive. Other smells, such as freshly baked bread or cookies, may continue to be pleasant and bring back pleasant memories but will not cause salivation or temptation. Being on a raw diet at that point is hardly a "sacrifice." In fact, if someone paid you to do so, you would still not eat cooked "treats."

Reentry into the world of cooked foods, with its deadly aura, would make you miserable. You have absolutely no temptation to return, and you know it would be painful to do so. Even one serving of cooked food would leave your sensitive body, with sensitivity you have cultivated, in a state of sleepiness, heaviness, depression and constipation. Your body is now so sensitive that the slightest bit of toxin is propelled swiftly outward, possibly leaving the body in pain and agony, heaviness and plugged-up-ness for hours.

Congratulations! You have now become as your ancient ancestors, a truly raw, natural food eater! You know you are quite well and healthy at this point in your journey back to how we evolved to eat. You know you are healthy when you feel no temptation whatsoever to indulge in the perverted, cooked, adulterated, processed foods of modern society.

Paradise Health

Some argue that without extremely high quality food and even super foods along with supplements, ideal "paradise health" is no longer possible due to all of the airborne toxins. This may be the case, but compared to eating a diet of cooked food, the change in one's health level will seem astounding after switching to a 100% (or nearly so, like 95%) raw diet.

After you have been a raw eater for several years, eating as closely as possible 100% live foods, you will find yourself in extraordinary health. What were formally minor complaints that you viewed as nuisances are now gone, things such as athlete's foot, acne, mild headaches, grogginess after meals, aches and pains, bouts of constipation and so on.

You will also find that you are much less thirsty. Cooked food is deficient in water and needs a lot more water to digest it. It is toxic, and toxins need water to flush them out. Eating fresh fruits, you will find you may need to drink only half as much water, or even less, as when cooking your food.

Body odors may vanish or become drastically reduced, proving that they originate from the internal putrefaction of cooked, processed or otherwise indigestible, food. Some long-time raw fooders can go days, even weeks, without a shower, and no one notices. Once totally cleaned out, you will not have bad breath or body odor. Your unwashed feet will not stink.

Even your sweat, sputum, vaginal discharges, stools and other body emissions may become odorless.

Note: If there is an occasional odor even though you have been "clean" for years, it may mean your body has been digging deeper for childhood toxins to get rid of. It could also mean that you were just exposed to some pollution or that you aren't digesting your food well due to emotional or other reasons, such as poor food combining, as will be discussed in Chapter 12.

Digestion, which once took up to 100 hours on a cooked food diet, will be 18-40 hours. To check transit time, eat some beets. When you see red in the stools, that will indicate the elimination, and you can calculate the transit time. New raw fooders, including myself once, are sometimes a tad alarmed upon seeing this for the first time, thinking it is blood!

Other foods you can use to check transit time are whole sesame seeds, flaxseeds or fresh corn, some of which will remain intact in the stools and be visible. Charcoal supplements from a health food store are yet another substance that can be used for this purpose.

Your stools will likely be looser and much more frequent. Whereas before you eliminated once or twice a day, you may now find yourself eliminating three or even four times a day. Elimination will be very fast and easy. You will no longer have time for "the bathroom reader."

You will no longer be clogged with phlegm. Your tongue will be much cleaner. With this accumulated congestion gone, your assimilation of nutrients will be much improved.

Your fear of germs and disease will vanish. You will now feel in near total control of your health!

As your body becomes more alkaline due to the raw food diet, your mood will improve. Because of increasing well-being and energy, your confidence will soar.

Now that you are feeding your body with live food, you will feel more alive than you ever dreamed possible.

12
Controversial Nutritional Issues

A veteran USDA meat inspector from Texas describes what he has seen: "Cattle dragged and choked ... knocking 'em four, five, ten times. Every now and then when they're stunned they come back to life, and they're up there agonizing. They're supposed to be re-stunned, but sometimes they aren't, and they'll go through the skinning process alive. I've worked in four large [slaughterhouses] and a bunch of small ones. They're all the same. If people were to see this, they'd probably feel really bad about it. But in a packing house everybody gets so used to it that it doesn't mean anything."

—*Slaughterhouse*

There are various nutritional recommendations and guidelines that not everyone agrees with. In this chapter, I have tried to present some of these differing points of view, especially when they appear convincing. You must ultimately do your own research and find out what makes the most sense to you.

This chapter's purpose is to inform you about choices you will have to make if you go raw. Don't use these issues as an excuse not to change your diet! *Most of them are things you need to consider even if you do not go to a raw diet.* <u>*Ignorance is not bliss when it comes to your health*</u>. Get informed, and don't stop with this book!

The Ratio of Carbohydrates, Fats and Proteins

Research by modern diet authors Dr. Robert Atkins and Dr. Barry Sears, advocates of low carbohydrate diets, has indicated that the ratio of macronutrients (carbohydrates, fats and proteins) in the diet can play an important role in one's health and feeling of well-being.

Some people are genetically predisposed to need a lesser amount of carbohydrates than the average American eats and function better with a combination of nearly equal caloric percentages of these three macronutrients. Eating a high percentage of carbohydrates can cause the pancreases of some people, especially those with pre-diabetic conditions, to secrete excess insulin, which has been found to be implicated in accelerated aging. Excessive insulin secretion may also induce fatigue, brain fog, weight gain and mental confusion.

Everyone must find by trial and error what the approximate ratio is that makes him feel best. Some people do well on a high carbohydrate diet that includes a lot of fruit, while others need a lot of protein along with the fat that typically accompanies it. Some people have intermediate requirements for each.

Although the book is not about raw diets in particular, *The Metabolic Typing Diet* by William Wolcott and Trish Fahey provides tests and explanations that enable one to determine which metabolic type he is, and the corresponding ratio of macronutrients he needs. They found three main types: the carbo type, the protein type and the mixed type.

Another book to guide you in learning what ratio of macronutrients is best for you and which also includes a great deal of information about the raw food diet is *Conscious Eating* by Dr. Gabriel Cousens. This comprehensive nutritional book includes a thorough analysis of the topic and provides information for determining your own individualized dietary needs.

David Wolfe also deals with the macronutrient ratio issue in his book *The Sunfood Diet Success System.* In years of talking with many long-term raw fooders, he found that all of them had the three macronutrients in their diet most of the time: raw fats (nuts, seeds, avocados, olives), raw carbohydrates (fruits) and raw proteins (green leafy vegetables).

At times, they would go for brief periods omitting one group, but after some days or weeks, they would again return to a balance of all three groups. He refers to "the sunfood triangle" and points out differing macronutrient ratios for various purposes, such as losing weight, gaining weight, detoxifying, overcoming candida infection, enhancing mental clarity, gaining the competitive edge in athletics and enhancing spiritual clarity.

He stresses that these are to be used strictly temporarily, or else an imbalance would result. For example, minimizing fats to 0% or close to it enhances both spiritual clarity and the detoxification process. This is why a diet of fruits and vegetables only, especially in juice form, is potent in cleansing while greatly enhancing spiritual inspiration and insight as well.

Controversy surrounds the optimal ratio of macronutrients within raw food circles. While at the 2004 Raw Food Festival held annually in Portland, Oregon, I had the opportunity to listen to Dr. Doug Graham speak in a lecture called, "Fruit or Fat?"

I knew that he advocated an 80% carbohydrate diet composed largely of fruit. I went as a last resort because there were no other speakers I hadn't heard already apart from culinary artists, who didn't interest me, as I was gathering scientific information for this book.

I had read a bit about his theory and felt it would never work for most people. "80% carbohydrate?" I used to joke. "That would send me into insulin shock, maybe even diabetic coma!"

Having read nearly every book by Dr. Sears before going raw, I was thoroughly convinced this high-carb diet theory was totally outdated. And having heard Dr. Gabriel Cousens lecture for five hours the previous day, I was well versed in the perils of most fruits with their high glycemic indexes.

Dr. Graham sported a shirt that had a King Kong-type gorilla on it with the words, "I get my protein from fruit." I must say I was extremely impressed with his energy.

I had expected some older, professor-type who hadn't bothered to keep up with modern times. Frankly, the photo on his web site makes him look about 15 years older than he does in real life. Instead, I saw a most energetic, vivacious speaker, with youthful energy and his active runner's physique. The man was bouncing with energy and even continued speaking and answering questions an hour into the lunch break!

Once I understood the science behind his theory, it made sense. Dr. Graham had interviewed thousands of people on all types of diets: the omnivorous SAD, vegetarian, vegan and raw food. He found that everyone ate too much fat, according to Dr. McDougall's studies. The average intake for most groups was 42% fat, 16% protein and 42% carbohydrate. But raw fooders ate even more fat, sometimes an average of 60% of our calories coming from fat!

The reason is that most of us are convinced that the only way to get enough protein is to eat a large quantity of nuts (often consisting of 80% fat) and seeds (about 70% fat). Also, we tend to eat a lot of salads and put salad dressings on them that contain pure, refined fat. As he pointed out, we would never dream of taking in pure, refined carbohydrates (sugar) nor pure, refined protein (protein powder). After all, these do not occur naturally and are highly processed. Yet most of us love to consume large quantities of refined fat (oils)!

Now, when I first heard the idea that raw fooders overeat fats, while superficially reading some of Doug's web pages, my reaction was, "So what? Aren't raw fats good for you? A lot of the harm from fats is because they are cooked." But as he went on, I began to see that the reason I hadn't had the super-high energy that I get from a diet of only fruit and vegetable juices was because of the fats I consumed on the raw diet.

Dr. Graham had been eating raw for many years as an athlete and was not satisfied with his energy levels. He noticed that after eating fats he did not feel like running. About 17 years ago, he discovered this diet: He found that by eating fruit for breakfast and lunch — and sometimes even dinner — he always maintained his energy. If he got hungry, he simply ate more fruit. For dinner he often ate salads and some nuts and seeds.

I too, have wondered, "If a high proportion of fruit is so bad for us, *why do I feel so great when that is all I eat,* as on a juice diet? And why is fruit such a large part of the diet of other primates, as well as instinctive eaters?" (See Appendix C for information on instinctive eaters, who tend to eat about 66% of their diet in fruit, as do chimps.)

I also wondered why we shouldn't eat something that is so delicious and is so quick and easy for us to digest. Furthermore, humans don't make Vitamin C, and fruit is our main source of it. The idea that we shouldn't eat much fruit if we want to be healthy just didn't make sense from the viewpoint of a naturalist.

According to Graham, we don't need more than 10% fat and 10% protein calories. Much of the protein we get can come from fruit. Chimps are our close relatives, and their diet consists mainly of 50-60% fruits and 35-45% greens. About 5% is insects, seeds, and on rare occasion, even monkeys. Gorillas are the strongest animals on the planet, and they build their muscles on greens and fruit.

As Dr. Graham explained, when we eat a high-fat diet, which he defines as being above 10-12%, the fat lingers in the bloodstream. It coats the sugars and slows down their assimilation by interfering with insulin's ability to latch onto them.

The resulting accumulation of sugar causes several things to happen: The pancreas sends out more insulin to attach to the sugar, which also gets coated by fat. The microbe *Candida albicans*, which is beneficial at normal levels since it consumes our excess sugars, then proliferates to unhealthful levels.

Furthermore, the receptor sites at which the insulin would leave the blood get clogged up with fat too so that as more sugar accumulates, still more insulin is secreted, causing Syndrome X, or insulin resistance syndrome. The resulting oxygen deficit from too much fat in the blood causes fatigue, as do the insulin and candida.

In an excerpt from an upcoming book, Graham explains, "Not only is the oxygen capacity of the individual red blood cell reduced as blood fat levels rise, the actual number of viable red blood cells is also reduced. In nature, we note that mammals that thrive on high fat diets rely upon anaerobic bursts (using no oxygen, or less oxygen than is required for the exertion) in order to acquire their dinner, whereas mammals that eat low-fat diets have tremendous aerobic capacity."

He goes on to point out that it would be more innately characteristic of man to walk from fruit tree to fruit tree to find his food (aerobic endurance) than to use one major exertive effort to chase and kill a wild animal (anaerobic burst).

The proof that at least part of this theory is correct is seen in the results Dr. Graham gets. He has successfully treated people with Type I, as well as Type II, diabetes. They have gotten off insulin within *three days.* Now, I have heard of raw food curing diabetes, but never in this time frame (usually several months).

In addition, *Candida albicans* overgrowth has been cured on a diet of 80% carbohydrates, mainly fruit! Those with candida are usually told *never* to eat fruit in the common treatment modalities.

As explained in Chapter 9, Doug also works with athletes, including Olympic trainers, to get maximal performance results.

Dr. Graham disagrees with the idea that there are significant differences in the ratio of macronutrients that individuals need, according to genetics. He explains this on a web site article called, "Half Fast Test." (Read the title fast for the intended pun!)

According to his research, sports physiologists have found only a plus or minus 5% difference between the very slowest oxidizer, who would need more carbohydrates, and the fastest oxidizer, who would need more protein. Therefore, he concludes that everyone should get between 75% to 80% carbohydrates.

Doug also claims that the glycemic index for foods is the least reliable of nutritional indexes.

Critics say that Graham's high-carbohydrate, high-fruit diet works only with athletes. They say that burning sugar for energy is a different metabolic process from storing sugar (turning glycogen into fat) when you eat more sugar than you burn. Perhaps the process of storing sugar requires more minerals than burning it. Hence, most fruit does not contain enough minerals for the average person, and the body has to compensate for the resulting acidity by leaching minerals from the teeth and bones. Tooth sockets also appear to be weakened on a high fruit diet, according to some anecdotal reports.

I asked Doug what he thought about the theory that we shouldn't eat so much fruit because today's fruit is too acidic and lacking in minerals. He replied that if the soil does not contain enough minerals to grow the fruit, it will simply grow a plant without bearing fruit. He also suggested that fruit that is in season would be higher in minerals.

Nonetheless, if you purchase an optical refractometer, one with a 0-36° brix range, you can get some indication of the mineral content. Manual refractometers are cheaper than digitals and don't require batteries. It soon becomes very clear that the mineral content in our soil has been radically depleted (as will be explained later in this chapter), and our produce is lacking. This is a common explanation for all the reports of losing teeth among raw fooders who eat primarily fruit.

You may partake of his diet and eat nothing but low glycemic fruit and vegetables, of course, but then you would have to consume vastly larger amounts of produce since higher glycemic fruit is also higher in calories. Sweet fruits contain much more calories than non-sweet fruits and vegetables, and so you will likely need to include some of them in the diet also.

If you are interested in trying his diet, I recommend you get a consultation with Dr. Graham. At the very least, read some of the articles on his web site (www.foodnsport.com) and his upcoming book on what he calls the "80/10/10 diet." People who have applied his concepts incorrectly have gotten themselves into serious health difficulties due to nutrient deficiencies.

Since attending his lecture, I have experimented with the diet myself. I feel positively fabulous after reducing my intake of fat, and this took my raw diet to a whole new energy level. I didn't realize that about 50-60% of my calories were coming from fat until his lecture. Since reducing fat means eliminating many of the salad dressings and gourmet foods, I find myself eating much more simply. Within one day of reducing my fat to 10-20%, I found that I needed much less sleep, six hours instead of eight.

I have heard other raw fooders besides Doug Graham say they have found through experience that fats and fruits, when either is taken in large quantities, are incompatible. If you are going to eat a lot of fruit, go easy on the fat and vice versa.

I know eating too much fat definitely saps my energy. Yet I am reluctant to eat as much fruit as Doug recommends, at least not without consulting with him as a patient, because I feel my one hour of walking and 20 minutes of yoga per day don't qualify me as an athlete.

My own feeling about the diet is that it would work best in a tropical paradise in which all fruit is more highly mineralized. Here in North America, such fruit is not prevalent. Commercial fruit is bred for its sugar content, shelf life and transportability and not for increased vitamin and mineral content. Moreover, commercial fruit is usually picked unripe in order to facilitate shipping long distances, and the plants have not had enough of a chance to add the full allotment of vitamins and minerals to them.

While this diet may nonetheless work for many people here in America, especially serious athletes, for most it might be best to reduce fat to 10-25% and not take in quite so much fruit. The body requires minerals to make use of the sugar the fruits contain. If they have a lot of sugar but few minerals, the body may leach out minerals from the bones, resulting in tooth and bone problems. (See Chapter 13 for more on that topic.)

Critics of Doug's controversial diet include some who tried it and felt great the first year or two but had bad results later on. They experienced hair loss, loose teeth, cavities, protein and/or essential fatty acid deficiency and loss of muscle. Perhaps this diet is not meant for everybody, at least not for the long term.

Regarding teeth, if you notice that they are becoming translucent or feel rough to the tongue instead of smooth, they are demineralizing. In that case, reduce the amount of fruit, especially acid fruits like lemons, and eat more of the vegetables or the highly mineralized "super foods" mentioned later in this chapter that you should be eating every day anyway.

I find that I still receive much of the benefits Dr. Graham speaks of even when I don't eat that much fruit — maybe only two or three pieces a day. I simply reduce the percentage of calories I get from fat to about 20-25% and save those for the late afternoon or evening. And *my energy is soaring throughout the day* when I save nearly all my fat calories for the evening meal. It violates all the rules of Atkins and Sears, but my body feels a million times better!

David Jubb, PhD and live food expert, concurs that our diet should be slightly less than 10% fat, slightly less than 10% protein and the rest complex carbohydrates. He is also very adamant about avoiding hybrid produce, which contains "runaway sugars" that can upset the liver and pancreas. (See more on that topic later in this chapter.)

Perhaps more important than the ratio of carbohydrates, fats and proteins is the ratio of fruit, seeds, and greens. For more details, see Appendix C.

Vegetarianism vs. Meat-Eating

Many people think humans are vegetarian by nature, though most of us are omnivorous, eating both plants and animals, by practice. The clues that we are biologically vegetarians include the facts that we have a relatively long digestive tract through which meat would putrefy before leaving and a lack of claws and fangs with which to cut up meat.

In *Sick and Tired?* Robert Young argues, "All the longest-lived and healthiest cultures on the planet are almost exclusively vegetarian, and I have yet to see any culture using animal food come remotely close to their healthy longevity" (p. 116).

Paavo Airola, author of *Are You Confused?* pointed out that the longest-lived people around the world — the Bulgarians, Hunzakuts, East Indian Todas, Yucatan Indians and Russian Caucasians — were either vegetarians or consumed very little meat.

Our genes and digestive tracts are most similar to chimpanzees, especially bonobos, which share 99.4% of our genes. Chimps in the wild eat a mostly fruitarian diet of fruit, green leaves, vegetables, nuts and seeds. But a small volume percentage of their diet is insect matter and even, by some estimates, 2-5% meat when they kill and eat colobus monkeys occasionally because their customary foods are unavailable. As stated earlier, there is a belief that we are biologically primarily frugivores like chimps and apes.

Some anthropologists believe that Cro-Magnons, who lived 40,000-20,000 years ago, ate meat. Yet Robert Leakey, a highly esteemed authority on the evolution of the human diet, has stated that Cro-Magnons did not have canine teeth. He concluded that they were not equipped to eat wild game and likely ate a primarily vegetarian diet, as did chimpanzees.

A popular diet book called *Eat Right for Your Type* claims that those with blood type O cannot be healthy without meat. Yet three prominent raw fooders who have the O blood type do not eat meat. Dr. Cousens has been a vegetarian for over 20 years, Lou Corona for 31 years and David Wolfe for over a decade. I have met them all personally and can say they are all very healthy and energetic.

Meat is among the most toxic of naturally occurring foods. Eating raw meat presents some potential dangers to one's health, as discussed in Appendix C. The occasional contamination of raw meat by parasitic bacteria and worms has been recognized for many years, but cooked meat creates mutagens that can lead to cancer. (See Chapter 6 and Appendix D.) The fat in commercially sold meat contains ten to fifteen times the pesticide concentration of plant tissues since fat stores toxins.

In *The China Study*, it is documented that a diet high in animal protein promotes cancer and other diseases of affluence, such as heart disease. A diet high in plant protein does not have these adverse effects. It was documented that nutrients from animal-based foods increase tumor development while nutrients from plant-based foods decrease tumor development.

Furthermore, it was found that anyone interested in obtaining optimal body size, height, weight and muscles, can achieve maximal potential on an exclusively plant protein diet. It may take longer to build muscles with plant protein than with animal protein, but their quality is superior. Slow and steady wins the race.

Another concern with meat consumption is the modern practice of rendering, whereby whole, dead animals are boiled in vats of acid; then the remaining hooves, fur and bones are removed and the acids neutralized with lye to create a "food" for farm animals. So animals are fed dead animals, sometimes sick ones, from road kill or euthanized pets, whose carcasses contain the poisons that were used to euthanize them.

This "food" is fed to animals that are natural vegetarians, such as cattle, and sometimes animals are even fed animals of their own species, which is totally unnatural. This is what is thought to have caused mad cow disease, the human variant of which is expected to kill many people in the next 15-20 years, due to its long latency period. Will we see "mad chicken disease" emerge in future years as well since many chickens are fed dead chickens?

Dr. Gabriel Cousens stated in a lecture that, according to studies, 3-13% of what is diagnosed as Alzheimer's is actually mad cow disease. We also have "mad fish disease," "mad deer disease" and even "mad squirrel disease," although none of this is being reported officially.

Many people have chosen not to eat meat at all because they believe we can expand our consciousness by eating vegetarian diets. Living food indeed seems to have a higher spiritual vibration, imparting that to the one who ingests it. Dead animals lack the life force that a living plant food diet provides.

Jubb writes, "Life force is the electric energy a living animal has between its nerves and blood. When the animal is dead, this force is no longer present. Yet in vegetation, the sun's light (life force) remains within it after it has been harvested. Each cell of the plant stores the energy of the sun within it" (*LifeFood Recipe Book,* p. 2).

When you eat meat, even raw meat, you are losing much of the advantages of a raw food diet, as discussed in Chapter 7. As Cousens explains in *Spiritual Nutrition* (p. 222), the sunlight energy is stored as activated electron energy in the carbon/hydrogen bonding we find in organic, live, plant foods. These foods boost our electrons and oxygen. They contain biophotons from the sun. When the food is metabolized by animals, they too get these benefits of direct sunlight plant energy.

Furthermore, in the USA, most animals are raised in very cruel conditions and slaughtered in such a horrific manner that anyone seeing it would be repulsed into vegetarianism. By purchasing such meat, we are voting with our dollars that this brutality continue. Recent research has shown that animals, like people, have a wide variety of emotions and even exhibit their own forms of laughter.

Most meat is laden with harmful ingredients. It is high in nitrogen compounds that are metabolized into uric acid, which deposits in our tissues if we eat more than a few ounces of meat a day. Unless we purchase kosher meat, we are also ingesting the adrenaline that was flowing through their bodies when they realized they were being killed. Many believe there is bad karma (an energy that brings back to you what you put out, good or bad) in eating such meat.

These poor animals are also drugged with steroids and antibiotics, in addition to being forced to eat an unnatural diet of inferior food full of pesticides and so forth. The pesticides and herbicides from all the plant food the animal ever ate are concentrated in its fats. All of those pollutants reach the body of the person consuming the animal, thus injuring him or her also.

In addition, not eating meat benefits the planet because of the huge resources that go into feeding and giving water to an animal compared to growing plant foods. As discussed in Chapter 1, we are literally robbing water from future generations with every hamburger we eat.

According to Dr. Cousens, *a vegan saves about 1½ million gallons of water per year when compared to a flesh and dairy eater.* Some may argue that water is recycled anyway, and so it doesn't matter. However, there is a real shortage of unpolluted fresh water. Some say wars will be fought over water in the future. *Even now such water costs more than oil since it has to be transported large distances using oil.*

Another resource wasted in raising meat to eat is land that could be used to grow plant food for people. Fourteen vegans can live off the land that it takes to feed one meat eater. According to John Robbins (*Diet for a New America*), *if meat eaters in the USA would reduce their meat consumption by a mere 10%, the resources saved could feed the 60 million people who starve to death annually.*

A third wasted resource from raising livestock is oil. According to Cousens, for each calorie we derive from beef, 78 calories of fossil fuel are consumed, compared to less than four calories of fossil fuel burned for each calorie of plant food.

Finally, raw plant food simply *tastes better!* Even if it were discovered that raw meat were definitely healthful and better for the ecology, I would remain a vegetarian because of the sheer pleasure of eating that way.

Nonetheless, some raw fooders, after remaining raw vegans for several years, have concluded that they needed to add some raw meat to their diets (most likely to get Vitamin B_{12}). You may not agree with this, but it was nonetheless their experience, and they certainly did not wish for that to be the case. Perhaps we are not all genetically alike in regard to this controversial issue.

If you are interested in learning more, there are more pro and con arguments relating to eating raw meat, as well as other raw animal products, such as dairy and eggs, in Appendix C.

Vegans and the Vitamin B_{12} Issue

There are over a dozen studies showing that it is very difficult for vegans to get sufficient Vitamin B_{12}. While our gut bacteria make it chiefly in our large intestines, according to Dr. Cousens, it is absorbed only from the small intestine, and so we cannot profit much from it.

Some people get enough of this vitamin by eating unwashed green, leafy vegetables since they contain bacteria that make it. But most of us do not have our own gardens. Furthermore, if you have ever eaten unwashed greens straight from the garden, you are also likely to be eating insects and their eggs. This is what our primate cousins do, but for most of us this idea would be rather disgusting.

Some people think they can get B_{12} from sea vegetables, such as blue-green algae or spirulina. But recent studies have shown that the B_{12} in sea vegetables is often an analog form of B_{12} that cannot be used by the human body. Since analog B_{12} competes for the same receptor sites as the truly usable B_{12}, it may in fact create a situation in which you have *less available* B_{12}. But with raw nori, B_{12} levels in the blood were shown to be neither increased nor decreased.

The liver can maintain a storage depot of up to ten years' supply of Vitamin B_{12}, but more typically 2-5 years, which is why many vegans take years to feel the effects of B_{12} deficiency. The longer one has been a vegan, the greater the chance of suffering B_{12} deficiency. This is especially true of raw vegans since many "cooked vegans" eat foods fortified with B_{12}, such as nutritional yeast or soymilk. I have talked to and read about long-term raw fooders who have experienced this.

B_{12} deficiency results in one or more of these neurological symptoms: extreme fatigue, achy joints, depression, numbness and painful tingling in feet and hands, nervousness, paranoia, impaired memory and/or behavioral changes.

Some of this damage can be almost irreversible, according to Cousens, if it becomes chronic. In *Spiritual Nutrition*, he cites three cases in which large groups of people went on a fruitarian diet devoid of B_{12}: Johnny Lovewisdom's vegan community in Ecuador, a fruitarian community in Australia and a group of African Americans who migrated to Israel. Each group suffered severely, especially the children, whose nervous systems were still developing.

B_{12} deficiency is especially problematic in a growing fetus or even a growing child, as it can permanently arrest brain and peripheral nerve development. Every pregnant or nursing woman, *regardless of the diet she is on*, should consider taking B_{12} supplements to avoid this possibility.

Dr. Cousens found that in his clinical experience, even meat eaters have a high rate of B_{12} deficiency. There are other causes of deficiency, such as malabsorption, exposure to radiation, drugs or other toxins, oral contraceptives, fungal infections, tobacco smoking, Vitamin B_6 or iron deficiency, mental stress, liver or kidney disease, pancreatic tumors or failure of the small intestine to contract and move food.

Dr. Gabriel Cousens has done extensive research with vegans and B_{12} and has concluded that about 80% of the vegan and live-food population are B_{12}-deficient. He points out a high homocysteine level in the blood is associated with a lack of B_{12}. Diseases associated with high homocysteine levels include heart disease, Alzheimer's, age-related hearing loss and many more.

Although supplementation with B_{12}-fortified nutritional yeast, which is next to impossible to find raw due to FDA regulations, may help, he does not recommend it because it increases internal acidity. Instead, he advises taking B_{12} supplements, saying, "This is the first time in history that we can be completely successful live food vegans. What I mean by being successful is completely healthy, including no B_{12} deficiency and no elevated homocysteine levels."

Others would argue that modern agricultural methods have utterly destroyed the bacteria that produce this important vitamin at the same time that air pollution has also placed excessive demands on our bodily supplies of it.

When he stated the above in a lecture, I asked him if he thought that genetically we were meant to be vegans. His reply was that originally we probably were, but when we got kicked out of the Garden of Eden, things changed (perhaps a DNA mutation). Now we are trying to get back to the Garden of Eden; so we should be vegan, especially if practicing yoga. He explained that yoga opens up the 72,000 nadis (the spiritual nervous system). If we eat animal products, we take in the animals' experience of cruelty, suffering and misery. The energy of death literally permeates our inner being.

There are several schools of thought on the whole veganism/B_{12} issue. Some are strict vegans due to philosophical or ethical reasons, believing it is very bad karma to eat any animal products. When you see how badly animals we eat are treated, as depicted in some of the videos like *Meet Your Meat* or *Eating*, it doesn't take much to convince you that this is the case. Even if this is not the way our ancestors ate, the technology of supplementation may help us remain healthy vegans. Another reason to be vegan is spiritual, as stated above. A vegan diet enhances one's meditations and yoga practice.

Another school of thought is that it is neither genetically natural nor healthful to be strictly vegan. Vegetarian species often eat eggs, insects, small vertebrates or soil. This includes gorillas, another primate closely related genetically to humans. Genetically, it may appear that we might not be suited for veganism — vegetarianism, yes, but maybe not complete veganism. Or perhaps in an environment of high quality food grown in cobalt-rich soil and unwashed greens, we could be truly vegan without supplementation.

Adherents to the no-supplement philosophy point out that vitamins have only been discovered within the last century or so. New nutrients are being discovered all the time. You may take a B_{12} supplement, but what if, down the road, they discover some other nutrient you are missing because you are eating true to your philosophical code but not to your genetic code?

Many people believe that it is safer to eat your nutrients in whole foods for this reason. Nutrients work together synergistically. The whole is greater than the sum of its parts. Therefore, it is always optimal to obtain missing elements from natural foods in order to get the as-yet-undiscovered nutrients. (See Chapter 14 and Chapter 5, study 13 for more discussion on this topic.)

Brother Nazariah, a leader of the Essene Church of Christ, had been a raw fooder for five years when he became very weak, with painful feet and hands. His central nervous system became damaged from running low on B_{12}. He added fermented, raw, dairy products (yogurt and kefir) and eggs to his diet. The symptoms disappeared.

In the 30-some years of his raw food experience, he came across many vegans who were suffering similar symptoms of Vitamin B_{12} deficiency; yet they would stubbornly cling to the idea of veganism because in theory it was best, and they didn't want to violate their philosophy.

In an interview with Frédéric Patenaude, Nazariah addresses the issue of veganism. He points out a study published in *Ahimsa Magazine,* a pro-vegan periodical, that actually concludes that vegans have a high incidence of degenerative brain diseases, such as Alzheimer's, dementia and others. He says that in the 1990s, the magazine *Vegetarian Times* published the results of a study claiming that lacto-ovo-vegetarians (those consuming dairy and eggs) lived longer than meat-eaters, but meat-eaters actually lived longer than vegans.

It appears that perhaps a few people may need, or feel that they need, small amounts of raw animal products, such as eggs or meat, for at least limited times under certain conditions, and we should not condemn them for it. My theory is that perhaps some people are poor absorbers of Vitamin B_{12} and perhaps some other, yet-to-be-discovered nutrients from plant sources.

Some people want to be raw fooders for optimal health and don't care about being strict vegans. I know someone who eats raw liver, where B_{12} is stored, from cattle naturally raised on pasture, but only a pound a month. The rest of the time he is a raw vegetarian. He began doing this only after eating raw for years, once he began exhibiting B_{12} deficiency symptoms.

Another solution is to mix raw egg yolks into smoothies, but it might take several eggs a day to get enough B_{12}. Some people find the egg whites to be too phlegm-producing. (See Appendix C for how to make sure your eggs come from healthy chickens.)

If someone already extremely healthy wishes to follow the vegan philosophy, he can supplement with nutritional yeast even though it isn't raw. One study done at Hallelujah Acres (see Chapter 5, study 5) showed that the use of one tablespoon a day of Red Star Vegetarian Support containing 5 mcg of B_{12} was enough to keep 85% of the vegans with a serum level of 200 pg (that's picograms, billionths of a gram!) B_{12} per milliliter of blood. Though a serum level of 200 pg keeps most deficiency symptoms at bay, Cousens now thinks 340-405 is optimal since it keeps the homocysteine level within the normal range.

In either case, if a person is still struggling with health issues, he should not add more acidity or fermentation with eggs or yeast. In that case, one could take B_{12} sublingual supplements, the methylcobalamin form of which is often recommended as the best, or injections. However, the toxic preservative chemicals present in the injections sometimes produce side effects, up to and including sudden death! You may find that B_{12} supplement pills contain much more than what you need, but only about 1% is actually absorbed; so you will probably need to take a pill at least every three days or so.

Victoria Boutenko is convinced we can get sufficient B_{12} if we eat large amounts of greens. She often eats about two bunches of kale a day for many of the health benefits such a diet provides. The greens must be organic. Pesticides probably destroy B_{12}-producing bacteria. I have read, however, that washing the greens removes B_{12}, and many stores also spray their greens for bugs. Perhaps buying organic greens from a local farmer who doesn't wash them would solve that matter.

Another concern of great significance, however, is that today's soil is very depleted of minerals, including the cobalt upon which B_{12} production depends. The main reason vegans are having such a tough time getting B_{12} — and minerals such as zinc and selenium — might not be a sign that we are meant to eat animal products but that our soil is hopelessly mineral-depleted. Another factor is that while the supply of B_{12} is down, the demand is greatly increased by auto exhaust, mercury from dental fillings and other environmental pollutants.

Several studies have been published which discuss the need for B_{12} supplementation in raw vegans. One is "Vitamin B_{12} status of long-term adherents of a strict uncooked vegan diet ('living food diet') is compromised." It was published in *The Journal of Nutrition* (October, 1995, Vol. 125, Issue 10, pp. 2511-2515, PubMed ID 7562085). Another is "Metabolic vitamin B_{12} status on a mostly raw vegan diet with follow-up using tablets, nutritional yeast, or probiotic supplements," published in *Annals of Nutrition and Metabolism* (2000, Vol. 44, Issue 4-5, pp. 229-234, PubMed ID 11146329).

Restrict Your Calories for Longer Life

UCLA researcher Dr. Roy Walford discovered that by reducing caloric intake by about 30%, one might extend his middle years by up to 40% toward maximal life span. He wrote about this in *Maximum Life Span*. Since the publishing of that book, his research on rats has been duplicated on primates.

One's diet must not only be restricted in calories, but also rich in nutrients, and so he recommended nutritional supplements.

According to Gabriel Cousens, MD, there has never been an incident in the history of medicine when such effects in so many different species could not be applied to humans as well.

Unfortunately, Dr. Walford himself died while still in his late 70s. According to research on animals, his diet may still have extended his remaining years even though he started it so late in life. You can still turn on the youthing gene even if you start the calorie-restriction diet when you are middle-aged. But Walford missed an important piece of the puzzle by continuing to eat cooked food. Another question about his diet arises: In his quest for low caloric intake, did he consume a lot of mercury-laden fish, leading to his Parkinson's disease?

Raw fooders like David Wolfe often combine reduced caloric intake with raw foods for maximal health and longevity. He is fond of saying that he eats less in order to live longer so that he will be able, in the long run, to eat more.

Man has intuited this simple health secret throughout the ages. An ancient Egyptian transcription translates, "Man lives on one quarter of what he eats. On the other three quarters lives his doctor."

Benjamin Franklin said, "To lengthen thy life, lessen thy meals." It just makes common sense. No one who is obese lives to 100. Toxins are stored in fat; therefore, whoever is overweight carries around a life-threatening toxic accumulation.

The longest living societies, such as the Hunzas, ate diets low in calories.

Dr. Cousens pointed out in a lecture that eating raw enables us to cut our calories in half since so many micronutrients, and even the macronutrient protein, are destroyed by cooking. Cooking ruins 100% of the enzymes, 50% of the protein, and 70-80% of the vitamins and minerals. Much more than that is destroyed, as pointed out in Chapter 7.

By eating raw foods, Cousens claims, we can get complete nutrition *even on a diet of eating 50-80% less food* (*Spiritual Nutrition*, p. 301). He cites research by Stephen Spindler showing that calorie restriction turns on the anti-aging genes and that such a diet can reverse age-related degenerative changes and thus reverse the aging process to some degree. It promotes the self-suicide of cancer-producing cells.

Research at Harvard Medical School and BIOMOL Research Laboratories has shown that taking the supplement resveratrol may even turn on the anti-aging genes, much like a low-calorie diet. If you prefer to get this phytonutrient in whole foods, it is found in organic grapes, red wine, pine tree bark and other plants, such as Japanese knotweed (*polygonum cuspidatum*). Of course, cooking will destroy this nutrient.

Food Combining

Generally, fruits should be eaten at least 30 minutes before other foods. This is because they pass into the small intestine quickly, requiring very little stomach digestion at all and would sit in the stomach and ferment if mixed with denser foods that take longer to digest.

This is why such combinations often cause gas, bloating, acid reflux or upset stomach. The exception is greens, which combine well with most fruits (Appendix C), especially when blended.

A hydrotherapist with 30 years of experience found that many people actually need up to two hours to digest fruits before they should eat other foods, and she saw quite a few of them give up on the raw diet because they didn't know that this was their problem.

Melons should be eaten alone, not even with other fruits. However, since melons are rapidly digested, other food may be eaten 20 minutes later.

It is also considered inadvisable to mix starches and proteins together in the same meal. If they are to be consumed together, the starches should be eaten first.

There is much more to proper food combining, and a good booklet is Dr. Herbert Shelton's *Food Combining Made Easy.* There is also Dr. Bass' "sequential eating" method as described on www.drbass.com.

Many people experience that proper food combining becomes less important when one is eating 100% raw since the body does not have to use as much of its own digestive enzymes. Nonetheless, it does seem that eating only one type of food at a time is easiest on the digestive system. Therefore, some advanced raw fooders eat "mono meals" consisting of only one type of food at a time, perhaps followed slightly later by a second kind of food. This is also how instinctive eaters eat. (See Appendix C.)

Nuts and Seeds: Hard to Digest?

Nuts and seeds contain enzyme inhibitors that make them difficult to digest. The enzyme inhibitor keeps the nut or seed from sprouting before conditions are right for the baby tree to grow. They should be soaked in pure water for eight to ten hours and then rinsed and drained before eating. Many people like to soak them overnight, then rinse them in the morning and store in the refrigerator covered in pure water.

Seeds can also be sprouted in a sprouting jar over the course of several days. If you do not like the light, "sprouty" taste of sprouted seeds or soaked nuts, dehydrate them for a few hours in a temperature-controlled dehydrator.

You can even add a bit of Celtic sea salt to them to give them that "store packaged" taste. They will also keep longer in the refrigerator if dehydrated. If you don't have a dehydrator, let them dry on non-bleached paper towels.

But even after soaking, nuts and seeds (especially nuts) are difficult for most people to digest simply because they are high in fat, with a high density and low water content. Macadamia nuts are about 90% fat! So you should limit your intake of them. Most people do well eating up to two to three ounces of nuts a day. However, if you eat a lot of the raw gourmet dishes, you may end up with more than this.

One factor that contributes to the difficulty of digesting nuts is that many of them, even those purchased from health food stores, are not really raw. Most have been heated somewhat to dry them to inhibit mold growth. Since a salmonella infestation in some almonds a few years ago, many nuts are heated beyond the temperature that would destroy enzymes despite having labels that boast "raw." It is often necessary to ask the distributor if the nuts are truly raw.

Many raw fooders are finding greater health by making nuts and seeds only a small part of their diet. Victoria Boutenko found that by making greens and fruit the vast majority of the diet and allowing only 5% or so of our diet to come from seeds, we match our diets to the natural diets of our closest relatives, the chimpanzees. (See Appendix C.)

Organic Food: Is It Really Necessary?

One thing people tend to become more aware of when they switch to raw diets is the superiority of organic produce. It costs more because it is not government subsidized like conventional chemical agriculture. *Government officials, receiving campaign contributions from agribusiness, pass laws subsidizing only toxic commercial farming and cattle ranching practices! In other words, your tax dollars are assisting in poisoning you.*

Because of the higher retail cost of organic produce, the advice to go organic is often met with resistance. When most people think of organic produce, they think it simply means "pesticide-free." But there is a whole lot more at stake.

Nutritional Value

You might buy a pound of organic apples for $1.29 or a pound of commercial apples for 59¢. While you save a little money on the commercial variety, you may get only half the nutrients plus a number of unwanted toxins that accumulate in your body and slowly poison you over the years.

Organic foods appear to contain on the average twice the amount of nutrients as commercial produce, but in some cases it is three or four times as much. David Jubb (*LifeFood Recipe Book*, p. 5) points out that in at least one study, organic spinach was found to have twice the calcium, four times the magnesium, three times the potassium, 69 times the organic sodium, 117 times the manganese and 80 times the iron of its commercial counterpart! Note, however, that this was just one small study. There are great variations in nutritional value among different crops of both commercial and organic produce.

Organic berries were found to have up to 58% more antioxidants than those grown conventionally, according to another study published in the February 2003 issue of the *Journal of Agriculture and Food Industry.*

A 1993 study published in the *Journal of Applied Nutrition* proved that over a two-year period, organic foods contained up to four times the amount of trace minerals, 13 times the selenium and 20 times the calcium and magnesium of commercially grown food. They also had less of the toxic metals lead and aluminum.

As Dr. Cousens points out, these remarkable differences, based on a fresh-weight (not dehydrated) basis, are not as obvious on a dry-weight (dehydrated) basis. As a result, scientists hired by chemical-based farming companies will use dry-weight comparisons.

Besides inferior nutrient content, commercial produce lacks in bio-energetic values. (See Chapter 7.) European tests on the bio-energetic values of foods proved that chemically grown foods are inferior to those cultivated organically.

It boggles my mind that people would go to all the trouble of buying organic produce, even growing their own, only to cook out so many of those nutrients for which they are paying extra or working so hard to grow.

Toxins in Commercial Produce

If you do not buy organic food, you may save a little money in the short run, but *you will pay much more in the long run when your health suffers.* For one thing, the standards for commercial produce are very low. The food could have been sprayed with any number of toxic pesticides, fungicides and herbicides.

Some of the insecticides sprayed on commercial produce, such as DDT, are even banned here in the United States but are sold to countries in Latin America. So if you save a few dollars to buy the commercial melon imported from Mexico instead of the organically grown one, you may be ingesting toxic DDT that was banned here decades ago! Even among the pesticides legal in the USA, over 20% have been linked to cancer, birth defects, developmental harm and central nervous system damage.

Toxic limits are set for adults, not children, which means children are getting several times the alleged "safe" limit.

Before the widespread use of these poisons, high rates of cancer in children were unheard of. Since most pesticides and herbicides are neurotoxic, they are also thought to cause hyperactivity and attention deficit disorder in children. According to Dr. Cousens, children put on organic diets show a 50% cure rate from just this one change. Imagine if a drug could boast this rate of cure — it would be front-page news!

Some studies have shown IQ reductions in children reared on commercial produce. One study done in Mexico called, "An anthropological approach to the evaluation of preschool children exposed to pesticides in Mexico" (*Environmental Health Perspectives*, Vol. 106, Issue 6, June 1998, PubMed ID 9618351) involved 33 children. The study found a drastic reduction of intelligence compared to those eating food without pesticides.

There is only a certain amount of pesticides that a person can absorb without ill effect in a life span of seventy-five years. One study showed that in North America, most one-year-old babies have already acquired that seventy-five year maximum! ("Can environmental estrogens cause breast cancer?" *Scientific American*, October 1995, Vol. 273, Issue 4, pp. 167-172, PubMed ID 7481720). Even for adults, this accumulation of toxic pesticides can lead to horrific effects, such as cancer, reduced mental function, decreased mental clarity, poor concentration, attention deficit disorder and Parkinson's disease.

Meanwhile, many of the pests these chemicals are intended to kill are growing resistant to the pesticides, and so farmers are forced to use greater quantities. In the past forty years or so that pesticides have been commonplace, pesticide use has increased by ten times in some places. Yet the crops that have been destroyed by insects have nearly doubled.

Currently, 500 species of insects have become pesticide-resistant. Since their life spans are much shorter than those of humans, they are able to adapt to these toxins much faster than we can. This is because it takes many, many generations for a species to genetically adapt to something new in the environment.

As Howard Lyman points out in his book *Mad Cowboy*, pesticides and other toxins used on produce represent a huge industry. Interestingly, the same companies that produce toxic chemicals for pesticides, herbicides, fungicides and industrial and household products also produce prescription drugs! *Thus, they profit at both ends: poisoning the people and providing the drugs that reduce the symptom severity of those poisons.*

This circle of profit is no conspiracy theory, but an easily provable fact. For example, Monsanto, a leading company of pesticides and genetically modified seeds, was owned by the Pharmacia Corporation, which sells prescription drugs. Merck is a pharmaceutical company that also produces chemicals and precursors for pesticides and other neurotoxins.

Remember that these pesticides, herbicides and fungicides kill farm workers, who have high rates of cancer. Why would you want to support such an industry?

A friend of mine who traveled to South America says the locals in the country he visited don't eat the food that has been sprayed with pesticides. They can't afford that produce, as the local farmers don't have the money to buy the pesticides. The big farming operations use the pesticides only on the crops that are being exported.

Ironically, the common populace is saved by poverty: They don't have enough money to buy poisoned food. Thus, we "rich Americans" are privileged to eat only the most toxic stuff!

In addition, commercial produce is often covered with chemical waxes and preservatives to enhance shelf life and improve its appearance. Brenda Cobb, author of *The Living Foods Lifestyle*, mentions seeing some plump, luscious-looking nectarines that were still packed in the box at a grocery store. She read the ingredients list and recognized only two: varnish and shellac. "I don't know about you, but where I come from, we use these products on furniture. They're certainly not something we'd consider eating. If we're going to eat varnish and shellac, why not just go to the hardware store and buy a pint or gallon of each and turn it up and drink it?"

Unfortunately, even some of the organic produce has been covered with wax for longer shelf life. The organic label refers only to how it is grown and not what is done to it later. The only way to know for sure is to ask the store manager. One of the advantages of shopping at the local farmers' market is that the produce is very fresh and rarely covered with wax.

But wait, there is more! If the toxicity in commercial produce and the lack of nutrients are not enough to make you go organic, *read on!*

Genetically Modified Organisms (GMOs)

Commercial produce may have been grown from genetically modified seed, whereas organic produce, by definition, may not. So, if you are eating commercial produce, especially corn or soy, there is a good chance it was genetically altered, and there is no law in the USA requiring that this be stated on the label.

Genetically modified organisms (GMOs) have been found to be much less nutritious and even poisonous. In a study by Dr. Arpad Pasztai at the Rowett Research Institute in Scotland, animals fed diets of GMOs were found to have smaller organs than those fed with traditional foods. *Their hearts, livers and even brains shrank after eating genetically modified potatoes for only ten days.*

Companies like Monsanto have developed GMOs so that they could patent seeds, as selling unpatentable seeds has not been particularly profitable. Also, since GMO plants do not reproduce, farmers must purchase new seeds every year, resulting in a potential food monopoly akin to the oil and banking cartels.

This practice institutes a sneaky form of slavery that will only get worse and worse until a small elite control our entire food chain.

The way they try to persuade us that this is ethical is by claiming that we need this technology to feed the world's hungry, but the truth is that GMO crops actually yield 4-10% less than heirloom varieties (*Spiritual Nutrition*, p. 506).

Furthermore, since they have genes spliced from other sources, GMOs may contain any number of allergens that are not listed, thus inducing allergic responses in some people. For example, according to Jeffrey M. Smith, author of *Seeds of Deception: Exposing Industry and Government Lies About the Safety of the Genetically Engineered Foods You're Eating*, a gene from a Brazil nut inserted into soybeans made the soy allergenic to those who normally react to Brazil nuts. This type of thing happens a lot, and the vast majority of corn and soy is now grown from GMO seeds.

Some GMOs combine genes from both plant and animal species! In fact, the FDA and EPA even classify as insecticides certain corn and potato strains that were designed to produce toxins to kill insects. So when you eat commercial corn or potatoes, you could be unsuspectingly eating an insecticide!

GMOs accelerate aging. Because GMOs are unable to reproduce, their life force is weak. Dr. Cousens said in a lecture that *GMOs deregulate our cells' DNA into premature aging.*

Instinctive eaters claim that they cannot notice a proper taste change when eating GMO food because our genes simply haven't been programmed to recognize them.

Europeans are much more informed about these "Frankenfoods" than Americans are. In Europe, by law, they must be labeled as such. Most Europeans refuse to eat them. In the United States, no labeling whatsoever is required, and companies are certainly not doing it voluntarily because they know a lot of people wouldn't buy the produce if they did.

GMOs are destroying our eco-structure. Since the wind blows pollen from these plants, they combine with natural plants. Animals eating these hybrids have been harmed. Farmers have had their natural, organic seeds infected as well.

For more information, see the web site www.cqs.com/50harm.htm, which hosts the article, "50 Harmful Effects of Genetically Modified Foods."

As people wake up to the dangers inherent in GMOs, they are uniting to fight back. On August 3, 2004, Trinity County in California became the second county in the nation to ban the production of genetically engineered crops and animals. There have been several more since then.

Meanwhile, pressure from agribusiness has resulted in legislation being introduced in Congress to outlaw counties from banning GMOs.

Commercial Foods Taste Bad

Moreover, organic food tastes better, in addition to being more nutritious. It usually tastes richer for having been grown in soil with more minerals and nutrients.

Animals can tell the difference between organic and commercial produce. In 2002, the Copenhagen Zoo began to feed its animals at least ten percent organic produce. "For one reason or another, the tapirs and chimpanzees are choosing organically grown bananas over the others," keeper Niels Melchiorsen told the magazine *Økologisk Jordbrug* (Ecological Agriculture), "Maybe they are able to instinctively tell the difference, and their choice is not at all random... The chimpanzees are able to tell the difference between the organic and the regular fruit. If we give them organic and traditional bananas, they systematically choose the organic bananas, which they eat with the skin on. But they peel the traditional bananas before eating them."

In a Pinch...

Sometimes you might find yourself in a city where there is no organic produce available. In such a situation, it will be necessary to eat commercial produce.

It is good to keep in mind that produce covered with a shell or peel generally contains less pesticide residue provided you don't eat the peel. So you could buy bananas, citrus fruit, nuts, corn on the cob with husks or avocados. Figs, cauliflower, and peas are also relatively safe.

Studies have found that the produce items containing the greatest amount of pesticide residue are: strawberries, dates, carrots, grapes, peaches, nectarines, apples, raisins, cucumbers, celery, spinach and potatoes with peels.

It is worth mentioning here that Victoria Boutenko said in a lecture that her family was healed on a 100% raw diet that did not consist of organic food. They didn't know about organic food when beginning their raw diet. However, that was over a decade ago, and commercial produce has undoubtedly become much worse since then. As soon as they found out about organics, they made the switch.

Keep in mind that toxins accumulate in your body. You wouldn't consider eating "a pinch of arsenic" on a regular basis. Cultivate the same attitude with pesticides, herbicides and fungicides!

And a Final Warning...

The organic food industry is growing by 20% a year in the United States. Anything with that much economic potential attracts a lot of attention. Therefore, the federal government, influenced of course by greedy, big, food corporations, has assumed control over the definition of the word "organic" under the guise of standardization.

This is not good news. It means that lobbying efforts by commercial agriculture are well underway to gradually dilute the standards over time. Already an "organically fed animal" can be fed merely 70% organic feed. In October 2005, Congress voted to weaken organic standards still more by allowing numerous synthetic food additives and processing aids to be included in processed foods labeled "organic."

The consumer needs to be on top of these changes in order to know the current meaning of "organic." Soon, growers and consumers may have to come up with a totally different label, something like "super" or "pure," if we are to maintain high standards.

To find where you can purchase organic food locally, visit www.greenpeople.org and www.rawfoodplanet.com.

Nuking Our Food by Irradiation

The process of irradiation exposes food to a dose of ionizing radiation that is equivalent to millions of chest X-rays. The explanation given to pacify consumers is that this destroys the "harmful bacteria" in meat and imported produce.

As always, the real reason is economic: The increased shelf life of hermetically sealed irradiated food allows for long-distance shipping and storage so that large agricultural corporations can grow food in countries with much lower environmental and worker safety standards. As a result, smaller local farms will suffer economically, and unsuspecting consumers will suffer physically from the radiolytic byproducts of this process.

Another reason is political: to assuage our fears of germs and "predatory" insects, while protecting these companies from related lawsuits.

When industries find their waste products like fluoride and chlorine too expensive to dispose of, they convince government that they have potentially "healthful" uses and sell them for huge profits. Why not put toxic fluoride and chlorine in the water? Why not sell radioactive waste, the byproduct of nuclear energy production, for irradiation of meat, grains and other foods at a profit of $50,000 a pound?

Irradiation kills not only bacteria, but also most nutrients. The food is left with no energy, no life force. It doesn't even ripen properly. According to Dr. Cousens, between 20% and 80% of the vitamins are destroyed, along with all of the enzymes and biophotons (*Spiritual Nutrition*, p. 507).

The irradiation process also creates the known toxins benzene and formaldehyde in the food, as well as unknown chemicals that are potentially toxic. According to research, animals consuming irradiated foods have suffered early death, stillbirth, genetic damage, cancer, stunted growth, organ malfunctions and vitamin deficiency. Germany experimented with irradiated food and has decided to ban the process.

Dr. Gabriel Cousens cites a study in India in which researchers fed irradiated wheat to children. After a month, leukemia-like changes occurred in the children's white blood cells and chromosomes. When they stopped eating the irradiated wheat, their blood parameters reverted back to normal.

Cousens cites five studies that claim irradiation is safe; yet all have been found to be invalid studies (*Spiritual Nutrition*, pp. 507-508). Two of the studies were found to be flawed. One study found that the animals eating irradiated food lost weight and had miscarriages, and two more studies used irradiated foods well below the FDA-approved levels. In spite of all this, the FDA approved the use of irradiation in our food supply!

There is a radura symbol on some food packaging to indicate irradiation. This looks a bit like a flower with two leaves surrounded by a circle. No labeling is required on processed foods or spices; so we cannot always know if something is irradiated. See www.exo-labels.org/label.cfm?labelid=173 for more information.

Recently, irradiated foods have been permitted in school lunches. Severen Schaeffer predicted that as irradiation of fresh produce becomes widespread, city dwellers will have access to no fresh food, and new forms of pathology will appear.

Sadly, even organic food might become irradiated. This is because organic laws pertain only to how the food is grown, but not to what happens to the food later. The best way to prevent eating irradiated food is to speak to the manager of the store.

Find a food co-op of politically aware and health conscious people who would never allow such food to enter their store. Purchase organically grown food from the local farmers' markets. Ask them how it is grown and treated. Some of them use organic growing methods but cannot use the organic label due to the red tape and expense involved in the certification process. It is highly unlikely that local farmers irradiate their food.

High vs. Low Glycemic Index Food

High glycemic index (GI) food is food that is high in fast-digesting sugars that cause the body to release excessive insulin, resulting in fat storage, fatigue and accelerated aging. If one consistently eats a lot of it, he or she will not feel good at all.

Some sweet fruits, melons in particular, score high on the GI scale; most others are in the mid-range. Root vegetables, such as potatoes, beets and carrots, are often considered high, although testing is usually done on the cooked versions of these foods. Raw starches are actually low GI foods. Note that *cooking* approximately *doubles the glycemic response* of a food in many cases! This is yet another reason to stop eating cooked food.

Hybrid plants (see next section) tend to have higher glycemic indices than their heirloom counterparts. In general, minimize high GI produce, which includes melons, cooked root vegetables, cooked grains, honey and sugar. If you are particularly sensitive, avoid just about anything that tastes sweet.

Dr. Gabriel Cousens has found that carrots, though traditionally thought to be a high glycemic index food, are not a problem when eaten raw.

As stated earlier in this chapter, Dr. Douglas Graham believes the glycemic index to be the least reliable of nutritional indexes. He says that this issue is less relevant on his 80/10/10 diet. I have found that on days in which I eat only fruit until dinner, including lots of high glycemic fruit (with the exception of dates), that I seem to be immune to the negative effects, just as Graham has stated.

Nevertheless, an illustrative glycemic index chart for selected food items is presented on the next page for those of you who may be interested.

Technically, the glycemic index is a measurement of the type or quality of carbohydrate in a food and how much 50 grams of it raises blood glucose levels over a two-hour period, with the consequent release of insulin from the pancreas as it is digested.

There are some variances in the figures depending on the soil in which the food is grown and the particular plant variety, so these numbers are approximations only. You will find somewhat different values given in different charts and databases because of these variations.

A high GI is defined to be over 70. Medium is in the range 56-69. A low GI is 55 or under. These numbers correspond to a reference standard that is arbitrarily assigned the glycemic index value of 100. To further confuse matters, some researchers use white bread as the reference standard; others use glucose.

I attempted to construct the following chart for raw foods, but data is sparse. Those items marked with an asterisk are either definitely or likely cooked.

Glycemic Index Chart

Sweet Fruits		Vegetables and Greens	
Apple	38	Bean sprout	25
Banana	52	Beet*	64
Cantaloupe	65	Cabbage	10
Cherry	22	Carrot juice	43
Date*	103	Carrot	16
Fig, dried	61	Celery	0
Grapefruit	25	Corn*	37
Grape	46	Lettuce	10
Kiwi	52	Mushroom	10
Mango	55	Onions	10
Orange	43	Parsnip*	97
Papaya	58	Peas*	48
Peach	42	Spinach	15
Pear	38	Squash	0
Pineapple	66	Turnip green	15
Plum	39	Watercress	15
Prune	29	Yam*	37
Raisin	64	**Nuts**	
Strawberry	43	Almond	0
Watermelon	72	Brazil nut	0
Non-Sweet Fruits		Cashew*	22
Avocado	0	Hazelnut	0
Bell pepper	10	Macadamia	0
Cucumber	15	Peanut	14
Red pepper	10	Pecan	0
Tomato	15	Walnut	0

*definitely or likely cooked

Hybrid vs. Wild Produce

For centuries, farmers have bred crops to make them taste and look better. This upgrading was a primitive kind of genetic engineering, but without mixing genes of differing species.

Through the methods of selection, grafting and crossbreeding, farmers hybridized foods to make them taste sweeter. Hence, we now have foods that taste very sweet compared with their wild forebears, as with beets, carrots and bananas. They also made hybrid plants for other commercial purposes, such as cold-resistance, fewer seeds, ease of harvesting and transportation, longer shelf life, fewer imperfections in shape and other aspects of appearance.

There are hundreds of varieties of potatoes. Yet, as a result of hybridization and standardization, we are able to find only a few at the grocery. The same goes for most other crops.

The downside of this trend has been that most of our commercial produce is much less nutritious. For example, hybridized fruits without seeds cannot even reproduce themselves. Such seedless foods have reduced life force. From a bio-energetic point of view, hybridized crops have not been an improvement at all. Biophotons are stored in the DNA. (See Chapter 7.) "Upgrading" crops means altering their DNA, which creates a serious loss of bio-energetic value.

This is why wild food is superior to cultivated or hybrid food. Dr. Popp of Germany found wild organic foods gave off twice as many biophotons as cultivated organic foods.

Exactly which foods are not good for you is a matter of debate, however. David Jubb highly recommends avoiding bananas and carrots, among other things. But Dr. Doug Graham is a big believer in bananas, even hybrid sweet ones. Dr. Cousens believes even hybrid sweet carrots are great, as does Rev. George Malkmus.

No one disputes the value of eating wild plants, however. You may wish to experiment with eating wild plants, which are much more potent in biophotons and nutrients. A book by Bradford Angler, *Field Guide to Edible Wild Plants*, can guide you as to which are safe to eat. Just be careful. Go out into the countryside, as plants in the city will probably have been sprayed or otherwise polluted. Furthermore, the chemicals may have caused mutations.

Aajonus Vonderplanitz describes eating a mushroom he thought was safe only to fall extremely ill, requiring eleven years to fully recover! He figured that the plant mutated from its original form, which is why he was unable to properly identify it. It wouldn't hurt to stay away from wild mushrooms altogether.

A friend of mine got sick immediately after eating a few ounces of a wild tuber that later turned out to have been pokeweed, a poisonous plant. He fasted for a few days, which relieved most of the problem, but didn't feel completely normal again for a couple of weeks. I asked how he could have avoided it. He said he should have tasted just a nibble and then waited to see how he felt.

Nibbling and then waiting awhile, even a whole day, may be the best solution when in doubt. This is what wild animals do, and this is what Igor Boutenko did when out in the wild with his family.

The Boutenko family, Victoria, Igor and their two children, went on a hike for several days and ran out of food. After fasting several more days, they became very hungry and realized that various animals were surviving on food in the forest; so why couldn't they?

They each gathered plants that looked good but didn't eat any. Then they all got together and rubbed the plants, smelled them, and tasted tiny bits under their tongues. Igor, as head of the family, got to try a full test of the plants that had passed every preliminary test of all four family members. They waited thirty minutes after he ate, and when he did not get sick, they all ate that plant sprinkled with olive oil and sunflower seeds, which they had brought with them.

If you are not that adventurous, you may wish to grow your own crops from heirloom seeds. One company that sells these seeds is Seeds of Change in New Mexico. (See their contact information in the Bibliography and Other Resources section.)

You could also sign up for an herb or wild plant walk with an experienced guide in your local area.

And if you have a garden, eat the weeds! The lamb's-quarters and other weeds you once pulled are higher in nutrients than many of the things you are intentionally growing.

The Acid/Alkaline Balance

A very important factor in health that is discussed very little in mainstream medicine is the acid/alkaline balance of the body. Yet in 1931, Otto Warburg received the Nobel Prize for discovering that cancer cells thrive in an acidic environment. In a speech, he claimed that nobody could say we do not know the prime cause of cancer, and that was 75 years ago!

Since then, acidity has become associated with numerous other diseases. As Victoria Boutenko points out, why aren't medical doctors routinely checking for our acidity levels when this is such a crucial health factor?

On the pH scale of 0-14, seven is defined to be neutral, whereas anything above seven is alkaline, or basic, and anything below seven is acidic. When we eat too much food that leaves an acidic residue, the body must deplete its limited alkaline reserves to keep the body from over-acidifying. According to Robert Young, PhD, our blood pH is ideally maintained at 7.365, mildly basic. According to Brian Clement, urine and saliva should test at an average of 6.5 in a healthy body. To maintain optimal health, we must eat at least 80% alkaline-residue foods and not more than 20% acidic-residue foods.

Acid-forming elements include sulfur, phosphorus, chlorine, bromine, fluorine, copper, silicon and iodine. Processed and artificial foods, foods high in protein (such as meat, seeds, nuts, eggs), drugs (prescription and recreational), soft drinks, air pollution and coffee are some of the main factors in swinging us toward acidity.

Alkaline-forming elements include potassium, sodium, calcium, magnesium and iron. Not all authors are in agreement as to which fruits and vegetables are alkaline-forming. Perhaps this is because each individual piece of produce varies vastly from its kin, depending on the soil in which it grew. However, everyone agrees that greens, and especially sea vegetables, are very alkaline-forming and help us balance our pH. Note that citrus fruits, such as lemons, are initially acidic in the mouth and stomach but leave alkaline residues in the blood.

To envision what body acidity is like, think of the calcifications that form on your car battery, and imagine the same thing accumulating in your digestive, nervous and circulatory systems! An acidic body at first leads to minor health complaints and later to major diseases and depression. If one becomes too acidic, he or she will die.

The body must compensate for acidity in order to save the life of the organism by leaching important alkaline minerals, such as calcium, from the bones to create a tolerable blood pH. Therefore, an acidic diet eventually leads to more serious complications, such as osteoporosis.

An acidic environment in the body is also conducive to the growth of health-destroying microorganisms. Dr. Theodore Baroody points out that as acidic wastes attack the joints, arthritis results (*Alkalize or Die: Superior Health through Proper Alkaline-Acid Balance*, p. 20). As they attack the muscles, they cause muscle aches. As they attack glands and organs, they cause disease in those organs.

Normal alkalinity in the body is characteristic of great health, leading to a blissful "high" feeling. The reason people self-medicate with recreational drugs is to become more alkaline, but the effect is fleeting and ultimately leads to a much more acidic state, hence the big crash after the high. It is best to eat raw fruits and vegetables, especially green, leafy vegetables, to achieve a sustained alkaline high and superior health.

Other factors that will increase your alkalinity are long, slow, deep breathing, Kundalini yoga and positive thinking.

To learn more about this complex topic, read *The pH Miracle: Balance Your Diet, Reclaim Your Health* by Robert Young, PhD, DSc, and *Alkalize or Die* by Dr. Theodore Baroody.

Drinking Water

Some raw fooders recommend drinking most of the water for the day in the morning. This helps to wake up and cleanse the body of toxins accumulated the day before. Paul Nison recommends drinking six to eight glasses upon rising.

Other raw fooders feel we do not need eight glasses of water a day. Gorillas and other apes in the wild drink almost no water relative to their size. The usual eight glasses a day recommendation is for cooked fooders. Cooked food is full of toxins that need to be flushed out. Cooked food is also relatively dehydrated. Furthermore, a diet high in processed foods contains huge amounts of sodium, which causes water retention and creates thirst.

My own experience is that I drink probably half as much water as I did when eating cooked foods. Nonetheless, during the detoxifying transition period, one may still need eight glasses a day in order to dilute and remove toxins.

For some raw fooders, drinking water can even deter cravings. Frédéric Patenaude, in his book *The Raw Secrets: The Raw Vegan Diet in the Real World*, refers to a friend experiencing this. His friend felt that cravings were his body's way of crying for water to help flush out the toxins of the food craved.

Raw fooders have observed that as the body detoxifies something, one will crave that thing.

Drinking water within an hour of eating (before or after) is thought by many raw fooders not to be a good idea, except for maybe a few sips, because it dilutes the stomach's hydrochloric acid needed for digestion.

However, on the other side of the controversy, both Roman Devivo and Antje Spors, authors of *Genefit Nutrition*, recommend drinking water right before eating. Noted author Dr. Fereydoun Batmanghelidj writes that drinking water an hour after eating food actually aids in its digestion.

Everyone who is educated on the topic agrees that tap water, contaminated by fluoride, chlorine, lead and numerous other toxins, is out of the question. Anyone who still believes fluoride belongs in the drinking water should read *The Fluoride Deception* by award-winning investigative reporter Christopher Bryson or *Fluoride the Aging Factor* by John Yiamouyiannis.

To mention just a few things, fluoride was used in Nazi Germany's concentration camps to pacify the prisoners. It permanently damages part of the brain that has to do with willpower. It lowers thyroid function, which is why cities that have it in their drinking water tend to have higher obesity rates. A Chinese study on the effects of fluoride on the nervous system found that it creates learning disabilities, including attention deficit disorders, and can be a danger to the fetus if a pregnant woman consumes it (*Neurotoxicology and Teratology*, Issue 17[2], 1995).

Chlorine is also toxic and causes scarring of the arteries. It kills living organisms, including people. Both were toxic industrial-waste byproducts. Companies that were looking for cheap disposal methods found ways to make waste disposal actually profitable: convincing people that it would be healthful to have it in their water! Since taking a shower is like drinking five glasses of water through skin absorption, one should have a water filter on the shower.

At the very least, one needs a reverse osmosis filter for drinking water. Yet many prefer to drink water that is even closer to its natural state, such as spring water.

There seems to be a controversy among raw fooders and other health-conscious people about which water is best: distilled, spring or some other water. The argument for distilled is that this has almost no toxins in it, and rainwater is naturally distilled by solar evaporation. The argument in favor of spring water is that this is what people have traditionally drunk, water from springs and streams from melted snow coming down mountains.

Some feel that drinking distilled water alone can even be dangerous, as it can, by osmosis, cause the body to leach out minerals. Promoters of distilled water have claimed that the only minerals leached out are toxic, denatured and not absorbable by the body and therefore needed to be removed.

Promoters of spring water, on the other hand, claim that it contains minerals, while those who promote distilled water argue that these minerals are not absorbable and are in nutritionally minuscule amounts compared to what fruits and vegetables contain.

Dr. Joseph Mercola advises us to "avoid distilled water, as it has the wrong ionization, pH, polarization and oxidation potentials, all of which damage your health and drain minerals from your body" (*The No-Grain Diet*, p. 151).

On the other hand, Dr. Baroody, who has a PhD in nutrition, claims that the idea that distilled water causes the body to leach out minerals is a myth. He claims he could not find even one reputable source for this information. In his book *Alkalize or Die* (p. 123), he claims, "Only distilled water produces a completely negative ion reaction in the system. And negative ions are alkaline-forming. All other forms of water contain varying amounts of positive (acid-forming) ions, except alkaline-restructured water."

He goes on to claim that distilled water creates a more alkaline internal environment in the body. He does not recommend spring water because of the heavy pollution it contains, explaining that toxic wastes have been buried in the earth for many years, contaminating the ground water. There is evidence that detergents, farm chemicals — and even radiation — have contaminated many spring sources. He also recommends water filtered by reverse osmosis, as well as electronically restructured alkaline water.

Yet, although Baroody claims that distilled water is negatively charged, it too takes on a positive charge in the presence of polluted air, which includes most indoor and outdoor urban air. This is why ionized (negatively charged) water is becoming more and more popular. First it is distilled, then ionized.

In a lecture, David Wolfe condemned well water for having too many minerals, rainwater for being aggressive and pulling out minerals (as he says people in Hawaii have found) and distilled water for being "corrupt, dead and dangerous." He claims that spring water is "intelligent" and has information in it. He says he has researched this so thoroughly that he cannot settle for less and actually goes directly to springs and fills up bottles.

The best, and most healthful, water I have ever tasted is Trinity water. It comes from a 2.2-mile deep, crystal-lined, granite source. You can purchase it in both spring and distilled forms. At the risk of its price going up even more, I highly recommend it. It tastes fantastic.

I have a friend who swears that any time he feels ill, one liter makes him feel great again. And my husband, who drinks exclusively Trinity water, says the taste of it has ruined the taste of all other waters for him! But since it comes in both spring and distilled form, you still have to decide between those two. (Note: As this book goes to press, Trinity has lost their funding, but they may yet make a comeback.)

Another issue of vital importance is that with all this bottled water, we are ingesting toxic amounts of xenoestrogens, which leach from the plastic water bottles — and other plastic food containers, for that matter, including the ubiquitous Saran Wrap. These lead to cancer, especially of the breast and prostate. The solution is to get a reverse osmosis filter for your kitchen and carry your water around in a food-grade stainless steel container such as that found at www.enviroproductsinc. com. Consuming raw broccoli, kale and cauliflower help protect from these foreign particles that mimic estrogen.

Salt

Nearly everyone is aware of how bad table salt can be. Entire books have been written on the topic, and it has long ago entered mainstream knowledge. But raw fooders debate whether Celtic sea salt, Himalayan rock salt and other forms of natural salt are healthful. Some believe we should avoid them altogether. Others claim they are a great source of minerals. According to Dr. Cousens, a vegan diet tends to wash out chlorine, the natural chlorine found in plant foods and needed by the body, not the harmful form found in tap water and swimming pools. He says we can bring in chlorine and sodium salts through Celtic sea salt or Himalayan salt.

Eating Foods in Season

It is always best to eat locally grown foods in season. For one thing, this can help you make sure you are not eating highly pesticided food. If you eat melons when they are out of season, and they are not labeled organic, they could have been imported from a third-world country where they are in season and where laws for pesticides are very lax.

Second, eating foods in season encourages you to eat fresh local foods. One advantage of that is supporting the local farmer. When you support your local farmer, you not only profit by eating food that is fresh and in season, but you also help reduce the profits of giant food corporations that really don't care about your health as much as they care about profits.

A health benefit is that food that originates nearby is also fresher and therefore higher in nutrients and biophotons than food that has been trucked or shipped from far away. Studies have shown that the sooner after picking something is eaten, the higher its nutritional value; it is always best to eat your foods freshly picked — the fresher, the better.

Another advantage of eating foods in season is sparing the planet from more air pollution and oil usage due to the vast amounts of fossil fuels burned up in shipping food thousands of miles to the market. This is an issue that is growing in political significance, as many believe we have reached, or are on the verge of reaching, "peak oil," after which oil prices will sky-rocket.

Supplements and Super Foods

No one disputes the fact that most of our farm soil is minerally deficient. Even a study done as early as 1936, reported in Senate Document 264, 74th Congress, second session, found that 99% of Americans are mineral-deficient. It announced that our soil is severely deficient in minerals. According to this document, "Our physical well-being is more directly dependent upon minerals we take into our systems than upon calories or vitamins or upon precise proportions of starch, protein or carbohydrates we consume. ... Disorder and disease result from any vitamin deficiency. It is not commonly realized, however, that vitamins control the body's appropriation of minerals, and in the absence of minerals, they have no function to perform.

Lacking vitamins, the system can make some use of minerals, but lacking minerals, vitamins are useless."

More reports followed. The 1992 Earth Summit Report indicated that the mineral content of the world's farm and rangeland soil had decreased dramatically. In 1993, the World Health Organization reported that our soil is 95% depleted of basic survival nutrients. These reports also explained the danger to our health and lives. Despite both public reports, nothing has been done. It is up to each of us to fend for ourselves, educating ourselves and finding out how best to mineralize our bodies.

I heard David Wolfe state in a lecture that he believes the lack of minerals in our soil has not been corrected intentionally. The government and "powers that be" would like us to remain mineral-deficient as that makes us easier to control. Raising the amount of minerals in your body, according to Wolfe's research, will increase your consciousness level. It takes your awareness and aliveness to a higher level than the raw food diet alone will do.

One way to correct this, if you live near the ocean, is to water your plants with diluted ocean water, which is mineral-rich. Read the book *Sea Energy Agriculture* by Dr. Maynard Murray in order to learn about this. If you don't dilute the sea water enough it will kill the plants, but you need a certain amount in order to remineralize the soil.

Some raw fooders say we should not take any supplements in the form of pills, as these are not natural. In fact, some of them, especially when not coming from a reputable company, may have toxic fillers. Instead, one can replenish his minerals with "super foods." These super foods include bee pollen, goji berries (a sweet Chinese herb), sea vegetables like dulse and nori, spirulina, noni juice, blue-green algae from Upper Klamath Lake, Peruvian maca, sprouts, raw cacao (chocolate) and wheatgrass juice.

In his book *Naked Chocolate*, David Wolfe cites evidence that raw chocolate (cacao nibs) is one of the earth's greatest nutritional offerings. It is high in magnesium, making it a powerful brain food and natural laxative. Ten percent of its contents are antioxidants, making it a leading longevity food. Research has shown that it benefits the cardiovascular system, increases the ability of blood vessels to dilate, decreases hardening of the arteries, prevents platelet aggregation, and thins the blood. A Harvard University study of 8,000 males found that chocolate lovers lived longer.

Chocolate has earned a reputation as "Nature's Prozac." It keeps up levels of phenylethylamine (PEA), which increases the activity of neurotransmitters (brain chemicals). This increases the activity of dopamine, epinephrine and norepinephrine, hormones that keep us feeling alert, alive, joyful and happy. Chocolate contains anandamide, a lesser-known neurotransmitter that creates bliss and a "high" feeling. High doses can mimic a cannabis high. It is believed to contain monoamine oxidase inhibitors (MAOI), which keep our neurotransmitters plentiful like those of children so that we can be as joyful, curious and excited about life as children are.

Chocolate is also known to be an aphrodisiac, hence its popularity as a Valentine's Day gift, and an appetite suppressant, which is why it is found in many weight-loss products.

According to Wolfe, "Cacao imparts an ennobling energetic creativity upon the consumer, allowing information to be downloaded from a higher dimensional space that surrounds us all the time. This creativity comes in a frequency that particularly suits the alchemist, astrologer, writer and orator. This property is esoteric and may never be precisely pinned down" (*Naked Chocolate*, p. 71).

Cacao is not without controversy in the raw food community, however. There are those who believe it is a stimulant causing "fight or flight" syndrome and the adrenal glands to secrete cortisol.

My own experience with cacao would indicate that even if this is the case, the effects of about four tablespoons of raw cacao nibs (one serving for me) is about ten percent, or less, the "fight or flight" of a 16-ounce mocha latté from Starbuck's. The only sign of addictive properties I have noticed is that I do not feel as noticeably fantastic if I take it *every day* as I would taking it only *two or three times a week*. But there is no letdown, withdrawal symptoms or addictive cravings that I have found with other stimulants, such as coffee. So I would term it a rather innocuous addiction and a powerful transition food to a raw diet. Some may even choose to make it a staple in a long-term diet.

Wolfe claims that the top three super foods, in terms of their association with longevity, are goji berries, royal jelly and cacao beans.

David Jubb, PhD, encourages the use of bee pollen, claiming that two tablespoons of this food contains more nutrients than two weeks' worth of eating at fast-food restaurants.

Personally, I take the super foods spirulina, bee pollen, raw cacao, dehydrated but living wheatgrass and others. I take some supplements as well, such as B_{12}, resveratrol, enzymes, probiotics and a live dehydrated green drink that is concentrated in minerals and greens. I also take angstrom minerals, minerals that are much smaller than colloidal minerals and are therefore much more absorbable. When I'm under a great deal of stress, I sometimes take the hormone DHEA to counteract the cortisol my body produces.

Other raw fooders say we need additional supplements. Many recommend additional enzymes. I heard Brian Clement say in a lecture that he takes 20 enzyme pills per day.

Lou Corona, a prominent raw fooder who has been on a raw diet for 31 years, promotes the use of enzymes and takes 30 enzyme pills a day. He also recommends probiotics, which help us maintain healthy intestinal bacteria.

He traveled all over the country, talking with many organic farmers, and learned that the demand for organic food was increasing so fast that many of them did not have time to grow the food properly. He also claims that the raw fooders who do not take supplements, while being free from disease, are not experiencing their maximal health potential.

One super food I learned from Lou to take is cayenne pepper. If I mix a teaspoon of it — which you should work up to gradually! — with vegetable juice, I suddenly have enough energy to complete any task before me, regardless of how tired I may have been. I later learned that hot chilies and chili peppers produce endorphins.

Dr. Gabriel Cousens says that he has observed in his clinical practice that the healthier a person becomes, the less supplementation he has to take. This is probably because as one becomes cleaned out, nutrient absorption is enhanced.

For further discussion of supplements, see Chapter 14.

Fiber: How Much Is Necessary?

The average American eats about 10 grams of fiber a day, although around 30 is recommended. Fiber is essential for cleaning our digestive systems. It is like a sponge that absorbs toxins. Victoria Boutenko discovered in her research that wild chimpanzees, our closest relatives, eat 300 grams of fiber a day! She has concluded that we should be getting around 70 grams per day. Most people don't get that much, even eating 100% raw.

We can get more fiber by not juicing with traditional juicers, but rather blending in a Vita-Mix or K-Tec machine, leaving the fiber in the drink. We can add flaxseeds to the mix. Psyllium husk is pure fiber. Victoria goes so far as to say that fiber deficiency is "the main reason for aging in humans," noting that it is difficult to guess the age of an animal in the wild, as wild animals only slow down during the final weeks of their lives.

13
Common Pitfalls to Avoid

We are living in a world today where lemonade is made from artificial flavors and furniture polish is made from real lemons.
—Alfred E. Newman

There are a few errors that people typically make in implementing the raw food diet, at least at first. Some of these make it harder to stay on the raw path. The purpose of this chapter is to make you aware of them so that you may take precautions.

Assuming a Food Is Raw When It Isn't — Although It May Be Labeled "Raw"

Anything heated above 118° F (48° C) is not considered raw by our standards, as enzymes have been destroyed. It is preferable not to heat anything above 105° F (40° C), if possible, in order that all enzymes may be preserved because some of them will be destroyed between 105° F and 118° F.

Arguably, some enzymes remain intact at higher temperatures than 118° F because these can withstand somewhat higher temperatures, but unless you are sure, it is best to err on the side of caution. The extent of destruction also depends on how long they are heated.

The word "raw" means different things to different people. For several cheese companies, for example, "raw" meant that the cheese was pasteurized at lower than the usual temperature. Raw fooders were purchasing this "raw" cheese until, after calling the manufacturer, they discovered it had actually been heated to 135° F.

I used to think dehydrated fruits were always raw until I called a company that sold dehydrated fruits and asked which raw fruits they had. I eventually learned that some they classified as "raw" had been heated from 120° F to 140° F!

Thus, it is crucial not to assume an item is raw by our definition but rather to call the processor to find out the exact temperature to which it is subjected. The retailer is not likely to know, nor often the distributor.

In her recipe book *Hooked on Raw: Rejuvenate Your Body and Soul with Nature's Living Foods*, Rhio explains that she called numerous food suppliers to research whether their food was truly raw. She discovered that figs, dates and prunes are often steamed. Sometimes, "raw" tahini has been heated to 150° or 160° F in processing. "Raw" groats are often pre-heated as well.

Rolled oats are sometimes thought to be raw, but the intense pressure applied to the oats by the rollers effectively creates enough heat to render them non-raw.

Nuts can also be deceptive. If you find a bag of commercially grown nuts or seeds at a grocery store, chances are they have been fumigated at temperatures above 118° F in order to destroy molds, often in the country they were imported from.

Therefore, nuts should be purchased in bulk from a reliable vendor and kept in the freezer to remain fresh. Freezing causes little damage to their enzymes because they do not contain water. You can also buy them in bulk at a health food store, but they will not be as fresh and may not even be raw.

Cashews are almost never *truly* raw, though labeled so, because they have to be heated to 156° F in order to get them out of their shells while neutralizing the poisonous sap that surrounds them. There are, however, a few raw food vendors that guarantee them to be truly raw, and they are listed in the Bibliography and Other Resources section. Their suppliers painstakingly and carefully separate them from their shells by hand. Because this process is so time-consuming, truly raw cashews are expensive.

Oils are nearly always pasteurized. Unless their labels specify the temperature at which they have been heated, they have been heated above 118° F. Even those labeled "cold pressed" are generally heated to at least 160° F.

You may have to shop online (see the Bibliography and Other Resources section) or in a health food store to find truly raw oil, which can only remain so without going rancid if the vendor sells it in dark containers from the refrigerated section. Olive oil seems to be stable enough to keep for a time unrefrigerated.

Maple syrup is never raw. Sometimes you may be able to purchase the unboiled tree sap directly from a grower, but it will be much less sweet than the concentrated syrup.

The jarred honey in commercial distribution has nearly always been heat processed, even when labeled "raw." The best places to find truly raw honey are health food stores, local farmers' markets and beekeepers themselves.

Even then, you must determine whether the honey was extracted by the more modern heat method (140° F) or by the old-fashioned centrifugal method. Sometimes, truly raw honey might be labeled "unheated" or "really raw." You can always ask the store for the beekeeper's telephone number, call him, and ask which extraction method he uses.

Better yet, go visit him and buy your honey directly from the beekeeper. Not only will you save money, you might also get an education in beekeeping. Beekeepers love to talk about their bees. Keeping your own small hive is always an option.

If you buy your honey still in its comb, then it is truly raw.

Juices can be very deceiving, appearing to be raw when they are not. People new to the raw diet might assume that bottled fruit juices are raw when they are almost invariably pasteurized.

Due to regulations that reflect a phobia of *E. coli* bacteria and potential lawsuits, it is now nearly impossible to find raw juice. It has usually been at least flash-pasteurized. The surest way to get truly raw juice is to have the store make it right in front of you or make it yourself.

Even then, at many of the juice bars, you have to make sure they are not adding "extras" to your fresh-squeezed juices. Some add yogurt, for example, to smoothies. I once had fresh-squeezed lemon juice at a juice bar. My husband said I acted "spaced out" later. Then he realized they probably had added sugar to the lemon juice.

I once ate some raw wild rice at a raw food restaurant that was simply divine! I went home and sprouted a bunch for myself. I got constipated and upon researching it, I learned that wild rice is always dried at 150° F for an hour or so; so it is never raw. When soaked, wild rice appears to sprout, but it is actually just tearing. I went looking for sources of wild rice that were truly raw and could find none.

Another word that can be deceptively misjudged for "raw" at times is "fresh." If you go to a restaurant and ask for what the menu calls "fresh guacamole," for example, it may mean that the powdery mix was made that day rather than made from fresh, raw avocados and other raw items.

Finally, because of our country's obsession with germs, you can safely assume that most imported, packaged or bottled foods have been pasteurized.

Judging the Diet before You Give It a Chance

Oftentimes, people try the raw food diet awhile and decide it is not for them — although genetically, *it is for everybody* — because they run into some of the following problems and are not educated enough about the diet to realize what is happening.

First, many are frustrated by detoxification symptoms, such as diarrhea, oversleeping, colds, fever, flu-like symptoms and headaches. Some people say, "I cannot do the raw diet because it gives me diarrhea," blaming the diet for the detoxification symptoms that result when the body is actually healing itself.

These detox symptoms may come and go, and it is important not to try to stop them with medications, which will not only stop the body from detoxifying but also add to the body's toxic burden that pollutes it and causes illness. Just keep eating raw, and review Chapter 11. The symptoms will go away, and you will feel better than you ever have if you persist with the raw food diet.

Second, many believe they cannot digest raw vegetables. Some people, unaccustomed to such large amounts of fiber in their diets, get bloated a lot in the beginning. If this is the case, you may juice them or blend them into soups or purées. This will make them much easier to digest.

Some raw fooders believe we are not even meant to eat very many raw vegetables. They claim that only herbivores can digest them well, as they have several stomachs, and their digestive tracts are twice as long as ours. They have 60 times more digestive juices to break down cellulose.

Others say that we can digest raw vegetables but must adapt to some degree, as we have eaten so many foods low in fiber for so long while on cooked diets.

Dr. Cousens acknowledges that, through so many generations of eating meat, some people seem no longer to have the digestive power to assimilate all their nutrients from a vegetarian diet immediately and may require several years to transition.

Victoria Boutenko believes that through eating so much cooked food we have lost our ability to make sufficient hydrochloric acid in the stomach. She has researched her theory that we can correct this deficiency by eating large quantities of green leafy vegetables, which are much more nutritious than other vegetables. (See Chapter 5 and Appendix C.)

Third, many, especially men, find that they lose too much weight. This is only temporary and will pass. You may need a year in which to lose weight and then regain until you achieve your ideal weight. When you rebuild, it will be with much healthier tissue since the building blocks are richer.

It is important to realize that the weight lost is almost entirely fat and that to build healthy muscle mass requires more than diet. It requires persistent resistance training exercise.

Fourth, many people find nuts, a major protein source on a raw diet, difficult to digest. Excessive nut consumption can even cause constipation or bloating in some people. So don't overdo them. Two to four ounces a day is plenty for most people. Also, be sure to soak nuts and seeds for about eight hours, then rinse thoroughly in order to rid them of enzyme inhibitors that impair digestion.

Some raw fooders who have found nuts difficult to digest have concluded that they shouldn't eat very much fat. Actually, that is not the case; raw fats are very good for us. People eating a lot of olives, avocados or coconut cream won't get that sluggish feeling that they might get from nuts and seeds.

Fifth, many are frustrated over the preparation time required for some of the complicated transition recipes in which everything must be made from scratch, such as salad dressing, barbecue sauce, mustard and so on. They don't realize that after six months to a year they will become very content with raw food in its simplest form.

Sixth, many feel chills and, because their body feels cold, they interpret that to mean their body is crying out for cooked food. This is simply a temporary phase in which the body is sending a great deal of its energy and blood inward to heal its vital organs, leaving little to warm the extremities. This condition will pass in a matter of months. Experienced raw fooders actually tolerate temperature extremes much better than cooked fooders do.

See a lot more information on these topics in Chapter 14.

Overeating Nuts, Seeds and Dehydrated Fruits

Some people actually gain weight on raw food diets by over-eating nuts and dried fruits. While transitioning to raw, they want to keep that stuffed, heavy, full feeling they got from cooked foods. This may be okay for the first six months or so, but after a while one expects to sustain increased energy. As discussed in Chapter 12, overeating fats or sugars fatigues in a variety of ways.

You wouldn't overeat nuts or seeds if you were out in the wild and had to crack their shells by hand. It would be too much trouble. You wouldn't even find them except in the fall season. But they can be very easy to overeat once shelled.

Likewise, if you were eating fresh fruit, it is unlikely you would eat five mangoes at a time. The water in them would make them too filling, and peeling them would be too trouble-some. Yet it is easy to sit and eat five sun-dried mangoes. They are pre-peeled and less filling without the high water content.

Water from fruit is about the best, purest water you can get. If possible, eat your fruit fresh. Dehydrated may sometimes be necessary for traveling or for storing out-of-season fruits.

Eating Too Much Fruit or Failing to Brush Teeth after Eating Acidic or Dehydrated Fruit

A number of raw food experts believe that humans are ge-netically frugivores, as are apes. This means that their primary food is fruit. Gorillas and chimps will eat plenty of greens, but given the choice they prefer fruit. In theory, we humans are also frugivores that can subsist on a diet mainly of fruit. Humans don't make Vitamin C like most other animals, and fruit is our best source of Vitamin C.

One of the most unforgettable moments of my life was when, in a forest in India, I took dozens of bananas to feed the wild monkeys. I envisioned them shyly begging, but instead they came down from the trees in droves and snatched the ba-nanas from me aggressively. I was so scared I dropped the six or seven bunches that I had left. It was like something out of a Stephen King movie!

Jan Dries writes, "The famous paleontologist Richard E. Leakey has proven that [we are frugivores] beyond a doubt. Why else does the digestive tract of modern man — if we study anatomy and physiology — still resemble that of the chimpanzee? There have been hardly any mutations" (*The Dries Cancer Diet*, p. 12).

A diet of nearly 100% fresh fruit has worked for some well-known raw fooders and was highly touted in the earlier days of the movement. Entire books, such as *Fruit: The Food and Medicine for Man*, heralded the healing potential of fruit. Joe Alexander tells about a time he spent 56 days eating only juicy fruits: no bananas, avocados or vegetables. He claims he never felt stronger in his life.

Ironically, it has been observed that excess fruit can ruin one's teeth. A diet excessively high in fruit can cause demineralization of the teeth with resulting serious dental problems.

Certainly one should brush her teeth after eating citrus fruits or dried fruits because their acidity may destroy the enamel. The tips of the teeth may become translucent, and then they start to chip. Bits of dried fruit get stuck between the teeth, and, as you learned as a kid, bacteria love to eat sugar.

But there appears to be more going on than this. Our soil is dangerously depleted of minerals. (See Chapter 12.) Since sugar binds to minerals, and there are no longer enough minerals in the soil for the fruit to have sufficient minerals, this means minerals could be leached out of our bones and teeth in order to digest them and to neutralize the acids. Our modern, hybridized fruit trees may also fail to extract enough soil minerals.

This phenomenon has been verified in an experiment. An article entitled, "Dental erosions in subjects living on a raw food diet" was published in *Caries Research* (1999, Vol. 33, Issue 1, pp. 74-80, PubMed ID 9831783). Over a period of many months (median duration 39 months), 130 people eating a diet at least 95% raw were compared to 76 control subjects eating a standard diet. It was found that those on the raw diet had significantly more dental erosions. They were eating 25-96% fruit (median 62%), and the daily ingestion of citrus fruit was 0.5-16.1 whole fruits (median 4.8).

Dr. Doug Graham's theory of the reason behind the fruit/erosion connection was explained in Chapter 12. His lecture "Fruit or Fat?" clearly placed the blame on overeating nuts and seeds, which are high in fat and very acidic, causing the bones to leach out calcium. Indeed, a diet high in fruit but low in fat seems to work well for serious athletes, according to his research.

Nonetheless, Dr. Cousens and other raw fooders place the blame on fruit. Dr. Cousens points out that although a diet high in fruit may have been excellent fifty years ago, we now need to shift to a diet lower in sugar content, which would create less fermentation and therefore not feed mycotoxic bacteria (*Rainbow Green Live-Food Cuisine*, p. 9). He attributes this need to lessen our fruit consumption to increased physical, mental, emotional and spiritual toxicity in the world and in ourselves.

As mentioned previously, he pointed out that several small groups of people who ate primarily fruit had to stop due to numerous health problems. Dr. Cousens is quick to note that just because something feels good in the short term, such as a primarily fruit diet, doesn't mean it's good in the long run.

As discussed in Chapter 12, another perspective on why eating a high percentage of fruit is no longer viable is that nowadays fruit is picked before it is ripe for commercial reasons in order to lengthen its shelf life, as well as make it easier to harvest and ship.

Fruit that is not vine- or tree-ripened tends to be lower in minerals than fully ripened fruit. Fruit picked prematurely tends to be more acidic than fruit that is vine- or tree-ripened. In addition, as mentioned previously, the depleted soil in which fruit grows lacks minerals. The extra acidity of unripe and/or mineral-depleted fruit is at least part of the cause of dental problems. Lack of minerals also makes them taste much blander, which is why fruit grown in mineral-rich soils tastes so much better.

In her book *Errors in Hygiene?!!?* Dr. Vivian Vetrano blames a sugary diet high in fruit and low in protein for the premature death of raw food guru T. C. Fry. He died at 69 with symptoms of B_{12} and protein deficiency because he refused to eat more than a very few nuts and seeds in addition to a mainly fruit diet. She objected when he kept offering to share his delicious, sweet fruits with her: "Sure you can stay off nuts, but look what it makes you do: overeat on sweet, dried fruit!" He also suffered from bad teeth and gums, perhaps partly from overeating fruit, although jaw injuries from a near-fatal car accident may have had something to do with it.

Another problem with overeating fruit is that it may cause a hypoglycemic reaction from too much insulin secretion. One may experience fatigue, irritability and excessive hunger and thirst.

On the other hand, as we saw in Chapter 12, Dr. Graham says that eating too much fat with the fruit is the cause of the problem! I have found, personally, that by reducing my fat intake I can now eat a lot more fruit and not experience hypoglycemia.

Before, when I ate considerably more fat, I would often experience low blood sugar symptoms after eating only a small amount of high glycemic fruit. I experienced fatigue, lethargy and sometimes cravings for more sugar.

Not Getting Enough Protein

There is a danger of not getting sufficient protein if you eat a diet of fruit alone and omit sufficient quantities of nuts, seeds, sprouted grains or sprouted legumes. For more information on protein, read the Chapter 12 section "The Ratio of Carbohydrates, Fats and Proteins," and the Chapter 14 section "How Do You Get Enough Protein?" As you eat raw, you absorb more of the protein so you need a lot less. But if you don't get enough, you will experience some of the symptoms described in Chapter 14.

Eating Too Much Fat

Often there is a great sigh of relief when switching to a raw diet because now you can eat formerly forbidden fatty foods, such as olives, nuts, avocados and seeds. Raw fat is wonderful for you. Most of the bad reputation of fat comes from cooked and rancid fat, which is dangerous to the heart, much more readily stored as fat rather than metabolized, and is implicated in numerous disease states. However, raw fat is actually good for you, enhancing hormone production and improving your skin. Some raw fooders believe that eating raw fat helps you metabolize or eliminate the stored cooked fat residues stuck inside you.

Traditional Eskimos ate a diet of up to 80% fat, and since it was raw, they remained very healthy. This is often used as an example that we need not limit our fat intake, or at least the ratio of fats to carbohydrates and proteins, on a raw food diet, but traditional Eskimos did not combine fruit with their fat either since fruit was unobtainable.

However, as discussed in Chapter 12, when transitioning to a raw diet, raw fooders often eat way too much fat, leading to negative consequences. They indulge in fat because they want that heavy, satiated feeling in their stomachs. They eat too much of the gourmet raw counterparts to cooked food, like crackers, cakes, pizzas and so forth, as well as refined oils, nut butters, nuts and seeds.

Overconsumption of fats will slow down weight loss or cause weight gain, increase the likelihood of hypoglycemia when you eat high glycemic fruits the same day (according to Dr. Graham), and increase your need for sleep. Although, to my knowledge, no studies have been done on people who overeat raw fat, Dr. Graham's clinical observation is that it is not good for the heart.

Overeating and Under-Sleeping

Raw diet promoter Paul Nison claims that the most common mistakes raw fooders make are eating too much and sleeping too little. Overeating or not getting enough sleep can create fatigue. Some beginners may mistake this for detoxification. Just remember that the main symptoms of detoxification will be over in one to six months. Any significant fatigue after that is due to overeating, not getting enough sleep or nutritional deficiencies, especially of Vitamin B_{12}.

If you eat too much fat, especially from nuts, you may get tired due to the difficulty of digesting them and the relatively long time it takes to digest fats. I have noticed that when my fat calories are only 20% of my total intake, I need only six hours of sleep instead of eight.

Also, overeating in general (cooked or raw, fats or fruits) causes the pancreas to release excess insulin, which causes fatigue and is thought to increase the rate of aging. Therefore, be careful not to overeat!

Eating fruit at night may cause insomnia. Garlic, spices, onions and condiments eaten at night may also disturb sleep. Drinking wine in excess of a glass or two is a great sleep-interrupter, especially if it is not organic and contains sulfites.

The old adage that the hours before midnight count for double has great merit. If you need to catch up on sleep, try going to sleep at 9 or 10 PM, and you will be amazed at the results. Before the widespread use of electric lighting, people usually went to bed shortly after sunset, rising at dawn. An excellent book on how the invention of the light bulb has contributed to modern-day health hazards is *Lights Out* by T. S. Wiley.

One great bonus about the raw diet is that if you do miss a good night's sleep, you won't feel nearly as fatigued as you did when eating cooked foods. Even if you sleep for only a couple of hours, you can still feel great the next day! You will still need to catch up on missed sleep eventually. Sleep deficits are bad for the brain.

After years of being 100% raw, you will find you need less sleep, as your body no longer needs so much detoxification.

Succumbing to Social Pressure

People often feel snubbed if you reject their food offerings. It is considered extremely offensive in some cultures. On the other hand, in places like California, people are used to seeing a myriad of diet variations and are not surprised by any of them.

Victoria Boutenko reminds us to say "thank you" in at least three different ways if someone goes out of his way to make you cooked food. Then, politely explain why you won't eat it. People need to feel appreciated and acknowledged more than they need you to eat their food. Victoria reminds us that if you went to Russia, and someone offered you a bottle of vodka, you would likely find some way to excuse yourself from drinking it. Therefore, you could find a way out of eating the food too. For more information on handling social situations gracefully, read the section "How to Stay Raw in a Cooked World" in Chapter 11.

Buying and/or Preparing Too Much Food

One of the biggest mistakes I made was buying too much produce or preparing too much food. Much of it went to waste. All of my food-preparing life, I was used to the mentality of saving time by whipping up huge batches of food and storing it in the refrigerator or freezer to reheat later.

On the raw food diet, food will keep in the refrigerator for about a week, but you do want to eat it as fresh as possible. Cutting and chopping it makes it lose some of its nutrients, as does storing it too long. Besides, fresh food always tastes best.

I encountered this problem while feeding only my husband and myself. Of course, if you are feeding children or others, this will probably not be a problem.

As cooked fooders, we were used to storing vast quantities of food. If some emergency came along, no problem: I always had at least a month's supply of pasta, grains, beans, canned goods, frozen entrées and such.

As a raw fooder, you won't find that many things you can stockpile. Basically, you have to let go of the hoarding mentality. The only food items I stockpile now are jars of olives, raw nut and seed butters and nuts and seeds that I keep in the freezer. If dehydrated fruits have been dried thoroughly enough, they may also keep for a long time, even when unrefrigerated.

Failing to Study the Raw Food Diet

Those who don't study the raw food diet may lose their inspiration or even forget why they went on it. When the going gets tough, they may cave in to cooked food. See the section "Educate Yourself" in Chapter 10.

Failure to Plan Ahead

Because raw, organic food is not found ubiquitously, as cooked food is, you will need to pack some food or plan ahead when traveling or even going to work or shopping. I have met a lot of raw fooders who, at least temporarily, fell out of the living foods lifestyle for the simple reason that they did not plan ahead, taking raw food with them on trips or while visiting others. See the section "How to Stay Raw in a Cooked World" in Chapter 11.

Not Eating Enough Greens

I recently attended a workshop by Victoria Boutenko in which she outlined the seven most common mistakes made by raw fooders. She mentioned many of the things I have already written about here, including something else — not eating enough greens. She explained that chimps and primates in the wild thrive on greens. She and her family felt something was missing until they started eating more greens and adding them to smoothies with fruit. Greens are one of the main foods that alkalize our bodies (see Chapter 12) and are extremely important for our physical health and sense of well-being. You will find more about her recommended green diet in Appendix C.

Neglecting Other Areas of Health

Some raw fooders conclude that now that they are eating healthfully they no longer need to exercise or go out for fresh air. There are many other factors in maintaining superior health besides nutrition.

First of all, anything that goes into or touches your body will affect your health. You need to remove all toxic shampoos, soaps, make-up, moisturizing lotions, household cleaning supplies and the like. Don't put anything on your skin that you wouldn't eat! (See Chapter 11 for more on this topic.)

Stagnant, polluted air is another source of toxins. Since air inside the house is usually even more toxic than the polluted urban air outside due to plastics and other unnatural products used in the home, it is advisable to spend more time outdoors and to buy an air purifier of good quality for use indoors.

Don't buy synthetic carpets, which emit toxic fumes for at least the first year, and avoid common paints. One company that sells nontoxic paint can be found at www.afmsafecoat.com.

Water is another source of toxins. You need to drink pure water (see Chapter 12), not unfiltered tap water. You also need a good shower filter since several glasses of water are absorbed through the skin during a shower.

You need to exercise at least half an hour a day. Exercise should vary and include stretching (as in yoga), walking and anything else you find fun. I also recommend a mini-trampoline, which cleanses and exercises every cell in the body by stimulating lymph flow.

A proper amount of sleep, as mentioned earlier in this chapter, is certainly critical for health. Sleep is when the body regenerates and heals.

Everyone needs to go out into the sun for about 20-30 minutes a day, longer if you are of African descent. Most of us are deficient in Vitamin D. The sun is the source of life, energy and healing.

Don't let all the talk of skin cancer scare you. One of the main causes of skin cancer is sunscreen, which is full of chemicals! Sunscreen also blocks out the absorption of the beneficial aspects of the sun, including the rays we use to produce Vitamin D. People deficient in sunlight often become depressed.

A good book on the topic is *The UV Advantage: The Medical Breakthrough that Shows How to Harness the Power of the Sun for Your Health* by Michael F. Holick, PhD, MD. He has published hundreds of studies on the beneficial aspects of the sun, claiming that they are not advertised because no one can make money from the sun! Another is *Into the Light — Tomorrow's Medicine Today!* by Dr. William Campbell Douglass, MD.

And what good does it do to stop eating cooked food if you are cooking your brain with cellular phone radiation? Cell phones are so bad, especially for children and teens whose brains are still developing, that studies in Europe, where only adults are allowed to use cell phones, indicate that massive numbers of these young people will have Alzheimer's in their 30s! In the US, cellular service providers protect themselves from future litigation by printing disclaimers in fine print in their manuals or contracts.

One reputable company that has devices that help keep radiation from the head of cell phone users is Biopro. For information, contact Dr. Dan Harper at 858-259-5945, ashu-harper@hotmail.com or www.mybiopro.com/drdan. Also see the products listed at www.midwestbioresonance.com.

Finally, negative thinking, including worrying, reacting, resentment and anxiety, creates an acidic condition within the body. Work on cultivating acceptance for the present moment, however dire it may seem, and create a positive attitude. Gratitude for whatever you have is a powerful and fast route to positivity.

14
Frequently Asked Questions

He who does not know food,
how can he understand the diseases of man?
—Hippocrates (460-377 BC), the father of medicine

Isn't a raw food diet boring?

A common misconception about the raw food diet is that it must be horribly boring. Even I, months before trying the raw diet, asked a long time raw fooder, "Don't you get tired of eating the same things all the time?" I envisioned a life of eating nothing but salads and fruit, maybe an occasional smoothie or some trail mix.

The truth is, when you switch to a raw diet, you will discover a vast number of totally new food combinations and taste sensations. Raw eating has enjoyed renewed popularity long enough that, at the time of this writing, there are more than twenty recipe books out, with new ones coming out every year. Just about any native or ethnic food you now enjoy has a raw counterpart. I enjoy raw versions of Thai, Indian, Chinese, Italian and Mexican dishes, although at this point I am quite content to savor simple salads.

Cooked food is pale, whereas raw food is bright, colorful and extremely attractive. Much of cooked food becomes mushy, whereas raw food comes in many different textures varying from crunchy to soft. Cooked food has lost its original flavor, making it bland. Most of it is so bland that spices and condiments, often toxic, must be used in its preparation; otherwise, we would not find it at all interesting.

After your body has detoxified itself of spices and condiments, including table salt, plain raw food will begin to taste much more interesting. For instance, a piece of celery will taste much saltier than it did when you ate salt.

Victoria Boutenko was eating 100% raw plant foods when she wrote, "There are thousands of different tastes in natural food" (*12 Steps to Raw Foods,* p. 75).

Fresh, unaltered raw foods offer vastly distinct flavors. As Victoria points out, no two apples taste alike; so biting into one that is especially high in nutrients, and thus flavor, is a delightful surprise. If you eat two different Snickers bars, they will taste alike. You know what to expect. But if you eat two different dates, they may taste perceptibly different.

My friend Marie Tadič, whose testimony appears in Chapter 2, says that people often ask her if she gets bored on the raw diet, and she replies, "No, I got bored eating all the same cooked foods all my life. This is totally new!"

In her book *Eating in the Raw,* Carol Alt says that as a cooked food eater and model under pressure to stay thin, she constantly felt deprived. It was only after switching to a raw diet that she was able to indulge in foods formerly forbidden without fear of excess weight gain, foods like raw cheeses, cookies, pies and other desserts. Indeed, a raw diet is anything but boring.

If we've been eating cooked food throughout history, what's the big deal?

So, what is the big deal, we might ask, if we have been eating cooked food "forever" and are living to be about 70 or 80 years old?

First, we have been brainwashed into believing that it is "normal" to live merely for 80-100 years. Longevity researchers have come to realize that our potential life spans are much longer than that. Researchers such as Dr. Roy Walford have found it to be a minimum of 120 years, but some feel it is longer still. Some intriguing human longevity records are presented in Hilton Hotema's *Man's Higher Consciousness.*

Second, we have been misled into believing that the absence of observable disease symptoms equates to health. This is because doctors don't study health but rather disease. People who have devoted their lives to studying health have found that there is almost no limit to the potential of super or "ultrahealth." One can keep improving by, for example, harnessing more and more of the body's or mind's innate potential.

Sometimes people would tell Zephyr, author of *Instinctive Eating: The Lost Knowledge of Optimum Nutrition,* that they felt they were adequately nourished already, and the proof was that they were still alive, after all. He would respond that, years ago, before his raw instinctive diet, he had a vastly more limited view of what it is to experience "being alive." Many raw fooders view their former lives as "the walking dead" or "the sleepwalking."

We have been brainwashed into believing it is "normal" to get sick periodically and even to have minor health impairments that we can live functional lives with, such as constipation, allergies, acne, headaches, premenstrual syndrome, aches and pains, indigestion and more. We are told that half of those who live beyond age 85 will suffer Alzheimer's, and nearly half will have cancer in their lifetimes.

We all take for granted that it is our destiny to eventually succumb to a lethal illness before actually dying. We assume that to spend the last ten years of our lives in horrible suffering, using up our children's inheritance for health care, is "normal."

Consider that illness may not be natural. Maybe it is not what nature intended for us at all. Perhaps, instead, radiant health is the norm and our birthright if we live a toxin-free life or close to it. Certainly, the primary sources of toxins we encounter come from that which we put directly into our bodies daily through our mouths and lungs.

Third, since the onset of electric cooking gadgets, as well as all the processed, packaged, foods we buy, we are eating more cooked foods than ever. Whenever food is canned, packaged, boxed or bottled, it has nearly always been pasteurized, irradiated or heated in some way and then vacuum sealed in order to preserve its shelf life.

I remember, as a cooked fooder, that I was often too busy to prepare dishes from fresh produce. To save preparation and shopping time, I would fill a cupboard with canned vegetables. Then I would make stir fry, heating it up with tofu. The next day, I would reheat some leftovers in the microwave. By that time, the food had been cooked *three times*!

We are also cooking at much higher temperatures than in the recent past, which produces a lot of acrylamides and AGEs (Chapter 6). While the techniques of cooking at high temperatures (grilling, frying and baking) have been around a long time, in most societies they were not used so frequently as now. They were reserved for special occasions, such as for guests and special celebrations. Daily cooking, even just a few generations ago, consisted mainly of boiling, steaming and lightly frying. Sixty years ago potato chips were uncommon, as were fast-food restaurants with their french fries.

The current generation probably eats about 95% of its diet cooked. For some, the only raw food consists of the lettuce and tomato on the burger at the fast-food restaurant! When my grandmother was on her deathbed, she craved strawberries. I wonder what this generation of Americans will crave: Pop•Tarts? Twinkies? Big Macs?

The current generation is not very healthy. Obesity has escalated to a point that, according to statistics from the National Institute of Diabetes and Digestive and Kidney Diseases, as of 2001, 58 million Americans were classified as overweight; 40 million were obese (30% or more over target weights). The Centers for Disease Control and Prevention (CDC) reports that the average American was 24 pounds heavier in 2002 than he was as recently as the 1960s.

Overweight is a major factor behind 80% of Type II diabetes, 70% of heart disease, as well as a major factor in cancer. According to the CDC, obesity is about to surpass tobacco as the leading cause of preventable death.

Younger and younger people are becoming overweight. Currently 9 million children over the age of six in the USA are obese, while another 15% are borderline and at risk according to the National Center for Health Statistics. Sixty percent of children ages 5-10 had at least one risk factor for cardiovascular disease according to 2004 data from the Institute of Medicine report *Childhood Obesity, Health in the Balance,* 2004. In children as young as eight years old, the increase in Type II diabetes is so high that it can no longer be called "adult onset diabetes."

People are getting cancer and even heart disease at younger and younger ages. Sometimes athletes even drop dead in their teens.

Furthermore, the alarming increase in the percentage of adults of childbearing age who are sterile, as high as 30% by some estimates, has some people thinking we may be on our way to extinction. Incidentally, Hallelujah Acres (see Chapter 9) has had great success in treating sterility issues with the living food diet.

It is well known that wild animals thrive on exclusively raw diets. Yet, if you captured a wild animal and fed it a cooked meal, it would not die immediately. It would take years of cooked meals, during which time it would suffer progressive degenerative disease long before actually dying.

This is also the way it happens with humans. The deadly effects of cooked food are cumulative. This means the toxins build up gradually as the body's digestive enzyme-making capacity is depleted slowly over the course of decades. This "aging process" proceeds so imperceptibly that the cause/effect relationship remains virtually unnoticed.

People tell me, "Oh, I don't care how old I live; so I may as well eat what I want." I then reply that this diet is not just about living a long, healthy life, but about adding energy and zest to the present years. It is about avoiding a future of living in a nursing home or hospital with tubes attached, having crippling arthritis, being a "shut-in" in old age, spending one's last years with Alzheimer's, and so on.

According to an article in *The Wall Street Journal* (February 21, 2001), more than half of all women and a third of all men who survive to age 65 are expected to spend time in nursing homes for the remainder of their lives.

The Health Insurance Portability and Accountability Act of 1996 makes it clear that the people, not Medicare or Medicaid, will have to foot the bill for their own nursing homes. How many Americans from the Baby Boom generation will be walking around homeless as a result?

One could die at middle age from a car accident yet, nonetheless, have no regrets about eating properly, as her life will have been much richer while it lasted on a raw food diet. People who eat living foods are full of life and vitality.

Though it may at first appear so, this diet is not one of great sacrifice. The message that I try to convey is that this is not a diet of deprivation. In a few weeks, cravings for cooked and unnatural foods greatly diminish, returning perhaps for a matter of a few seconds or minutes every week or so the first year. You quickly get to the point where you simply don't want to eat the old way. There is no sacrifice here once you adjust to the new, healthful way of eating.

Can't I just eat cooked foods with vitamin, mineral and enzyme supplements?

Countless people, myself included once, have thought, "Well, I will just supplement with a multi-vitamin/mineral tablet to compensate for any lost nutrients." But it is not so simple.

For one thing, nutrients from food are much more absorbable than those from pills. As pointed out in Chapter 7, new vitamins and nutrients continue to be discovered; so the pill may not contain all of them. Supplements are generally dead, lacking the life force of raw food. Micronutrients ingested in supplement form also arrive in unbalanced combinations our biology doesn't handle well. The questions with supplements are always, "which ones?" and "what doses?" Nobody knows. In fresh, raw foods, Nature has provided its nutrients in the proper balance needed for us to digest and utilize them.

I personally do not feel that all supplements are worthless, however. As an acupuncturist and herbalist, I have found a number of herbal remedies that help the body heal. However, they would work even better if they could be available in raw form rather than the pill form commonly found in jars or the brewed herbal teas used in traditional Oriental medicine.

I am convinced that a cooked fooder is better off adding certain supplements, but a raw fooder taking no supplements gets much better results than a cooked fooder taking hundreds of dollars of supplements each month.

My husband and I used to be supplement junkies. We should have joined "Supplements Anonymous" if it had existed. Yet both of us agree that we feel much better now that we are eating raw without about 75% of the supplements we used to use. Raw food simply works better than any number of supplements you could buy!

Nonetheless, as discussed in Chapter 12, our soils are extremely mineral-deficient. Mineral deficiency throws everything off, including our enzyme balance. Because of this, even some prominent raw fooders take supplemental enzymes, minerals and mineral-rich super foods.

Recall from Chapter 5 that Dr. Kollath found that only raw foods, not vitamin and mineral supplements alone, could restore his animals to full health.

Furthermore, researchers from the Linus Pauling Institute reported that a raw diet fed to mice had the same anticancer properties as high doses of Vitamin C, indicating that supplementation was not necessary when eating raw. (See Chapter 5.)

Dr. Campbell relates in *The China Study* that his work in the 1982 report *Diet, Nutrition and Cancer* led to a huge boom in the supplement industry. He attributes this to the fact that the committee organized the scientific information on diet and cancer by nutrients, with separate chapters for each nutrient.

He now feels this was a mistake. They did not emphasize that the nutrients should be obtained from *whole foods*. He feels that everything in a whole food works together synergistically, that it is misguided "scientific reductionism" to think that we can obtain proper nutrition merely by adding supplements to our diets.

Of course, if you are on a cooked diet, taking enzyme supplements is better than eating cooked food without them, as they help digest the cooked food. But they do not fully compensate for all of the enzymes, biophotons and other ingredients of live food, many of which, undoubtedly, have yet to be discovered. I have taken cooked food with literally dozens of enzyme supplements at one meal and still suffered that sluggish, "cooked food" feeling.

Several raw food authorities, including Aajonus Vonderplanitz, claim that unheated honey is so rich in enzymes that it may assist in the digestion of cooked food. Wolfe found that it might even be better than enzyme supplements. The problem with taking extra honey instead of enzyme supplements is that if it is over-consumed, it can cause hypoglycemic reactions. Of course, unprocessed, unheated honey is less damaging than what you normally find in the store, and truly raw honey is the only kind that has enzymes.

Additionally, consider that supplementation may compensate for some lost food value, but it does not negate the fact that the cooked food contains toxins. So even if you supplement with enzymes to compensate for enzymes lost in cooking, you are still ingesting cooked food toxins. (See Chapter 6.)

Many supplements are inorganic and therefore are poorly utilized by the body, but they can help in cases of severe deficiency. For example, inorganic iodine added to salt helped give thyroids a boost in areas of the country where iodine levels were low. But in order to obtain the ideal amount of iodine, one would have to take doses from *inorganic* sources that would be seriously toxic, or nearly so.

Jan Dries says, "Only natural food supplements contain substances that are accepted by the cells. All other substances are rejected or lead to pollution of the body" (*The Dries Cancer Diet*, p. 103). He shows that supplements, though correcting one area, may wreak havoc on another area. For example, frequent use of carotene stimulates lung cancer in smokers, and megadoses of Vitamin C in supplement form can negate the positive effects of selenium.

Most supplements also contain binders (glues), fillers (so-called "inert" ingredients that have no business being in the human body) and sometimes toxic "preservatives" or "natural" flavorings. Great liberty can be taken with the word "natural."

Even the vitamin "nutrients" themselves are often chemically created and don't have the correct geometric configurations of naturally occurring vitamins. Some of these "isomers" are toxic. Nor do they contain all the natural cofactors that occur in whole foods that enable these vitamins and minerals to be optimally utilized by the body; hence they may be poorly assimilated as well. A concern for vegans is that they usually contain animal or insect extracts among their unlisted ingredients. For example, gelatin capsules are made from horse hooves.

If you use supplements, try to get them in as natural a form as possible. For example, take dehydrated fruits and vegetables like "Juice Plus" instead of a "dead" vitamin/mineral pill. Take dehydrated living grasses if you don't have time to make wheatgrass. If you use hormonal therapy, take bioidentical hormones from plant extracts that your body can recognize, as recommended by Suzanne Somers in her book *The Sexy Years.* But never fool yourself into believing that what you are doing by taking supplements, even in their most natural forms, is as good as obtaining your micronutrients from whole, fresh foods.

What if I lose too much weight or muscle strength?

People who are naturally thin may fear getting too skinny eating raw diets. What happens with many of them is that they actually reach their ideal weight, putting on some pounds, but if this does not happen automatically, they can always eat more fat (avocado, nuts, olives, seeds) or sprouted grains and legumes to reach desired weights.

Victoria Boutenko found that when people who had become too emaciated on raw food diets began drinking her green smoothies (Appendix C), their increased hydrochloric acid secretions improved nutrient absorption so much that they reached and maintained healthy weights.

Typically, if someone who does not need to lose weight goes raw, he may lose a few pounds initially but eventually regain it.

As for muscles, their fat and water content diminishes, but their strength increases! My husband certainly noticed that. Lou Corona has described this as an increase in "core strength." Although he has not worked out in years, he can do a yogic posture which many heavyweights and athletes cannot:

that of sitting down, legs extended in front, hands by the sides, followed by raising the body and legs using only arm strength.

Can't I just go on a diet of 50-95% raw food?

Sure you can, but studies show that seriously sick people recover on 100% raw food diets. A number of experts feel that chronic illness calls for nothing less, as this is what best promotes healing. If you are seriously ill, I recommend you obtain guidance from a naturopathic or other holistic physician or from a healing center. (See the Bibliography and Other Resources section.) Most likely your initial healing diet will consist exclusively of raw fruits and vegetables, omitting even nuts and seeds, in order to impart extra cleansing energy.

On the other hand, there are some who believe that while a serious illness calls for great diligence, discrimination and direction with every morsel of food entering the body, it should not be 100% raw initially. Nutritionist Natalia Rose feels that "cleansing foods can release too much waste matter into the bloodstream and eliminative organs" and that those organs may not be strong enough to keep up with the increased load. A condition known as "autointoxication" could result as the toxins cycle through the bloodstream (*The Raw Food Detox Diet*, p. 46).

Frankly, my strong suggestion for *healthy* people would be to go 100% raw because that is the surest way for cooked food temptations to disappear. It is also the fastest way to rid the body of toxins accumulated over a lifetime. Once you eat cooked food, your body stops eliminating old debris in order to work on the incoming arrival of the new toxins.

Or you could do as I did for some time and go 95% raw, allowing that 5% for special occasions when a loved one makes you a treat that you will politely nibble at or for that favorite food on a special occasion. Just be sure that the definition of "special occasion" doesn't become diluted until it's every day! One woman I know stays 100% raw except for Christmas, her husband's birthday, and her daughter's birthday. Because she has set these limits, she is not tempted to let her mind trick her into eating cooked food on other days.

It will be much easier for you not to have to battle the urge to eat favorite cooked and processed "goodies" if you commit to going *radically raw*. Knowing this, I was tempted to leave out advice on how to manage a less than 100% uncooked diet.

However, I also know that many people simply won't go for the 100% raw diet. People already relatively healthy may not have the necessary motivation to commit to a 100% raw diet. Obviously, it is better to eat 50% raw than only 5%.

I have counseled people willing to commit only to 50% raw, and yet, even then, they delighted in their improved health and newfound energy. The greater your percentage of raw food, the more you are avoiding toxic cooked foods, and the more you are nourishing your body with nutrients found only in raw food.

So, the greater the percentage raw, the better your health will be. You will benefit accordingly — the more raw, the better. Researchers and raw food advocates have found that a diet of 75-85% raw foods calorically is sufficient for reasonable health maintenance. Dr. Gabriel Cousens has found that he cannot get results with anything less than 80% raw food. Rev. George Malkmus, who attributes his cancer recovery to the raw food diet, found that once he became cancer-free, he could maintain his health on an 85% raw food diet.

A friend of mine suggested I write a section about "how to cheat" on the raw food diet. I would say that, if you are only committed to being say, 90% raw, just don't keep any cooked food items in your house. Save them for special occasions: a baked potato when dining out, steamed vegetables when visiting a friend or other occasional indulgences at parties and potlucks. If you keep "cheat food" in your cupboard, you will easily slip back into a greater percentage of cooked foods.

If you decide to eat only partially raw, it is best to decide beforehand exactly which cooked foods you will allow yourself to eat. For example, if your goal is 90% raw, you could calculate the number of calories you need and pick something each day that you eat cooked. For cxample, one item could either be steamed vegetables, a baked potato or some stir fry. But under no circumstances would you consume dairy, junk food, cooked sugary desserts, candy bars, potato chips, baked bread, cooked meat or other very unhealthful foods.

If you select a more ambitious goal, such as 95% raw, you might want to be very precise and only allow for a few of your favorite cooked foods and only seldom when eating or dining out. For example, the first year I went raw, I was committed to staying 95% raw. I figured this way I could have my occasional baked potato, a favorite food, despite its 450 novel chemical by-products.

I also wanted to have popcorn when going to the movie theater a couple of times a month. I knew that the popcorn at theaters had hidden MSG, and so I smuggled in my own dry air popped corn. But I prevented myself from falling back into an all-out cooked food addiction by limiting myself to those two cooked foods: dry air popcorn and potatoes fixed any way, with each consumed but once a week.

The reason I chose those two was that they were my favorite foods, and I could not find any raw counterpart. I was not tempted to eat a baked cake, for example, because I knew I could have my raw cake, and it tasted even better. I almost never allowed myself to eat cooked food even while at a party.

Once I ate some cream-cheese icing off a piece of carrot cake and, on a few occasions, croutons or turkey dressing. But the price, with my newly awakened sensitivity, was heavy for eating wheat: a sluggish mind and extremely slowed digestion that included being constipated for a day. In addition, I acquired an intense craving for wheat for several days thereafter due to its physiologically addictive nature. (See Appendix A.)

If you aspire to 99% raw, that does not give you much leeway. In that case, the 1% might consist of occasional irradiated spices showing up in otherwise completely raw dishes at raw food potlucks. Or it could be for when the salad bar looks bleak except for the coleslaw with its pasteurized mayonnaise. It might even be comprised of food you eat that you think is raw, but isn't. So, in that scenario, you should never consciously eat anything cooked, but don't get fanatically upset if you do so inadvertently.

Also, remember that *even at raw potlucks*, you will invariably end up eating a small percentage of cooked food. You can only avoid this if you become a "raw food Nazi," drilling every contributor over whether he had checked with his supplier to verify the oil was unpasteurized, the tahini not heated (which many labeled "raw" are), the fruit was not irradiated, and so on.

Yet there is a big health difference between a 90-95% raw food diet and a 100% raw food diet, and so the goal is worthwhile. The difference is much more than 5-10%. This is because on a 100% raw food diet, your body is continually detoxifying old toxins stored in your body for years or decades, and you are rejuvenating. The moment you eat cooked food, the detoxification of the old stuff stops because your body will be busy detoxifying the incoming toxins. You may still detoxify some of the old toxins at night to a certain degree, but overall it will be a much slower process than that of a 100% raw fooder.

Nonetheless, there are many people who say that they feel just as good while eating 90% raw as they did when eating 100%, providing the 10% cooked is not processed foods, but rather something much less toxic, such as steamed vegetables.

Another concern is that the 90-95% raw fooder still has one foot in both worlds, which makes it much easier to backslide, especially during holiday seasons. For one thing, unless you border on obsession with calculations, you won't really know exactly what your percentage of cooked foods is. It may become easy to deceive yourself.

Eventually, the partial cooked fooder may encounter the frustrations of "yo-yoing" back and forth between a healthful diet and a cooked food one. Whereas a 100% raw fooder eventually completely loses all desire for dead food, one who is less than 100% will be continually battling cooked food addiction.

Raw fooders who remain 100% or very close can go to cooked parties, potlucks and restaurants and have no temptation to eat those foods. They may enjoy some of the aromas, but they don't salivate and don't feel deprived.

How do you get enough protein?

Initially, obtaining sufficient protein is a great concern for many approaching the raw food diet, especially those embarking on a vegetarian or vegan raw diet. However, it has been shown that the body does not need as much protein as formerly thought. As Dr. T. Colin Campbell says, "The story of protein is part science, part culture and a good dose of mythology." (*The China Study*).

In the late 1800s, the dairy and meat industries in Europe popularized the idea that we needed lots of protein. The average American eats about 60-120 grams of protein per day. It has been proven that we need only 25-45 grams a day and maybe even as little as 15 grams.

Certainly, dietary protein is essential, but that does not mean we need excessive amounts of it. The truth is that most Americans eat far too much protein, which leaves us with acidic residues that cause numerous diseases.

In an excellent Internet article entitled, "Protein — How Much is Right for You?" Dr. Robert Sniadach explains that the heavy amount of protein that Americans eat is hazardous to our health. "The metabolism of proteins consumed in excess of the actual need leaves toxic residues of metabolic waste in tissues, causes auto-toxemia, over-acidity and nutritional deficiencies, accumulation of uric acid and purines in the tissues, intestinal putrefaction, and contributes to the development of many of our most common and serious diseases, such as arthritis, kidney damage, pyorrhea, schizophrenia, osteoporosis, arteriosclerosis, heart disease and cancer. A high protein diet also causes premature aging and lowers life expectancy."

Dr. Sniadach believes we need but 20-40 grams of protein a day. He also points out an article in a 1978 issue of the *Journal of American Medicine* that states that athletes do not need any more protein than non-athletes. It is a myth that protein increases strength. In fact, excess protein takes greater energy to digest and metabolize. In his Natural Hygiene course, he explains in detail that the body is actually able to recycle proteins.

Dr. Gabriel Cousens also notes that research on people fasting on water indicates that their serum albumen levels (the amount of protein in their blood) remained constant during fasting despite no protein being eaten.

We maintain a pool of amino acids that continually sends free amino acids or protein complexes to wherever they are needed for tissue repair. This is explained in the classic physiology textbook authored by Dr. Arthur Guyton.

Also, keep in mind that cooked protein is only about 50% assimilated; so on a raw diet, you only need half of what you needed on a cooked diet. Not only is the cooked protein less assimilated, but much of it is also denatured or lost in cooking. When you cook protein, you lose half of it in its true form, according to research at the Max Planck Institute in Germany.

In his Great Experiment (see Chapter 5), Dr. Szekely invariably found that less food heals the body faster and that thirty to forty grams of protein from uncooked and unadulterated foods was as efficient as sixty to eighty grams from cooked food.

If you are a vegan, you will get enough protein from leafy green vegetables, nuts and seeds. Even fruit is about 1% protein by volume — it has much more, up to 30%, if you go by caloric content. Denser sources of protein include sprouted grains and beans, although those are difficult to digest and should be used only in small amounts, such as a few ounces in one day.

Human mother's milk is only about 5% protein by calories. Keep in mind that this is consumed during the time when the human is growing most rapidly! I am not saying that 5% is the optimal percentage of protein, but only that we could survive on that, if necessary, providing that our digestive tract has been cleaned out for optimal absorption.

In *Errors in Hygiene?!!?* Dr. Vetrano points out that we should not totally neglect getting sufficient protein. She feels that Natural Hygiene leader T. C. Fry died prematurely at age 69 because he insisted that his diet of fruit and vegetables alone would contain sufficient protein. Even though it was going against the teachings of Natural Hygiene, which he dedicated his life to promoting, he refused to eat more than minimal nuts and seeds.

She asks all to take heed of "the early symptoms of a low protein diet: listlessness, apathy, slow healing of wounds, edema, skin and hair changes" (p. 253). When people with these symptoms consult her, she advises them to eat nuts and seeds in addition to fruit. The symptoms then disappear almost overnight. She also notes that increased stress in one's life increases the amount of protein necessary. Stress also contributed to T. C. Fry's early demise, and at a time when his protein needs were increased, he still refused to eat much of it.

In *The China Study*, Dr. Campbell points out that the most efficient (i.e., fastest) way to provide building blocks for our replacement proteins would be to eat not only animal flesh, but *human flesh.* However, the greatest efficiency doesn't always lead to the greatest health, and in the case of protein, plant protein shows that "slow and steady wins the race." In his exhaustive research, he found those depending on plant foods for protein were able to achieve their height and weight potentials, even if it took a bit longer. Yet they remained free of degenerative diseases like cancer and heart disease, which eventually manifest in those who eat meat heavily.

In her book *Green for Life,* Victoria Boutenko mentions that dieticians have lumped greens in with other vegetables in their food charts, and so their high protein content has been largely hidden from us. Greens are a way to put on quality muscle since they contain pure amino acids freshly made by the sun as opposed to "secondhand" proteins from meat.

I would like to add here that my husband's biggest fear of eating raw was getting insufficient protein. He is a bodybuilder. He has been nearly 100% raw for close to four years now and realizes that his fear was unfounded. He lost weight initially and then gained most of it back. Although he does not weigh as much as he used to, he is stronger and can actually lift more weight than when he ate cooked food. (See Chapter 2.)

Won't I miss my comfort foods?

Because we often eat for emotional reasons, you may initially miss some of your favorite "comfort foods." However, as you learn to prepare some of the popular raw food recipes, including rich desserts and gourmet dishes, you will soon realize that raw foods can be equally comforting. Although they may not be what your mother fed you, you will soon find that eating things like delicious, raw, creamy, carob mousse will taste just as decadent as chocolate. Better yet, see the recipe for raw chocolate in Chapter 15. Even a few medjool dates will usually hit the spot.

Whenever you feel you need a special treat, you can buy a large-size juice from a juice bar. Just make sure they don't add anything like sugar, protein powder or yogurt. Buy that instead of the white chocolate mocha latté from Starbuck's. Or treat yourself to an organic melon, which might be too expensive to buy on a daily basis.

Since I became raw four years ago, the movement has caught on to such a degree that there are now tremendous numbers of gourmet raw packaged treats that can be purchased at health food stores or online. These are usually dehydrated and high in fat. They therefore should not be eaten as a dietary staple that replaces fresh, whole produce. But they do make wonderful comfort foods or treats.

What about my family? How can I ever get my family to eat my raw food dishes?

At first, when I told my husband I intended to become a raw fooder, he was very much opposed to it. "I will not eat a diet of rabbit food!" he complained. But he had to, by default, because I was the only one willing to do any food preparation.

I made sure the dinners were very elaborate and tasty so that I would not be tempted to return to cooked food myself. So of course, he also relished the raw gourmet "stir fry," raw "meatloaf" made of nuts and seeds, raw avocado salad dressing, raw carrot cake and all the other dishes I delighted in experimenting with.

After a few weeks, he grew very excited. "I have so much energy! I am never tired! I feel younger! We need to go all the way with this raw food thing!" Now he is even more fanatical than I am about staying 100% raw. So, I am convinced it is sometimes easier to make converts with the taste of the food than the logic behind the diet.

For those who have teenagers or kids, I recommend the recipe book *Eating without Heating*, written by two teens, Sergei and Valya Boutenko. Of course, written by kids, many of the recipes are for cakes, cookies, candies and raw burgers. But these use high quality ingredients: nutritious dates, honey, nuts, seeds and such. More delicious than any junk food, these are also quite valuable to the body.

For pre-adolescent children, involving them in the process of preparing raw food recipes will engage their interest. This is what Victoria Boutenko did, as her kids were only eight and nine years old when they started. She purchased for them their own blender, for example, so that they could make their own smoothies. When their friends visited them, they loved to "play" at making raw food dishes.

Make food a "game" for the kids, and make it look especially pretty, such as making a flower out of a tomato. Be creative and decorative, just as you would be with cooked food on special occasions. For example, make a face on an orange, using toothpicks to attach olives as eyes and berries to form a mouth.

If your kids get teased for being "different" because of their diet, invite their friends over for a party, lunch or picnic. They will love the raw goodies too, and your kids will gain new respect. You might even have to watch out for other kids wanting to trade lunches with them!

Remember to be gentle with your family. Pushing them will not convince them. Think of all the times someone preached to you about something. Did it make you want to do what they insisted you needed to do? Chances are you felt they were controlling you. Only your example of superior health, as well as superior food, will inspire them. Your partner is an adult and has to make his/her own decision.

As for your children, *you were the one who got them addicted to cooked food*. So, you can also condition them to eat healthfully. But don't expect them to change overnight. Instead, prepare scrumptious goodies that will win them over and gradually substitute "treats" and cooked dishes with raw ones, slowly increasing the number of raw snacks and main dishes.

In her book *I Live on Fruit*, Essie Honiball tells how she converted her husband to fruitarianism without being at all pushy or preachy. She started by serving him fruit with every meal, gradually replacing cooked food with more fruit. When one morning as a test she fed him a former favorite meal of eggs and ham without any fruit, his reaction was, "Do I have to eat this slop? Can't I just have fruit?"

Rhio explains in *Hooked on Raw* that she did the same thing with her boyfriend, serving him his cooked food and also some of her raw gourmet dishes until all he wanted was the raw food.

Tanya Zavasta cautions newly raw women: *Don't give up a good man just because he won't eat grass with you!*

If your family refuses to switch, stick with your own resolve to stay raw. Sooner or later they will catch on. Of course, it will not be easy at first if you have to prepare your own food plus the cooked dishes. But it has been done. If you stay 100% raw, the cooked food temptations will gradually dissipate. You might also strike a deal with your family that if they choose cooked food, they must contribute to most, or all, of its preparation, providing they are able.

A word of caution: If you decide to put your children on a 100% raw diet, I would advise against telling others. We live in a society in which "authorities" tend to interpret this as "child abuse." They have a way of believing that veganism is somehow bad, which it can be if kids are not getting sufficient Vitamin B_{12} and sunshine (Vitamin D).

If they are old enough, teach them to be discreet. When the "authorities" came knocking on the Boutenkos' door after hearing reports that the family was on a weird diet, the kids, who were home alone at the time, answered the caseworker's query with, "We just got back from Burger King!" After she left, satisfied that they were eating "nutritious" fast food like everyone else, the kids would jokingly refer to it as "Murder King."

Does my pet need to eat raw? If so, how can I get my pet to eat raw food?

Animals in the wild do not suffer degenerative diseases, but those eating table scraps or processed foods — bagged, canned or boxed — do. Such foods have been heated and had inorganic mineral supplements and preservatives added to them. Another reason is that owners wouldn't be able to stomach feeding their beloved pets such garbage if it weren't disguised by processing.

If your pet is young, it will naturally prefer raw food. If, however, you have gotten the poor creature addicted to cooked food, you will have to transition it back to raw. You cannot reason with it the way you can a human.

There are two possible methods to do this: the gradual way and the fasting method. With the first way, you will gradually mix raw food into their customary chow. For example, one week you might try 10%, then the next week, 20-30% raw. Eventually, your pet will be eating 100% raw. You will observe that its energy and vitality will increase. Its excrement will no longer stink! The animal itself will also not smell so bad, either.

Pets need live enzymes too, which is why they eat grass and even the excrement of other animals, which contain digestive enzymes. Often an animal will eat so much grass that it vomits. This is believed to be because it is detoxing too quickly. The same happens to people who drink excessive wheatgrass juice during transition to raw diets.

A quicker way to transition your pet would be to fast it on water for several days. This is something to consider, especially if it is sick. Even if it is healthy, fasting will speed up the detoxification from all the cooked food. You will not know how many days the creature needs to fast, and so it is best to put out fresh pieces of raw food for it after a couple days and let the pet decide when to break its fast.

I have a long-time raw food friend who once "cat-sat" for two obese cats. He decided to give them "tough love" and put them on a water fast! They lost weight, and one of them was converted to eating raw meat within three days.

However, when the owner returned from vacation, despite their admittedly healthier appearance, he decided it would be too much trouble to keep buying fresh, raw meat. So, the poor felines were forced to resume their former kibbles diet that had caused worms, indigestion and numerous vet visits for one of them. No doubt, they went back to being lazy and fat.

Whenever people or animals revert to cooked food, the change reminds me of the movie *Awakenings*, in which catatonic people were given a brief chance to live again but eventually had to go back to their former catatonic condition.

Bruno Comby points out that animals in the wild, eating natural diets, can remain very healthy despite harboring a virus that would greatly sicken the same animal living on processed foods designed for pets. He explains, *"The animal whose diet has not been changed fares better every time.* Again and again, one finds a kind of peaceful coexistence between the virus and the animal that eats a natural diet" (*Maximize Immunity*, p. 27). He also cites the case of a veterinarian who fed a natural diet to two cats, and after four months, there was a complete remission of "feline AIDS" in both cats.

If you are not convinced your pet needs to eat a raw diet, read the animal studies referenced in Chapter 5, especially the one on the cats. I showed this study to a good friend of mine about a year ago. She said it couldn't be true because her cats all ate processed food (which was organic, but still heat-treated), and her three cats were all very healthy. A year later when she complained about how sick they were and how much her vet bills were, I reminded her of the study. Now she wants to try the raw diet on her cats!

Another friend of mine spent a great deal of money to get orthodox drug treatment for her cat that came down with leukemia. The cat recovered, and my friend asked, "Now, how can you be so strongly opposed to drug treatment? Look at her; she is playing like a kitten!"

Six months later, the cat died of another form of cancer. This happens to humans all the time. Give them chemo or radiation, and one cancer goes away. Then, due to the resulting weakened condition of their bodies, a few years later another cancer kills them. This doesn't happen on raw food. The body strengthens and regenerates on a raw food diet. People and animals alike, once cured by the body's innate healing mechanism empowered by natural food, may live out their normal life spans even after full-blown cancer.

A woman I met at the 2004 Raw Food Festival in Portland, Oregon told the wonderful story of adopting a very sick dog, Pepper, which had also suffered burns. Veterinarians said he had a fatal disease. She fasted him, then fed him a 100% raw diet, and he recovered completely. He is still very healthy today. His story is found on www.healthyhealing.org. Unlike most people I have come across who feed their pets raw food, this dog owner was smart enough to get onto a raw diet herself!

One note of caution: Some of the meat you buy at the grocer's has been irradiated. If it comes in hermetically sealed plastic, your suspicions should be aroused, but the only way to tell for sure, since its appearance is often unchanged, is to talk with the store manager. You may have to go directly to a butcher to make sure the meat has not been irradiated. If it has been irradiated, it won't have enzymes or some of the other important nutrients of raw meat and will contain a new class of toxic compounds called radiolytic byproducts.

Aren't you hungry all the time?

Actually, I get hungry less often on a raw diet because my body is being better nourished. Before, I always felt hungry for something, usually not even knowing what.

Initially after switching to a raw diet, I often needed fat in my diet — nuts, avocados, olives, seeds, coconut butter — because fat stays in the stomach longer than carbohydrates. Now I can have nothing but juice all day and not feel hunger.

When we were cooked fooders, my husband would always crave two big platefuls of whatever we were eating. After we switched to raw, I marveled that one plate was usually enough for him. I figured it would be the opposite, that he would want more of the raw food. But his body was being fully nourished, and so he grew satisfied with less.

We have been eating raw for close to four years at the time of this writing and notice that our grocery bills have diminished, despite the use of more organic food, because our appetites and need for food have diminished.

This may sound unappealing because we Americans love to eat. But when eating a primarily raw diet, the desire for food diminishes naturally, and so there is no feeling of deprivation.

Famous model Carol Alt explains, "When I was eating cooked food and starving myself to stay thin as a model, I was very literally hungry almost all of the time. I am never hungry now. I eat all the time. I feel great. I have lots of energy. I'm thin now, but not hungry at all" (*Eating in the Raw*, p. 102).

If this diet is so great and healing, why doesn't my doctor know about it? Why isn't it all over the news?

Medical schools are funded primarily by pharmaceutical companies that have little interest in teaching future doctors about healing methods from which they will gain no profit. (See Appendix B.) Most doctors receive a matter of a few course hours of instruction in nutrition during the entire four years (or more) of medical school. They are taught that diet is not important to health and that drugs and surgeries must be their main tools.

A few doctors have heard about raw food healing but have been trained by their instructors to think of it as quackery. They ask if there is any research to prove the raw diet heals.

This is really a catch-22 situation because no one wants to fund the expensive research. _No one profits from this diet except the person who employs it_. Even organic farming is not a highly profitable industry unless done in high volume.

Also, doctors have invested all their adult lives in their method of pharmacology. It can be a radical ego blow to learn they have been on the wrong track, or at least, not on the highest track.

Guy-Claude Burger worked with a medical doctor who had lost his hearing in his left ear and couldn't move or feel anything in two of his fingers. The cardiac nerve that controlled his heartbeat was also seriously affected. After six months on the instinctive raw diet, he was back to normal. Yet Burger felt the doctor was _annoyed_ at his recovery because it proved to him that food was more important than medicine!

What most people don't realize too is the tremendous pressure medical doctors are under to maintain their status quo protocols. As Rev. George Malkmus says, "They find themselves in a very difficult dilemma because the laws protect them from the adverse side-effects and deaths that occur from the dispensing of drugs and the other accepted medical treatments. But if they prescribe God's Natural Laws and simple health principles to their patients, they can, in some states, lose their license to practice medicine, go to jail and be fined" (_God's Way to Ultimate Health_, p. 48).

One friend of mine was lamenting that the people in the raw food movement who get publicity are portrayed as "weird" and not "mainstream." I told her that even if there were a (pre-scandalous) "Martha Stewart" of the raw food movement, she would never get big and good publicity from the media. Trillions of dollars are at stake to keep the masses misinformed. It's really too bad that these major corporations couldn't channel their energies and money into the higher road of healing the planet, but that's the way it is, at least right now.

The raw food movement has always been a grassroots movement and probably always will be. It will never be promoted by mainstream government agencies or the corporate-controlled media. There are too many political and industrial interests involved in keeping people on the SAD that makes all too many people *feel* sad!

As Dr. David Darbro wrote in the foreword to Rev. Malk-mus' book *God's Way to Ultimate Health*, "Powerful political and economic forces exist throughout the land which thrive upon the public's health misfortunes. These vested interest groups, because of financial reasons, do not wish to see these people freed from disease and pain. They hire expensive lawyers, influence the media, and bitterly oppose those who say there is a better way."

Dieticians and nutritionists also receive their fair share of brainwashing. Food companies, such as the sugar industry, often subsidize university nutrition departments the way drug companies support medical schools. (See Appendices A and B.) Look at the food served to hospital patients! One friend of mine who considered becoming a nutritionist remarked, "I don't want to go to school only to prescribe Jell-O to hospital patients."

As for the news media, newspapers and television treat the raw food movement as an eccentric fad or oddity rather than the real solution to many of our physical, mental and societal problems that it is. This is understandable when you ask who funds the advertisements that ultimately fund the media. TV, newspapers and magazines are largely funded by pharmaceutical corporations, restaurants and processed-food companies through their advertising.

These companies also prepare press releases with "news stories" by "experts" touting the latest drug or processed-food product. Such releases are often shown on the news, actually becoming free commercials for the sponsoring company! This is done mainly because people will believe a seemingly "objective" news story more readily than a paid advertisement.

The main thing that is helping people find out the truth about how drugs and foods affect our health is the Internet since people can erect web sites at little cost. Big money is not necessary. Before the Net, the only people who really had freedom of speech were those who owned the mass media or controlled them with money. Now the big corporations are even trying to buy out the Internet, our last vestige of free speech. The government is threatening to use "terrorism" as an excuse to censor it!

Personal-care product companies are also major players in the media industry, and of course they would be none too happy if the healing power of the raw diet ever caught on. Who would need drugs? Who would buy Coca-Cola? Who would even need deodorant or mouthwash after a few years of detoxifying?

And because a raw food diet makes one ever more health-conscious, many other products would also lose their markets: toxic cleaning products, shampoo or toothpaste with toxic ingredients and so on.

Moreover, after a year or two of eating raw diets, many people no longer care to watch much TV, preferring instead to use that time tending to their gardens, growing their own food, spending quality time with their families, taking hikes in the wilderness, indulging in creative projects or writing books to tell others about the miracles of eating raw food.

Cooking is deeply ingrained in the psyches of everyone everywhere. People don't want to give up their favorite foods. Addiction can be blinding to even the most sincere seekers of health and the fountain of youth. Most people will scoff at the idea of a raw food diet's healing power, even relegating it to quackery, rather than give up their potatoes, hamburgers, steaks, pasta, convenience foods, popcorn and the rest.

Finally, the idea that one can heal herself with natural food sounds rather simplistic. Most people think life is cruel. *We are meant to suffer and fall ill.* Scientists believe they must create the elixir of health in a chemical lab, and the public think they must pay huge sums of money for health care. In her book on her own raw food recovery from cancer, Dr. Nolfi quotes Goethe: "Mankind is annoyed because the truth is so simple."

Don't wait for scientific research to confirm these truths! What good will it do you if, fifteen years from now, it is mainstream knowledge, but you are six feet under?

Don't you miss eating something warm?

At first I missed hot food. I would eat things straight from the dehydrator, just to get the warmth. But later I no longer did. I was about 95% raw my first year. Sometimes I would eat a baked potato while dining out. Often, after a few months, the heat annoyed me, and I would wait for it to cool down to room temperature to eat it.

Heat actually harms the gastric mucus lining. After a few months of eating raw, I found the heat annoying to my tender lips and the tissues of my mouth lining.

We associate warmth of food with comfort. But this association can be easily broken.

Shouldn't I wait until the summer, or at least spring, to begin eating raw? Won't I be too cold eating raw in the winter?

For psychological reasons, people think they need hot food to warm them up in the winter, making it too difficult to eat only raw food in the winter. By such logic, however, one would never eat *hot food* during the *summer*!

In all fairness, people in transition often do feel chilled. However, these same people may feel that same chilliness even in the summer if they decide to transition during that season.

This feeling of chill is believed to be part of the healing process, as the body is directing the blood, warmth, oxygen and nutrients inward to heal the most vital organs and tissues first, cleansing and rebuilding the body from the inside out. It disappears in time, the length depending on the individual's state of health going in. In my case, it only lasted about a month. It is definitely profound, however, when fasting.

Jan Dries writes, "What is important about the thermodynamic aspect is that it stabilizes the central temperature by activating the capillaries. Both the organs and the tissues receive more blood, larger quantities of oxygen, warmth and nutrition, while the discharge of homotoxins improves. In the beginning, switching over to the diet can lead to chills, but only until the thermoregulation has adjusted itself" (*The Dries Cancer Diet*, p. 184).

Dr. Gabriel Cousens writes that he felt somewhat colder on raw foods until the second or third year, after which he grew comfortably warm and could even go out barefoot in the frost. He also met some raw fooders in Alaska who reported feeling warmer in the cold Alaskan winters after being on a raw diet for some time.

Victoria Boutenko wrote about this topic and explained that a hot meal, cup of coffee or even a shot of ice-cold vodka warms up the body a bit via the same mechanism: They are toxins that the body is trying to get rid of. In the process, they irritate the adrenals, which respond by producing epinephrine, norepinephrine and a variety of steroid hormones.

"These hormones stimulate our sympathetic nervous system, which is why we feel awake at first. They also force our heart to beat faster and to pump larger amounts of blood through our body, which makes us feel warm. This feeling doesn't last long, and we pay a high price for it. After 10-15 minutes, our body gets exhausted from performing extra work."

She goes on to explain that over the long haul, the weakened adrenals leave you feeling colder, which is why older people have to wear sweaters even in the summer. Conversely, by healing yourself with a raw food diet, you become better able to tolerate extreme cold much better. So, to feel warm, you should actually eat a raw diet!

Eighty percent of all blood in the body is in the capillaries and only 20% in the arteries. If the capillaries are clogged by cooked food remnants, the blood doesn't circulate efficiently. If the blood is cleansed by a 100% raw diet, circulation increases, along with tolerance to cold weather. Boutenko writes further that her raw family jumps into icy-cold mountain rivers year round, sleeps outside under the rain or snow, and her son even goes snowboarding wearing only shorts.

In *Fruit: The Food and Medicine for Man*, the author quotes one Dr. Barbara Moore as follows, "I have found that neither energy nor heat of the body comes from food."

She goes on to relate that she spent three months in the mountains of Switzerland and Italy, eating nothing but snow and water, yet walking 15 miles to the foot of the mountain and climbing to at least seven or eight thousand feet. Then she would come down and walk another 20 miles to her hotel. She did this year after year, but found that she could not do this in civilization because the air was not pure enough.

Additionally, Iranian American Arshavir Ter Hovannessian, author of *Raw Eating*, regularly slept outdoors without feeling too cold.

People also report being able to tolerate heat and humidity better. In general, a raw diet enables one to better tolerate both temperature extremes. This is why we never see wild animals with coats or air conditioners.

Acupuncturists I know will think I am a heretic for believing in a raw food diet since Chinese medicine advocates the macrobiotic diet, a diet of whole foods, most of which are cooked, especially when a patient has what is termed a "cold condition" (not to be confused with the common cold).

My former partner in an acupuncture business, in fact, asked me how I could promote a diet that went against the ancient Chinese tradition. I pointed out what one of our teachers once said. He had asked a Chinese acupuncturist master why they had the liver pulse on the left hand when the liver organ is located on the right side of the body. "We were wrong," was the humble reply of the Chinese master.

If they were wrong about that, then they could also be wrong about their diet. And it is not just the Chinese; virtually every culture has been entrenched in cooked food culinary arts for tens of thousands of years.

Nutritionist, author and raw food chef Brigitte Mars has a lot to say on the topic. She studied Chinese herbalism under Michael Tierra and Bob Flaws, two of the American masters in the field. When she went raw several decades ago, they warned her about eating cold food in a cold climate, and so she switched back to cooked food.

Decades later, her daughter went raw. At first, she felt a need to rescue her daughter from this "error," but then she began to wonder, "If the diet in the health food stores is so great, why are there so many supplements for sale there? And if the Chinese diet is so great, why do they need so many herbs?"

So she again took up the raw diet and noticed that she actually began to feel *less cold* than usual because her circulation had improved. She now declares, "Raw food is the perfect marriage between yin and yang." She explains this is because "yin" represents (among other things) the fluids, and "yang" represents (among other things) the life force and energy. Cooking destroys both of these in the food.

Joe Alexander has some interesting comments about people who use climate to delay their journey to raw diets (*Blatant Raw Foodist Propaganda!* pp. 116-117, quoted with permission):

> I have met many people who say that they would like to live on raw food if they lived in a warm climate, but it is too cold where they live. When I lived in Canada, I met such people. Then in Northern California, where there is hardly any winter at all, compared to Canada, I met people who said it was too cold there to be a raw fooder. Now here in Arkansas, which, to me, coming from Canada, is like a tropical jungle, I still meet people who say it is too cold here to be a raw fooder. And when I have visited the area around Austin, Texas, which is so far south that I was able to stand outside all day painting a landscape between Christmas and New Years, I still met people who said it was too cold there to be a raw fooder, which makes me wonder where these people think it is warm enough to be a raw fooder — the center of the sun maybe?

I have never had problems being a raw food eater in cold weather. In fact, it helps me stand cold weather better. As a cooked food eater, my hands and lips used to crack and bleed when it got cold. That doesn't happen when I stay on raw food. And I have more energy to run around and be active to generate body heat. There are millions of wild animals living in Canada. Every one of them is a 100% raw food eater. So what makes people think they are special and need cooked food? Eating raw food doesn't mean you have to eat it ice cold from the refrigerator. You can warm it up to room temperature or body temperature. Anthropologists have apparently discovered that cooking began in northern Europe, where people would put frozen foods over a fire to thaw them out. Fine. Then they got careless and left them over the fire too long, and that's when our troubles began.

Conversely, raw food diet helps me to stand extremely hot weather better, too.

All that having been said, I can suggest ways to cope with the winter cold better during and after transition to raw eating. When indoors, add more clothing layers or blankets; turn up the thermostat; take your food out of the refrigerator a couple hours before you eat it to let it warm up to room temperature; and exercise until you sweat whenever you still feel cold.

Spend some time daily outdoors running, jogging, or walking briskly. The heat of exercise will warm your body. Prepare for the cold season by exercising outside in the fall long enough each day to work up a sweat, wearing as little as possible to permit your bare skin to adjust to colder temperatures. You will be surprised at the difference this makes.

Why does cooked food seem to taste better?

Cooked food does *not* taste as good as raw food once you have successfully transitioned to a 100% raw diet. However, at first, during the first few months or even the first year, there may be some cooked foods you miss or even give in to the temptation to eat. But if you allow your tastebuds time to adjust, you will eventually come to prefer raw food over cooked.

For example, I used to love a spicy, baked, carrot cake. But once I tried the raw carrot cake recipe in Juliano's *Raw: The Uncook Book*, I was delighted with it. People get so excited when they find a baked cake that is moist. Baking dehydrates nearly all of the moisture from a cake. But a raw cake is always very moist. There is no comparison!

Cooked food is caramelized from the interaction of heated sugars and amino acids. Even though these are toxic, mutagenic substances, they taste good to jaded appetites.

Cooking also releases very strong aromas, making the food smell stronger, and much of what we think is taste is actually smell. As we have observed with instinctive eaters, our instincts associate smell with desire to eat. Instinctively, we associate strong-smelling food with its nutritional value. Cooked foods have much stronger aromas because the heat disperses food molecules into the air. So the smell of cooked food deceives us. However, I suspect that as the heat disperses aromas into the air, much of the flavor is also being dispersed. Arnold Ehret opined that cooking sends the most vital nutrients out of the food and into the atmosphere!

Cooked, processed foods often contain additives and flavor enhancers, many being unsafe excitotoxins like MSG and aspartame, as explained in Appendix A. Food companies add these to their foods to make them addictive.

Dairy, wheat and sugar are put into nearly all processed foods for their subtle, sometimes not so subtle, addictive qualities. Unfortunately, after decades of eating food strongly overwhelmed with condiments, spices, additives and artificial flavorings, our over-stimulated tastebuds can barely discern the delicate natural flavors of raw foods.

The main reason cooked food tastes good is because we have been conditioned to believe so. If you take a baby and wean her from mother's milk with cooked, processed, commercialized baby food as most mothers do, chances are she will spit out the food repeatedly. If forced to eat dead food, she will likely cry. Only after repeated attempts at rejection will she give in.

Instinctively, she knows it is not good, doesn't taste good, and isn't good for her. She may cry, get rashes, and fall ill, but eventually her body gives up struggling against it and attempts to adjust to it. It's "eat this awful stuff my mother is forcing on me or starve."

Those feeding their babies a 100% raw food diet have observed that they go through none of these stages and in fact avoid all the childhood illnesses thought to be "normal," such as rashes, earaches, fevers, frequent colds and the like, even named diseases like mumps, chicken pox and measles, without the need for vaccinations.

Cooked food is addictive and disturbs our normal instincts. As Guy-Claude Burger says, after one has been eating "initial foods" and then eats a bit of cooked food, one is soon "completely taken over by cooking. Cooked foods jam the instincts, overload the body, and make initial foods quickly lose their appeal; one compensates by adding more cooked foods, and it soon turns into a vicious cycle." He reports that the pleasure of raw, whole foods is much more complete and intense than that of cooked foods, but not at first. It takes time and occurs only after not having eaten cooked food for some time.

Finally, eating hot foods burns off your tastebuds! When you stop destroying tastebuds, food will begin to offer much more flavor as the tastebuds regenerate.

Doesn't cooking result in better digestion and allow for absorption of certain nutrients?

Once you are accustomed to the raw diet, you will find uncooked food is easiest to digest. After all, raw, living food has food enzymes within it to assist in its own digestion, whereas cooked food pulls much more from your body's limited ability to produce these enzymes. This is why you feel fatigue after a cooked meal, but light after a raw one.

People mistakenly think that raw food is hard to digest because they may have some initial difficulty. The truth is that their "digestive fire" has been weakened by so many decades of eating cooked food. Thus, they may experience some gas or stomachache. Or they may experience diarrhea, which is a sign that their bodies are detoxifying — which is good!

People who begin raw diets in their forties or older often would do well to eat their vegetables in raw, blended soups or juice them, making them easier to digest. With time, their digestive systems will strengthen, and they can eat more raw vegetables. (See the Roseburg study in Chapter 5.)

Even experienced raw fooders may have to limit their intake of raw vegetables that are difficult to digest, such as broccoli or cabbage. Some people do not consider raw vegetables an "original food" but believe we started eating them only since 10,000-20,000 years ago when civilization and agriculture began. Vegetables contain a lot of cellulose, which is not always easy to have in your digestive system unless you are a cow. Such fiber may cause stomach bloating.

Yes, cooking will make it easier to absorb certain nutrients from broccoli and cabbage, but it also destroys most of the other nutrients and creates toxic byproducts. Better to avoid certain vegetables entirely, getting nutrients from fruit and other raw foods, than to eat them cooked!

Media reporters always have to show a "downside" in order to display their "objectivity." In nearly every newspaper or magazine article I have read about the raw food movement, the authors use as an example that cooked tomatoes allow for more lycopene absorption. But what about the Vitamin C and other nutrients destroyed in the cooked tomato? What about the toxins that go along with the cooked tomato?

The reduced lycopene concentration in raw tomatoes does not warrant cooking, especially since there are many ways to get sufficient lycopene, such as eating watermelon or strawberries. According to Dr. Atkins, *blending* the raw tomatoes releases the lycopene just as well as *heating* them anyhow.

Another example sometimes cited to indicate the superiority of cooked food is that cooking a carrot softens the tough cellulose cell wall, thus enabling more absorption of beta-carotene. Yet cooking the carrot denatures or destroys other nutrients, such as Vitamin C, and completely kills all the enzymes.

One solution to this pseudo-problem would be to blend the carrot in a heavy-duty blender, which breaks down the bulk of the cellulose cell walls without destroying nutrients.

Another criticism of raw food is that cooking starches converts them to sugars that are easier to digest. While this is true, vitamins, minerals and enzymes are destroyed and toxic by-products produced, as discussed in Chapter 6. Besides, given the obesity rampant in many "civilized" countries, maybe some of the calories in these starchy foods are best left undigested and unassimilated. Many raw fooders believe that starchy foods, such as beans, rice and many grains, are simply not our genetically ideal foods to begin with and better left to the birds!

George Meinig writes, "There is a common misconception that cooking makes food more digestible. While this is true in a few isolated instances, on the whole it is utterly false. Cooking or heating often makes a bad food safe to eat, but it never makes it a better food."

He goes on to suggest taking the following test: Eat some cooked corn and notice the undigested corn kernels in your stools. Then eat the corn fresh from the cob without cooking it. This time you will not see as much undigested corn. Go to www.price-pottenger.org/articles/rawfoods.htm for his article.

What if I just *have to* eat some cooked foods? Which ones are the least bad?

If you find yourself in a situation in which you must eat cooked food, wok cooking and steaming are preferred, as much of the insides of those foods will still contain enzymes. Boiling would be acceptable, as far as cooking goes, if you then drink the cooking water, where many of the nutrients went. But food cooked at very high temperatures, prepared by deep-frying, barbecuing, pressure-cooking, grilling and baking, is best avoided. The resulting advanced glycation end products are very toxic.

Probably the worst form of cooking is microwaving, which severely deranges food molecules, creating a toxic mess! Dr. Hans Hertel of Switzerland carried out a small, but well-controlled, study on the effects of eating microwaved food and was fired from his job as a food scientist because of it.

He learned from his experiment that microwaved food causes abnormal changes in human blood and the immune system. Additionally, microwave appliance leakage, which often goes undetected, can cause skin cancer, birth defects, cataracts, dizziness, headaches and blood disorders.

If you must eat cooked foods, try to eliminate the very worst ones, such as dairy, wheat, processed foods, cooked meat and table salt. (See Appendix A.)

Try to eat only one cooked food per meal. That would mean, for example, cooked eggs but no cooked cheese mixed in. Eating simply like this will aid digestion. Always have a salad with it, along with enzyme supplements or unheated honey, which is rich in enzymes. If you choose to have only one cooked item per day, eat it in the evening so you can still feel light and energetic throughout the day.

Finally, carry enzyme supplements with you so you can take a dozen or so before eating any cooked food. Honey may be even richer in useful enzymes; so carry a small container of unheated honey to restaurants or parties.

If raw food isn't available, isn't it better to eat cooked food than to eat no food?

Guy-Claude Burger ran an experiment with some field mice. One group was fattened up with cooked food. The other was lean, having been fed only raw food. Then he enforced a "famine," fasting them on water for some time. One might think that the cooked food eaters, being fatter, would have withstood the famine better, having more body fat to live on.

However, when eating was resumed, the cooked eaters didn't fare as well, and some even died, whereas none of the raw eaters died. His conclusion was that the stored fats from cooked food are toxic, which make them lose any advantage they might provide during a famine.

Of course, in a prolonged famine in which one is faced with death from months of starvation, it might be wise to compromise on a 100% raw diet if given the chance to eat cooked food. Hopefully, few of us will ever face such drastic situations.

From a raw food chat room, I did hear of a 100% raw woman imprisoned unjustly for being a whistleblower. She chose to water fast rather than eat the prison food! She managed to get released on bail before having to eat anything cooked.

I also know of long-term raw fooders who find it much more appealing to fast a few days when there is no raw food around.

Isn't there a danger of bacteria in raw food?

Raw food is not dangerous. Bacteria, such as salmonella, are present in small quantities in all foods. As explained in Chapter 4, bacteria and other microscopic "critters" are only dangerous to a body with a weakened immune system — a toxic environment. If bacteria were so dangerous as we have been brainwashed to believe, why aren't all the wild animals dropping dead from bacterial infections? They have no stoves and no means of sterilizing their food.

Humans, on the other hand, eat very little raw food and have lost much of their immunity to bacteria. Their defense systems are weakened. The whole obsession with the "war on germs" has led to a very weakened population. We actually need to replenish ourselves with good bacteria by eating raw food!

You may get ill from food bacteria if you have an untrained defense system from having eaten too few raw foods or having destroyed too many friendly bacteria with excessive antibiotics.

You can also be harmed by consuming foods containing far too many bacteria of the wrong types. Such food would smell rancid and might even look spoiled and partially decomposed.

Bacteria are in you and all around you. There is no way to get rid of bacteria unless, as Aajonus Vonderplanitz says, you cook yourself to death! All the evidence to date points to the fact that humans and other animals have adapted to bacteria and other microorganisms through millions of years of cohabitation with them. But we have not adapted to the thousands of years of cooked food. The foreign molecules created in heating food are dangerous to us.

As explained in Appendix C, however, raw animal foods, such as meat, dairy and eggs have the potential to contain much, much more pathogenic bacteria than raw plant food.

Does this diet cost more money?

Initially, after you switch to organic produce, you may become alarmed at the amount of money you are spending. (Review Chapter 12 for a list of reasons to eat only organic.) Yet you will spend far less than eating out. You will save a lot by not buying meat. You will also save the cost of buying processed, prepared foods. After a few years of eating a raw diet, you will need to eat far less. Review Chapter 1, point 6 ("Economy") for more information. But in general, good, raw, organic food *is* more expensive than junky, processed, dead food made mostly out of grains.

Your body is worth it. You wouldn't put junk in your gas tank, and your body is the only vehicle your consciousness or soul has in this lifetime.

Can I drink alcohol?

Of course, alcohol is toxic, killing brain and liver cells, but if you want to enjoy an occasional drink, drink organic wine. Wine is fermented and has enzymes to help digest at least the non-alcoholic part of it. Non-organic wine is full of toxic sulfites, which may disturb your sleep and give you a hangover.

Be aware that you will not be able to handle as much alcohol as you used to. It will go through you faster since your body is more efficient at detoxifying. It also may interfere with your sleep, especially if you eat food along with it.

Guy-Claude Burger says, "There are better things than that [wine]. Fermented coconut milk, for instance — it's light, sweet, pungent and pleasantly alcoholic. It tastes better than champagne when instincts like it."

I also have found that a bit of kombucha tea, a raw drink of fermented mushrooms, satisfies my desire for a drink. There is just a tiny bit of alcohol in it.

One thing to consider about drinking alcohol: If you drink enough of it to impair your judgment, you may lose your will to avoid eating cooked food.

Victoria Boutenko reminded us in a lecture that no matter how much money we pay for that organic wine, alcohol is the one "food" item highest in acidity!

Can I drink tea or coffee?

Some raw fooders are not ready to give up other addictions, such as cigarettes or coffee. Joe Alexander said that even as a raw fooder he was addicted to coffee until he got an ulcer from it. He defends the use of hot drinks, including vegetable broth from boiled vegetables, saying, "My experience is that drinks consisting almost entirely of boiled water don't spoil the raw food high" (*Blatant Raw Foodist Propaganda!* p. 117).

Many report that these desires fade away on their own. As your body becomes more pure, even one cup of coffee a day can feel very toxic and acidic. Some raw fooders enjoy a cup of green tea, although drinking caffeine is less than ideal. Others enjoy herbal tea. Some wean themselves from coffee and tea but drink warm water with lemon, which is quite cleansing.

According to Frédéric Patenaude, "Anything liquid is better than anything solid, as far as cooked food is concerned, and with few exceptions. Solid food has to be turned into a liquid for your body to absorb it. ... Tea, while not viewed as a 'living' food, is nothing more than herbal flavoring steeped in warm water" (*The Sunfood Cuisine*, p. 220).

Personally, I have found the psychological addiction to a hot drink (especially containing caffeine) much harder to give up than cooked food. When I went raw, I gave up coffee and switched to the milder organic green tea for my morning brew. Later, I had to wean myself off green tea after learning that both green and black teas contain high concentrations of fluoride, which causes osteoarthritis and hypothyroidism, along with other maladies. Since making this discovery, I sometimes have yerba mate. I also occasionally indulge in a cup of coffee, half decaf.

I enjoy occasional herbal tea as well but find that I can no longer tolerate those with "spices" or "natural flavorings" in them, as I get a reaction like the one I get after accidentally ingesting MSG, which is often hidden in the most innocuous-sounding ingredients.

Be sure to drink your hot brew plain or sweetened with unheated honey — after the drink cools a bit — or stevia. If available, use raw cream instead of pasteurized. If not available, use nut milk.

Nonetheless, the goal should be to eventually wean oneself off hot drinks. According to a study in the British medical journal *Lancet*, hot beverages and food irritate the throat and tongue and are associated with increased throat and tongue cancers (*Lancet*, Dec. 1973, p. 1503). According to the author, Dr. McCluskey, we should dip our little finger in the hot drink for ten seconds and drink only if the finger is not scalded. Another *Lancet* study, cited in *Life in the 21st Century*, associates drinking hot beverages with gastric enzymatic abnormalities.

Be aware that coffee, even decaffeinated, and tea are also very acidic and mucus-forming. This is the biggest price to pay. If I indulge in an occasional cup of brew, I feel the adverse effects within an hour and sometimes immediately.

Another big price to pay by drinking hot drinks: Your taste-buds continue to be burned off, just as they are with cooked foods; so you never really get to experience the full flavor of food that a strict raw fooder does.

A final word about hot drinks that contain caffeine: Caffeine is a potent addictive substance. Most people are unaware of just how bad it is. Stephen Cherniske explains in his book *Caffeine Blues* that this seemingly innocent drink can create a very unhealthy condition within the body.

Caffeine causes energy swings, fatigue, depression, headaches, diarrhea, tension in the neck, PMS, fibrocystic breast disease, insomnia, anxiety, tooth grinding, irritability, irregular and accelerated heartbeat, ulcers, memory loss, ringing in the ears, panic attacks, osteoporosis and anemia.

It also causes high blood pressure. In fact, I know someone who used a lot of coffee to pump up his blood pressure so he would fail the medical test after being drafted to Viet Nam: It worked!

It can even lead to heart attacks. It raises blood levels of cortisol, which lowers levels of the hormone DHEA, thereby accelerating aging. Because it increases cortisol, it accelerates the progression of AIDS. It is perhaps the main cause of chronic fatigue rampant in America because it interferes with the deepest stage of sleep, exhausts the adrenals, and causes blood sugar abnormalities.

Think about that the next time you pass by a Starbuck's!

Can I eat frozen foods?

Freezing destroys 30-60% of the enzymes in fruit; so eating them frozen is not really ideal. However, during the transition period, a frozen banana can satisfy the urge for ice cream. It tastes wonderful in a smoothie.

The enzymes in frozen foods without much water content, such as nuts, are more immune to destruction; so it is not so bad to freeze nuts as it is fruit. Nuts do not contain water.

Unlike most other chemical compounds that contract when they freeze, water expands as it forms ice, and the tiny ice crystals in all cells that contain water are like little bombs going off inside the food. These destroy enzymes, vitamins and all sorts of other molecules. Therefore, nuts, seeds and dehydrated foods are not much damaged by freezing, and their enzymes are not destroyed because they have no water. If you freeze a sunflower seed, it will still sprout later. Try it!

If you want to maximize the nutrients in frozen fruit, dehydrate it first. Of course, doing so will cause it to lose that creamy texture reminiscent of ice cream.

What do *you* eat?

It always seems so funny when, after I tell someone I am a raw fooder, her face scrunches up in bewilderment and she asks, *"What do you eat?!"*

This makes me laugh because we have gotten so far from natural food that most people cannot even imagine going without processed, refined or cooked food.

So I answer with whatever happens to be my routine at the time. But in the years spent researching and writing this book, I have had to revise this section about three or four times because I keep changing my eating habits, fine-tuning them.

This is what I wrote a few years ago:

> Usually, I have fruit with nuts for breakfast. Later I had heard that this was 'bad food combining,' so decided to just have fruit. But then I found I got very hungry soon after. So I went back to the raw trail mix idea of fruit and nuts.

In proper food combination, fruit should be eaten alone or 20-30 minutes before another food, but if the fruit is dehydrated it seems to work okay. The nuts slow down the fruit's digestion so that I don't get hypoglycemic reactions. The fat in the nuts stays in my stomach for hours, and so I don't get hungry. It works out fine. Just be sure to floss after eating dehydrated fruit, as it can get stuck in the teeth, feeding bacteria.

For a snack, I have about 10-20 raw olives or maybe more fruit.

For lunch, I have a salad. At first, I used to make elaborate raw salad dressings. After a few months, I got tired of that and simplified things by just having a mixed green salad with a cucumber and avocado. The fat in the avocado kept me full until I got home for my mid-afternoon snack.

For my late snack, I may have a smoothie. Or, I may have flaxseed crackers with nut butter. Sometimes I put honey on it, and it tastes like the peanut-butter-and-honey sandwich that my mother used to make.

For dinner, I will have a raw food recipe dish. Often, I will make a simple dish or eat leftovers from the day before. Sometimes, however, I will not be in the mood to plan or prepare a meal for days or even weeks. In that case, I will just munch on more olives, nuts, fruits or vegetables.

Now for my updated version: Like so many raw fooders, I have found that I require and crave much less fat than when I initially switched to raw. I have found that I can get through a stressful workday with relative ease if I eat almost no fat until dinner.

So I start the day with a green juice mixed with cayenne powder to wake me up. It works as well as caffeine without the downside! Or I have the "Super Smoothie" that is listed in the recipe section in Chapter 15.

For a snack, I love my chocolate. (See recipe in Chapter 15.) Raw chocolate gives the brain a boost and is a natural re-uptaker of neurotransmitters. It is Nature's Prozac, and I feel it! With raw chocolate, I get an emotional, as well as mental, boost. It's funny, because cooked chocolate, usually processed with milk and sugar, never did anything for my brain or emotions, and I didn't even like the taste.

For lunch, I will have a salad with minimal or no dressing or other fat. Sometimes I will put a few olives or soaked and dehydrated sunflower seeds in it to spark up the taste.

For dinner, I will have raw soup or whatever leftover gourmet dishes I have around from the weekend. I sometimes go out to eat, now that more places serve raw entrées.

I used to eat popcorn at movies. My first year of raw food, I was only 90-95% raw, and so I smuggled in some dry air popped popcorn, as the theaters sell only popcorn loaded with MSG. Later it seemed too bland, and I realized it was just the habit of eating little bits of food while in a movie that mattered to me. So now I smuggle in cherry tomatoes, olives, flax crackers, sprouts, baby carrots or even a bag of raw, organic greens!

My diet is slowly becoming more simplified. It is always evolving. Currently, I prepare or eat the fancy gourmet dishes only when I have guests or attend a potluck. I enjoy the time saved by not fixing food and therefore have time for other activities, such as writing this book!

A lot of times, I just relish an avocado or a couple of pieces of produce. It might not sound exciting to you, but it tastes great. Furthermore, as I become healthier, less and less of my excitement in life depends on food.

Shortly before going to press with this book, I read Victoria Boutenko's *Green for Life* and have begun experimenting with a gallon of green smoothies every day. By the time you eat that, there isn't much room for anything else. I have enjoyed much more alkalinity, weight loss and a feeling of well-being. I plan to make this the mainstay of my diet.

Why should I go on a raw diet if I am young and healthy?

Many people think they are quite healthy already and thus do not need a raw food diet. Some people I counsel say that they will wait until they are older. This is especially true with young people, who produce so many hormones and enzymes that even though they eat a diet of 90% cooked food, they maintain a surplus of energy.

But I always tell them, *"If you feel great now, just think of how much better you would feel on a raw diet!"* and, "You are only 20-something now. What if you could look and feel the same, or only slightly older, when you are in your 50s?" And, "Just think of the edge you'll have at work!"

Indeed, I marvel at what I might have accomplished in life had I learned about this diet several decades ago!

One's life goals on a raw diet typically change for the better. One gets in closer touch with her true nature. Mental or emotional problems get solved that otherwise wouldn't. This is an especially important factor for young people who are struggling to find meaning in their lives.

If you want to *remain* young and healthy, this is the secret. I surely wish I had discovered this secret when I was in my twenties or even younger! This diet not only prevents disease but also slows aging. I have *seen* people who are in their 50s who started this diet in their 20s; so I *know* this is a fact.

Moreover, there are higher levels of health to be attained, as mentioned in Chapter 1. It is truly an adventure to see how much you can improve your health. Your vision can improve; you can lessen your need for sleep; and you can heighten your senses. Your athletic abilities can be further enhanced. Perhaps best of all, you can experience a deeper spiritual awakening.

It is exciting to be on the cutting edge of health! We have been poisoned and held back by cooked food for so many generations that we raw fooders are all pioneers in this arena. Indeed, we have barely tapped into our "health potential."

Can I start this diet while pregnant?

One school of thought claims that while the raw diet is an excellent way to cleanse the body and prepare for pregnancy, as well as a superior way to eat while pregnant once you have already cleansed, pregnancy is not the best time to start.

The argument is that while you are heavily detoxifying, you may stir up toxins that will cross the placenta and affect the fetus. The more toxic accumulation you have stored in your body, the greater the danger. But even those who conservatively take this stance will agree that you may begin a *60% raw* diet while pregnant since such a diet will benefit you and your unborn child while not stirring up many toxins.

On the other hand, there are those who say it is safer for the baby as well as the mother to begin a 100% raw diet while pregnant than to continue eating cooked food.

Indeed, there are people who began nearly all-raw diets while pregnant and delivered very healthy babies. (See Chapter 2.) The reasoning here is that toxins from the daily incoming cooked food would otherwise cross the placenta and injure the fetus.

In fact, a recent study of the umbilical cord blood of ten American newborns commissioned by the Environmental Working Group proved that pesticides and other chemicals are found in the blood of newborns. The analysis found 287 chemicals, and the babies averaged 200 contaminants each!

Ideally one should come to pregnancy having already been raw and cleansed for years. But that is not always possible, as in the case of unplanned pregnancy. In such a case, there are those who feel pregnancy is nonetheless *a great time* for a woman to go raw. Food instincts become sharpened and clear-cut as the mother's body tries to build the best possible nest for the incubating fetus. If the well-known food cravings that occur during pregnancy are satisfied in the context of whole, fresh, raw food choices only, a woman would be most likely to succeed as a disciple of the instinctive nutrition branch of raw foodism. (See Appendix C.)

For example, a pregnant woman may crave pickles or potato chips because the body knows that more sodium is needed during pregnancy and is suggesting foods that it "remembers" as being high in what's needed. But if raw foods that are naturally high in sodium, such as celery, spinach or seaweed, are presented for smell/taste testing, the mother's body will likely choose one of those instead.

The morning sickness problem has a ready-made solution in Natural Hygiene, which is fasting! The nausea is the body's only way of communicating its desire to stop the feeding process while it proceeds to clean house. Any form of eating while a major cleanup operation is in progress would just interfere with it, and the body often responds by immediately ejecting these intrusions via vomiting.

While the body is thus loudly proclaiming the need for a fast, the woman's rational mind, the one that always gets us into such trouble, is fearful that she would be starving the fetus by fasting. Wrong! There is a reason that morning sickness is primarily limited to the first trimester of pregnancy when the size of the embryo/fetus is smaller than a marble. Sure, it's growing, but the fasting mother's stored up nutritional reserves are more than adequate to meet the challenge of feeding such a tiny being.

The reason this nausea occurs in the morning is because the body had already entered fasting mode overnight during sleep. It has found projects to work on that it wants to complete. Ideally, the woman would repair back to bed and stay there until this feeling of nausea passed, however long it took, and a clear-cut call for food came from her body.

Some people fear that episodic detox reactions induced by a sudden switch to raw foods might poison the fetus and cause a miscarriage. These people do not understand the nature of detox reactions, which are merely symptoms of the healing process in action. The real danger lies in continuing to eat in the old, habitual, toxic way, which continues to poison the fetus throughout the entire pregnancy period.

The bloodstream detoxifies very rapidly once a shift to raw foods occurs. It is this purified bloodstream that permits gradual dissolution of excess fat tissue and other sequestered toxic matter slowly into the blood and lymph and elimination via the kidneys and bowels, thus eventually removing impediments to the proper functioning of all the body's tissues and organs.

This deeper level of detoxification may take months or years to complete, but while it is in progress, the mother's bloodstream is still in a purer condition than it would have been had she done nothing to reform her diet.

Is it advisable for a lactating mother to go raw?

It is true that infants have been known to refuse the nipple at times when the raw-eating mother is going through an acute detoxification crisis. This is because some of those toxins are being ejected into the milk, souring its taste, but these episodes are only temporary, whereas the quality of the milk that follows is being raised to a higher, more healthful level of purity. The persistent mother and patient infant win out in the long run. See "The Prisoner of War Diet" in Chapter 5 for a case of breast-feeding on a raw diet.

Is this diet healthful for my kid?

It cracks me up when someone asks me this. Do you really think that, after all the research you have seen so far, that it could possibly be healthful for your kids to eat *cooked* food? Furthermore, if it were not healthful, how do you think children survived over the eons of time on raw food diets prior to the invention of cooking?

I saw a CBS news segment on the raw diet in which someone said it was "unsafe" for children to eat this way. Someone who knows the facts would say that the odds of a child on a raw, plant-based diet getting sick from bacteria are insignificant. The odds of the child getting slowly poisoned from a diet of cooked food, however, are 100%.

Gabriel Cousens, MD, saw the need for a study on this subject because too many parents are being harassed by the government when they put their kids on a living food diet. He therefore has begun one of the few studies being done on raw vegan children. Preliminary results of his study were given to those who attended his lecture at the annual Raw Food Festival in Oregon and are summarized in Chapter 5.

Dr. Cousens also informs the parents of the need to be sure their children get enough Vitamin B_{12}, which is often lacking in vegan diets (as discussed in Chapter 12).

I have seen kids who were raised eating 100% raw food diets, and they never got sick. No earaches, no fevers, no colds! None of the usual childhood diseases! And most amazingly, they do not crave or want cooked or junk foods. Even given the choice between a raw, gourmet, pizza dish, or something fancy like that, and Nature's cuisine of plain, simple produce, they prefer the latter!

Victoria Boutenko relates that the raw diet radically improved not only her kids' physical health, but also their mental abilities and behavior. Once, she invited 18 raw teens over to her house, kids that her children had been corresponding with on the Internet. Although she was apprehensive about having so many American teenagers at her house at one time, she said they all behaved like "angels."

Addiction to cooked food begins shortly after weaning from mother's milk. For those not breastfed, it begins even sooner with pasteurized milk or formula. This is why babies get colicky, suffer from rashes and so on. It explains the phenomenon that when you try to feed them their first cooked food, they spit it out. This is why they cry.

Rev. George Malkmus says, "One of the most cruel injustices we commit as parents is when we place cooked (pasteurized) milk, cooked cereal and cooked baby foods into the beautiful living body of little children designed by God to be nourished _only_ with raw, living foods!" (*God's Way to Ultimate Health*, p. 83).

Natalia Rose explains that it is important not to be obsessively strict with kids, however. There will be times that they will go to parties in which others are eating cakes, pizzas and sodas. She explains that it is important psychologically to let them make their own decisions, and if they eat right at home, chances are they won't even like the cooked, chemicalized stuff anyway. The amount they eat on such occasions will be minimal, and once they are home, it's back to the good food (*The Raw Food Detox Diet*, p. 87).

There is even a book on helping your kids make the switch to the most healthful diet on the planet: *Raw Kids: Transitioning Children to a Raw Food Diet*, by Cheryl Stoycoff.

15
Raw Pleasure

What we eat is more than nutrients or even the particular energy of the food. We also eat the mental state of those who grew the food, picked the food, prepared the food, and of the one who is eating the food. Food that is grown with love, picked with love, prepared with love, and eaten with love has a different quality than food that goes through those stages with a different consciousness relating to it. —Dr. Gabriel Cousens, (1943—) *Spiritual Nutrition and the Rainbow Diet*

Now that we have learned all about the benefits of eating raw, the raw food movement, the scientific explanation for the health benefits of eating raw and how to go about changing one's lifestyle to eat raw, *let's eat!*

If someone had told me four or five years ago that I would become a quasi-chef, I would have had a good laugh. My life was always too active to get excited over a recipe. In fact, as a cooked fooder, I don't recall ever inventing a recipe in my life. I don't even recall exchanging recipes with anybody. Let others do the cooking; my life was too full to be messing around in the kitchen. Yet here are my now-favorite recipes that I have fine-tuned over the years and are always popular with guests.

At first, I dreaded the idea of preparing my own food. My idea of preparing my own food before was sticking a TV dinner into a microwave. For special occasions, I might have made some stir-fry or baked potatoes. Often, I just ate out.

How and why did I get over my aversion to food prep and even go so far as to make my own mustard, salad dressings and even soup from scratch? *Only the desire to attain new levels of health motivated me.*

But I knew I had to change my attitude and make it _fun_. *Music, in my case, was the key.* I went out and bought some CDs that I knew would put me into a high, yet energetic, state of consciousness: Enya, Basia, Al Jarreau, Ronnie Jordan's "smooth jazz," as well as the ethnic music by Strunz and Farah worked great for me. More recently, I enjoy fixing food to Joan Kurland's awesome CD, "Looking Up."

But everyone has her own taste in music. The more you can sing and dance around while fixing food, the more fun it will be, the more you will actually enjoy it, and most importantly, *the more love you will transmit to the food*. Although there hasn't been a lot of research in that area, I am sure that food prepared with love is much more healthful to eat than food prepared by someone stressed out.

At first going raw may seem like a lot of work since you have to make so many things from scratch that you would normally buy prepared, such as crackers and salad dressing. But to quote Tonya Zavasta, "The day will come when you will no longer care for recipes. At first you cannot stand the lightness that consumption of the raw foods produces, but after several years on this lifestyle it is the fullness that becomes insufferable" (*Beautiful on Raw*, p. 13).

Note: Some of these recipes use nama shoyu, which is unpasteurized soy sauce made from cooked soybeans. If you are extremely sensitive to MSG, I would leave this out, as it does contain a little MSG, just as soy sauce does. If you are unable to get unpasteurized miso, you may use a pinch or so of Celtic sea salt. Any time you are unable to use lemon, lime or grapefruit juice, use raw apple cider vinegar.

If you are a strict vegan, there are numerous things you can substitute for the honey. You can use agave, which comes from cacti. Or you could use dates or raisins or other sweet fruit, but dried fruit is more concentrated than fresh fruit.

Stevia extract is especially good as a sweet substitute if you are sensitive to sweets and don't want any excess insulin output from your pancreas. Stevia is a plant. Though it is probably not raw when you get it from the store, stevia extract is used in such minute quantities that it won't matter too much. Since it is 200 times sweeter than sugar, less than one teaspoon is often all you need. It is also very easy to grow your own stevia plant. However, many find that it leaves a bitter aftertaste.

As you can see from the following recipes, I adore cilantro! It is said to be a good heavy metal chelator to aid in detoxification. I put an entire bunch of it in almost anything that is not a dessert. Feel free to reduce the amount. You could also use parsley or your own favorite herb as a substitute.

When I first started preparing raw dishes, I omitted many of the fresh herbs because I didn't want to pay two dollars for some fresh organic herbs when the recipes called for so little of them. Then I started buying my own pots of herbs, such as oregano, thyme, basil and parsley, and plucking a few leaves as needed.

I found that herbs make all the difference! They are truly the spice of raw food. Once I made nut and seed cheese with a handful of thyme and basil and discovered it had an over-whelmingly familiar taste. I closed my eyes and tried to remember where it came from. It was the bologna I ate as a kid! To think, all that time it was not the pork or beef that was tasty, but the hint of herbs they mixed into it.

I highly recommend that you purchase herbs in pots so that you can keep growing your own. Fresh herbs cost several dollars at a grocery, and that is a needless expense when so many recipes call for such small amounts. Grow your own and you can pluck a few leaves for extra flavor in whatever dish you are making.

Eventually you will want to alter these recipes or experiment with creating your own. The rule used by successful chefs is to attempt to excite all the tastebuds. To get that "wow!" reaction, you need to have a bit from each of the five flavors: spicy, sweet, salty, sour and bitter. Many herbs are spicy, and you can also use organic spices. Use agave, honey, stevia, fresh or dried fruit for sweet. Use Celtic, Himalayan or other natural, unrefined salts for a salty taste, or use kelp, dulse or unpasteurized miso. Lemon, lime or grapefruit juice or raw apple cider vinegar hits the sour spot. For bitter, add green, leafy vegetables.

When dehydrating, keep the temperature at 100°-105° F since the enzymes start to die off at about 105° F. You may even want to tape down the thermostat so it won't accidentally be bumped.

Note: Unless otherwise stated, _store all the leftovers in the refrigerator_, and try to use them up within the next few days for best flavor and health benefits. Generally, most raw dishes will keep three to six days, but the fresher, the more nutritious and better tasting.

Soups

Everybody's Favorite Celery-Cilantro Soup

1 bunch celery (about 8 stalks)
1 bunch cilantro
1 bunch fresh dill
1 cup unpasteurized olive oil
½ cup raw almond butter or raw tahini
3 cloves garlic
2-4 T unpasteurized miso
2 T nama shoyu
¼ cup lemon juice (if not available, raw apple cider vinegar)
8 cups water

Blend in a K-Tec or Vita-Mix, adding a little of the ingredients at a time until creamy. This is a big hit everywhere I have taken it. I always get requests for the recipe! If you want to make it creamier, simply add more celery stalks and a little more almond butter or olive oil.

Serves about 10.

Creamy Carrot Soup

3 cups carrot juice
8-10 T raw almond butter
1½ avocados
4 T nama shoyu
2-3 garlic cloves
2 T honey
1 bunch celery (about 8 stalks)
6-8 cups water

Blend in a K-Tec or Vita-Mix, adding a little at a time until creamy. Use the leftover carrot pulp from the juice to make almond carrot cookies. (See "Desserts.")

Makes about 10 servings.

Cream of Tomato Soup

3 tomatoes
2-3 celery stalks
½ red bell pepper
Small handful of sun-dried tomatoes
1 t Celtic sea salt
Juice of 1 lemon
6 dates, pitted
5 oz raw cashews
¼-½ cup unpasteurized olive oil
Enough pure water to make it as thick or thin as you like

Blend in K-Tec or Vita-Mix, adding a little at a time until creamy.

Makes about 5 servings.

Cream of Celery Soup

1 bunch celery
1 bunch parsley
2 cups water — use sesame milk for creamier taste (see "Beverages")
¼ cup olive oil
1 tomato
1 T honey
Juice of 1 lemon
1 t Celtic sea salt

Blend in K-Tec or Vita-Mix, adding a little at a time until creamy.

Serves about 4-6.

Vegetable Chowder

Everybody's Favorite Celery-Cilantro Soup
2 zucchinis, grated
2 carrots, grated
2 avocados, cut up into chunks
Corn kernels from 3 ears of corn
1 bell pepper, chopped

Put the vegetables into the celery/cilantro base. Gently stir. This is a big hit at potlucks, even cooked ones! People like this one for winter and the celery/cilantro base alone for summer.

Serves 10-12.

Cream of Spinach Soup

1 avocado
1 cup water
2 cucumbers, skin and all
2 cups spinach
2 cloves garlic
1 bell pepper
1 bunch cilantro

Blend in K-Tec or Vita-Mix, adding a little at a time until creamy. You may need to add more water.

Serves 4.

Corn Chowder

4 cups corn kernels
1 avocado
1 cucumber
¾ cup almonds, soaked 6-12 hours, rinsed and drained
1 bunch cilantro
3 T dulse flakes
1 T Celtic sea salt
4 cloves garlic
Enough pure water to make it as thick or thin as you like

Blend in K-Tec or Vita-Mix with water, adding ingredients a little at a time, using only enough water to blend. Add more water until it is the right consistency, thick and creamy.

Serves 5-8.

Creamy Cauliflower Soup

5 cups sesame or almond milk (see "Beverages")
1 medium or small cauliflower, chopped up
1 bell pepper, any color
½-1 avocado
Juice from 1 lemon or lime
3 T raw tahini or nut butter
3 T unpasteurized miso
½ jalapeño pepper
3 cloves garlic

Blend in K-Tec or Vita-Mix until creamy.

Serves 5-8.

Lorenzo's Tomato Avocado Soup

A friend of mine serves this soup every time we go to his house, and my husband and I can't get enough! He says he has experimented with it a lot and found that the only crucial ingredients that cannot be omitted or substituted are the avocado and tomato, which is why I gave it this name.

2 cups water
1 large tomato
1 ripe avocado
2 cloves garlic
Juice from a small lime
¼ onion
½-¾ cup broccoli
1 big red kale leaf
4 small chilies or 1 jalapeño
4-5 stalks bok choy
1 inch fresh turmeric
1 red bell pepper
¼ cup flaxseeds
1 t Celtic sea salt
2 T raw apple cider vinegar
2 T nama shoyu (optional)

Blend ingredients in K-Tec or Vita-Mix until very creamy.

Serves 2-4.

Entrées

Spaghetti

Squash, zucchinis or daikon radishes (about 8-12 inches of any of these for each serving)
Tomato Sauce (see "Sauces, Salad Dressings, Condiments")
Tahini Sauce or Pesto Sauce (see "Sauces, Salad Dressings, Condiments")
Parmesan Cheese (see recipe under "Salads and Salad Trimmings")
Bits of vegetables, such as bell pepper or broccoli, chopped into small bits, or cherry tomatoes sliced into two (optional)

Using the Saladacco spiralizer, make spaghetti out of the vegetables. This wonderful gadget will make long, stringy strands just like spaghetti! If you have a large group to feed, this can be quite tiresome, as the spiralizer is a hand-crank gadget. Perhaps as this diet catches on, someone will invent an electric one or at least a spiralizer attachment to the food processor. If you do not have a spiralizer, or if you simply don't have the time or energy to crank out the spaghetti strands, you can use the grating attachment of the food processor to get mini-strips. Next, add tomato sauce and top with tahini sauce. Sprinkle with Parmesan cheese. Top with vegetable bits.

Chinese Stir "Fry"

1 foot long daikon radish
4 carrots
1 bunch green onions
5-6 stalks celery
½ head small cabbage
2 zucchinis
1 red bell pepper
1 cup mung bean sprouts
¾ cup watercress
3 stalks broccoli
1½ cups snow peas
Slivered raw almonds or raw cashews
Sesame seeds
Tahini sauce (see "Sauces, Salad Dressings, Condiments")
Tempeh (optional)

With the food processor, grate the daikon radish, and slice the carrots, celery, green onions, cabbage, zucchinis and bell pepper. (This is one time you will be especially thankful for your food processor: A job that could otherwise take an hour will be finished in minutes!) Put into a large bowl. Cut off florets from broccoli and toss into the mixture. Chop off tips of watercress and toss in, along with mung bean sprouts. Cut off stringy ends of snow peas and toss in. Fold in about a cup of tahini sauce. Top off with almond slivers (or truly raw cashews, sliced) and sesame seeds. Chop up tempeh and fold into mixture.

Serves 8-10.

Buddy and Cherrie's Barbecue Chicken Nuggets

This recipe was contributed by Buddy and Cherrie. (See Chapter 2.) They used it in one of their workshops on how to have a "raw picnic in the park." It is so delicious you'll swear it's chicken! I personally prefer to double the amount of curry and poultry seasoning given in their recipe below.

2 cups carrots
2 cups almonds, soaked and drained
¼ cup orange juice
¼ cup onion
¼ cup olive oil
2 T agave
1 T poultry seasoning
2 t Celtic sea salt
¼ t black pepper
½ t curry powder
1 recipe Barbecue Sauce

In a food processor, process carrots until diced. Add remaining ingredients and process until well blended. Add remaining ingredients and blend until well mixed. Mold into nugget-size shapes and place on Teflex sheets. Brush with Barbecue Sauce. Dehydrate at 105° F for about 5 hours, flip onto a mesh screen, spread with more sauce and dehydrate about 5 more hours until dry but not crisp. Serve with additional sauce as dip, if desired.

For a plain nugget, leave the Barbecue Sauce off and dehydrate the plain nugget.

Yield: 37 nuggets, using a 2 T-size scoop

Barbecue Sauce for Nuggets:
1½ cups sun-dried tomatoes, soaked
1 cup chopped tomatoes
1 clove garlic
¼ cup dark agave
1 t Celtic sea salt
3 T lemon juice
¼ t dry mustard powder
1 t Chili Powder
1 T liquid smoke (optional — not a raw product)

Combine all ingredients in a blender and blend until smooth.

Yield: 1 cup sauce

Burritos

Tortillas: To make the burrito tortillas, mix the following ingredients and dehydrate at 105° F for 12-24 hours until completely dry. Cut with scissors into squares for wraps. Store the remainder in a sealed container.

3 cups pure water
4 carrots, chopped
4 T unheated honey or raw agave
4 tomatoes
1 cup sun-dried tomatoes, soaked for at least 30 minutes and cut into
    pieces with scissors
2 celery stalks
¼ cup nama shoyu
1½ cups flaxseeds, soaked overnight and rinsed
1 t cayenne powder
½ bunch cilantro (optional)

Filling: "Sunflower Seed Pâté" or any of the other dips listed under "Appetizers and Dips."

Top off with alfalfa sprouts (or shredded lettuce) and roll into a burrito shape. These are always a big hit at potlucks!

Note: When you don't have time to make the burrito tortillas, you can use raw nori sheets instead.

Serves 10-12. You can make them smaller and have a great deal more if this is served as an appetizer instead of a main course.

Nori Rolls

This is the "fast food" of the raw diet. It is like making a sandwich.

1 Nori sheet (Note: The green ones found at Oriental groceries are
    much cheaper, but heated. Black ones are truly raw.)
Sprouts of any kind, a small handful
Tahini sauce (see "Sauces, Dressings, Condiments") or
Sunflower Seed Pâté (see "Appetizers and Dips"), about ½ cup
Grated or thinly chopped carrots, bell peppers, zucchini or beets
Small handful chopped green onions (or red onions), 1 T per serving
Chopped avocado (optional), ¼ avocado per serving

Put the Nori sheet on a plate. Put a tablespoon or two of sauce in the middle, followed by some sprouts, onions and chopped vegetables.

Note: This recipe cannot be made ahead of time, as the sheet will get very damp from the sauce and break. Therefore, you must make them just before serving. This recipe makes great appetizers as well as a snack or lunch entrée.

Raw Pizza

1-2 medium, ripe eggplants (note: skin should be wrinkly; if green inside, they are not ripe and may be harder to digest)
Tomato sauce (see "Sauces, Salad Dressings, Condiments")
Deluxe macadamia nut cheese (see "Appetizers and Dips")
1 bunch green onions, chopped
½ cup fresh olives (more likely to be raw if from a jar, as canned olives are usually heated)
1 bell pepper, grated and chopped into small pieces

Remove the skin from the eggplants, and slice about ½ inch thick. Cover little mini-pizza circles with tomato sauce. Next, add a thin layer of deluxe macadamia nut cheese. Top with chopped green onions, bell peppers and olives. Dehydrate for about 4 hours at 105° F. What's really amazing is that the eggplant shrivels up and tastes almost like wheat! These can be refrigerated and taste really great even if you don't heat them up again in the dehydrator. These are a big hit, especially for pizza lovers. They can also be used as appetizers. The following is an optional crust that actually looks and tastes remarkably like cooked pizza:

Optional crust:
2½ cups buckwheat groats, soaked 6 hours, rinsed, drained and sprouted 24 hours
½ cup unpasteurized olive oil
1 bunch cilantro

Dehydrate until dry, which may take at least four hours. The only caveat about this kind of crust is that grains are much harder to digest than eggplant, even when sprouted. Digestion will probably get easier the longer you are eating a diet close to 100% raw.

Serves about 8-10 people, or use the little pizzas as an appetizer.

Tomato Raviolis

Tomatoes
Hummus (see "Appetizers and Dips")

Slice tomatoes about ½ inch thick. Put hummus between two slices of tomato, like a sandwich. Dehydrate at about 105° F for several hours.

Beet Burgers

1 cup pulp left over from beet juice
1 cup ground sunflower seeds (soaked, rinsed, dried, then ground in
    coffee grinder)
½ cup finely chopped celery
¼ cup finely chopped green onion
½ bunch cilantro
3 T flaxseeds, ground in coffee grinder
½ cup water
¼ cup finely chopped bell pepper
1 T unpasteurized miso or 1 t Celtic or Himalayan salt

Mix everything in a food processor using the "S" blade. Form patties on a dehydrator and dehydrate about eight hours.

Serves about 10.

Desserts

Carob Cream

This tastes and looks like chocolate mousse. You won't be tempted to eat chocolate with this dessert! It can be eaten alone or used as an icing for a cake or a dip for strawberries, bananas and so on.

1 avocado
½ cup raw carob
¼ cup raw coconut butter
½ cup unheated honey

Blend in food processor with the "S" blade until mixture is creamy and it looks like Hershey's chocolate. If it doesn't taste sweet enough, add another tablespoon of honey. Alternatively, you can thicken this with coconut butter or sweeten it with agave.

Serves 6-8.

Ice Cream

1½ cups nut or seed milk (see "Beverages")
2 cups pulp left over from nut or seed milk (use half as much if you
    want a less "pulpy" texture)
2 T coconut butter or oil
½ cup unheated honey
1 T organic vanilla extract

Blend in food processor with the "S" blade until creamy. Then pour into
ice-cream maker. In a Cuisinart, it will take about ½-¾ hour for it to become ice cream. If you want chocolate flavor, add about ½ cup raw
carob powder. Store any leftovers in the freezer, but it will get very
hard and be difficult to eat; so best to use it up now.

Serves 6-8.

Raw Candy

Nuts, soaked 6-12 hours, rinsed and drained
Dates
Raw carob powder, to taste (optional)
Raw shredded coconut or unhulled sesame seeds

Mix nuts, dates and carob in food processor. Mix in a food processor
with the "S" blade until the mixture forms a ball that bounces around
inside that machine. Remove and form little balls. Roll the balls in sesame seeds and/or raw shredded coconut. These keep a long time in
the freezer. Experiment with ingredient proportions and quantities to
suit your own taste.

Frozen Fruit Ice Cream

Handful frozen strawberries (or blueberries)
1 frozen banana
Juice from 1 orange
8-10 grapes, frozen or fresh

Blend in food processor with the "S" blade until creamy. Or, if you have
a centrifugal type juicer, push ingredients through, using the blank
screen. The consistency will be like soft-serve ice cream. Store any
leftovers in the freezer, but it will get very hard and difficult to use; so
best to use it up now.

Serves 2-3.

"Pumpkin Pie" Pudding

5 figs
10 pitted dates
1 cup walnuts, soaked 6-8 hours, rinsed and drained
¾ cup grated carrots
¾ t each of cloves, nutmeg, cinnamon (or just use "pumpkin pie spice")

Blend in food processor with the "S" blade, adding ingredients a little at a time. Blend until creamy.

Serves 4.

Raw Cake

Crust: Blend until creamy 2 cups almonds (soaked overnight, rinsed, drained), 1 cup finely ground almonds (ground in coffee grinder or K-Tec or Vita-Mix), 4-5 T unheated honey, 1 t cinnamon.

Icing: Carob Cream (see above).

Serves 10.

Carrot Almond Cookies

4 cups grated carrots
4 cups almonds, soaked overnight and rinsed, drained
3 inches fresh ginger, chopped
¾-1 cup unheated honey
¾-1 cup sun-dried raisins
4 T unpasteurized white miso (optional)

Slowly blend the mixture in a food processor, using the "S" blade. Take heaping tablespoons and put on the dehydrator sheets. Flatten them with the back end of spoon so that they are about half an inch thick. Dehydrate them 4-8 hours at 105° F. They will be nice and crunchy if dehydrated enough. Store in the refrigerator and eat within three or four days. Makes about 4 dozen. For fewer, simply halve the recipe.

Raw Chocolate

The following recipe is such a brain booster and mood elevator that it is my snack of choice nearly every day! Below is the recipe for just one serving:

3 T raw cacao nuggets (taken from the bean — available at www.rawfood.com or www.livingtreecommunity.com)

1 T raw coconut butter

1 T raw agave nectar (or unheated honey)

Grind cacao into fine powder using coffee grinder. Mix with a fork or blender with butter and agave sweetener. This makes one serving and will taste remarkably like (indeed, much better than!) commercial chocolate that is made with milk and sugar. Raw cacao nourishes the brain and is a natural antidepressant as it reuptakes neurotransmitters!

Peppermint Patties

For the chocolate layer, make recipe for raw chocolate. Make 6-7 times the amount, possibly even a bit more.

For the white-colored peppermint layer, blend in a food processor using the "S" blade:

3 cups shredded dehydrated coconut (call the company to be sure it is truly raw)

$^1/_3$ cup raw honey or agave nectar

1 t peppermint or mint extract

Spread thin the layer of coconut mixture for the peppermint part on the bottom of a container, topping it with a thin layer of chocolate. Freeze for several hours. This tastes better than the peppermint candies you buy in wrappers; yet it is much, much more healthful!

Serves 10.

Peanut Butter & Chocolate Cups

This is the raw version of Reese's peanut butter cups. Take paper cupcake or confection holders such as the ones that cupcakes come in or the smaller ones that chocolates come in. Fill the bottom half with raw almond butter. Then fill the top part with the raw chocolate recipe in this section. Freeze and keep frozen until you serve them.

Buddy and Cherrie's Carob Nut Taffy

This recipe was graciously contributed by Buddy and Cherrie (aka the "Rawdaddy" and "Rawmomma" of Chapter 2).

1 cup walnuts, soaked, dehydrated and chopped into large pieces
1 cup almonds, soaked, dehydrated and chopped into large pieces
1 cup brazil nuts, soaked, dehydrated and chopped into large pieces
½ cup agave or unheated honey
2 T raw carob powder
2 T cacao nibs, crushed or ground

Chop the nuts coarsely. I do it by hand so that the chunks are in large pieces. Place in a bowl and mix well with remaining ingredients. Place on Teflex sheet and dehydrate for 8 hours. Remove from sheets and place on mesh screens and dehydrate for 24 hours. They will be soft but will harden up as they cool. Store in an airtight container. They will be a little sticky. If you are looking for a crunchy, chocolate type of treat, this is wonderful.

Buddy and Cherrie's Cashew Ice Cream

Here we go again with another fantastic recipe from Buddy and Cherrie. This is their favorite raw ice cream.

3 cups raw cashews, soaked overnight and drained
3 T raw carob powder
3 T raw cacao powder (buy it that way or grind the cacao nibs in a coffee grinder until powdery)
4 cups coconut milk
1¾ cups raw agave nectar
½ t vanilla extract

Blend ingredients in food processor with the "S" blade or in a K-Tec or Vita-Mix until creamy. Put into an ice-cream machine.

Sandy's Apple Pie (10 minutes)

This was contributed by Sandra Schrift from Chapter 2:

Crust: Soak 1 cup of pecans and 1 cup of walnuts for a few hours. Drain and mix with four coconut-covered dates in food processor. (I buy mine in bulk at Whole Foods Market.) Place mixture in a glass pie plate (use your hands) and refrigerate overnight if possible.

Filling: 3 apples chopped (with their peels) in food processor. (In summer time use peaches.)

½ t cinnamon
¼ t nutmeg
1-1½ t lemon juice

Spread the filling over the crust.

Toppings: Sliced strawberries, blueberries, kiwis or any fruit you wish. This makes it look pretty ... and taste good.

Beverages

Nut or Seed Milk

1 cup nuts or seeds (sesame seeds or almonds are especially good)
6 cups water

If you are using sesame seeds, be sure to get the unhulled kind, as they are richer in calcium. Mix seeds or almonds with water in K-Tec or Vita-Mix or use the non-heating option of the Soyajoy machine. If you use the K-Tec or Vita Mix, strain with cheesecloth. (A Soyajoy has a built-in strainer.) Use the pulp to make ice cream. (See "Desserts".) Or use the pulp to make spinach dip under "Appetizers & Dips." The milk keeps for three days.

Makes about 6 servings.

Banana Milk Shake

1 frozen banana
1 cup nut or seed milk
2 dates or 1 T unheated honey

Blend in K-Tec or Vita-Mix or food processor (using the "S" blade) or blender.

Serves 1.

Smoothie

2 frozen bananas
Juice from 2-3 oranges
2 T bee pollen or spirulina flakes

Blend in K-Tec or Vita-Mix or food processor (using the "S" blade) or blender.

Serves 2.

Chocolate Mint Soda

1 cup nut or seed milk (see recipe in this section)
1 T unheated honey or ½ T stevia extract (liquid)
2 T raw carob powder
½ capful peppermint extract

Blend in K-Tec or Vita-Mix until it is foamy like a soda.

Serves 1.

Super Smoothie

This is the best breakfast ever! It really gets you going. Who needs a latté? This will get you through the most stressful job ever. If you live alone, save half for lunch or to get a second wind when you get home. Upon taking this drink, I have experienced being able to clean my condo or do the laundry after working 11 hours straight at a stressful job!

1 bunch kale
2 cups fresh juice from sweet-tasting fruit (e.g., orange juice)
1 banana
2 T bee pollen
1 pinch cayenne (Start out with this until you can gradually build up to more. I now use a teaspoon of cayenne per serving, but it took months to get to that point.)
4 T raw cacao nibs

Blend in a Vita-Mix or K-Tec machine, adding water as needed to achieve your preferred consistency.

Serves 2-4.

Green Drink

1 bunch kale
1 cup freshly squeezed fruit juice or carrot juice
1 dash cayenne

Put all ingredients into a Vita-Mix or K-Tec machine. Fill close to the top with pure water. Blend until creamy.

Serves 2-4.

Sauces, Dressings, Condiments

Tahini Sauce

1 cup raw tahini
¾ cup unpasteurized olive oil
$^2/_3$ cup orange juice (about 2 medium-sized oranges)
3 cloves garlic
1½ inches fresh ginger
1 T nama shoyu (optional)
1-2 t Celtic sea salt
¼ cup fresh cilantro (optional)

Mix in food processor with the "S" blade, adding ingredients a little at a time. Mix until creamy. This is great on raw Oriental vegetables for a stir-fry or on Nori Rolls.

"Thousand Island" Salad Dressing

2 oranges, pulp, seeds and all
4 T unpasteurized olive oil
2 T unheated honey
2 T nama shoyu
¼ cup raw almond butter
2 T raw apple cider vinegar
4 cloves garlic

Blend in food processor with the "S" blade, adding ingredients a little at a time. Mix until creamy. Add a bit of water if needed to thin, or add more oil.

Honey Mustard Dressing

½ cup raw mustard (see recipe in this section)
½ cup unpasteurized olive oil
½ cup unheated honey
½ cup water (less makes it more creamy)

Blend in food processor with the "S" blade until creamy.

Oil and Vinegar

1 cup unpasteurized olive oil
1 cup raw apple cider vinegar
1 T finely chopped fresh basil (optional)

Mix the ingredients and shake or blend in blender or food processor.

Curry Spinach Dressing

2 cups spinach
1 cup cilantro
1 T curry powder
2 T unpasteurized miso
2 T raw almond butter
½ t Celtic or Himalayan salt
½ t cayenne
¼ cup water
¼ cup unpasteurized olive oil
¼ cup raw apple cider vinegar
¼ cup agave nectar
¼ cup water (if you want to make it thinner)
1 avocado (if you want to make it thicker)

Blend in a food processor with the "S" blade. This is great to pour over a tossed salad and mix thoroughly.

Raw Mustard

8 T whole yellow mustard seeds
4 oz mineral water
3 oz lemon juice
2 T unheated honey

Soak mustard seeds in water and lemon juice overnight. Add honey and blend in food processor with "S" blade until creamy. Keeps for months in the refrigerator.

Tomato Sauce

1 cup fresh tomatoes
½ cup sun-dried tomatoes
½ cup pitted dates
½ bunch cilantro
3-4 cloves garlic
¼ cup chopped red onion
4 leaves basil
1 t Celtic sea salt
3 T unpasteurized olive oil

Blend in K-Tec or Vita-Mix until creamy. You could blend it in a food processor with the "S" blade, but the dates and sun-dried tomatoes will be very hard to blend, causing the machine to vibrate, and the ingredients may even splatter! But this splattering can be avoided if you soak both the dates and sun-dried tomatoes for at least two hours first.

Parmesan Cheese

½ cup ground flaxseeds
1 T dehydrated cilantro or parsley flakes
½ t garlic powder

Mix the ingredients evenly. Sprinkle on vegetable spaghetti, salads or other main dishes.

Appetizers and Dips

Raw Hummus

2 zucchinis
¾ cup unhulled sesame seeds, soaked 6-12 hours, rinsed, drained
¾ cup raw tahini
¼-½ t cayenne
½ t celery salt
3-4 garlic cloves
1 t Celtic sea salt
¼ cup lemon juice

Blend in a food processor with the "S" blade, adding ingredients a little at a time until creamy. Serve on flax crackers or use as a vegetable dip with sliced zucchini, baby carrots, sliced bell peppers and fresh broccoli.

Nori Rolls

See "Entrées."

Creamy Spinach Dip

½ lb spinach (about 5-6 cups)
½ red onion
3 cloves garlic
¾ cup raw tahini or leftover pulp from nut or seed milk
½ bunch cilantro
3-4 T lemon juice
½ t Celtic sea salt

Blend in food processor with the "S" blade, adding spinach a little at a time. Mix until creamy. Serve on flax crackers, or use as a vegetable dip for sliced zucchini, baby carrots, sliced bell peppers or fresh broccoli.

Deluxe Macadamia Nut Cheese

12 oz (3 cups) macadamia nuts, soaked 6-12 hours, rinsed and drained
1 t Celtic sea salt
2 cloves garlic
1 T fresh cilantro
¼ cup lemon juice
$^3/_8$-½ cup unpasteurized olive oil

Blend in food processor with the "S" blade, adding the nuts a little at a time. Mix until creamy, the texture of cream cheese.

Note: For a creamier mixture, you could put the nuts through a juicer with the blank screen before putting them into the food processor. In that case, you will need about half the olive oil! You might have to add one or two tablespoons more of oil.

Blend until it has the creamy texture of cream cheese. Serve on flax crackers, or use as a vegetable dip with zucchini, baby carrots, sliced bell peppers, fresh broccoli and so on.

Pecan Pesto

2 cups pecans, soaked 4-8 hours, rinsed and drained
1 bunch cilantro
1 medium red onion
4 cloves garlic
4 T ginger
Juice of 1 small lemon or lime

Mix in food processor using the "S" blade. Use just as you would pesto sauce. It is great over zucchini or squash noodles.

Pumpkin Seed & Macadamia Nut Cheese

1½ cups macadamia nuts, soaked 4-8 hours, rinsed and drained
1½ cups pumpkin seeds, soaked 4-8 hours, rinsed and drained
Juice from small lemon
3 T unpasteurized olive oil
3-4 fresh basil leaves
3-4 any other fresh herbs (tarragon, mint, thyme)

For best results, put nuts and seeds through the blank screen of a juicer (e.g., Omega or Champion). Then mix everything until very creamy (with a texture like cream cheese) in a food processor using the "S" blade. If you do not have a juicer, simply put the nuts and seeds into the food processor right away with the other ingredients. You may have to add more olive oil, though, to help it get creamier.

Guacamole

2 Roma tomatoes or ½ cup other tomatoes
2 large avocados
½ bunch cilantro
Juice from ½ small lemon
1 t jalapeño, chopped
2 cloves garlic
1 t Celtic sea salt
½ red bell pepper

Blend in food processor using the "S" blade. For a chunky texture, cut the pieces first into small chunks; then blend for only about 3 seconds to get slightly smaller chunks. For a creamy texture, blend longer.

Sunflower Seed Pâté

1 cup sunflower seeds, soaked overnight, rinsed
1 cup pumpkin seeds, soaked overnight, rinsed
½ cup pitted olives
2 red bell peppers
½ bunch cilantro or favorite fresh herb
1 t Celtic or Himalayan salt
½-1 cup sun-dried tomatoes, soaked for 30 minutes and cut into small
    pieces with scissors

Put the seeds through a blank screen of a juicer. If you don't have a juicer with a blank screen, you can use a food processor with the "S" blade to blend them, but it won't be as creamy. Then, mix all other ingredients in the food processor with the "S" blade.

Salads and Salad Trimmings

Arabian Salad

2 tomatoes
1 bell pepper, green or red
1 cucumber
¼ bunch cilantro
1 bunch green onions
Unpasteurized olive oil
½ t Celtic sea salt
1 lemon

Chop cilantro finely. Chop other vegetables into bite-size chunks. Add salt. Sprinkle on olive oil, but don't let it be so much that vegetables get soggy. Squeeze lemon juice over salad. Gently stir. This is a tasty, cool salad enjoyed in Middle Eastern dinners.

Serves 2-3.

Cheesy Spinach Salad

½-¾ cup unpasteurized olive oil
Juice from one lemon
1 cup pumpkin seeds, soaked 6-8 hours, soaked and rinsed
1 T mustard (see recipe in "Sauces, Salad Dressings, Condiments")
4 garlic cloves
½ t Celtic sea salt
1 lb chopped and cleaned spinach
1 red onion

Mix all ingredients except the spinach and onion in food processor with the "S" blade or in a K-Tec or Vita-Mix. If the dressing is too thick, you may have to add more oil or a tiny bit of water. Chop the red onion, and put it with the spinach into a big bowl. Pour the dressing over it and toss.

Serves 6.

Coleslaw

1 cabbage (green or purple)
½ red onion
1 red bell pepper
1 green bell pepper
3 carrots

Dressing:
$^1/_3$ cup raw apple cider vinegar
$^1/_3$ cup unpasteurized olive oil
$^1/_3$ cup unheated honey
1 T mustard or mustard seeds
1 t Celtic sea salt

Grate the carrots with the food processor using the grating blade. Slice the other vegetables using the slicing blade. Next, blend the dressing using the "S" blade and pour over the salad.

Serves 8-10.

Waldorf Salad

1-2 apples, grated
1-2 sprigs asparagus, grated or sliced in small pieces
½ cup sun-dried raisins
½ cup walnuts
3-4 cups lettuce and/or spinach

Toss salad ingredients. Top with honey mustard dressing (see "Sauces, Dressings, Condiments").

Holiday Salad

5-6 cups spinach (about ½ lb)
1 cup pecan croutons (see recipe in this section)
½ cup raw olives
½ red onion, sliced into halved ringlets

Toss pecans, olives and onion ringlets into spinach. Top with oil and vinegar or dressing of your choice.

Serves 5-6.

Marinated Kale

1 bunch kale (stems removed and saved to put later into a juice)
1 small red onion
2 carrots
1 red bell pepper
2 zucchinis
1 bunch cilantro or mint
½ cup red cabbage or 2-3 stalks celery

Chop in a food processor using the slicing blade. Then the dressing (below) over it and let it marinate overnight. Sprinkle with raw sesame seeds before serving.

Dressing for Kale:
½ cup coconut oil or unpasteurized olive oil (Note: if you plan to store this in the refrigerator, I would avoid using coconut oil as it congeals.)

2 cloves garlic
2 inches ginger
½ cup lemon or lime juice
2 T nama shoyu
1 dash cayenne

Chop the garlic and ginger, then blend with the other ingredients using a food processor with the "S" blade.

Serves 6-8.

Arame Salad

This makes a large salad. You might want to cut the recipe in half.

1 head green cabbage
1 head red cabbage
2 beets
5 carrots
3-4 bell peppers (red and green)
1 red onion
½-¾ cup arame seaweed (sun-dried)
½-¾ cups sesame seeds (soaked overnight and rinsed)
½ cup each of agave or unheated honey, raw apple cider vinegar and
    unpasteurized olive oil

With a food processor, slice the cabbages, bell peppers and onions. Grate the carrots and beets. Sprinkle in the arame and sesame seeds. For the dressing, mix the agave or unheated honey, raw apple cider vinegar and olive oil. Pour over the salad.

Serves 15-20.

Pecan Croutons

1-3 cups pecans
Cinnamon
Unheated honey

Soak the pecans overnight, rinse and drain. Roll them in a mixture of honey and cinnamon. Dehydrate them for four hours or so until they are dry. Toss them in a salad.

Salad Sprinkles

Soak overnight a few cups of flaxseeds, sesame seeds or sunflower seeds. If you like, you can soak them in Celtic sea salt or Himalayan rock salt. Rinse and thoroughly dehydrate. Sprinkle onto your salad for extra flavor and crunch.

Snacks

Cauliflower Pâté ("Mashed Potatoes")

3 cups cauliflower, cut up
1 cup macadamia or pine nuts, soaked 4-8 hours, rinsed and drained
¼ cup lemon juice
¼ cup water
¾ T Celtic sea salt
½ T garlic

Put into food processor, using the "S" blade, adding cauliflower a little at a time. Blend until the mixture looks light and fluffy like mashed potatoes. The mixture will not only look like mashed potatoes, but the taste will also be reminiscent of mashed potatoes!

Serves 8.

Garlic Cilantro Flax Crackers

2-3 cups of flaxseeds, soaked overnight (note: seeds will expand with water; so it will become 4-6 cups the next day.)
1 bunch cilantro, chopped
1 T Celtic sea salt
5-6 cloves garlic
5-6 T nama shoyu

Blend cilantro, salt, garlic and shoyu in the food processor, using the "S" blade. Put the seeds into a big mixing bowl and fold into the mixture, mixing until it is spread throughout the seeds. Put onto dehydrator sheets, and dehydrate until it is completely dry on both sides. (Some people like to turn the cracker over after 6 hours or so, but it is not absolutely necessary.) It may take up to 24 hours to dry completely. Store in a closed, airtight container with some moisture absorption packets. (These are often found in supplement or vitamin bottles.) The crackers can keep a month or so if dry.

Barbecue Flax Chips

$^1/_3$ cup flaxseeds (soaked overnight)
$^1/_3$-$^2/_3$ cup pulp from carrot or orange juice (if not available, use another
    $^1/_3$ cup flaxseeds)
3 dates or ¼ cup agave nectar or unheated honey
1 celery stalk
2 tomatoes
1½ cups water
$^1/_2$-$^2/_3$ cups sun-dried tomatoes (if a heavy-duty blender is not avail-
    able, such as a Vita-Mix or K-Tec machine, be sure to soak them
    for an hour before blending to soften them)
1 dash cayenne powder
1 t Celtic or Himalayan salt
2 carrots

Blend all ingredients except seeds. Then add seeds, blending mixture
until it is smooth. Dehydrate in the shape of small crackers or large
ones that can be broken later. Dehydrate at about 105° F for about 24
hours until very dry. Store in an airtight container with moisture absorption packets such as found in vitamin and other nutritional supplement
containers. This will enable them to keep much longer.

Breakfast Dishes

Any of the drinks listed in the "beverage" section are also a
great way to start out the morning. But if you need something
to munch on...

Allen's Cereal

1 banana
2 heaping T sun-dried raisins
1 heaping T bee pollen
1 heaping t almond butter
1 heaping T hemp seeds

Mash the banana with a fork until it is creamy. Stir in other ingredients.

Serves 1.

Trail Mix

1 cup almonds, soaked, drained, rinsed and dehydrated or left out until
    dry
½ cup sun-dried raisins
½ cup shredded coconut
½ cup sunflower seeds, sprouted and dried

Mix together. This is also great as a snack or travel food.

Serves 6.

Appendix A

Killer "Foods" to Avoid

If you're going to America, bring your own food.
—Fran Lebowitz (1951—), US journalist

Some "foods" are simply not man's natural foods. They slowly poison us and are therefore deadly. "But aren't we omnivores?" you might ask. Most of us are omnivores in practice, but that doesn't mean our bodies are omnivorous by nature.

You might decide to call your car an "omnivore" and mix some other ingredients into your tank along with the gasoline, but how long would it take before the engine would be messed up? How much mileage would you get for the gallon? How long would your car last?

Most people would never imagine doing that to their vehicles yet think nothing of doing it to their bodies. They worry about the financial cost of repairing or replacing their ruined cars, rarely pondering that their bodies are irreplaceable regardless of the amount of money they have.

Nutritionists point out that we have expanded our range of foods throughout history. Chefs are proud of their culinary creativity. Food corporations tempt us with their sweet and salty inventions. Yet few have realized the correlation between our degenerating health and all the new food variations.

"Well, I have to die someday," is a common response when someone is made to think that just maybe these innovative food novelties contribute to bad health. It is true; we are all destined to die. But how many of us want to spend our final years with crippling arthritis, diabetes, Alzheimer's and the numerous other pathologies of old age? Wouldn't it be prudent to find out what some of the dietary blunders of modern man are so that you could remain in great health right up to the end?

There is an old saying, "The history of disease is the history of agriculture." Humans did not begin eating grains until the dawn of agriculture, which was only 10,000-20,000 years ago, not much time compared to our millions of years of evolution. The development of grain use, along with its processing and preparation techniques, led to the use of sugar, salt and alco-

hol. It also led to the refining away of most of whatever nutrition these grains contained.

Adherents to the paleolithic diet are quick to point out that
heart disease, cancer, obesity, diabetes, osteoporosis, rheumatoid arthritis and other diseases of affluence were very rare
among recent hunters and gatherers, such as the Bushmen,
Amazonian Indians and Australian Aborigines, until they
started to eat Western foods and adopt our lifestyles.

Around the same time that agriculture began, people started domesticating cattle and consuming their milk. They made
vessels to store it in. Various experts have concluded from both
anthropological research and nutritional research that very few
people can properly digest the milks of other species. Cow's
milk is excellent for a baby calf but can be quite detrimental to
a baby, child or adult human.

In addition, few of us can adequately digest grains, in particular gluten grains, especially wheat, one of the most common
foods we eat. Grains are for the birds; birds are graminivores.
Severen Schaeffer (*Instinctive Nutrition*) believed that the two
classes of foods that contribute most severely to stress are cereals and dairy.

You might think, "Wait a minute! But I learned about the
four food groups in school, two of which were dairy and bread!"
(And cooked meat, don't forget, was another.) Internationally
known nutritionist Dr. Mary Ruth Swope says that the Four
Basic Food Groups were nothing but the result of a clever advertising ploy designed primarily to benefit the dairy and meat
industries. I would add that it benefited the grain industries
too, although they probably didn't invest as much money in its
publicity.

In fact, the dairy industry uses the public school system as
their primary advertising target. They give free "educational"
(marketing) materials to teachers, who are often overwhelmed
with curriculum development and welcome ready-made materials. They have a web site containing over 70,000 lesson plans
for teachers to use! Their marketing is so effective that even the
most health conscious people, even the author of this book,
cannot easily erase the implanted idea that "milk does a body
good."

As David Klein says, "Our commercial masters, who endow
our educational institutions and pay for most advertising, control the American dietary profession and almost totally determine the pathogenic American diet" (*Your Natural Diet*, p. 13).

The food pyramid is not much, if any, better than the four food groups, and the "new" food pyramid is more of the same. *It actually includes salt, sugar, condiments, candies, syrups and other man-made atrocities as a food group!*

The biggest change from the old one is that the food groups are no longer presented horizontally. Now a colored rainbow, vertical stripes represent much the same disastrous diet, all with official government approval.

Through studies, such as those done by the Food and Nutrition Board, the government tells us that a diet high in refined sugar, fat, animal protein and dairy is good for us. Most people don't realize the power wielded by the food industries over the conclusions reached in these studies. They are nearly always funded by food corporations, and the "independent" researchers involved know that their future grant money depends on their coming up with industry-favorable results.

Food corporations lobby politicians to set government dietary standards in their favor and buy influence by contributing to their election campaign funds. As the documentary *Eating* points out, "There's a politician in your kitchen, and he's already decided what you'll be eating tonight!"

Because unsuspecting people trust government to look out for their health and believe in these studies, *they affect the health of most Americans by influencing the food served in schools, hospitals, orphanages, prisons, mental institutions, day-care centers and nursing homes and the diets recommended by trained nutritionists and dieticians.*

Dr. T. Colin Campbell served on the committee that wrote the report *Diet, Nutrition and Cancer,* one of the first investigations of the relationship between diet and cancer. He quickly learned that scientists in the world of health and nutrition were not free to pursue their research wherever it might lead.

"Coming to the 'wrong' conclusions, even through first-rate science, can damage your career," he wrote in *The China Study* (p. 265). He learned that the career of a sincere scientist, trying to get the truth out for the sake of people's health, would be damaged due to the powerful forces of the food and drug industries that would lose huge profits if people actually ate better.

We are living in a world in which people subsist on what can barely be called "food." Some foodstuffs have been so tampered with, such as sugar beets/cane and wheat, that they bear almost no resemblance to their original forms.

To top it off, non-food chemicals have been refined or manufactured and added to nearly all processed and many restaurant foods. Most prominent and dangerous among them are salt, MSG, aspartame, various "preservatives," hydrogenated oils and "natural flavors."

As a teacher in the public school system, I always knew it would be much harder to teach after lunch. The easiest day I ever had teaching in the public school system was when I was substituting at a Los Angeles school in which the children ate lunch one hour before going home. More usual is two or three hours.

Teachers everywhere try to save the least important material for after lunch. The children become extremely hyperactive from having ingested all of these abnormal molecules that interfere with their brains' functioning.

It is particularly difficult at the high school level where the kids can buy chips and sodas instead of the less harmful sandwich option. Some of them become hyperactive, while others fall asleep from hypoglycemia.

Schools earn sales commissions by selling these junk foods, and they rationalize that the kids would buy it anyway so they may as well be the ones that profit from it.

However, there was one alternative school in Wisconsin that was smart enough to change this by practice offering only totally unprocessed, whole food, albeit cooked. (Search the Internet for "Miracle in Wisconsin.") The school was also filmed in the documentary *Super Size Me*.

The kids in this school shaped up, focusing on their schoolwork, and achieved better grades. The school ended up saving so much money from lack of vandalism that they still came out ahead despite paying more for the wholesome food and losing out on junk food kickback money.

Even if you decide not to pursue paradisiacal health with a raw food diet, you would do well to avoid these "*killer foods*":

The Four White Evils: Wheat, Dairy, Sugar and Salt

Even if you don't go the raw route, you can gain tremendous health benefits by omitting the "four white evils" from your diet: wheat (and other gluten grains), dairy, sugar and salt.

Many times, it is not just what we eat that keeps us healthy, but also what we omit from our diet.

These four "foods" have been so highly refined and processed that they can no longer be considered real foods. Before the food pyramid, schools taught that we needed to get a certain number of daily servings of (1) dairy, (2) bread and cereals, (3) meat and (4) fruits and vegetables.

Decades later, there was an attempt to update the recommendations with development of the food "pyramid," but the food industry didn't approve release of its initial version — it was *too healthful,* which would have lost business for them! — so we ended up with a much watered-down revised version, which has recently been revised again.

Mental and emotional health is very negatively impacted by these "foods." A chief probation officer, Barbara Reed Stitt, was able to get the criminals she worked with to turn their entire lives around simply by omitting these unnatural foods! She proved that the delinquent mind could be healed by diet change alone and that the biochemistry of the criminal mind is created in part by the insane American diet. She wrote all about her work with criminals in her book *Food & Behavior.*

Grains, but especially wheat!

Dr. Joseph Mercola points out in *The No-Grain Diet: Conquer Carbohydrate Addiction and Stay Slim for Life* that nutritional anthropologists have compiled data from fossil records and other sources that indicate humans are designed to fare better on a hunter/gatherer's diet than on an agricultural one. Since we began eating grains 10-20 thousand years ago, there have been increases in infectious diseases, tooth decay, osteoporosis and diabetes. Even the organic, unhybridized grains of ancient times caused these negative health consequences.

Our genetic makeup is still that of the paleolithic hunter/gatherer, according to Dr. Loren Cordain, PhD, author of *Paleo Diet: Lose Weight and Get Healthy by Eating the Food You Were Designed to Eat.* In other words, we are meant to eat wild meats, fruits and vegetables, but not cereal grains.

Dr. Mercola believes that one of the most critical problems with grain consumption is the blood glucose elevation that it causes. This triggers cravings for sweets, which further exacerbate the problem.

During the last few decades, doctors have recommended cutting back on fat, and the result has been disastrous. Americans have consumed cooked grains and other highly glycemic carbohydrates more than ever, thus contributing to diabetes and obesity. "Fat-free" packaged foods are notoriously high in sugars and carbohydrates, which stimulate insulin release, causing fat storage and leading to diabetes.

High levels of blood insulin also suppress human growth hormone and increase hunger. They are believed by longevity experts to be a key factor in aging, as excess insulin raises blood pressure and cholesterol, shortens life span, increases food cravings, stimulates cancer cell growth, increases osteoporosis, and causes adult onset diabetes.

Another problem presented by grains is that they are high in yeast/fungus/mold. (See Chapter 4.) Commercially stored grains ferment in 90 days, during which time mycotoxins are produced. Grains that are not stored for long periods in grain elevators — spelt, amaranth, quinoa, millet, buckwheat and wild rice — do not present such a mycotoxin hazard.

Most grains are also acid-forming, which, as shown in Chapter 4, can be very bad for health when overindulged. Amaranth, millet, buckwheat and quinoa are among the few grains that are alkaline-forming.

Most people are more or less "gluten intolerant" and should not eat the following grains: wheat, rye, barley, spelt, triticale, kamut and farina. Severe gluten intolerance without a proper diet leads to celiac disease or dermatitis herpetiformis. Celiac disease is characterized by diarrhea, weight loss, irritable bowel syndrome and/or other signs of indigestion. Milder forms of gluten insensitivity include allergies and asthma.

Many holistic doctors believe that grains are also implicated in autoimmune diseases, such as rheumatoid arthritis, MS, underactive thyroid and skin rashes.

When wheat is referred to as the "staff of life," remember that a "staff" is a crutch, and a crutch is not something one needs for support when times are good. Grains have long shelf lives, thus proving vital in times of famine, thereby offering crutch-like support in the face of starvation.

While wheat may contain many nutrients, this does not mean it is good for us or easy to digest. In fact, wheat is second only to dairy in the number of illnesses, both physical and mental, it has produced in unsuspecting victims.

According to Carlton Fredericks, author of *Psycho-Nutrition*, "In Europe during World War II, when wheat imports were reduced by 50%, schizophrenic admissions to the mental wards fell by nearly the same percentage. In Formosa, the natives eating very little grain are reported to have a schizophrenic rate nearly two-thirds less than that of northern Europe."

Grains are not considered an initial food by instinctive eaters (Appendix C) since, as mentioned previously, humans have been eating them for such a brief time period. If you find a raw grain, it will probably taste bitter. Even if you sprout it, it won't taste that wonderful. Grains need a lot of processing to become tasty and edible. Because of this, the wheat we use today is so highly processed and genetically manipulated that the body does not even recognize it as a real food.

According to Severen Schaeffer, the wheat eaten today is so hybridized that it will not produce a taste change among instinctive eaters. Even chickens, which eat instinctively, will gorge themselves upon it.

The processing of grains employs many toxic chemicals, including mercury, cyanide, salt, chlorine, alum, aspartame, ammonium, mineral oil and fluorine.

Wheat contains morphine-like opioid peptides, which are addictive and increase the appetite. This explains why food manufacturers put wheat in everything. It is even hidden in items like ketchup under names like "modified starch." Gluten was found to contain fifteen different opioid sequences. These opioids also cause learning disabilities.

In an article entitled, "Schizophrenia and dietary neuroactive peptides," T. C. Dohan discusses how wheat and other glutens create endorphic activity, which is probably what makes them addictive, and also cause schizophrenia in people who are particularly sensitive. Whole wheat contains more fiber and nutrients than refined wheat, but it also has more gluten, which wreaks havoc on our nervous systems.

In a lecture, Dr. Gabriel Cousens described watching a normal, healthy woman being injected with a wheat extract. Within three minutes, the woman became schizophrenic, complete with hallucinations!

Wheat is found in nearly every American meal in the form of bread, pasta, pizza, cereal, cake, cookies, doughnuts and more. It can also be constipating.

I like to say, "Bread makes you dead." My mother was a big bread eater, and it clogged her colon. Naturopathic doctors say that "death begins in the colon" because the intestines are primary cleansing organs. If they do not work, toxins accumulate in the body. My mother died of cancer, and I believe her high wheat diet had a lot to do with it.

Grains also contain phytic acid, making them acid-forming and therefore potentially disease-producing. Excess acidity means the body will excrete important alkaline minerals, like calcium and magnesium, to maintain blood pH neutrality, thus leading to osteoporosis. Grains also may ferment in one's intestines, producing alcohol and gas.

David Wolfe, in *Eating for Beauty*, writes that products with wheat seeds can make the face puffy and the skin pale and pasty.

In *Grain Damage*, Dr. Douglas Graham explains why the government convinces us that grains are healthy. It is because all governments know that they must feed the people in order to stay in power, and grains are cheap foods with long shelf lives. If people were told that they needed fresh produce for optimal health and didn't have the money to feed their families accordingly, there might be a revolution. Therefore, generations upon generations have been convinced that wheat is healthful. Now even government officials have been fooled into believing it.

On an ecological note, before the agricultural revolution's advent, the world's human population remained almost stable for about 200,000 years, doubling about every 20,000 years. Today, because grains are such cheap sources of food for the masses, our population doubles about every twenty years.

Thom Hartman, author of *The Last Hours of Ancient Sunlight*, predicts that when we run out of oil to run the agricultural machinery, millions, if not billions, will starve. Perhaps this could be averted if we focused on growing fruit trees, which feed many more people per acre than grains do and don't rely as much on heavy farm machinery that depends on oil.

Dairy

We have been conditioned by the powerful dairy lobbyists to think that milk is healthful by intense marketing that begins in preschool. Probably no other food has been associated with health as much as milk! Yet, according to *The China Study*, casein, the protein that makes up 87% of cow's milk protein, is one of the most dangerous foods you can eat. The author says that dairy is probably *the most relevant cancer-causing substance that we eat* (p. 104).

In a study conducted in India, mice were divided into two groups, one eating a diet of 20% protein and the other consuming only 5% protein. The protein used was casein. Both groups were exposed to equal amounts of the cancer-causing agent aflatoxin. One hundred percent of the group eating a diet of 20% casein got liver cancer, whereas none of the ones eating a diet low in this protein got cancer (*The China Study*, p. 47).

Casein affects the way cells interact with carcinogens, the way DNA reacts with carcinogens and the way that cancer cells grow. A diet high in casein allows more carcinogens to enter into the body's cells. This allows more carcinogens to bind to the DNA, fostering more mutagenic reactions that turn the cells cancerous, which allow faster growth of tumors once they have been formed.

By adjusting the amount of dairy that we eat, we have the power to turn off or on cancer growth and to override the cancer-causing properties of aflatoxin and possibly other carcinogens!

The China Study also implicates dairy in Type I diabetes, MS, osteoporosis, prostate cancer, breast cancer and other diseases.

The web site www.notmilk.com lists numerous diseases and ailments that have been eliminated by people who merely stopped consuming dairy. What more evidence is needed that dairy is not a natural human food?

According to the documentary *Eating*, 70% of the population is lactose intolerant, especially people of color. Yet due to the strong dairy lobby in the USA, milk is required drinking for all kids enrolled in federal lunch programs, "which amounts to nutritional persecution of minorities due to their high rates of lactose intolerance."

When babies are given cow's milk to drink, they often become colicky. *Yet something is thought to be wrong with the baby rather than with the drink!*

Dairy is not only almost always pasteurized, but it comes from sick cows that are pumped up with antibiotics and hormones. In fact, milk is filled with pus cells from these sick cows' udders! This situation was exacerbated when Monsanto's artificial growth hormone began to be fed to dairy cattle to boost milk production. Their milk began to routinely exceed FDA guidelines for pus cell content. Rather than ban the growth hormone, the FDA increased the allowable pus cell content to match what the dairy industry was producing.

Dr. Cousens cites studies that show a correlation between an increased incidence of leukemia in cows and in children who drank these cows' milk, as well as a study in which 100% of the chimpanzees drinking milk from leukemic cows for one year also came down with leukemia themselves (*Spiritual Nutrition*, pp. 261-2).

A woman wrote this about her children's experience with dairy:

> My two children are now in their 20's, but when they were little, every kid I knew was having tubes put in their ears because they all kept getting ear infections, and the parents got tired of giving them so many rounds of antibiotics for years and years.
>
> Mine would get the same ear infections; so with my son, I made an appointment to have the tubes put in (a surgical procedure in which they create a drain in the ears). A friend asked me why would I have tubes put in when all I had to do was take my son off dairy.
>
> I'd never heard this before. I canceled the appointment, took my son off dairy, and he never had another ear infection. I did the same for my daughter: no more dairy, and she stopped getting ear infections and strep throat.
>
> Dairy and soy just breed infection; it's as simple as that.

It is ridiculous to believe we need dairy to get enough calcium. Tall human skeletons have been found dating back millions of years, while man has been raising cattle and drinking their milk for a mere 10,000 years. By eating nuts, seeds and greens, we can receive adequate calcium that is actually much better absorbed than that from cow's milk.

The documentary *Eating* points out that *there has not been a single case of calcium deficiency of dietary origin in the entire history of the human race.* The milk industry created this myth. Osteoporosis is caused largely by lack of weight-bearing exercise, insufficient Vitamin D, and bone demineralization due to consumption of excess protein and mineral-poor junk foods.

If milk were so good for our bones, you would think that we would have one of the lowest rates of osteoporosis in the world. In fact, those countries and regions that consume the most dairy have the *highest* rates of osteoporosis: the USA, England and Scandinavia.

Dairy, like meat, is high in protein, which causes the bones to leach alkaline minerals in order to neutralize this acidity. Furthermore, dairy is low in magnesium and high in phosphorus, which makes its calcium less bioavailable. Twenty-five to thirty million Americans have been diagnosed with osteoporosis. Of that figure, a quarter will end up in nursing homes, a quarter will never walk again unassisted, and a quarter will die of conditions related to bone fracture.

Osteoporosis is extremely rare in cultures that eat traditional plant-based diets. The best sources of bioavailable calcium are green vegetables like lettuce, broccoli, spinach, kale, dandelion and Swiss chard, as well as nuts and seeds. Greens can be juiced or blended to make them quick and easy to consume.

Sergei Boutenko broke his clavicle in a snowboarding accident, and subsequently he constantly craved sesame milk, which is rich in calcium if unhulled seeds are used. The doctors said it would take eight to twelve weeks for him to heal. However, the sesame seeds sped up his healing. After two weeks, he actually grew a calcified ball over the injury that isolated the bones so they could knit properly (12 Steps to Raw Food, p. 14).

In the book Biological Transmutation, Louis Kervran describes using the herb horsetail grass, which is high in silica, to recalcify broken bones. This worked much better and faster than calcium supplementation. In a lecture, David Wolfe talked about a woman who used this method with amazing results to reverse her osteoporosis, astonishing her doctors, who said she would never recalcify to that extent.

Dairy has been found to influence mental as well as physical health. "When I investigated hyperactive children, I found that many of them were 'wild and crazy' because they were sensitive to dairy products," wrote Lendon Smith, MD, in Dr. Lendon Smith's Low-Stress Diet Book. Alexander Schauss, author of Diet, Crime and Delinquency, worked with juvenile offenders and found that 90% had milk intolerance or allergy. Many of these also drank twice the amount of milk that others their age did.

Interestingly, Severen Schaeffer reported that all cancer patients examined under instinctive eating conditions carried very unpleasant odors, often reminiscent of putrefied milk. When the tumors shrank, the odors faded. The same odor of putrid dairy products was observed among autoimmune patients.

It appears there *may* be some people, however, who are genetically adapted to *raw* dairy, at least to some extent. These are mainly people of Northern European ancestry, especially from Scandinavian countries. However, the milk should be raw and from animals that have not been given steroid hormones, antibiotics, or unnatural feed.

For more information on the perils of dairy, see Appendix C.

Table Salt

Sodium chloride, the primary constituent of table salt, is a very toxic, inorganic compound. You can get plenty of sodium in its organic form from celery and various other vegetables. You can get iodine, which is added to table salt, from sea vegetables, such as dulse or kelp. Substitute Celtic sea salt, sea vegetables or Himalayan rock salt in all recipes requiring salt. You can also make celery salt from dehydrated, ground up celery, or you can purchase it ready-made.

Nearly all processed foods contain huge amounts of added salt, listed as sodium on the labels, in order to extend shelf life, enhance flavor, create addiction, and thus increase profits. Salt adds flavor to bland, lifeless food. The body needs only 200-280 milligrams of sodium daily; yet the average American takes in 4,000-6,000 milligrams. Some eat 10,000 mg in one day, which is $1/8$ of the fatal dose!

Since salt in the body holds 96 times its weight in water, the average American carries about 10-15 pounds of edema, or excess water weight, due to salt accumulation. This disrupts fluid balance, increases blood pressure and causes dehydration of blood capillaries. Half of Americans have high blood pressure by the age of 65, and high blood pressure is called a "silent killer" since one in four doesn't even know he has it.

According to Aajonus Vonderplanitz, four grains of salt (and he includes sea salt) destroys approximately two million red blood cells. It takes three hours to replace them and 24 hours to clear out the dead cells. Because nutrients are leached from the body and blood during these processes, salt speeds the aging process.

In her book *The Salt Conspiracy*, Victoria Bidwell argues that for all practical purposes, there is a conspiracy to keep salt in so many foods. When health professionals petitioned in 1981 for a bill to limit and label the sodium in processed foods, over 100 Representatives signed on as co-sponsors of the legislation, and numerous health organizations, including the American Medical Association, were in favor of it. But it was withdrawn after Congressmen were wined and dined by food producers.

Sugar

Since the early 1900s, sugar consumption in America has increased tremendously. The average American today consumes 150 pounds of sugar a year. When sugar was rationed during World War II, the rate of diabetes dropped sharply. Refined sugar is largely responsible for the rise in processed carbohydrates that Americans eat, which raises insulin levels, increasing obesity, heart disease and diabetes. Author T. S. Wiley declares, "*We are as addicted to a low-fat, high-sugar diet as alcoholics are to alcohol* because high insulin levels create the same brain state that alcohol does."

Most experts view refined sugar, or table sugar, as a drug rather than a food. In 1973, a Senate committee declared it to be an anti-nutrient. An anti-nutrient is defined as any substance or drug that is in some way antagonistic to nutrients, interfering with their use or metabolism.

At least 78 ailments have been linked to sugar consumption, which has skyrocketed in America the last few decades. Sugar suppresses the immune system, upsets the body's mineral balance, and promotes dental decay. It is often a factor in alcoholism, obesity, diabetes, arthritis, asthma, hyperactivity, kidney damage, cancer, hypoglycemia, varicose veins, osteoporosis, depression, headaches and many other ailments and diseases.

Yet sugar continues to be one of the main "comfort foods" of Americans. We crave it because the fungi in our bodies (see Chapter 4) love sugar and will push us to eat sweets so that they can survive. Eliminating sugar and even sweet fruits spells death to the fungi!

A good book on the pitfalls of sugar is *Lick the Sugar Habit* by Nancy Appleton.

Excitotoxins

"Excitotoxins" are toxic, addictive chemicals, such as aspartame and MSG, commonly added to foods to excite the brain. They trick the brain into thinking the food is delicious, provoking addiction while causing cumulative damage to the nervous system over many years. Thus, we have advertisements for chips that say, "I bet you can't eat one," meaning you cannot stop at just one chip.

Most people have complete trust that if a food additive were harmful, it would be outlawed by the FDA, but in actuality this organization works for the food and drug companies. (See Appendix B.) As Howard Lyman puts it, "[The] American people have been raised to believe that someone is looking out for their food safety. The disturbing truth is that the protection of the quality of our food is the mandate of foot-dragging bureaucrats at the US Department of Agriculture and the Food and Drug Administration who can generally be counted upon to behave, not like public servants, but like hired hands of the meat and dairy industries" (*Mad Cowboy*, p. 20). In fact, there have been cases in which someone working for the food industry temporarily got a job at the FDA in order to get a chemical approved for consumer use and then went back to the more lucrative position with the food company!

In the book *Excitotoxins: The Taste That Kills*, Dr. Russell Blaylock, MD, documents the cover-up to keep these chemicals legal despite the evidence that they are toxic to the brain and nervous system. Some of the potentially severe forms of damage include Parkinson's disease, Amyotrophic Lateral Sclerosis (ALS) — also known as Lou Gehrig's Disease — Alzheimer's, Huntington's disease, brain tumors, seizures and learning and emotional disabilities. A pregnant woman consuming excitotoxins risks damaging the brain of her unborn child. This is thought to be one of the major causes, along with mercury from vaccinations, of the increase in learning disabilities and autism among children.

MSG has been used by food companies for about 50 years. Reactions vary from person to person. They intensify when one has not been ingesting it for several weeks. Reactions may include headache, insomnia, itching, nausea, vomiting, diarrhea, asthma, anxiety, panic attack, mental confusion, brain fog, mood swings, neurological disorders — Parkinson's, MS, ALS, Alzheimer's — behavioral disorders (especially in children and teens), skin rashes, runny nose, depression, bags under the eyes and more.

You might read a food label and think the product is safe if it does not list MSG. However, this is absolutely not the case. The FDA does not require the labeling of MSG if it is blended in with a mixture of spices or food additives; so it is usually hidden. This is because, in the 1970s, consumers became aware of the damage it does.

It is definitely hidden in anything labeled with the following: hydrolyzed protein, sodium caseinate, calcium caseinate, autolyzed yeast, yeast extract or gelatin. It is quite possibly in anything labeled with the following ingredients: textured vegetable protein, carrageenan, vegetable gum, seasonings, spices, flavoring, natural flavorings, chicken, beef, pork, smoke flavorings, bouillon, broth, stock, barley malt, malt extract, malt flavoring, whey protein, whey protein isolate or concentrate, soy protein, soy protein isolate or concentrate, soy sauce or soy extract. One of the most common forms is "hydrolyzed vegetable protein." In other words, MSG is in nearly all boxed, canned and bagged foods unless you buy them at a health food store, where it is less likely to be an ingredient.

MSG is commonly found in soups, Chinese food, chips, processed foods (anything pre-made and packaged), nearly all fast foods and nearly all chain sit-down restaurants. It enhances the flavor of dead, bland food. Many restaurants also use it to give their food a burst of flavor. It's what gives foods such as the skin of Kentucky Fried Chicken, most potato chips and microwave popcorn that strong, addictive flavor.

A research assistant at the University of Waterloo, John Erb, was wondering what was causing the massive obesity epidemic. He went through scientific journals and was shocked to learn that hundreds of studies around the world have shown that MSG is both toxic and addictive.

He learned that MSG is injected into rats and mice to make them obese when overweight rodents are needed for experiments since these animals are not naturally obese. *The MSG triples the amount of insulin the pancreas secretes*, and insulin is a hormone that causes *fat storage*. In his book *The Slow Poisoning of America*, John exposes the food industry for getting people addicted to their food by adding this known poison.

Two good web sites to further educate you on this very important matter are www.nomsg.com and www.msgtruth.org.

Sadly, the FDA has no limits as to how much MSG may be added to food. As a result, more and more gets used over the years. This has doubtless added to behavioral and health problems among children. Think of all the pregnant women eating at fast-food restaurants, risking their babies' health!

Aspartame has been used for years as a sweetener in soft drinks and has lately been put into numerous other foods. It is hidden in canned juices, protein powders, protein bars and much more. It is thought to be linked to MS symptoms, brain tumors, sudden death in athletes, Parkinson's disease, brain fog, learning disabilities, ADHD, birth defects, diabetes, emotional disorders, seizures, migraines and more. Diabetics and young women are at particular risk, as they drink a lot of diet soft drinks.

A good web site for information on aspartame is www.dor way.com. A good book on its perils is *Sweet Poison* by Dr. Janet Starr Hull. There is also a movie documentary about it entitled, *Sweet Misery*.

After being about 95% raw and cleaned out for some time — and therefore acutely sensitive — I unknowingly drank something with a bit of aspartame in it. I experienced, for a brief flash, a loss of muscle control, spilling a container of raw soup all over the floor! I knew it was not "clumsiness" on my part but rather a brief experience of what it was like to have MS. My husband reported similar nerve problems after taking the same beverage. This chemical is insidiously being sneaked into processed foods in America without even being labeled as such.

Not only is aspartame deadly, but also this "diet" product actually makes you *gain weight*! It suppresses thyroid function. Aspartame is thought to make you store fat. Kevin Trudeau describes an experiment he conducted in which people replaced their diet sodas with regular sodas, and 80% of the people lost weight after two weeks (*Natural Cures "They" Don't Want You to Know About*, p. 160).

For those seeking low-calorie, low-carbohydrate substitutes, Splenda — the brand name for sucralose — is also very unhealthful. Some of its side effects include: a shrunken thymus gland, enlarged kidneys and liver, atrophy of lymph follicles, decreased red blood cell count, aborted pregnancy, decreased fetal weight, diarrhea and more. "Splenda is not Splendid" is one of the web site articles that expose its toxic qualities, located at www.wnho.net/splenda.htm. Just plug "toxic reaction Splenda" into an Internet search engine to learn more.

The best low-calorie sweetener is stevia, a natural and nontoxic plant that is 200 times sweeter than sugar, and so only small doses are needed. Because it often has a bad aftertaste, many people are replacing stevia with raw agave nectar. It is very sweet and does not induce low blood sugar since it does not stimulate the pancreas to produce or release insulin.

Processed Foods

Americans eat more processed foods than ever: foods from boxes, cans, bags, jars and the like. Most of these foods have the life force cooked out of them several times over and are loaded with salt and sugar to enhance their taste and preserve them. In addition, most contain excitotoxins, wheat, sugar, salt and other chemicals to enhance taste, create addiction for the consumer, and/or preserve the food. Processed foods have no food value apart from calories. They do not enhance life but only destroy health, slowly sucking out your life force. As Jack LaLanne says, "If man made it, don't eat it!"

America's processed foods are so bad that many overweight people could eat the same exact food types living abroad and yet lose weight! This happened to me when I lived in Mexico. It also happened to Kevin Trudeau, as he explains in *Natural Cures "They" Don't Want You to Know About* (p.157). This is because the chemicals found in our domestic processed-food products wreak havoc on our digestive organs, preventing them from operating correctly.

According to Trudeau, who has talked to many food industry insiders, *there are over 15,000 toxic chemicals added to our food that do not require labeling.* Since our brains are mostly fatty tissue, a large chunk of those chemicals are stored in the brain, leading to depression, stress, anxiety, learning disabilities and possibly Alzheimer's disease. He estimates that over 95% of all food purchased has up to 300 chemicals added to each product that are not even listed on the label. The power of the food lobbyists working for the food industry rivals that of the drug companies. (See Appendix B.)

Most of the sugar Americans eat is concealed in processed foods. Of the 2½ pounds of sugar the average American eats per week, 1½ pounds comes from high fructose corn sweetener used in processed foods, and it is six times as sweet as sugar. Low-fat or zero-fat foods are especially high in this sweetener to compensate for the loss of flavor from omitting the fat.

Processed foods are also loaded with hydrogenated fats. During the process of hydrogenation, the shape of the fatty acid changes into a dangerous "trans" configuration, or "trans fat." Hydrogenated soy or palm oil is in most packaged foods, as this extends their shelf lives. The body simply can't handle hydrogenated oils.

Research shows conclusively that they cause Type II diabetes. They also increase the risk of heart disease, cancer and autoimmune disease. Over 100 studies have been ignored by the FDA and mainstream media because of the potential economic impact on food industries. Furthermore, as a person continues to eat fat in this form, he is getting even less of the essential fatty acids needed for mental and physical health.

Processed foods may also contain Olestra (also known as "Olean"), a substance found in fat-free snack foods. It is a fat substitute that goes through the body undigested but unfortunately takes fat-soluble vitamins with it. Because it is a fat substitute, it becomes a large percentage of the food item. As a result, large quantities of what T. S. Wiley calls a "nonfat, two-molecules-away-from-plastic solution" are consumed.

For example, one fat-free potato chip with Olestra is made up of one-third Olestra. When Olestra is allowed to be placed in non-snack foods, Americans who fall for the fat-free gimmick will find themselves slowly dying of vitamin and essential fatty acid deficiencies — if they aren't already.

Those who consume Olestra are also denying themselves the health benefits of real, raw, healthful fat. Real fat is needed to create hormones, feed the brain, and perform many other vital bodily functions. Real fat is also needed to control the glycemic response to food, slowing down the absorption of sugar so that hypoglycemia and, later, diabetes do not ensue.

Additional killer ingredients in processed foods are: sucrose, fructose, maltose, dextrose, polydextrose, corn syrup, molasses, sorbitol, maltodextrin, high fructose corn syrup, margarine, BHA, BHT, sulfates, sulfites, dyes and colorings.

Here is the list of ingredients for the popular cake snack "Twinkies:"

Ingredients: Enriched bleached wheat flour (flour, ferrous sulfate [iron], "B" vitamins [niacin, thiamine mononitrate {B_1}, riboflavin {B_2}, folic acid]), sugar, water, corn syrup, high fructose corn syrup, vegetable and/or animal shortening (contains one or more of: partially hydrogenated soybean, cottonseed or canola oil, beef fat), dextrose, whole eggs. Contains 2% or less of: modified cornstarch, cellulose gum, whey, leavenings (sodium acid pyrophosphate, baking soda, monocalcium phosphate), salt, cornstarch, corn flour, mono- and diglycerides, soy lecithin, polysorbate 60, sodium and calcium caseinate, soy protein isolate, sodium stearoyl lactylate, wheat gluten, calcium sulfate, natural and artificial flavors, sorbic acid (to retain freshness), color added (yellow #5 and #6, red #40).

The only ingredient that is really a natural, unadulterated food is the "whole eggs," which comprises only a minor part of the recipe and is no doubt also cooked.

Now compare that with this recipe for a delicious raw cake:

Body of cake: Mix in blender or food processor 2 cups raw tahini (sesame butter), 3½ cups shredded coconut, ½ cup agave, ½ t Celtic sea salt, ¼ cup sun-dried raisins or dates.

Icing: Blend together 2 cups raw cashews, 4 T raw agave nectar, 2 t vanilla extract, ½ cup fresh coconut butter (use fresh dates if not available), 1 t Celtic sea salt, ½ cup water.

This recipe takes 15 minutes to prepare.

Which one do you think would taste better, the raw cake or the processed cake? Which one do you think would be more health-enhancing to your body? Of course, the raw, natural cake does cost more. It won't keep for more than a week. Which one would be cheaper and more profitable to mass-produce?

Here is something Dr. Max Gerson said in a speech in 1956. If it was that bad in 1956 — the year I was born! — think how bad it must be now!

But our modern food, the "normal" food people eat, is bottled, poisoned, canned, color added, powdered, frozen, dipped in acids, sprayed — no longer normal. We no longer have living, normal food. Our food and drink is a mass of dead, poisoned material, and one cannot cure very sick people by adding poisons to their systems. We cannot detoxify our bodies when we add poisons through our food, which is one of the reasons why cancer is so much on the increase. Saving time in the kitchen is fine, but the consequences are terrible. Thirty or fifty years ago [and remember, this speech was written in 1956] cancer was a disease of old age. ... Now one out of three dies of cancer.

This was published in *Physiological Chemistry and Physics*, 1978, Vol. 10, Issue 5, pp. 449-464.

Now, thanks to the wonders of processed foods, we are experiencing a nearly 50% rate of cancer in the USA. Soon, it will be much worse if people don't wake up and reclaim their health from the food industries!

Appendix B

The Drug Story

The whole imposing edifice of modern medicine
is like the celebrated Tower of Pisa — slightly off balance.
—Charles, Prince of Wales, (1948—) *Observer*

You might wonder why I am going into the "dirt" on the pharmaceutical industry. It is because of Claudia. Claudia was one of my first raw food students. She was enthusiastic about the diet but couldn't let go of her chemotherapy to treat her breast cancer so insisted on using both. I tried to warn her that even a raw food diet could not compensate for the toxicity that she would be exposed to. She died about a year later. I suspect it was *from the treatment,* not the cancer. You will understand when you read this chapter.

In writing this brief exposé of the pharmaceutical companies, *I do not wish to imply that no one has ever been helped by drug therapy, toxic as it may be.* Even if drugs don't *cure* disease, they can alleviate symptoms. Be aware, however, that the symptoms are part of the body's natural healing process. If you don't want to give up your barbecued spareribs, you may choose to take drugs to relieve the symptoms that will eventually arise before you age and die prematurely.

<u>But in a society that professes to be free, there should be no tolerance for suppression of alternatives that are far more healthful, and in fact, unlike drugs, do cure disease</u>. Drugs should be a *choice,* not a *forced option.*

Drugs are flat out toxic. Just flip through the *Physician's Desk Reference* and see for yourself! Just as humans have not evolved to incorporate and benefit from the thousands of new chemicals produced by cooking, we have not evolved to be able to tolerate drugs, which are just as unnatural to our bodies. So how did this penchant for drug taking come about?

In the book *The Drug Story,* Morris A. Bealle explains how John D. Rockefeller built perhaps the most lucrative industry in the history of the world. Americans now spend about half a trillion dollars ($500,000,000,000) on pharmaceuticals every year.

Because Rockefeller interests owned, or controlled through lavish advertising, most of the mass media, Bealle had to self-publish his book. It was first published in 1949, and even though it received no media attention, it was already into its 33rd printing in the 1970s.

Rockefeller was once perhaps the wealthiest man in America, owning Chase National Bank and Standard Oil. He wanted to make even more profit from the waste products of petroleum refining; so in the 1860s, he patented bottled, raw petroleum as a cure for cancer and the popular maladies of the day. The "miracle cure," called "Nujol" (from "new oil"), had a placebo effect, meaning that the belief people had in it created a certain amount of results. His cost to produce it was $1/5$ of a cent, and it sold for $28^2/3$ cents for eight fluid ounces.

Of course, some of these petroleum-based drugs had a certain value, such as for enabling insomniacs to sleep. But soon enough people would experience a huge price to pay in "side" effects.

Rockefeller nurtured his drug industry until there were 12,000 drugs in the early 1900s. His "charitable" Rockefeller Foundation became an instrument for "educating" medical students into his excessive — and exclusive — patented pharmaceutical therapy. With some of his drug profits, he granted scholarships to medical students, but not one penny did he give to any of the chiropractic or natural therapy schools, even though he himself used homeopathy, knowing full well that the drug empire he was erecting was a scam. One way he helped build his medical monopoly was funding, with millions of dollars, only those medical schools that made medical students memorize the uses of his thousands of patented drugs.

Knowing the power of the written word, Rockefeller then set out to control the media, making sure that only drug-friendly articles were printed and that anyone promoting an alternative, natural, therapy would be labeled a "quack." Newspapers and magazines dependent on him for his bountiful drug advertisements would not dare print anti-drug articles. *He controlled about 80% of all advertising by 1948.*

He put his men on the directorship of the Associated Press, thus controlling the "news" on health matters so that, of all the healing modalities, only drug treatments were published in a favorable light. One of his puppets, Morris Fishbein, director of the American Medical Association, was made the official "science editor expert" of *The Journal of the American Medical Asso-*

ciation, even though he never practiced medicine a day in his life and in fact did not even complete medical school! Several mainstream magazines were purchased with Rockefeller money: *Time, Newsweek, Life* and *Fortune*. Thus began the pro-drug brainwashing of the public via the media.

Furthermore, The House of Rockefeller got its hooks into the FDA, using its political power and leverage to influence it to become one of the drug cartel's puppets. To this day, this government bureau covertly works for the food and drug companies, not the public. They keep drugs and practices legal that should not be and outlaw or persecute those that should be.

They crack down on those who impinge upon the Drug Trust's self-defined domain. Former FDA Commissioner Herbert Lay, MD, once said, "The thing that bugs me is that the people think the FDA is protecting them. It isn't. What the FDA is doing and what the public thinks it's doing are as different as night and day."

In *The Drug Story*, Bealle has this to say about the FDA: "This Bureau — known as the Food and Drug Administration — is used primarily for the perversion of justice by 'cracking down' on all who endanger the profits of the Drug Trust. The Bureau occasionally prosecutes, on its own initiative, small-time opportunists who should be prosecuted. Thus, in a few small cases, the Bureau does good work. Its principal activities, however, are as servants of the Drug Trust. Not only does the FDA wink at violations by the Drug Trust (such as the mass murders in the ginger Jake and sulfathiozole cases), but it is very assiduous in putting out of business any and all vendors of therapeutic devices which increase the health incidence of the public and thus decrease the profit incidence of the Drug Trust" (pp. 39-40).

After a thorough investigation of the FDA, Elaine Feuer exposed the truth about it in *Innocent Casualties: The FDA's War Against Humanity*. She documents that the FDA goes after the companies that offer natural cures for those diseases most lucrative to the drug companies. An example of their hypocrisy is their making *herba ephedra* illegal after 153 deaths were linked to it; yet every year thousands of people have died from taking *recommended amounts* of *aspirin*.

Bealle wrote and published another tell-all book, *The House of Rockefeller*. He documents how they set up stooges and puppets not only in the FDA, but also in the US Public Health Service, the Federal Trade Commission, the Better Business Bureau, the Army Medical Corps, the Navy Bureau of Medicine, the Centers for Disease Control and among thousands of health officials all over the country.

An updated version of the story that reveals more of this corruption is found in the writings of Dr. Leonard Horowitz, Harvard-educated public health researcher, who wrote *Death in the Air: Globalism, Terrorism & Toxic Warfare* and *Emerging Viruses: AIDS and Ebola*, among other titles.

With his enormous wealth, Rockefeller founded and lavishly endowed education boards, thus gaining control of federal government health policy and also the output of the intellectual and scientific community. In fact, no Pulitzer, Nobel or any similar prize endowed with money and prestige has ever been awarded to a declared foe of the Rockefeller system.

Thus began the brainwashing of the American public and eventually the world, as Rockefeller's empire spread worldwide. It didn't matter that most of the drugs were not only worthless for healing, but actually harmful and even dangerous.

Studies have shown that vaccinations are a major cause of learning disabilities, autism and mental retardation in children. *Evidence of Harm: Mercury in Vaccines and the Autism Epidemic: A Medical Controversy* by David Kirby is one of several books exposing this danger. The drug companies even lobbied to get a rider attached to the Homeland Security Bill that prevents people from suing them for the damage done by vaccinations!

Furthermore, a number of antidepressant medications have actually been proven to arouse suicidal and homicidal tendencies in users. Hormone replacement therapy has been shown to increase cancer risk. If you still have doubts about the dangers inherent in drugs, just scan the *Physician's Desk Reference* for all the "side" effects of whatever drug interests you.

The brainwashing continues to escalate. Today, approximately two-thirds of all advertising is for drugs. People are convinced by TV ads that they need to see their doctors and demand various advertised drugs. People's minds are so altered by these ads that they feel that parents who don't give their children drugs or vaccinations are guilty of child abuse. Yet these drugs are harmful, and many are physically addicting.

Always remember: It was only half a century ago that medical doctors appeared in cigarette commercials and advertisements, advising which brand of cigarettes was good for digestion and stress and even advising pregnant women to smoke!

"One of the major reasons why there is so much sickness and disease is because of the poisons you are putting in your body. The number one poison you put in your body consists of prescription and nonprescription drugs!" says Kevin Trudeau. "That's right. The prescription and nonprescription drugs you are taking to eliminate your symptoms are, in fact, one of the major reasons that you get sick" (*Natural Cures "They" Don't Want You to Know About,* p. 33).

When Dr. T. Colin Campbell got on the committee to write the first report on the connection between diet and cancer (*Cancer, Diet and Nutrition*), he quickly discovered there existed a "Medical Establishment." He explains in *The China Study* that the hostility of Harvard Medical School and other medical universities surprised him. But when the American Cancer Society also joined in making the committee's life difficult, at that point he realized that a kind of medical mafia was in charge of things. Only after being in the system for many years did he learn that an honest search for truth in science is rare; powerful forces of money, ego, power and control take priority over the real quest for health.

Although more and more people are catching on to the importance of diet to good health, medical schools persist in failing to educate medical students about nutrition. Most doctors I have met took only two course hours of nutrition classes in their entire medical training.

Dr. Julian Whitaker, MD, president of the American Association for Health Freedom, said, "Many people are aware that doctors are woefully ignorant in nutrition. Only about one-third of the nation's 125 medical schools require students to take courses in nutrition, and most of those courses are very brief. This is a shocking statistic, considering that six out of the ten leading causes of death are directly related to diet."

Dr. Campbell points out that not only do medical students receive merely about 21 classroom hours of nutritional instruction, but also this "instruction" is largely influenced by the food corporations themselves! Joining forces to provide the Nutrition in Medicine program and the Medical Nutrition Curriculum Initiative are no less than the Dannon Institute, the Egg Nutrition Board, the National Cattlemen's Beef Association, the National Dairy Council, Nestlé Clinical Nutrition, Wyeth-Ayerst Laboratories, Bristol-Myers Squibb Company and others.

The reason that medical schools fail to teach medical students the truth about health is that drug companies fund them via scholarships and want to create doctors who function as professional and legal drug pushers. Yet, in prescribing drugs as primary treatment, doctors are breaking their Hippocratic oath, "First, do no harm." Since they are detrimental to, and cannot be assimilated by, the body, *drugs are worse than cooked food.*

As T. C. Fry stated, "In studying organisms, biology lays down its first law: that while a plant can make use of inorganic elements and by means of solar energy build them up into its own substance, animal organisms do not have this power and are dependent for their sustenance on the plant kingdom. ... Every inorganic material becomes a foreign element in the animal organism and consequently a poison to it" (*The Health Formula*, p. 122). Could this be where the raw food company "Nature's First Law" got its title?

Pharmaceutical companies cleverly use the term "side effects" instead of simply "effects" to explain the damage done by drugs. The use of the word "side" softens the impression, making it seem like a small, insignificant thing, like a small portion of salad dressing "on the side" or a "side dish," as opposed to the main course. Sometimes these "side" effects include cancer, heart attacks or even death, *symptoms much worse than the ailment being treated.*

In fact, a 2002 study published in *The Journal of the American Medical Association* (*JAMA*) indicates that one in five new drugs will either be withdrawn from the market or get a "black box warning" indicating a previously unknown, serious, adverse reaction that may result in death or severe injury. At the time of this writing, for example, Viagra has been implicated in causing blindness in some poor, unsuspecting men!

Another *JAMA* article ("Incidence of adverse drug reactions in hospitalized patients," 1998, pp. 1200-1205) showed that 20% of all new drugs have serious, unknown, side effects (on top of all the *known* effects), and more than 100,000 Americans die every year from *correctly* taking their *properly prescribed* medications! Remember, too, that this is a confession *from within the system.* Mightn't it be that the true situation is actually *even worse*?

Dr. Joseph Mercola, MD, who has one of the world's most widely read health Internet sites (www.mercola.com), writes in one of his Internet commentaries, "Unless we are able to break the connection to drug support of medicine, we are not likely to see much of a shift in the traditional paradigm. It is a very subtle, pernicious and persistent influence that is very difficult to break out of. In retrospect, I believe I was 'brainwashed' in medical school, and it took me nearly five years to break out of that mold, despite the fact that I was resistant to it going in."

In recent years, the drug push has gotten much stronger as billions are spent on TV advertising, as well as lavish gifts and incentives to medical doctors.

Orthodox medicine is quick to yell "quack" when unproven alternative methods are used for healing. The irony is that most of the dangerous and deadly drugs used in traditional allopathic medicine have not been proven. And of course those that *have* were proven using tunnel vision, looking only at the symptoms being treated and not at the overall resulting health consequences.

David Darbro, MD, wrote in the foreword to *God's Way to Ultimate Health*, "I learned that the Office of Technological Assessment of the United States Government had shown that 80-90% of the therapeutic approaches which were accepted by the medical profession as standard care *were actually unproven!* No wonder I wasn't seeing anyone cured! I suddenly realized that 80-90% of what I had been taught in medical school was UN-PROVEN!"

Dr. Mercola points out there are "hundreds of articles published in top medical journals claimed to be written by academic researchers that are actually written by ghostwriters working for agencies which receive large amounts of money from pharmaceutical companies to market their products. These are the very journals medical professionals rely on when determining treatment options."

Most of the studies done to prove drug effectiveness are funded by the drug companies themselves, which is like letting the fox guard the chickens. Can you spell "*conflict of interest*"?

A man I once talked to told me that he quit working for a drug company because he noticed that *doctors were encouraged to drop from studies patients who were not responding to the drug being tested* to increase the percentage of good results!

According to a recent report, *Death by Medicine*, the number one cause of death today in the USA is *iatrogenic*, meaning caused by errors made by medical caregivers. This study was compiled by Gary Null, PhD; Carolyn Dean, MD, ND; Martin Feldman, MD; Dorothy Smith, PhD; and Debora Rasio, MD, from government health figures and medical peer-reviewed journal articles.

They tallied up deaths from adverse drug reactions, medical errors, bedsores, infections, unnecessary procedures and malnutrition that occur in hospitals. They added in deaths of outpatients. The total for 2001 was 783,936, while the deaths from heart disease in 2001 were 699,697 and those from cancer were 553,251. They also estimated that the number of deaths due to errors is actually 20 times greater since many go unreported due to fear of lawsuits and confusion about the actual cause of death. Often, doctors mistakenly list the cause of death as the disease, when many times it is actually the toxicity of the drug treatment itself, as with the use of chemo-"therapy."

The study puts the blame for these needless deaths on the medical industry. Instead of teaching patients to minimize disease-causing factors like improper diet, pollution and insufficient exercise, current medical practice actually exacerbates illness via drugs, excessive surgeries, toxic and invasive diagnostic testing procedures and even counterproductive, harmful dietary advice! The pharmaceutical juggernaut and its pocketbook are *holding the medical field hostage.*

The report concludes that drug companies influence, via curriculum, the brainwashing of medical students as well as the outcome of "scientific studies." As the authors, three of whom are MDs themselves, are quick to point out, "It appears that money can't buy you love, but it can buy you any 'scientific' result you want."

Medical doctors are even complaining about this situation in medical journals, as in an article published in 1994 in *JAMA*, "Errors in Medicine." Author Dr. Lucian Leape calculated the 0.1% failure rate at intensive care units to be comparable to two unsafe planes landing at O'Hare Airport a day, 16,000 pieces of mail lost in the post office per hour or 32,000 checks deducted from the wrong bank account every hour! If six jumbo jets a day were crashing, wouldn't there be an outcry and a boycott of airlines until the situation were fixed?

The report by Null et al. points out that the equivalent is happening in modern medicine; yet the media will not give the issue feature coverage because they depend upon drug company advertisements. The entire report can be found at various Internet sites, including that of lead author and nutrition expert Gary Null, www.garynull.com/documents/iatrogenic/deathby medicine/deathbymedicine1.htm. (Note: A free login account must be set up on the web site in order to access this link.)

This danger of death at the hands of those who are supposed to heal us never existed before widespread drug usage; doctors and hospitals once employed gentler treatments, including herbal potions and fasting.

Nowadays, when hospitals or doctors go on strike, death rates drop in those localities. These strikes are always brief affairs lest people catch on to how dangerous their allopathic treatments can be.

In 1973, a strike in an Israeli hospital lasted a month, and the death rate dropped by 50%. Similar results happened again in Israel in 1983 and 2000. In 1976, doctors refused to treat all cases except for emergencies in Bogotá, Colombia for a period of 52 days, and the death rate fell 35%. In 1976, a slowdown of Los Angeles doctors resulted in 18% fewer deaths.

Patients trapped in the medical matrix must wake up. We should not have to fear entering hospitals. *Healing should not be life-threatening!* Healing centers should be places of *rest and relaxation.*

I remember spending nights in hospitals with loved ones. When my mother was on her deathbed, I was allowed to sleep over but wasn't able to get any actual sleep due to lights, noise and regular interruptions by nurses barging in. Even a healthy person like me would get sick after a few such sleepless nights added to the abominable hospital food and toxic drugs! So how can a sick person be expected to *heal* in a place like that?

Cancer treatment is perhaps the biggest example of the complete insincerity at the medical pyramid's pinnacle. As discussed in Chapter 12, the cause of cancer, systemic acidity, was discovered by a Nobel Prize winner in 1931, decades before the "war on cancer" began! The cure was also discovered — eliminating the cause by restoring the body's natural alkalinity.

There is simply too much money to be made in cancer treatment. Since it is a $120 billion dollar a year industry, the medical monopoly will let it go about as readily as a dog will release a juicy bone.

Yet Dr. Hardin B. Jones, PhD and professor of medical physics and physiology at U. C. Berkeley, found that people diagnosed with cancer who received *no allopathic treatment* (chemotherapy, radiation, surgery) actually lived longer than those who did! They lived an average of 12½ years longer. Those receiving no therapy lived, on the average, four times as long as those who paid huge sums of money for medical treatments

(*Transactions of the N. Y. Academy of Medical Sciences*, 1956, Vol. 6).

Though this research was published decades ago, today's "gentler, softer" toxic treatments are not much better because they are still based on the false premise that you can heal with poisons. The basic chemical used in chemotherapy is similar to mustard gas, a World War I weapon used to kill soldiers on the battlefield. It was so terrible that wartime treaties banned its future wartime use.

Radiation is nearly as bad. It is actually quite absurd to think that toxins that would kill *healthy* people with strong immune systems should heal very sick people with weak immune systems!

Orthodox cancer treatment consisting of chemo or radiation very often kills people before their cancer does. This occurs because the effects of the drugs include malnutrition due to loss of appetite, vomiting and destruction of the lining of the digestive tract, as well as destruction of the immune system as the result of killing blood and bone marrow cells. Hence, the patient often dies of infection before he dies of cancer.

Chemotherapy itself is quite carcinogenic, which is why the patient, even if pronounced "cured," will usually die of the same or a different form of cancer within a few years. In fact, the arbitrary definition of "cured" is that the cancer patient is still alive five years after the beginning of medical treatment, even if he dies the following week!

This is the real reason why early detection leads to more "cures." If the patient is going to die within six years, whether he gets the treatment or not, then detection within the first year may result in a "cure" since he will have begun treatment prior to five years before his death!

Even surgery, the third quiver in the oncologist's bow, yields less than optimal results due to its inherent limitations. Surgeons can remove only self-contained tumors, not cancers that have spread systemically throughout the body. Even then, they remove much healthy tissue along with the sick tissue, even entire organs that could have been saved by natural healing, which operates at microscopic levels that the surgeon's scalpel can't match.

Author Edward Griffin writes, "Excluding skin cancer, the average cure rate of cancer by medical doctors is 17%" (*World without Cancer: The Story of Vitamin B17*). So, not only is the cure rate low, but the definition of "cure" *hardly paints a healthy picture.*

It's strange that we have been blinded by the big pharmaceutical companies to believe that there is any merit in orthodox treatments for cancer when studies have in fact shown quite clearly the opposite to be true.

A German epidemiologist from the Heidelberg/Mannheim Tumor Clinic, Dr. Ulrich Abel, wrote up a comprehensive review and analysis of every major study on chemotherapy, even writing to 350 medical centers around the world to be sure he had everything published on the subject. After several years of study, he concluded that there was no scientific evidence anywhere that chemo could in any way appreciably extend the lives of cancer patients. He said it was like the story of "The Emperor's New Clothes."

Few mainstream journals published his data, naturally, since they are highly dependent upon pharmaceuticals for their funding. But by the time he published his report and subsequent book, *Chemotherapy of Advanced Epithelial Cancer: A Survey,* he knew more about chemotherapy than any person in existence. His report, published in *Lancet* in August 1991, described chemotherapy as a "scientific wasteland" that doctors were not willing to give up even though there was no scientific evidence that it worked.

T. S. Wiley points out, "A review article in the *Journal of Clinical Oncology* in October of 1998 compiled the results of a twenty-two year study following 31,510 women with breast cancer. Their overall conclusion was that over the course of twenty-two years of reviewing twelve different therapeutic regimens in various combinations, the cancer therapies only provided 'a modest improvement in survival rates'" (*Lights Out*, p. 144).

Ralph Moss, MD, has written several books exposing the cancer industry. Of course, these books are given no media attention. There are also several interviews with him on the Internet in which he blasts the cancer industry.

In his video "How to Eliminate Sickness," Rev. George Malkmus refutes the integrity of the alleged "war on cancer," which began when President Nixon was in office and has squandered to date over forty billion dollars in search of a cure.

"Research," he explains, "is nothing but a guise to keep the American people in ignorance." He is able to boast that people heal completely at his healing center, not only from cancer, but also from AIDS. "If the medical community were getting these results, it would be front page news."

At the end of the video, a medical doctor speaks about how he healed himself with the raw food diet and wished he had only known about this during his 30 years of medical practice.

When people used to ask me if acupuncture really worked, I answered, "Hey, it's been around for 5,000 years. Don't you think the Chinese would have figured it out by now if it didn't work?" Folks, the alleged war on cancer has been around about 30 years now. How many more people will have to die before we realize these methods are not working?

When Lorraine Day, MD, got cancer, she refused chemotherapy and radiation because she knew the statistics, and she wanted to live. For several years, her breast lump continued to grow. She became bedridden for six months as she tried 35-40 different alternative remedies, including the macrobiotic diet and supplements. When she hit upon what worked, live fruit and vegetable juices and wheatgrass, the tumor disappeared in eight months. She regained full health after another ten months.

She now promotes a living food diet. She has made quite a few videos, including "Cancer Doesn't Scare Me Anymore" and "Drugs Never Cure Disease." She remarks that the medical industry keeps looking for answers in the wrong places because they are stuck in the wrong paradigm. How ironic it is, she points out, that the medical establishment admits that people can *prevent* cancer with diet and lifestyle but maintains that they cannot *recover from* cancer with diet and lifestyle.

When Dr. William Donald Kelley found an enzymatic cancer cure that had a 93% success rate, including patients whose immune systems had been torn to shreds by chemotherapy, what was his reward from orthodox medicine? *He was jailed!* In order to continue his practice, he was forced to go to Mexico. His book, *Cancer: Curing the Incurable without Surgery, Chemotherapy or Radiation*, tells of his treatment and its success rate.

To me, it seems very strange that when orthodox treatment fails to cure cancer 80-90% of the time, it is said, "The cancer killed them." *But when an alternative approach works 93% of the time, the doctor is persecuted, accused of killing the 7% he failed to save, and jailed because he did not give patients the orthodox, toxic medicine that would have greatly increased their mortality!* Clearly, as far as the drug companies are concerned, *the issue at stake is money and not lives.*

Some people wonder why insurance companies do not sponsor fasting resorts and other alternative methods that work so well, when these methods are infinitely less expensive than standard treatments. The reason is simple: If people knew the truth about curing disease, they would refuse to pay hundreds of dollars a month for health insurance. People might pay a bit for accident insurance, but since the chances of a catastrophic accident are miniscule compared to the chances of developing a disease condition (nearly a 100% chance), then the insurance rates, and therefore insurance company profits, which are typically a percentage of insurance rates, would logically have to be much lower.

At the health care pyramid's peak, those who control the insurance companies are no dummies. They know that fasting and proper diet heal and prevent disease. But they are financially invested in keeping the masses locked in the wrong paradigm. Keeping people in fear that they have no control over their own health justifies large health insurance premiums.

In her book *The Medical Mafia*, Guylaine Lanctôt, MD, explains that our health care system is controlled by a group of three: the American Medical Association, the health insurance industry and, most of all, the pharmaceutical companies.

She once practiced medicine in the USA, as well as in France and Canada where medicine is socialized. She urges Americans not to socialize medicine, explaining that the only ones who profit are the pharmaceutical companies. Allopathic medicine focuses only on illness, not on creating health. Taxpayers' money would go much, much further in creating real health for the people by funding natural therapies and preventive measures via health education. Not only would this be cost-effective, but there would also be no adverse side effects. This is not happening because people have been brainwashed into believing that the men in white laboratory coats know best.

The pharmaceutical industry is a vast business, a dangerous cartel even to children. In fact, wise and loving parents who wish to provide their children with safe and more effective cancer treatments than chemotherapy or radiation often have to fight in court and *risk losing custody of their own children!* I heard of a case from a raw food teacher of mine who knew of a couple whose child had brain cancer. They had to give up their jobs, leave their home, and go into hiding in order to be able to heal their child with a raw food diet. The child was healed of cancer, but they lost everything in order to make that happen!

A case in which a young boy died because he was denied alternative treatment is presented on the web site www.ouralex ander.org/war1.htm.

The medical mafia appears to own a patent on the word "cure." Their servant, the FDA, has issued a ruling that states that the only thing that can cure or prevent a disease is a drug! There must be a lot of natural healers that are breaking this law by healing people, but they may not tell anyone.

Even though drugs do not cure, anyone who offers a real cure, such as a raw food diet, is putting himself in serious legal jeopardy if he claims that his treatment cures. In acupuncture school, we were sternly warned never to use the word "cure." This could cost us our licenses or even land us in jail.

The Federal Trade Commission (FTC) is another handmaiden of the medical mafia. Kevin Trudeau details how they harassed him when he was selling a natural remedy, coral calcium. He went to the FTC and asked if any of his ads would violate FTC or FDA regulations. They responded that the infomercial ads were acceptable.

Later, without warning, after profitable sales of this supplement, the FTC filed a lawsuit against him saying he was making unsubstantiated claims, *although they had approved these claims earlier!* They shut down his company and seized his assets.

He has since learned that this is their standard operating procedure. They wait until money is made so they can take it. And when the FTC files suit, it is not required to go to federal court. Instead, FTC suits are presented before an "administrative law judge" who is really an employee of the FTC. The "courtroom" is in the FTC building itself!

The media have relentlessly trashed Kevin for his bestselling consumer watchdog book, *Natural Cures "They" Don't Want You to Know About*. Shows like 20/20 that usually attempt to give both sides of a story refused to interview any of the tens of thousands of people who had written to Kevin praising his book for helping them find true healing. Instead, they tried to distract their audience from recognizing the validity of his message by focusing their efforts on assassinating the character of the messenger. He was, after all, attacking their drug sponsors.

The First Amendment to the US Constitution states, "Congress shall make no law prohibiting the free exercise of religion or abridging the freedom of speech or of the press."

Benjamin Rush, MD, who was a signatory to the Declaration of Independence and physician to George Washington, urged Congress to add the words, "or abridging the right of citizens to secure medical treatment from doctors of their own choice." He pleaded, "Unless we put medical freedom into the Constitution, the time will come when medicine will organize into an undercover dictatorship. ... To restrict the art of healing to one class of men and deny equal privilege to others will constitute the Bastille of medical science."

There may be some cases in which people's lives are prolonged or even saved by antibiotics or other allopathic interventions. But it is a very, very inefficient way to treat disease.

First of all, if one is eating properly and practicing good preventive medicine via a healthful lifestyle, he will not contract infection or disease.

Second, if he does become sick, fasting and eating properly works much better than drug therapy to restore health. These methods are also gentler, kinder, safer and much cheaper.

Yet the medical mafia would have people, during their last few months of life, spend their last dimes and even go hundreds of thousands of dollars into debt in order to prolong the dying process a few months longer in sheer agony. These cases happen all the time. It has been estimated that the average American outlays 50% of his lifetime medical expenditures during the last six months of his life. His children's potential inheritance is snatched up by the medical mafia so that he may endure a rather unsavory existence, hooked up to machines and barely conscious, for another six months or so. The cost of this is bankrupting Medicare and Medicaid.

Painkillers are perhaps the most seductive of all drugs because pain is the most unbearable of all disease or injury symptoms. But even pain medications are not as necessary as one might think. On a raw diet, especially an instinctive one (see Appendix C), one experiences vastly less pain from injuries. Acupuncture is also remarkable in pain management.

For those who are extremely sick and hooked on morphine, coffee enemas reduce pain incredibly well. Dr. Max Gerson weaned all of his cancer patients from pain medication with the use of coffee enemas, which he explains in "The cure of advanced cancer by diet therapy: a summary of 30 years of clinical experimentation" (*Physiological Chemistry and Physics*, 1978, Vol. 10, Issue 5, pp. 449-464). Medical monopolies don't like that kind of competition. Is it any wonder he was forced to move his clinic to Mexico?

Dr. J. W. Hodge, MD, of Niagara Falls, NY, has this to say of the medical monopoly:

> The medical monopoly, or medical trust, euphemistically called the American Medical Association, is not merely the meanest monopoly ever organized, but the most arrogant, dangerous and despotic organization which ever managed a free people in this or any other age. Any and all methods of healing the sick by means of safe, simple and natural remedies are sure to be assailed and denounced by the arrogant leaders of the AMA doctors' trust as fakes, frauds and humbugs. Every practitioner of the healing art who does not ally himself with the medical trust is denounced as a "dangerous quack" and imposter by the predatory trust doctors.
>
> Every sanitarium who attempts to restore the sick to a state of health by natural means without resort to the knife or poisonous drugs, disease-imparting serums, deadly toxins or vaccines, is at once pounced upon by these medical tyrants and fanatics, bitterly denounced, vilified and persecuted to the fullest extent.

In her book *Dying to Get Well*, Shelly Keck-Borsits talks about her nightmarish experience with FDA-approved birth control injections of DepoProvera that were supposed to be "safe." She experienced migraines, fibromyalgia, loss of libido, chronic pain, muscle weakness and a huge list of other problems resulting in several years of hell until she discovered Natural Hygiene, with its inclusion of the raw food diet.

She documented this horrible nightmare of drug-induced symptoms, along with those of many other women, and sent it all to the FDA, thinking they would be concerned enough to do something about it. She never heard a word back from them.

Shelly laments that we are a drugged nation, constantly bombarded with brainwashing commercials to convince us that drugs are the answer to everything from A to Z.

We are taught not to deal with our emotions, but to pop a Prozac. We are taught not to eat right and exercise, but to run to the doctor for a quick-fix prescription drug. We are pressured, even by teachers, to drug our kids with Ritalin instead of finding the underlying causes of their hyperactivity, which are usually refined sugar, food additives and dyes (Appendix A) or pesticides (Chapter 12).

Take no responsibility for your health! Just pop a pill! And when you don't get well, it's the doctor's fault or the drug's fault or the hospital's fault. And when you have paid so much money for the treatments that didn't get you well, complain to the government that health care should be paid for by taxpayers, the health care that *didn't even cure you.* It's insane, totally insane!

The drug companies are worried because a growing percentage of the American health dollar is now being spent on alternative therapies. Twenty-six drug companies have banded together to form an organization, now known as the "quackbusters," that tries to discredit true healers. They call them "quacks" and even stoop to the low level of sending false complaints to the FDA and other federal agencies. Visit www.quack potwatch.org for more information.

On a positive note, many doctors and other health professionals are fighting back when the drug cartel hits them with accusations of quackery. The ongoing struggle between the "health freedom movement" and the "quackbusters" is covered by a newsletter entitled, "Millions of Health Freedom-Fighters Newsletter." Those who are persecuted for using non-drug treatments are now *fighting for the right to heal!*

Another problem we face is CODEX, an international regulatory body that, for over a decade, has tried to make dietary supplements available by prescription only. If you want an herb or mineral supplement, you would have to get it from an MD, and then it would be available only in miniscule doses. This is already happening in parts of Europe, and the World Trade Organization is trying to make sure it happens soon in the USA.

Yet another pressure group is Operation Cure All, which has a plan to restrict health information, supplements and natural therapies. The World Health Organization, the United Nations, international banks and the multi-national pharmaceutical companies are all working in concert to make this happen. This group has already conspired to outlaw all health claims for products sold on the Internet. Testimonials are not allowed, either.

For more information, read the aforementioned *Medical Mafia* and any of Ralph Moss' books exposing the cancer industry, as well as *Racketeering in Medicine: The Suppression of Alternatives* by James P. Carter, MD, and *Politics in Healing: The Suppression and Manipulation of American Medicine* by Daniel Haley.

Dr. Marcia Angell resigned from her editorial position at *The New England Journal of Medicine*. She explained in an interview with the LA Times on August 9, 2004 that she had no choice after writing an exposé about how drug companies manipulate clinical trials and about their influence on medical journals, doctors and government agencies.

Her book is called, *The Truth about the Drug Companies: How They Deceive Us and What to Do About It.*

Clearly, the "war on drugs" needs to include pharmaceuticals. Perhaps Nancy Reagan should have said, "Just say no to *prescription* drugs!" Maybe, as I once told a friend, we should all join in partnership for a prescription-drug-free America.

In conclusion, let's consider these 16 quotations regarding the use of drugs in medicine, most of them made by MDs themselves:

- "The cause of most disease is in the poisonous drugs physicians superstitiously give in order to effect a cure." —Charles E. Page, MD

- "Medicines are of subordinate importance; because of their very nature they can only work symptomatically." —Hans Kusche, MD

- "If all the medicine in the world were thrown into the sea, it would be bad for the fish and good for humanity." —Oliver Wendell Holmes, Sr., Professor of Medicine, Harvard University

- "Drug medication consists in employing, as remedies for disease, those things which produce disease in well persons. Its *materia medica* is simply a lot of drugs or chemicals or dyestuffs — in a word, poisons. All are incompatible with vital matter; all produce disease when brought in contact in any manner with the living; all are poisons." —Russell T. Trall, MD, in a 2½-hour lecture to members of Congress and the medical profession, delivered at the Smithsonian Institute in Washington, D.C. in 1862.

- "Every drug increases and complicates the patient's condition." —Robert Henderson, MD

- "Drugs never cure disease. They merely hush the voice of Nature's protest and pull down the danger signals she erects along the pathway of transgression. Any poison taken into the system has to be reckoned with later on, even though it palliates present symptoms. Pain may disappear, but the patient is left in a worse condition, though unconscious of it at the time." —Daniel H. Kress, MD

- "The greatest part of all chronic disease is created by the suppression of acute disease by drug poisoning." —Henry Lindlahr, MD

- "Every educated physician knows that most diseases are not appreciably helped by medicine." —Richard C. Cabot, MD, Massachusetts General Hospital

- "Medicine is only palliative, for back of disease lies the cause, and this cause no drug can reach." —Wier Mitchel, MD

- "The person who takes medicine must recover twice, once from the disease and once from the medicine." —William Osler, MD

- "Medical practice has neither philosophy nor common sense to recommend it. In sickness the body is already loaded with impurities. By taking drug-medicines, more impurities are added; thereby the case is further embarrassed and harder to cure." —Elmer Lee, MD, Vice President, Academy of Medicine

- "Our figures show approximately four and one half million hospital admissions annually due to the adverse reactions to drugs. Further, the average hospital patient has as much as a thirty percent chance, depending how long he is in, of doubling his stay due to adverse drug reactions." —Milton Silverman, MD, Professor of Pharmacology, University of California

- "Why would a patient swallow a poison because he is ill or take that which would make a well man sick?" —L. F. Kebler, MD

- "What hope is there for medical science to ever become a true science when the entire structure of medical knowledge is built around the idea that there is an entity called disease which can be expelled when the right drug is found?" —John H. Tilden, MD

- "We are prone to thinking of drug abuse in terms of the male population and illicit drugs such as heroin, cocaine and marijuana. It may surprise you to learn that a greater problem exists with millions of women dependent on legal prescription drugs." —Robert Mendelsohn, MD

- "The necessity of teaching mankind not to take drugs and medicines is a duty incumbent upon all who know their uncertainty and injurious effects, and the time is not far distant when the drug system will be abandoned." —Charles Armbruster, MD

Appendix C

Radical Branches of the Raw Food Movement

Extreme measures are very appropriate for extreme disease.
—Hippocrates (460-377 BC), *Aphorisms*

The Green Smoothie Diet

Victoria Boutenko (see Chapter 9) is heralding a new "green revolution" with her diet consisting mainly of green smoothies, as detailed in her book *Green for Life*. This is a pretty radical diet, not just in content, but also since it makes one become almost a "liquidarian."

It began when she was searching for answers as to why her family, having been 100% raw for over 11 years, nonetheless had minor health problems, such as fatigue, dental sensitivity and gray hair. In her quest for answers, Victoria thoroughly researched our closest living relative, the chimpanzee, which shares 99.4% of our DNA sequence. In fact, she found, chimps are so close to us, even intellectually (having their own sign language) and emotionally, that scientists at the Chimpanzee & Human Communication Institute at Washington Central University believe chimpanzees should be classified as people! Chimps even have the same A/B/O blood types and are used for studies on tissue transplants.

When studying their diet, Victoria learned that the diet of the average raw fooder was very different from that of the healthy wild chimpanzee. Typically, a raw fooder will eat a diet of about 45-50% fruit by volume, maybe 5-10% greens and 25-30% fats in the form of avocados, oils, nuts and seeds. The rest would be vegetables. On the other hand, chimps will eat a diet of 50% fruit, 40% greens and blossoms by volume and then about 10% pith, bark, seeds and insects or even — though rarely — small animals.

Victoria developed her green smoothies as a way for us to ingest such a vast quantity of greens and found that by mixing them with fruit they became not only palatable, but also very tasty.

People writing to Victoria were concerned that mixing fruits with greens was bad food combining, but from her research, she concludes that greens warrant being a food group by themselves since they differ so much from other vegetables.

For example, they are much higher in protein. One pound of kale has more protein than the USDA recommendation for one day. They match human nutritional needs the most closely of all foods, making them "the most essential food for humans." Greens contain chlorophyll, which is "liquefied sun energy."

Thus began her green smoothie diet, which is very close to the ratios of our chimpanzee relative, about 40% greens, 50% fruit and then some nuts and seeds.

Her family experienced dramatic health improvements after just a few weeks of consuming two bunches of greens daily. Warts and moles they had had since childhood fell off. Her husband Igor's beard turned black. Wrinkles vanished, vision sharpened, and nails grew stronger. The children's tooth sensitivity stopped, and they needed less sleep. Furthermore, the family's cravings for fat and spices vanished.

You may wonder, why smoothies? For one thing, chimps spend about six hours a day chewing, something few humans have time for. It is necessary to chew greens intensely into a creamy consistency in order for the strong cellulose walls to be ruptured, releasing their nutrients. Who has the time for that?

Secondly, as dentist Price discovered (*Nutrition and Physical Degeneration*), we have damaged our jaws and chewing capacities through decades of eating soft, processed foods. Most of us have had our wisdom teeth pulled due to this jaw deformation, and those teeth are also needed for such intense chewing.

Victoria recommends a Vita-Mix blender since a cheap blender's blades would go dull after just two weeks on this diet. The reason for using a Vita-Mix rather than a juicer is that we need the fiber that juicing eliminates. Chimps eat 300 grams of fiber a day, while the average American consumes only 10 grams. Though the usual recommendation for humans is about 30 grams a day, Victoria believes we need at least 70 grams.

Additionally, blending foods helps predigest them since most of us develop very low levels of hydrochloric acid production as we age. Yet the green smoothie diet has been proven to regenerate stomach acid production. (See "The Roseburg Study" in Chapter 5.)

Victoria found that the switch to a greens diet created much more alkalinity. Her family's urine used to test acidic despite their 100% raw diets. They had concluded there must be a glitch in the test since they were on the healthiest diet in the world. But since adding the large quantity of greens, they have tested consistently at perfect alkalinity!

She wondered why doctors don't routinely test for alkalinity. I think they do not learn its importance in medical school because the medical schools are funded by pharmaceutical companies that know how acidic drugs are. (See Appendix B.)

So many people have noted dramatic improvements so quickly on this diet that Victoria sees *the switch to green as more beneficial than even the switch to raw.*

One woman who had Stage IV pancreatic cancer tried a raw diet, but the cancer would not go away. She then tried the green smoothie diet, hoping to prolong her life a bit more. After her next tests, however, the doctor told her that not only was the cancer gone, but also her pancreatic juices were healthier than the average!

Other testimonials in her book describe no more cravings for coffee, meat, sweets and fats, freedom from need of a wheelchair, normalized B_{12} levels and healed eczema and cataracts.

Victoria notes that the jaw needs exercise. She sells a jaw exerciser that compensates for the lack of chewing. Most people would need this, even if not on her diet, since we no longer chew as much as we should. It improves bone density in the teeth just as walking improves leg bone density. It also firms up sagging jowls.

I first met Victoria and Igor three years ago, and I must say, they look ten years younger now! I learned from her book that I had not been doing the diet correctly. For example, I was only taking about a fourth of the amount of greens I needed. I was also not getting nearly the optimal amount of fiber, which, as she details in her book, is crucial for eliminating toxins. Additionally, it is necessary to rotate the greens to get as much variety as possible. I am beginning to experiment with this diet the correct way with great results. The feeling of ecstatic well-being from normalized alkalinity is astonishing.

Non-Vegan Branches

Even though I am a vegetarian, I feel that no book on the raw food movement would be complete without mentioning these other two groups of raw fooders. However, since the version of the raw diet I practice, teach and promote is vegetarian, I decided that presentation of these somewhat radical schools of raw diet belonged in an appendix.

The purpose of writing this is not to convince anyone to eat meat. That is a personal decision people often agonize over. Meat lovers will only painfully forgo meat for better health. A small percentage of long-term vegans sometimes agonize over the decision whether to eat small amounts of meat after their health fails due to strict veganism. The purpose of this writing is not to persuade you, but simply to inform you of the issues involved and conclusions that some people have made.

Perhaps the majority of raw fooders transition to raw eating after first being vegetarian, or even vegan, for a number of years. Because of this, many of the raw vegan promoters prefer to think of themselves as entirely separate from the somewhat radical branches of the raw food movement described below.

Vegans are usually religiously adamant that people are meant to be frugivores, not consuming any animal products at all. Many feel that it was the animal products that made them sick in the first place before they discovered the healing power of the raw food diet. They cannot imagine that it may not have been the meat in itself that caused their cancers or other serious illnesses, but rather the fact that the meat was cooked.

Some researchers have concluded that although we as humans are all part of the same species, we vary somewhat in our genetic backgrounds and metabolic needs. It appears that at least a *few* people seem to do better with at least *some* raw animal protein. Others do much better on raw vegetarian or vegan diets. The authors of *Nature's First Law* are fond of saying, "Raw is law," and it seems that even raw animal products are far superior to their cooked counterparts.

Are there people who genetically require meat? If you research both sides of the issue, you may become humbled enough, as I am, to say that you don't really know. But one thing I do believe: If we had the millions upon millions of funds at our disposal that the drug companies have to devote to research, we would be able to get to the bottom of this matter.

Beyond Raw Food: Guy-Claude Burger and Instinctive Eating

The instinctive diet is, in my opinion, possibly the *ultimate diet* in terms of getting back to the way we used to eat. It is the way we ate for millions of years, guided not by nutritional theory, but rather by sheer instinct. It is the lost art of trusting the nose and tongue to guide us to the exact food that produces optimal ecstasy and maximum health. But it is probably the hardest diet to adhere to now, as we are so far removed from natural settings. We have to unlearn so much of our food conditioning. We have to learn so much to return to our instincts.

Though the diet is practiced by animals in nature all over the world today, humans repopularized it through a book, *Manger Vrai: Instinctothérapie* ("Eating Correctly: Instinctotherapy"), written by the French author Guy-Claude Burger.

At age 26, Burger was told he had no hope of surviving cancer. Doctors said there was nothing they could do for him. So, with nothing to lose, he decided to look to nature, since he believed that cancer is a disease of civilization. Possibly nature could heal him. He went back to his native Switzerland to live on a farm. After observing how animals use their instincts to select foods, he began eating only fresh food that he instinctively desired. *Within months*, his cancer diminished, and eventually he became completely free of it.

According to Burger, "Medicine is a few hundred years old. Instincts, on the other hand, have millions of years of experience behind them — all of which has accumulated in our genetic memory."

Eventually, Burger established a center for instinctive healing and teaching called the French National Anopsological Center. There people were healed of nearly every kind of disease using the instinctive approach, which begins with sniffing the food as an animal does. One sniffs various foods from a smorgasbord and perhaps even tastes a bite or two until finding the one that smells and tastes the best.

Then, one consumes this food exclusively until there is a distinct taste change, which is called an "alliesthetic response." If satisfied, one stops eating at this point. If hunger remains, one repeats the sniff/taste process with the remaining available foods until he finds another food that smells and tastes more attractive than the rest, continuing to repeat the procedure to repletion.

Herein lies the difficulty: With the instinctive diet, the food must not only be raw, but also totally unadulterated. It must be as found in nature: unheated, uncut, unseasoned, unfrozen, not chopped, not dehydrated, not mixed, not genetically modified and without pesticides, chemical fertilizers, fungicides, wax and so on.

Such foods are considered "initial" or "original" foods because they are in the state in which our ancient ancestors ate them. So a "walk on the wild side" for an instinctive eater (sometimes referred to as an "instincto") would be to eat a mixed salad! An instinctive eater, upon backsliding, might eat something that is everyday fare for a typical raw fooder, such as a nut and date trail mix.

An instinctive eater must thrive by eating only one raw food at a time. It is important not to mix the food, as humans have traditionally done since prehistoric times. This is because the taste change does not occur if the food is altered in any way. Mixing just two foods together will get the smells and tastes confused, confusing the instincts.

Why is the taste change so crucial? While attractive smell and taste are the body's ways of telling the person she needs that particular food at that particular moment, the taste change is the body's instinctual way of telling her that she has had enough of that food. Eating more of it could be toxic.

Zephyr, author of *Instinctive Eating*, describes it as an intimate communication between "the eater's DNA and the food by way of a biochemical, sensual message. This type of communication takes place between two living entities — a food and an animal."

One never has to be afraid of overeating on this diet. The taste change, which becomes very distinct with practice, will let one know when to stop. The taste change will make it unattractive or unpleasant to continue eating that food. The books *Instinctive Nutrition* by Severen L. Schaeffer and *Genefit Nutrition* by Roman Devivo and Antje Spors have lists of foods and what the taste change for each particular food is. For example, cherries become bland tasting when no longer needed. Dates become sour. Plums lose their flavor or taste acidic. Other changes include tastes that become boring, biting, sharp, burning or dry. One's lips may even bleed (pineapple).

In the book *Manger Vrai*, Guy-Claude Burger recounts how this taste change is so reliable that it saved his children's lives when they tried some poisonous wild berries. The taste became bitter just before a toxic dose could be ingested. Conventionally eating neighbor children who ate from the same plants were not so fortunate.

An interesting thing about instinctive eaters is that they include raw meat as an initial food. Some of them let the meat dry in dehydrators or in the open air to enhance the taste, as it becomes similar to beef jerky. Perhaps this is because our ancestors scavenged meat from carcasses that may have been sitting around for a few days. Instinctive eaters do not believe we were hunters initially, but rather scavengers, and so our diet included carrion.

Instinctive eaters consider it important to consume flesh only from animals that were raised instinctively themselves. In France, a company called Orkos even sells meat especially for instinctive eaters from animals which themselves are third generation instinctive eaters, making the animals much healthier.

Although excess *cooked* meat in the diet is often associated with cancer, Burger noted that he knew of patients recovering from what was diagnosed as terminal cancer who would instinctively crave large quantities of *raw* meat. Some people believe that raw meat does not make the blood acidic, thus not creating or promoting degenerative diseases, such as cancer, arthritis, heart disease and osteoporosis, as cooked meat is notorious for doing.

Since it permits not only the vegan nuts, seeds, fruits and vegetables, but also the animal products meat, eggs, honey and even insects, the instinctive diet is one of the most all-inclusive of raw food diets.

However, most grains were found not to generate proper taste changes and were therefore relegated to the category of non-original foods, especially wheat, which has been quite genetically manipulated by agriculture over the centuries. Grains are therefore typically excluded from instinctive diets.

Dairy was also found to be a harmful "nonfood" unless one is a baby consuming the milk of his own species. Burger ran experiments with raw, organic milk, including goat's milk, which is easier to digest than cow's milk. He and his wife even milked the goats by hand themselves to assure its natural quality. Members of his family alternated monthly periods of drinking and abstaining from milk in order to avoid confusing possible causes of any symptoms in the body.

Without fail, the milk drinkers experienced faintness, sunken eyes, weakness, diarrhea, bad breath, coated tongues (indicating phlegm build-up), greasy hair, moodiness and infections appearing in minor cuts.

Burger implies that they were disappointed to discover that milk was not an initial food. As a Frenchman, he undoubtedly loved his cheese. While Northern Europeans may retain the enzyme lactase to help digest the lactose in dairy, its casein still presents a problem.

The most amazing thing about the instinctive diet is that those practicing it report levels of health that people have never even imagined possible, even beyond that of mere raw fooders.

For example, while a raw fooder may experience minimal labor time and almost no pain during childbirth, an instinctive eater does not even experience a water breakage until the moment of birth. Then the breaking water propels the baby hydraulically through the birth canal so that no pain is experienced! Labor becomes a matter of minutes rather than hours. This is no doubt what nature intended for us before we were "cast out of the Garden of Eden."

On the instinctive diet, pain, inflammation and infected cuts are almost nonexistent. After an injury, an instinctive eater will experience the initial pain, which is necessary so that the body can tell the person that it needs attention, but after a minute or so, the pain stops. Because there is no inflammation, the throbbing pain that most of us experience after an accident doesn't exist for one who eats this way.

For an instinctive eater, wounds no longer become infected. We tend to assume it is normal for germs to infect a wound if no disinfectant is used, but germs only thrive in the toxic internal environment of a malnourished body. They are nature's garbage collectors (see Chapter 4), and if there is no garbage to be collected, they do not proliferate.

Burger claims that he and his family never used disinfectant for over 20 years, despite cuts from rusty barbed wire and nails contaminated with manure, including pig's manure, which could theoretically cause tetanus. Yet they never got tetanus shots and never got tetanus.

Burger tells how surprised he was when his daughter had an injury that became inflamed and infected. She confessed that she had been eating cooked food at school, but her temptation ceased after experiencing so much pain!

Temperature extremes are well tolerated by instinctive eaters. Severen Schaeffer reports a man who fell into an ice-cold lake and spent the night clinging to his capsized boat until a morning rescue. After fifteen minutes in the ice-cold lake, he began to feel "warm all over" and suffered no lasting after-effects from being in the cold water all night. Animals in the wild, eating instinctively, tolerate cold temperatures well. Why shouldn't people too?

The healing power of the instinctive diet appears to be greater than that of a random raw diet. Dr. Catherine Aimelet, a consulting physician at the experimental Instinctotherapy Center near Paris, documented the case of a mother who refused surgery on her son's third-degree burned hand, which the doctors felt needed amputation. By the 30th day of an instinctive diet, he had no visible trace of burn, no scars, no aftereffects at all.

Within one year on the diet, a 7-year-old reversed a pre-autistic state and totally cured hemophilia. Rheumatoid arthritis in a 61-year-old woman regressed almost completely in nine months. Often a heavy smoker or alcoholic quits his vice completely within days. In some cases, hair even grows back on bald men's heads.

When other diets have failed, the instinctive diet works in taking off unwanted weight. Guy-Claude Burger tells of having known "300-pounders who had given up on everything — diets, fasting and drugs, all to no effect — lose up to 110 pounds within three months." He believes instinctotherapy enables the body to find the substances it needs to release metabolic deadlock.

Chimpanzees, man's closest relative, eat about 50% by volume, 68% by calories, of their diet in fruit. It has been observed by Burger that instinctive eaters eat about the same percentage of fruit.

Burger noted that when someone has overeaten a particular cooked food a lot, he or she would be repulsed by that food in the raw state for some time. Perhaps the toxic residues and overload of the cooked food must be detoxified before the body craves the food raw.

In France, scientist Bruno Comby has spent many years experimenting and researching the instinctive diet. It is extremely rare that someone with full-blown AIDS will return to the stage of symptom-free carrier; yet his work documents several such cases in his book *Maximize Immunity*. He even cites a case in which *the person became a non-carrier of HIV!* His research is respected by medical doctors in France.

Interestingly, Comby has concluded that humans, as well as chimpanzees, benefit from eating insects. He wrote a book about which insects are delicious, although it has not yet been published in English.

Perhaps best of all, this diet confers great pleasure and even euphoria. Eating denatured food to one's heart's content creates guilt and physical discomfort, whereas the opposite is true with original foods. A person gets to eat his fill of whichever food he finds most attractive in taste and smell at the time of eating. People have set the following records for the following one-ingredient meals, consumed all at one meal: 52 egg yolks, 156 oysters, 48 bananas, 120 passion fruits, 16 melons. Yet no digestive upsets occurred because the food was fulfilling what the body needed in each case. No one ate beyond the point of pleasure; no one forced himself to eat more.

Zephyr insists that he feels most alive and healthy when he stops eating a food when it no longer is totally pleasurable. He claims that if science were to suddenly prove that the standard cooked diet were the most healthful, he would plunge into depression because the pleasure from eating cooked foods pales in comparison to the pleasure found in instinctively eating natural foods. Although people on the outside may think so, this is not the diet of an ascetic!

Instinctive eaters, more than any other raw fooders, speak of euphoria. Burger says, "When one eats initial foods ... one is in a constant state of well-being. One can very well describe it as a form of euphoria, ecstatic joy that constantly wells up within."

Severen Schaeffer describes his delight in eating instinctively, "Once the senses have reawakened, the delight to be found in a native food the body truly needs can litcrally border on ecstasy."

Zephyr writes in his book *Instinctive Eating*, "My ecstatic experience those first few days of instinctive foraging was the undeniable 'proof' I had been searching for, the missing element of my other food experiments. ... The high I was experiencing had many of the qualities of psychedelics. I experienced playful lucidity, freedom from many cultural programs, a more visceral sense of my connection to source, a more natural slower rhythm and shift of focus towards timelessness. ... It was an intense awakening!"

Eventually, Zephyr came to eat insects and fruit skins. It has often been said by vegetarians that we shouldn't eat an animal unless we are willing to kill it; so he even describes the primal experience of killing some of his chickens by hand in order to be in moral integrity with eating meat.

Because of his interest in living communally, he became an active member of an instinctive community in Hawaii called Pangaia. More information can be found at www.pangaia.cc.

Perhaps the most difficult aspect of the instinctive diet is the lack of food variety we as individuals typically have available to us. We would certainly attract a lot of attention to ourselves if we were to start picking up, sniffing, and tasting produce at a grocery store in order to test whether or not it is what our bodies need.

A friend of mine saw someone doing this at an all-you-can-eat salad bar and thought the man was mentally retarded! Besides, the artificial chill of such foods weakens their odors.

Yet who can afford to buy large quantities of vast numbers of foods? If it turns out, for example, that a cucumber passes the test, you may need to eat quite a number of them before satiation or taste change. How would you know how many to buy?

Having a smorgasbord of raw, organic produce to select from while the rest of the food is left to rot is not economically feasible. Therefore, it would help either to live down the street from the organic grocery or to live in a community that practiced this together, everyone pitching in some food.

Nonetheless, practitioners of this diet say that once you have become trained to follow your instincts in a few workshops, you begin to notice what your body typically needs and develop a system so that this does not become a problem.

Aajonus Vonderplanitz and the Raw Animal Food Diet

Aajonus Vonderplanitz' raw animal food (RAF) diet is in a category of its own. He is perhaps the most controversial of all raw food leaders. His story is one of going from *eating rabbit food* to *eating rabbits!*

Aajonus suffered cancer as a child. A vaccination also caused him to become dyslexic and autistic. Yet, with great determination to restore his health, he recovered from all of these problems by means of a raw vegetarian diet, which he followed religiously. Nonetheless, he still retained some health challenges.

After being a raw vegetarian for quite a few years in California, he biked around North America for three years, living off the land, hoping to learn the truth about optimal health by living in the wild. Occasionally, he lived with Native American tribes for a month at a time.

He went on a vision quest for his health dilemma in the summer of 1975, meditating, praying, and fasting alone for four days and nights, at which time an Indian spirit named Elk-of-the-Black-Moon appeared to guide him. Conversing with Aajonus, he suggested that raw meat would make him strong.

Aajonus protested that he could not kill an animal for food. The Native American responded that there is a natural agreement among all species. "Death is quick in the hunt. Suffering is a lifetime in disease. You choose," he instructed, explaining that the American Indians had lived peacefully eating raw meat under harsh conditions for thousands of years. But Aajonus was not yet ready to hear the message.

He eventually decided he preferred to starve to death rather than return to Los Angeles, with its pollution and the survival-of-the-fittest rat race. So he began to fast himself to death.

Coyotes kept waking him up. This happened night after night. One night, a coyote rubbed his cold nose on Aajonus' leg and motioned with his head for him to follow. The coyote led him to the pack, and they all killed a rabbit in front of him. A female coyote placed the dead rabbit at Aajonus' feet.

He felt that the coyotes were helping him end his life faster since at that time he believed that eating raw meat would be toxic. Although Aajonus had not eaten meat in six years, it began to taste delicious after only five bites.

Aajonus woke up the next morning after what he describes as the best sleep of his life. He felt strong. He had found the missing link to his health recovery! He peddled back to Los Angeles to spread the great discovery. Everyone thought he was crazy. That was in 1976.

People who have seen Aajonus at work no longer think he is crazy. He is respected by medical doctors who have worked with him. He has touched many lives.

In his book *We Want to Live*, Aajonus relates that his teenage son was once brought to a hospital unconscious after a car accident. Several doctors claimed he would probably die, but if he survived, he would be brain dead.

Aajonus describes in mini-novel fashion, how when no one was looking, he emptied the drug bottles of their anti-seizure medications and replaced them with nutritious, raw, animal foods: honey, eggs and butter. His son came out of his coma within several days. Aajonus went on to feed him raw meat.

Eventually, the son regained speech and the use of his muscles and brain. Due to the raw meat, the son's muscles did not atrophy as commonly occurs among brain-damaged accident victims.

He completely recovered and went on to study at a university. Eleven years after the accident, his son remained free of any seizures or other complications from an accident in which doctors had left him to live the life of a vegetable.

Aajonus has worked with people having all kinds of ailments. In his book, he claims he facilitated 236 cancer remissions out of 240 cases. He has educated people and assisted them in beating chronic fatigue syndrome, hepatitis C, heart disease and more.

He describes many case studies, including that of a teenage girl who reversed her leukemia by eating fresh, raw, animal bones with organic, raw, ground beef instead of getting a bone marrow transplant. He even helped a man avoid surgery for his knees by having him eat raw animal food.

Aajonus' diet is radical, perhaps because it is almost the opposite of the vegan raw diet. The raw animal food diet, also known as the primal diet, consists largely of raw meat, raw eggs, unheated honey and raw dairy. Fruits and salads are kept to a minimum, as these create an alkaline environment in the stomach when a strongly acidic one is required to digest meat.

Aajonus notes that since we are not herbivores with several stomachs, many raw vegetables are difficult for us to digest and thus best taken as juice. Nuts and seeds are also considered difficult to digest and are to be taken sparingly.

Aajonus proved that a raw plant diet can facilitate self-healing from serious disease, but he also discovered that raw animal protein not only helps the body heal, but also reverses aging and regenerates the cells.

He claims not to have worked out or performed any other strenuous exercise in nearly twenty years while still maintaining a muscular physique. He also claimed in an interview with *Whole Life Times* that only about four percent out of 1,800 vegetarians he had known since 1969 did well on such diets, and only about 0.01% excelled.

I have met Aajonus on several occasions, as he attends potlucks and gives question and answer sessions in San Diego every few months. He has the muscles of a man who exercises and a very healthy, robust, youthful appearance for someone his age — about 56 when I last saw him. His hair is brown, and he has a youthful complexion.

However, as many have noted, most remarkable are his clear, radiant eyes. Iridologists have commented that his eyes indicate perfect health! But one need not be an iridologist to be dazzled by his eyes.

At the potlucks, I was amazed to meet a woman I had known from years earlier. She showed me photos of herself when she'd had cancer. After a few sessions of chemo, she had found it too invasive and tried the raw animal food diet instead. Within months, she was completely healed! She has been cancer-free for many years now. I have run into her from time to time, and she continues to radiate health.

I met another woman who had been saying her good-byes to everyone while dying of hepatitis C. She was in remarkable health when I last talked to her, thanks to her recovery on this diet.

Although raw dairy was impossible for me, as I explain in the next section, I couldn't question that it worked for Aajonus. He is very much in touch with his body. So, I cannot deny the facts: Dairy seems to be okay for at least a small minority of people, so long as it is raw and from organically fed animals not polluted with antibiotics and steroids.

On the other hand, who knows whether consumers of raw dairy will not encounter health problems down the road? It is questionable as to whether we are truly able to fully digest casein. The instinctive eaters are adamant that this creates health problems.

Even if you are a militant vegan, I would encourage you to read the book *We Want to Live*. It is a true testament to the power of raw food nutrition to heal not only disease, but also trauma — trauma so horrific that one may otherwise be forced to live out his life as a "vegetable"!

Before reading his book, I thought orthodox medicine was at least superior for accidents and trauma; now I am not so sure. The first half is written in the form of a true mini-novel that *you will not be able to put down*. I just *had* to read the whole thing in one day, which is rare for me. The second half consists of frequently asked questions and answers, as well as dietary remedies for particular ailments. Recipes are in a separate book, *The Recipe for Living Without Disease*.

Nonetheless, anecdotal reports on the Internet chat groups have stressed that some people have suffered heart disease and even liver problems on a diet of so much animal fat. There is probably only a small minority who can thrive on this diet.

Issues with Raw Meat, Dairy and Eggs

When the subject of eating raw meat comes up, the first fear that arises is that of bacteria. According to Aajonus, if one eats raw meat that is highly contaminated, the smell will be so putrid that no one would want to eat it. This instinctual warning signal of a strong, awful, odor given to us by nature is destroyed by cooking. Cooked food will accumulate 50-60 times the bacterial count that raw food gets before it gives off this putrid odor. Therefore, the risk of getting harmful bacterial infection from *cooked* meat is much greater, as it is harder to detect.

If bacteria from raw meat were so dangerous, why aren't all of the wild, carnivorous animals dropping dead from salmonella and other infections? You don't see too many of them sterilizing their food.

Raw meat, especially pork, is not advised for the beginner or part-timer. However, when one has healthy intestines, having been cleaned out on a raw diet for some time, intestinal parasites will theoretically not thrive. If one is still full of toxic debris from cooked or unnatural foods, worms and other parasites can flourish. A parasitic infection actually assists in cleaning up this debris by consuming the weak, dead and mutated cells of the intestinal lining. They break these damaged cells down into substances the body can eliminate.

Bruno Comby gives an account of a person with a tapeworm that wouldn't go away with medication, but it was completely passed in the stools after the individual switched to a raw, instinctive diet.

Guy-Claude Burger even ate raw pork without getting trichinosis. He maintains that on an instinctive diet, the parasites simply don't thrive. He gives an example of a man who had been suffering pinworms and couldn't get rid of them until he tried the diet. *Within days* of eating raw foods exclusively and instinctively, the worms flushed out, and he has been free of them since. Remember, however, that Burger and the people he worked with were eating only very healthy animals: third generation instinctive eaters.

Aajonus Vonderplanitz said in a 1998 interview with *Whole Life Times*, "Once I ate pinworm-infested salmon and ten weeks afterward did not prove positive for any kind of intestinal parasite. I have eaten raw meat since 1976 and have never suffered parasites." If one is clean inside, the parasites don't have an environment in which they can survive.

On the other hand, I received word that a noted instinctive eater and author of a book on instinctive eating nearly died of trichinosis from eating a raw, wild, mongoose. These creatures have been known to eat cooked food scraps from human trash. Carnivore, beware!

Another point I wish to stress is that while in theory it may seem healthful to eat raw meat, things have changed with our modern animal farming and meat distribution methods. As Dr. Lorraine Day, MD, points out in her video "Drugs Never Cure Disease!" meat inspectors tell us that all hamburger meat in this country is made from what they call "4-D meat," which means the animal was dead, dying, diseased or disabled.

In this video, Dr. Day explains that the chickens we buy at the supermarket have had their intestines pulled out in the slaughterhouse. The excrement pours all over the chickens, and the chickens are actually soaked together in a vat filled with the excrement until they absorb 10% additional weight from this fecal soup!

The government allows this practice because if they didn't, it would cost the chicken companies a lot of money. The Tyson company, for example, would lose 40 million dollars a year. You may be wondering why the government doesn't also consider the medical costs to the people eating this fecal-infested chicken. Perhaps it is because the people don't have the lobbying power of Tyson Foods.

Finally, for those who still think fish is a healthful alternative: Fish that are high on the food chain, i.e., tuna, shark, swordfish and other large ones, can have up to a million times the pollution of the water they swim in! This includes not only mercury, but also dioxins, pesticides, cadmium and petroleum hydrocarbons. Bon appétit!

Perhaps one of the most toxic of all raw animal products is dairy. *I remain unconvinced that there are very many, if any, people who can truly digest the casein in even raw dairy.* Humans stop making rennin, the enzyme needed to digest casein, at about age three, by which time they are weaned from their mothers' milk.

After being on the raw vegan diet for nine months, I read Aajonus Vonderplanitz' books and decided to try the raw animal food diet as an experiment. I was thrilled to be able to eat dairy again, for I had been a real cheese-lover, especially feta cheese. I placed an order with some Amish for raw cottage cheese, kefir, yogurt and several flavors of cheeses. I was in dairy heaven!

I had just gotten off a two-week juice-only diet; so I was very clean inside, and my sensitivity was therefore heightened. If something was bad for me, my body was going to reject it immediately; there would be no room for me to be in denial!

To my chagrin, I got asthma attacks as bad as when I was a teenager. The phlegm layers having been cleaned out, the toxins got to me more intensely. It felt like there was a tight band all around my chest, as if my lungs had been glued so that they could not expand! I couldn't sleep because if I lay down, I couldn't breathe. I could barely breathe at all.

I wish I had the mutated gene (if such exists) that accepts dairy from another species, but I don't. And breathing is really important to me. If you have ever suffered from asthma, you know how horrible it can be and how little sleep you get in the night when there is an attack.

I can still digest raw cream and raw butter because those are pure fat. It is the protein in dairy that contains casein, *which is what glue is made of.* It sticks to the digestive tract, forming abnormal mucus in most people who eat dairy.

In *The China Study*, casein is implicated as one of the major cancer-causing substances humans consume! For more on the negative effects of dairy, see Appendix A.

While I was in great pain from the asthma attacks, I kept thinking, "So, the main reason I got such bad asthma when I was young was simply due to the dairy!"

I was told that I "outgrew" the childhood asthma, but what had really happened was that my body had formed such a thick mucoid layer that the dairy was no longer absorbed so quickly as to give me such acute reactions. Instead, it was slowly poisoning me.

If only doctors were educated in nutrition! It would have spared me decades of pain and addiction to stimulants (asthma pills and *herba ephedra*) had I known how simple it would have been to avoid the asthma altogether. I often wonder what my life would have been like if doctors were educated about nutrition. How much more would I have accomplished had I not taken that detour in my life?

Raw eggs are, in my opinion, the least harmful of raw animal foods. They have gotten a bad rap because of salmonella infection. But salmonella, like other bacteria, is not the problem. It is only a scavenger that helps clean a toxic person out. Only a sick, toxic chicken is going to be infected with it anyway, and you shouldn't be eating the eggs of such chickens.

If you are not up for a major cleansing, simply avoid eating eggs that smell or look bad or have yolk membranes that break easily. Eat eggs only from organic, vegan-fed, free-range chickens, as these are much healthier. As with meat, the uncooked egg will smell much worse than a cooked one when it is highly infected.

Osteopathic physician Joseph Mercola claims from his research that only one in 30,000 eggs contains salmonella in high enough quantities to create illness. Check out his web site at www.mercola.com.

In *The No-Grain Diet*, he cites a study by the USDA in 2002 that found that 2.3 million eggs every year are contaminated with salmonella. But since *69 billion eggs* are produced annually, this means only one in 30,000 have salmonella. If you wish to minimize your chances of getting sick, buy eggs that come from healthy chickens. The carton should state "free range" and "vegan fed." These are not fed dead chickens or chicken excrement; so you don't have to worry about getting "mad chicken disease" in case that is later discovered to be a counterpart to mad cow disease, which reputedly arose from feeding infected, dead cows to live cattle.

Free range and vegan-fed, especially including flaxseeds, are always the best, as they are higher in beneficial omega-3 fatty acids, as opposed to the more common omega-6 fatty acids. Furthermore, such eggs taste much, much more delicious. The yolks are deep yellow and rich in flavor, whereas conventionally raised chickens lay eggs with pale yolks that are much blander in taste.

If you are avoiding eggs for ethical reasons, eggs from free-range chickens are not much better than from caged chickens. I have heard that for some factory farms, the poor chickens only get to roam out of their cages for as little as five minutes a day!

The cholesterol in eggs has also given them an undeservedly bad reputation. Our society is suffering from heart disease because nearly all of the fat we eat, and certainly *all of the animal fat* we eat, is cooked. Harmful cholesterol accumulations result from fats that have been cooked or are rancid.

Arterial cholesterol accumulations actually *decrease* with *raw* fats. According to enzyme expert Dr. Edward Howell, raw fats belong in a category of their own. They contain the enzyme lipase, which is destroyed by cooking or processing. This enzyme helps properly digest the fat. Raw fats have no harmful effect on the arteries or heart. The Eskimos lived on a diet very, very high in raw animal fats, including raw eggs, and suffered no heart disease until introduced to cooking.

According to Aajonus Vonderplanitz, raw fat is needed more than any other nutrient, even more than carbohydrates and protein. It cleanses, fuels, lubricates and protects the body.

Some people caution against eating raw egg white because it contains avidin, an enzyme inhibitor that interferes with the absorption of biotin, a B vitamin. Dr. Mercola used to recommend eating the whole egg raw until Dr. Sharma, PhD, who is a biochemist with Bayer, investigated the matter. He concluded that there is not enough biotin in an egg yolk to bind to all the avidin present in the raw whites. He found that 5.7 grams of biotin are required to neutralize all of the avidin found in the raw white of an average-sized egg. There are only about 25 micrograms — or 25 millionths of a gram — of biotin in an average egg yolk.

Nonetheless, animals in the wild consume the entire egg. Aajonus Vonderplanitz experimented with feeding people, as well as animals, yolks without the whites and found that eating both together was more conducive to metabolic and emotional balance. However, some people, including me, find the egg white to be mucus-forming.

One danger of raw animal foods is their high level of mycotoxins. (See Chapter 4.) Dr. Cousens is convinced that all animal products — no matter how raw, organic or home-reared — are high in mycotoxins. According to *The Fungal/Mycotoxin Etiology of Human Disease*, Vol. 2, 1994, a single egg contains 37 million pathogenic microorganisms. Even pasteurized milk has 5 million, and beef, poultry, lamb and seafood contain 336 million per serving. While an average American meal of animal products has 750 million to a billion of these pathogenic microorganisms, the average vegan meal has less than 500! When you compare a billion to 500, this is a most convincing argument in favor of being at least primarily vegan.

On other hand, let us not fall into the trap of being too germ-phobic, as we have been brainwashed to be. A certain amount of bacteria is actually good for us, and there is a theory that our immune systems have been weakened by our "war on germs" mentality.

Meat: To Eat or not to Eat

Man's digestive tract is long, like that of a vegetarian animal. Man likely originated in a tropical area, but as he migrated to colder climates, eating meat became necessary for survival because it was the only thing around to eat in the winter. In practice, if not in theory, there seem to be a number of people who fare much better with *at least some occasional* meat.

After many years on a raw food diet, some people feel deficient in something, even weak, perhaps due to Vitamin B_{12} deficiency. (See Chapter 12.) Aajonus Vonderplanitz claims that while initially the raw vegan diet improved his health, he deteriorated despite following all the rules to get complete protein.

Some would have taken that as a signal that they should eat some cooked food, perhaps even cooked meat. But could it be that their bodies really need not cooked food, not cooked meat, but meat in its natural, raw state? Eighty-five percent of the nutrition in meat is destroyed in cooking; the proteins are damaged, making them less assimilated and even quite toxic. Surely if meat is needed, it must be eaten from a healthy, organically fed animal and in its raw, natural form.

A dentist, Dr. Weston Price, lived with native peoples from all over the world before they were assimilated into modern society with its artificially refined diet. He found the healthiest people were not vegetarians, but meat eaters, especially the Eskimos, who were raw meat eaters and for whom 90% of their diet was raw animal food. Referring to the Eskimos, he wrote, "In his primitive state, he has provided an example of physical excellence and dental perfection such as has seldom been excelled by any race in the past or present."

On the other hand, it has been argued that Price studied only 14 groups of people, of which only a small minority were vegetarian. Perhaps those vegetarians did not have access to a wide enough variety of foods. Since his work did not really focus on the issue of vegetarianism, his remarks in that department do not carry as much weight as his main point that we need to go back to unprocessed, whole foods. Additionally, the Eskimos maintained glowing health mostly because they were eating everything 100% raw, and Price did not consider that a relevant factor, instead attributing it to the meat.

Those on the path of instinctive nutrition eat raw meat very moderately. Severen Schaeffer claims that it is regularly observed in instinctive eating conditions that healthy infants, children and adults are spontaneously attracted to the smells and tastes of meat. Guy-Claude Burger talked about feeding meat, which his wife chewed beforehand, to his newborn infant, who enjoyed it and slept peacefully that night.

Zephyr writes in his book *Instinctive Eating* that he once found his body craving something he hadn't been giving it. An inner voice told him to eat raw meat, and this turned out to be the missing link that liberated him from backsliding into cooked foods. He says that raw meat gave him power, drive and passion. He claims he has known only one person who has been able to remain consistently an instinctive eater for longer than a few years without eating raw meat and that certain states of consciousness are activated and nourished by eating and even killing animals.

Devivo and Spors point out in *Genefit Nutrition* that raw meat has tremendous therapeutic value under certain conditions but can also be the most dangerous of foods if overeaten. They even observed fast-growing tumors in people who ate excessively large amounts of raw meat over several years and attribute this to the accumulation of undigested foreign proteins that overload the system and create mutations, boosting the production of cancer cells. They claim that mammalian proteins are the worst "because they are closest to our own proteins; so the immune system might not always recognize them as foreign and might allow them to accumulate freely in the body" (p. 80).

Research indicates that some people fare better on vegetarian diets, while others appear to do better with some meat. This is thought to be related to the genes: Those with tropical genes can live as vegetarians, while those with Northern European genes might need meat. If you find that you are what the authors of *The Metabolic Typing Diet* call a "protein type," who needs more protein, it may be difficult to get enough protein on a raw vegan diet.

However, you can still remain vegetarian by supplementing your raw diet with raw eggs, sprouted legumes and grains and soaked seeds and nuts. A few people may even handle raw dairy if they have the genetic mutation to tolerate it.

As mentioned in Chapter 12, perhaps those who seem to require meat cannot assimilate sufficient Vitamin B_{12} any other way. There is a lot of controversy as to whether we can get enough B_{12} on a vegan diet.

Vegans even refuse any dietary supplements with gelatin capsules, which are made from animal protein. Some do it for health reasons and others because they believe it is immoral to eat animals or their products, possibly creating bad "karma," the notion that what you do, good or bad, comes back to you later. Probably most raw fooders fall into this category.

Personally, I do not believe there is bad karma from eating meat if one really needs it. But I do believe it is best to purchase only free-range animals; otherwise you are eating an animal that has been treated harshly, like a slave. The animal should also have been fed organic food and be free of antibiotics, steroids and other drugs, for your health as well as its.

If you do not eat organically fed or wild animals, remember you will be eating, by some estimates, ten times the toxic pesticides that you get from produce. This is because high concentrations of toxins are stored in animal fat, and meat is about 50% fat. Most of the fat is in the flesh itself and cannot be trimmed off, but wild and properly exercised animals will be leaner, with higher proportions of omega-3 fats.

Many spiritual traditions claim that eating meat increases the "density" of one's consciousness and can even "lower one's vibration," which inhibits spiritual growth. (There is a theory that our molecules vibrate at a faster, or higher, level when our consciousness expands, thus accelerating spiritual growth.)

This may be true, and it may be true for some people more than others. It may also be that certain animals, such as cows, create more density than others, such as fish. I once asked Aajonus Vonderplanitz what he thought about the spiritual side of eating meat. He answered that for him, he definitely became more centered and calm after incorporating meat, contrary to what he had been taught by his spiritual teachers! He said that the hypoglycemic effect of eating so much fruit created a lot of mood swings and even anger outbursts. Now, even when confronted by angry vegetarians, he remains unperturbed.

It is also prudent to point out that raw animal foods are not the highest form of living foods in the same way that raw plant foods are. The theory is that by eating living food, we increase our life force. As Dr. Gabriel Cousens points out, "The sunlight energy, when transferred to us indirectly through our food, is almost completely lost to us if the transfer of the vegetarian nutrients is second-hand through animal foods" (*Conscious Eating*, p. 575).

Another factor to consider is that meat, whether cooked or raw, is generally acidic. (See Chapter 12 for a discussion of the acid/alkaline issue.) It is undoubtedly less acidic than cooked meat, but protein in general tends to be acidic. In my opinion, if one decides to eat raw meat, it should be only a small percentage of the diet, such as the less than 5% or so that the chimpanzees eat.

A huge factor in considering significant flesh consumption is that even raw meat has large amounts of saturated fat. If you have seen the video "Diet for a New America," you will recall the scene in which Dr. Michael Klaper pulls saturated fat from the man's artery. Saturated fat is solid at room temperature, and it is implicated in heart disease.

Not much research has been done with raw meat eaters. Still, it can be argued that the Eskimos ate a lot of raw blubber and remained healthy. Raw meat contains no trans fat, and perhaps this is the real culprit in heart disease. Cooked meat is definitely dangerous in this area. Dr. Atkins, innovator of the famous Atkins diet, died indirectly as a result of his own heart disease!

My personal grand experiment with raw animal foods didn't last long. You already know the disaster that happened with raw dairy. While my encounters with meat were not as harsh, it quickly became apparent that it was not for me.

A few years ago, I decided to test the raw animal food diet for a month. I found that after eating raw meat, I maintained the light feeling that I had on a raw vegetarian diet. When I ate raw meat alone, it was actually easier for my body to digest than raw nuts, raw vegetables, raw sprouts or raw seeds. I even slept better, with no disturbances, on the days that I had meat instead of the usual raw vegan food.

I know a raw fooder who claims that eating raw fish soon after breaking a long fast brings his strength back much more quickly. It seems hard for me to believe that we as humans are not capable of digesting raw meat when so many other people I know have reported the same.

On the other hand, if I mixed raw meat with raw vegetables, such as eating a salad and meat both in the same day, my intestines apparently became too alkaline to digest the meat properly, and I became constipated, just as Aajonus Vonderplanitz warned.

On a diet rich in raw meat, one should have a salad only once in every two weeks or so. (Whereas, on a diet of cooked meat, salads help flush out the toxins.) Just think of the people who, in times before cooking, migrated to the Northern Hemisphere. In the winter, they ate animals. In the seasons when plants grew, they ate plant food. Originally there may not have been much mixing of the two.

I found that a diet of only animal products to be too limiting for me. I experimented with raw meat for a month and then gave it up with no desire for more. I just loved my salads too much. For me, it seems more natural to eat salads than meat. *Besides, raw vegan food tastes much better than raw meat.*

Another factor to consider in the decision whether or not to eat meat is its ecological impact. Forests and rainforests are being destroyed all over the world to raise cattle. Our limited fresh water is being depleted. *Soon, our land may be covered in desert largely as a result of meat eating!*

While eating meat, at least raw meat, may be in the best health interest for many individuals, it is not in the best interest of an overpopulated planet. Within decades, eating meat will likely become a luxury only the wealthy can afford. For most of the world, *it already is.*

To the uninitiated, raw meat sounds thoroughly disgusting. However, if the body needs it, it may taste better than any cooked meat you have ever had. If you decide to eat meat, by all means make it raw, as cooked meat has been proven to cause many diseases: heart disease, cancer, arthritis, kidney disease and gout, to name a few.

Even if you eat the best quality raw meat, be aware that it might be well to start off as a raw vegetarian for six to twelve months before adding meat. This is to ensure that you are cleansed enough so that any microscopic parasites in the meat will not have an environment in which to flourish within your body. Some people advise marinating meat in lemon juice overnight to kill parasites. This also makes raw meat look and taste more like cooked meat.

Keep in mind, too, that even the best meat is not usually very fresh. Some of it is imported from New Zealand, where cattle are grass-fed and free-range. Work carefully with a holistic doctor or health professional because eating raw animal products holds, perhaps, the only potential danger of the raw food diet.

Kosher meat is also advised for anyone eating meat, *cooked or raw.* This is because these animals have been slaughtered in a much more compassionate way. They are killed so quickly they don't even have time to realize it and therefore do not have adrenaline rushing through their veins. We produce enough adrenaline in our stressful lives without adding still more stress by consuming an animal's adrenaline.

Another benefit to kosher animals is how they are fed: There is no use of rendered feed, derived from dead chickens, cows, pigs, road kill and euthanized pets in place of their usual vegetarian food. The practice of rendering is said to be responsible for mad cow disease, and who knows how many other mad animal diseases will be popping up? Also, the animals are guaranteed to have been healthy. As stated earlier, much of the meat we see at the grocery comes from very sick animals. If you can, get kosher meat from animals that have been fed organic plant food.

Kevin Trudeau claims to have a source of organic, kosher meat. If you join his web site for a small monthly fee at www.naturalcures.com, you can learn where to buy it.

The web site www.eatwild.com provides a directory of numerous farms in the USA that sell eggs, meat and/or raw dairy products from naturally raised and/or organically fed animals.

If you live in Europe, it is best of all to get your meat from the third generation instinctive-eating animals sold by Orkos distributors. Their web site is www.orkos.com/home_EN.php.

Appendix D

Studies from Scientific Journals

It is inexcusable for scientists to torture animals;
let them make their experiments on journalists and politicians.
—Henrik Ibsen (1828-1906)

The following are excerpts from some scientific studies published in professional scientific journals, along with a few comments summarizing the findings. This list is by no means complete. Note that "mutagenic" means causing mutations, and "carcinogenic" means causing cancer. Mutagens are typically carcinogenic.

"Advanced Maillard reaction end products are associated with Alzheimer's disease," *Proceedings of the National Academy of Science*, June 7, 1994, Vol. 91 (12), pp. 5710-5714.

As explained in Chapter 6, cooked food produces Maillard molecules, abnormal molecules that are usually toxic to the body. In 1916, French chemist Louis Camille Maillard proved that brown pigments and polymers that occur in pyrolysis (chemical breakdown caused by heat — in other words, cooking) are formed after the reaction of an amino acid group with the carbonyl group of sugars.

This study presents evidence that "the characteristic pathological structures associated with Alzheimer's disease contain modifications typical of advanced Maillard end products: pyrraline and pentosidine, immunocytochemically labile neurofibrillary tangles and senile plaques in brain tissue from patients with Alzheimer's disease." The study found, in contrast, little or no abnormal staining in healthy neurons of the same brain. It was concluded that the Maillard reaction-related changes could be the cause of the biochemical and insolubility properties of the lesions of Alzheimer's disease through the formation of protein cross-links.

"Analysis of cooked meat muscles for heterocyclic amine carcinogens," *Mutation Research*, May 12, 1997, Vol. 376 (1-2), pp. 129-134.

The study concluded that cooking meat makes it carcinogenic. The most carcinogenic method of cooking of those tested was shown to be flame grilling.

"Carcinogens in foods: heterocyclic amines and cancer and heart disease," *Adv Exp Med Biol*, 1995, Vol. 369, pp. 211-220.

Carcinogens occur naturally in the foods we commonly eat, including a number of heterocyclic amines (HCAs) identified in beef, pork, poultry and fish as a result of cooking. These compounds are formed during the normal cooking process by the reaction of creatine with various other amino acids.

HCAs were singled out because of their high mutagenic activity in the Ames test, which involves feeding the chemicals to rabbits to see how much it takes to kill half of them. The HCAs can be separated into two types, nonimidazole and imidazole, the latter being the predominant type present in Western foods.

Both types of HCAs have been found to be carcinogenic in rodent bioassays. A high proportion of the nonhuman primates tested also developed myocardial lesions.

The conclusions were that consumption of the HCAs formed by cooking meat may constitute a risk factor for both cancer and cardiovascular disease in humans.

"Characterization of mutagenic activity in cooked-grain-food products," *Food and Chemical Toxicity*, January 1994, Vol. 32 (1), pp. 15-21.

The study tested wheat gluten or flour from several plant sources heated at 410° F (210° C) for one hour, as well as baked or toasted grains and a heated grain beverage. The study found that heated grain products form aromatic amine chemicals during heating that are mutagenic in bacterial mutation tests.

"Cooking procedures and food mutagens: a literature review," *Food and Chemical Toxicity*, Sept. 1993, Vol. 31 (9), pp. 655-675.

The abstract reads, "Commonly eaten meat products prepared from beef, pork, mutton and chicken show some level of mutagenic activity following normal frying. Food preparation methods have a significant influence on the formation of the mutagenic activity. The main food mutagens found in cooked meat products are heterocyclic amines. Several of them have been tested in long-term animal studies and shown to be carcinogenic in rodents. From a health point of view, it is desirable to reduce or prevent the formation of food mutagens. Therefore, a deeper understanding of the precursors and reaction conditions for mutagen formation during normal domestic cooking is very important."

The study goes on to show that several of the precursors in the formation of thermic mutagens are creatine or creatinine cross-linked with other amino acids and sugars.

"Determination of heterocyclic aromatic amines in food products: automation of the sample preparation method prior to HPLC and PHLC-MS quantification." *Mutation Research*, May 12, 1997, Vol. 376 (1-2), pp. 29-35.

The study found, "Heat-processing protein-rich foods may cause the formation of heterocyclic aromatic amines (HAAs), all of which are mutagenic, and some also have carcinogenic potential."

"Effects of heating time and antioxidants on the formation of heterocyclic amines in marinated foods," *Journal of Chromatography B*, March 25, 2004, Vol. 802 (1), p. 2737.

Marinated food samples were cooked at 208° F (98° C) for 1, 2, 4, 8, 16 and 32 hours. Results showed that heterocyclic amines formed during heating increased in amount for each increase in heating time. Antioxidants (BHT and Vitamins C and E) helped inhibit HCAs, but the effect was minor.

"Effects of temperature and time on mutagen formation in pan-fried hamburger," *A Cancer Journal of Clinicians Cancer Letters*, July, 1979, Vol. 7 (2-3), pp. 63-69.

Mutagenic activity was found in hamburgers during pan-frying. It increased with temperature and time, but especially with temperature.

Uniformly frozen patties were fried at varied temperatures. Mutagenic activity was not detected in the uncooked hamburgers. In hamburgers fried at 289° F (143° C), mutagenic activity remained low for those fried from four to twenty minutes. However, when fried at 375-410° F (191-210° C) for up to ten minutes, mutagenic activity increased considerably. Mutagenic activity in fried hamburgers sold at selected restaurants ranged from very low to moderately high.

"Food-derived mutagens and carcinogens," *Cancer Research*, April 1, 1992, Vol. 52 (7), pp. 2092s-2098s.

This study showed that cooked food contains a variety of heterocyclic amines (HCAs), byproducts of cooking found to cause cancer in animals. All the mutagenic HCAs tested were carcinogenic in rodents, most of these poor creatures ending up with cancer of the liver and other organs.

"Quantification of HCAs in cooked foods and in human urine indicated that humans are continuously exposed to low levels of them in the diet."

"Formation of mutagens in cooked food. II. Foods with high starch content," *Cancer Letters*, March 1980, Vol. 9 (1), pp. 7-12.

Mutagens are formed when starchy foods are cooked. The study included fried potatoes, toasted bread, baked bread and fried bread to produce mutagenically active substances. Toasting white and dark bread produces mutagens at the same initial rate, but dark bread produces much higher levels of mutagenicity when toasted for long times.

The study concluded, "Significant mutagenic activity is produced when starchy foods are prepared by common cooking procedures."

"Health risks of heterocyclic amines," *Mutation Research*, May 12, 1997, Vol. 376 (1-2), pp. 37-41.

The study found, "Common cooking procedures, such as broiling, frying, barbequing (flame-grilling), heat processing — any pyrolysis of protein-rich foods — induce the formation of potent mutagenic and carcinogenic heterocyclic amines."

The cooked proteins produced organ tumors in mice and rats, as well as in nonhuman primates. The differences of risk from heterocyclic amines range greatly among humans, depending on exposure and genetic susceptibility.

"Lipid extracts isolated from heat processed food show a strong agglutinating activity against human red blood cells," *Food Research International*, 2002, Vol. 35 (6), pp. 535-540.

Agglutination of the blood cells refers to their stickiness, the cells sticking together as if glued together. In this study, the hemagglutinating (blood stickiness) activity of several mass market oils and several lipid mixtures isolated from different food items was evaluated against human red blood cells and against hamster red blood cells.

Unheated oils had a low agglutination effect, but when the same foods were heated at a common cooking temperature for 24 hours, the isolated mixture of lipids and oils showed strong hemagglutinating activity, which shows that heated oils have a toxic effect on humans. Agglutination, or coagulation, of blood forms clots, and clots can block blood flow in arteries, leading to heart attacks and strokes.

"Metabolism of food-derived heterocyclic amines in nonhuman primates," *Mutation Research*, May 12, 1997, Vol. 376 (1-2), pp. 203-210.

The study found that the heterocyclic amines from cooked meat increased the risk of liver cancer in monkeys.

"Molecules heated in cooking generate compounds toxic for embryos," *Cahiers de nutrition et de diététique [Journal of Nutrition and Dietetics]*, March 1982, pp. 36-37.

In this study, a mixture of glucose (the most common sugar) and lysine (an amino acid) was heated for two hours at 194° F (90° C). Fifty percent of both compounds reacted, forming Maillard molecules. Then the resulting mixture was blended with food and fed to rats, using only $1/6$th part of the compound mixture together with $5/6$ths part food. Results were that the number of embryos per litter decreased from 9.8 to 3.75. The weight of the embryos decreased, while placenta weight increased.

The researchers interpreted the weight decrease of the embryos as signifying food poisoning rather than lack of nutrition. Teratogenic (interfering with normal embryonic development), vascularized, tumors of the navel were also observed.

"Occurrence of lipid oxidation products in foods," *Chemical and Food Toxicity*, Oct/Nov. 1986, Vol. 24 (10-11), pp. 1021-1030.

Lipid oxidation products were found in food that is dehydrated (which is normally done at temperatures higher than 118° F), fried and cooked in other ways. These contribute to coronary heart disease.

"Occurrence of mutagens in canned foods," *Mutation Research*, Nov/Dec 1984, Vol. 141 (3-4), pp. 131-134.

The study found mutagens in commercially heat-processed foods that are not present in the unheated raw material and appear to be produced during processing. Mutagens in these foods have been observed to display chemical behaviors and induce salmonella strains similar to those mutagens in grilled foods that have been shown to be mammalian carcinogens.

"Past, present and future of mutagens in cooked foods," *Environmental Health Perspective*, Aug 1986, Vol. 67, pp. 5-10.

Using a mutation assay with *Salmonella typhimurium*, the scientists who conducted this study detected various types of mutagens in cooked foods. Mutagenic heterocyclic amines were found in broiled fish meat and pyrolyzates of amino acids and proteins. Mutagenic nitropyrenes, some of which are carcinogenic, were found in grilled chicken. Roasted coffee beans contain mutagens, such as methylglyoxal. Mutagen precursors were found in food processing.

"Pyrolysis and risks of toxicity," *Cahiers de nutrition et de diététique* [Journal of Nutrition and Dietetics], 1982, Vol. 17, p. 39

Cooking has been proven to produce millions of different Maillard molecules. The research in this paper verifies that the numerous substances generated are endless chains of novel molecules that are toxic, aromatic, peroxidizing, anti-oxidizing, mutagenic and carcinogenic.

"Toxicity of dietary lipid peroxidation products," *Trends in Food Science and Technology*, July 1990, Vol. 1, pp. 67-71.

This study concluded, "Humans are exposed to oxidized fats from fatty fish, fish oils, deep fat frying and powdered foods." It found that even though primary hydroperoxides and lipid polymers produced from heated oils are not significantly toxic in themselves, toxic effects may be induced by secondary lipid peroxides. "Secondary" refers to products generated in the body when the initial substance is metabolized.

The study also points out that recent studies indicate that heated oils may play a role in the acceleration of atherosclerosis. "There is increasing evidence that cholesterol oxides found in deep fat fried and dehydrated foods can exert atherogenic effects."

If you want more studies...

These are but a small sampling of the available evidence of the toxic effects of cooked food. Search PubMed on the Internet at www.ncbi.nlm.nih.gov/entrez/query.fcgi if you would like to do some research on your own. Plug in keywords like "cooked food," "cooked meat," "cooked starches" and "cooked fats." Then use the word "heated" instead of "cooked." Next, plug in some of the toxic byproducts that you have seen in this section of the book, such as "heterocyclic amines."

Appendix E

Sample Menus for One Week

The following menus are suggestions that may be modified according to taste. Portion sizes will vary and hence were generally not specified since people have differing caloric needs according to their sizes, ages and activity levels. Many of the suggested menu items are described in the recipe section of Chapter 15.

These sample menus contain a wide variety of dishes. *In reality, however, your own menus will more likely consist partly of leftovers from the previous day* since it is so much easier to prepare a single dish that will last for several days.

If you are pressed for time, you might make a few raw gourmet dishes on the weekends with plenty of salad and just live on that for the week, along with raw fruit, raw trail mix and flax crackers. Every two weeks or so, make some flax crackers with your favorite spices and vegetables. If they are dehydrated enough they can last several weeks, even longer.

Believe it or not, it does not get boring to eat the same raw dishes a few days in a row. Most people already do that with cooked food.

I was encouraged by many people to make this section available for those of you who may need some guidelines to get started, but I encourage you to experiment and find the foods that resonate with you. For example, you may find that you want to drink the "Super Smoothie" every morning as I do.

One thing to remember is that after six months to a year, you will no longer crave complex recipes. You will be satisfied more and more with eating foods as just Mother Nature gives them to us in their simplest, most perfect, whole raw forms.

Day 1

Breakfast: ½ cantaloupe

Snack: 1 serving Raw Chocolate (see recipe)

Lunch: Cream of Spinach Soup (see recipe)

Dinner: Raw Pizza (see recipe)

Snack: Garlic Cilantro Flax Crackers (see recipe) with raw almond butter or Deluxe Macadamia Nut Cheese (see recipe)

Day 2

Breakfast: Banana Milk Shake (see recipe) or Super Smoothie (see recipe)

Snack: Fruit of your choice, one piece

Lunch: Arabian Salad (see recipe)

Dinner: Chinese Stir "Fry" (see recipe)

Snack: Frozen Fruit Ice Cream (see recipe)

Day 3

Breakfast: 3 T raw, dehydrated, green vegetable juice with a pinch of cayenne

Snack: Fruit of your choice, 1 or 2 pieces

Lunch: Coleslaw (see recipe)

Dinner: Nori Rolls (see recipe)

Snack: Garlic Cilantro Flax Crackers (see recipe) or other flax crackers of your choice with Guacamole (see recipe)

Day 4

Breakfast: Smoothie (see recipe)

Snack: Fruit of your choice, 1 or 2 pieces

Lunch: Fresh, green, leafy vegetable mix with Honey Mustard Dressing (see recipe), sprinkled with soaked and dried walnuts

Dinner: Vegetable Chowder (see recipe)

Snack: Raw Cake (see recipe)

Day 5

Breakfast: Fruit of your choice, 1 or 2 pieces

Snack: Trail Mix (see recipe)

Lunch: Holiday Salad (see recipe)

Dinner: Tomato Raviolis (see recipe)

Snack: Chocolate Mint Soda (see recipe)

Day 6

Breakfast: Trail Mix (see recipe)

Snack: Fruit of your choice, 1 or 2 pieces

Lunch: Everybody's Favorite Celery-Cilantro Soup (see recipe)

Dinner: Spaghetti (see recipe)

Snack: Cauliflower Pâté ("Mashed Potatoes") (see recipe)

Day 7

Breakfast: Allen's Cereal (see recipe)

Snack: Raw Candy (see recipe)

Lunch: Raw Hummus (see recipe) with fresh cucumber slices

Dinner: Creamy Carrot Soup (see recipe)

Snack: Freshly cut cucumbers, tomatoes, carrots and celery dipped in Creamy Spinach Dip (see recipe)

Bibliography and Other Resources

General Bibliography

Abel, Ulrich. *Chemotherapy of Advanced Epithelial Cancer: A Critical Survey*, Hippokrates Verlag: Stuttgart, Germany, 1990.

Abramowski, O. L. M. *Fruitarian Diet and Physical Rejuvenation*, Essence of Health Publishing Co.: Westville, South Africa, 1911.

Alexander, Joe. *Blatant Raw Foodist Propaganda!* Blue Dolphin Publishing: Nevada City, CA, 1990.

Alt, Carol. *Eating in the Raw: A Beginner's Guide to Getting Slimmer, Feeling Healthier and Living Longer the Raw-Food Way*, Clarkson Potter Publishers: New York, NY, 2004.

Angell, Marcia. *The Truth about the Drug Companies: How They Deceive Us and What to Do about It*, Random House: New York, NY, 2005.

Angler, Bradford. *Field Guide to Edible Wild Plants*, Stackpole Books: Harrisburg, PA, 1974.

Appleton, Nancy. *Lick the Sugar Habit: How to Break Your Sugar Addiction Naturally*, Avery Publishing Group, Inc: Wayne, New Jersey, 1988.

Arlin, Stephen. *Raw Power! Building Strength & Muscle Naturally*, Maul Brothers Publishing: San Diego, CA, 1998.

Arlin, Stephen, Dini, Fouad and Wolfe, David. *Nature's First Law: The Raw Food Diet*, Maul Brothers Publishing: San Diego, CA, 1996.

Baker, Arthur M. *Awakening Our Self-Healing Body: A Solution to the Health Care Crisis*, Self Health Care Systems: Los Angeles, CA, 1994.

Baker, Elizabeth. *Does the Bible Teach Nutrition?* WinePress Publications: Mukilteo, WA, 1997.

Baker, Elizabeth. *The Un-Diet Book: The All-Natural Lifestyle for Weight Loss and Eating, Good Health and Exercise by the Author of the Uncook Book*, Drelwood Communications: Indianola, WA, 1992.

Baker, Elizabeth. *The Unmedical Book: How to Conquer Disease, Lose Weight, Avoid Suffering & Save Money*, Drelwood Publications: Saguache, CO, 1987.

Baroody, Theodore A., ND, DC, PhD Nutrition, CNC. *Alkalize or Die: Superior Health through Proper Alkaline-Acid Balance*, Holographic Health Press: Waynesville, NC, 1991.

Bealle, Morris A. *House of Rockefeller: How a Shoestring Was Run into 200 Billion Dollars in Two Generations*, All America House: Washington, DC, 1959.

Bealle, Morris A. *The Drug Story*, Columbia Publishing Company: Washington, DC, 1949.

Bernays, Edward L. *Propaganda*, Ig Publishing: Brooklyn, NY, 2005.

Bidwell, Victoria. *The Salt Conspiracy*, Get Well, Stay Well, America! Freemont, CA, 1986.

Bircher-Benner, Ralph. *Dr. Bircher-Benner's Way to Positive Health and Vitality, 1867-1967*, Bircher-Benner Verlag: Zurich, Switzerland, 1967.

Bland, Jeffrey S., PhD. *Genetic Nutritioneering: How You Can Modify Inherited Traits and Live a Longer, Healthier Life*, McGraw-Hill: New York, NY, 1999.

Blaylock, Russell L., MD. *Excitotoxins: The Taste that Kills*, Health Press: Santa Fe, New Mexico, 1997.

Boutenko, Victoria. *Green for Life*, Raw Family Publishing: Ashland, OR, 2005.

Boutenko, Victoria. *12 Steps to Raw Foods: How to End Your Addiction to Cooked Food*, Raw Family Publishing: Ashland, OR, 2001.

Boutenko, Victoria, Igor, Sergei and Valya. *Raw Family: A True Story of Awakening*, Raw Family Publishing: Ashland, OR, 2000.

Bragg, Paul. *The Miracle of Fasting for Agelessness, Physical, Mental & Spiritual Rejuvenation: New Discoveries about an Old Miracle, the Fast Fasting Way to Health,* Health Science: Burbank, CA, 1966.

Brandt, Johanna. *The Grape Cure,* Benedict Lust Publications: New York, NY, 2001.

Bruce, Elaine. *Living Foods for Radiant Health,* Thorsons: London, England, 2003.

Bryson, Christopher. *The Fluoride Deception,* Seven Stories Press: New York, NY, 2004.

Burger, Guy-Claude. *Manger Vrai: Instinctothérapie,* Editions du Rocher: Paris, France, 1980.

Campbell, T. Colin, PhD. *The China Study: Startling Implications for Diet, Weight Loss and Long-Term Health,* BenBella Books: Dallas, TX, 2004.

Carper, Jean. *The Food Pharmacy: Dramatic New Evidence that Food Is Your Best Medicine,* Bantam Books, New York, NY, 1988.

Carter, James P., MD. *Racketeering in Medicine: The Suppression of Alternatives,* Hampton Roads Publishing Company, Inc.: Charlottesville, VA, 1992.

Cherniske, Stephen, MS. *Caffeine Blues: Wake Up to the Hidden Dangers of America's #1 Drug,* Warner Books: New York, NY, 1998.

Chessman, Millan. *Stay Young & Healthy Through Internal Cleansing,* Chessman: San Diego, CA, 1995.

Clement, Brian R. *Living Foods for Optimum Health,* Prima Publishing: Roseville, CA, 1996.

Cobb, Brenda. *The Living Foods Lifestyle,* Living Soul Publishing: Atlanta, GA, 2002.

Cohen, Robert. *Milk the Deadly Poison,* Argus Publishing, Inc.: Oradell, NJ, 1998.

Comby, Bruno. *Maximize Immunity,* Marcus Books: Queensville, ON, Canada, 1994.

Committee on Diet, Nutrition and Cancer, Assembly of Life Sciences, National Research Council. *Diet, Nutrition and Cancer*, National Academy Press: Washington, DC, 1982.

Cook, Lewis E., Jr., and Yasui, Junko. *Goldot: The Doctrine of Truth: Guidebook of Life — Doctrine of Truth: The Science of Man — A Fundamental Guidebook of Life*, Cook: Oceanside, CA, 1976.

Cordain, Loren, PhD. *The Paleo Diet: Lose Weight and Get Healthy by Eating the Food You Were Designed to Eat*, J. Wiley: New York, NY, 2002.

Cousens, Gabriel, MD. *Spiritual Nutrition: Six Foundations for Spiritual Life and the Awakening of Kundalini*, North Atlantic Books: Berkeley, CA, 2005.

Cousens, Gabriel, MD. *Conscious Eating*, Vision Books International: Santa Rosa, CA, 1992.

Cousens, Gabriel, MD. *Spiritual Nutrition and the Rainbow Diet*, Cassandra Press: Boulder, CO, 1986.

Da Free John, *Raw Gorilla: The Principles of Regenerative Raw Diet Applied in True Spiritual Practice*, The Dawn Horse Press: Clearlake, CA, 1982.

Devivo, Roman and Spors, Antje. *Genefit Nutrition*, Celestial Arts: Berkeley, CA, 2003.

De Vries, Arnold. *The Fountain of Youth*, Dunlay Publishing Company: New York, NY, 1947.

Diamond, Harvey and Marilyn. *Fit for Life II: Living Health*, Warner Books: New York, NY, 1987.

Diamond, Harvey and Marilyn. *Fit for Life*, Warner Books: New York, NY, 1985.

Douglass, William C., MD. *Into the Light*, Second Opinion Publishing, Inc.: Atlanta, GA, 1993.

Dries, Jan. *The Dries Cancer Diet: A Practical Guide to the Use of Fresh Fruit and Raw Vegetables in the Treatment of Cancer*, Element Books Inc.: Rockport, MA, 1997.

Dykeman, Peter A. & Elias, Thomas. *Edible Wild Plants: A North American Field Guide*, Sterling Publishing Co., Inc: New York, NY, 1982.

Ehret, Arnold. *Rational Fasting*, Benedict Lust Publications: New York, NY, 1971.

Ehret, Arnold. *Mucusless Diet Healing System*, Benedict Lust Publications: New York, NY, 1970.

Feuer, Elaine. *Innocent Casualties: The FDA's War against Humanity*, Dorrance Publishing Co.: Pittsburgh, PA, 1996.

Fredericks, Carlton. *Psycho-Nutrition*, Grosset & Dunlap: New York, NY, 1976.

Fry, T. C. *The Health Formula*, Health Excellence Systems: Manchaca, Texas, 1991.

Fry, T. C. and Honiball, Essie. *I Live on Fruit*, Life Science Institute: San Antonio, TX, 1991.

Fry, T. C. and Klein, David. *Your Natural Diet: Alive Raw Foods*, Living Nutrition Publications: Sebastopol, CA, 2002.

Fuhrman, Joel, MD. *Fasting and Eating for Health: A Medical Doctor's Program for Conquering Disease*, St. Martin's Press: New York, NY, 1995.

Gallo, Roe. *Perfect Body: The Raw Truth*, Promotion Publishing: San Diego, CA, 1997.

Gerson, Max, MD. *A Cancer Therapy: Results of Fifty Cases*, Whittier Books: New York, NY, 1958.

Graham, Douglas, DC. *Grain Damage*, Dr. Douglas M. Graham: Marathon, FL, 1998.

Gregory, Dick. *Dick Gregory's Natural Diet for Folks Who Eat: Cookin' with Mother Nature!* Harper & Row: New York, NY, 1973.

Griffin, Edward G. *World without Cancer: The Story of Vitamin B_{17}*, American Media: Westlake Village, CA, 1997.

Haley, Daniel. *Politics in Healing: The Suppression and Manipulation of American Medicine*, Potomac Valley Press: Washington, DC, 2000.

Hendel, Dr. Barbara and Ferreira, Peter. *Water & Salt: The Essence of Life — The Healing Power of Nature*, Natural Resources, Inc., 2003.

Holick, Michael F., PhD, MD. *The UV Advantage: The Medical Breakthrough that Shows How to Harness the Power of the Sun for Your Health,* Ibooks, Inc: New York, NY, 2003.

Horowitz, Leonard G. *Death in the Air: Globalism, Terrorism & Toxic Warfare,* Tetrahedron: Sandpoint, ID, 2001.

Horowitz, Leonard G. *Emerging Viruses: AIDS and Ebola: Nature, Accident, or Intentional?* Tetrahedron: Rockport, MA, 1997.

Hotema, Hilton. *Man's Higher Consciousness,* Health Research: Pomeroy, WA, 1962.

Hovannessian, Arshavir Ter. *Raw Eating,* Hallelujah Acres Publishing: Shelby, NC, 2000.

Howell, Edward, Dr. *Food Enzymes for Health and Longevity,* Lotus Press: Twin Lakes, WI, 1994.

Howell, Edward, Dr. *Enzyme Nutrition,* Avery Publishing Group, Inc: Wayne, New Jersey, 1985.

Howenstine, James A., MD. *A Physician's Guide to Natural Health Products That Work,* Penhurst Books: Miami, FL 2002.

Hunsberger, Eydie Mae. *How I Conquered Cancer Naturally,* Production House: San Diego, CA, 1975.

Jubb, Annie Padden and David. *Secrets of an Alkaline Body: The New Science of Colloidal Biology,* North Atlanta Books: Berkeley, CA, 2004.

Jubb, David. *Jubb's Cell Rejuvenation: Colloidal Biology: A Symbiosis,* North Atlanta Books: Berkeley, CA, 2005.

Keck-Borsits, Shelly. *Dying to Get Well: Conventional Medicine FAILED! How Raw Food Reversed My Disease Naturally — Are You Sick & Tired of Being Sick & Tired? — A Medical Cover-Up Exposed! — A Cure to Disease Revealed! — What Your Doctor Isn't Telling You Could Kill You!* Shelly Keck-Borsits: Rensselaer, IN, 2003.

Kelley, William Donald and Rohe, Fred. *Cancer: Curing the Incurable without Surgery, Chemotherapy or Radiation,* New Century Promotions: Bonita, CA, 2001.

Kennedy, Gordon. *Children of the Sun, A Pictorial Anthology: From Germany to California 1883-1949*, Nivaria Press: Ojai, CA, 1998.

Kenton, Leslie and Susannah. *Raw Energy*, Arrow Books Limited: London, England, 1984.

Kervran, Louis C. *Biological Transmutations, and Their Applications in Chemistry, Physics, Biology, Ecology, Medicine, Nutrition, Agriculture, Geology*, Swan House Publishing Co.: Binghamton, NY, 1972.

Kirby, David. *Evidence of Harm: Mercury in Vaccines and the Autism Epidemic: A Medical Controversy*, St. Martin's Press: New York, NY, 2005.

Krok, Morris. *Fruit: The Food and Medicine for Man*, Essence of Health: Wandsbeck 3631, South Africa, 1984.

Kulvinskas, Viktoras. *Life in the 21st Century*, 21st Century Publications: Fairfield, IA, 1981.

Kulvinskas, Viktoras. *Survival into the 21st Century: Planetary Healers Manual*, 21st Century Publications: Fairfield, IA, 1981.

Lanctôt, Guylaine, MD. *The Medical Mafia*, Here's the Key, Inc: Morgan, VT, 1995.

Lyman, Howard F. *Mad Cowboy: Plain Truth from the Cattle Rancher Who Won't Eat Meat*, Scribner: New York, NY, 1998.

Malkmus, George, Rev. and Dye, Michael. *God's Way to Ultimate Health: A Common Sense Guide for Eliminating Sickness through Nutrition*, Hallelujah Acres Publishing: Eidson, TN, 1995.

Malkmus, George, Rev. *Why Christians Get Sick*, Destiny Image Publishers: Shippensburg, PA, 1995.

Marcus, Erik. *Vegan: The New Ethics of Eating*, McBooks Press: Ithaca, NY, 2001.

McDermott, Stella. *Metaphysics of Raw Foods: Embracing the Natural Food Laws; the Fundamental Principles of Raw Foods; Their Comparative Nutritive Value; the Divine Laws of Dietetics; Methods of Preparing Raw Foods to Serve, Together with Numerous Menus*, Burton Publishing Company: MT, 1919.

Mercola, Joseph, ND and Levy, Alison Rose. *The No-Grain Diet: Conquer Carbohydrate Addiction and Stay Slim for Life*, Dutton Books: New York, NY, 2003.

Meyerowitz, Steve. *Sprouts, the Miracle Food: The Complete Guide to Sprouting*, Sproutman Publications: Great Barrington, MA, 1999.

Meyerowitz, Steve. *Juice Fasting & Detoxification: Use the Healing Power of Fresh Juice to Feel Young and Look Great: The Fastest Way to Restore Your Health*, Sproutman Publications: Great Barrington, MA, 1999.

Moss, Ralph W., MD. *The Cancer Industry: The Classic Exposé on the Cancer Establishment*, Paragon House: New York, NY, 1989.

Mosseri, Albert. *Mangez Nature Santé Nature*, Les Hygienistes, 1992.

Murray, Maynard, MD. *Sea Energy Agriculture*, Acres, USA: Austin, TX, 2003.

Nison, Paul. *Raw Knowledge II: Interviews with Health Achievers*, 343 Publishing Company: Brooklyn, NY, 2003.

Nison, Paul. *Raw Knowledge: Enhance the Powers of Your Mind, Body and Soul*, 343 Publishing Company: Brooklyn, NY, 2002.

Nison, Paul. *The Raw Life: Becoming Natural in an Unnatural World*, 343 Publishing Company: New York, NY, 2000.

Nolfi, Kristine, MD. *Raw Food Treatment of Cancer*, TEACH Services, Inc.: Brushton, NY, 1995.

Oldfield, Harry and Coghill, Roger. *The Dark Side of the Brain: Major Discoveries in the Use of Kirlian Photography and Electrocrystal Therapy*, Element Books, Inc., 1991.

Oski, Frank, MD. *Don't Drink Your Milk! The Frightening New Medical Facts about the World's Most Overrated Nutrient*, TEACH Services, Inc: Brushton, NY, 1983.

Oswald, Jean A. and Shelton, Herbert M. *Fasting for the Health of It*, Franklin Books: Bayonet Point, FL, 1983.

Ott, A. True, PhD. *Secret Assassins in Food: The Ninjas of Taste,* Manna Publishing: Ogden, Utah, 2005.

Patenaude, Frédéric. *The Raw Secrets: The Raw Vegan Diet in the Real World,* Raw Vegan: Montreal, QC, Canada, 2002.

Pearson, R. B. *Fasting and Man's Correct Diet,* Health Research: Pomeroy, WA, 1921.

Pfeiffer, Carl C., PhD, MD. *Nutrition and Mental Illness: An Orthomolecular Approach to Balancing Body Chemistry,* Healing Arts Press: Rochester, VT, 1987.

Pottenger, Francis M., Jr. *Pottenger's Cats: A Study in Nutrition,* The Price-Pottenger Nutrition Foundation: San Diego, CA, 1983.

Price, Weston A., DDS. *Nutrition and Physical Degeneration: A Comparison of Primitive and Modern Diets and Their Effects,* P.B. Hoeber, Inc: New York, NY, 1939.

Rampton, Sheldon and Stauber, John. *Trust Us, We're Experts! How Industry Manipulates Science and Gambles with Your Future,* Tarcher/Putnam: New York, NY, 2001.

Robbins, John. *Diet for a New America,* H. J. Kramer: Tiburon, CA, 1998.

Rose, Natalia. *The Raw Food Detox Diet: The Five-Step Plan for Vibrant Health and Maximum Weight Loss,* Harper-Collins Publishers, Inc: New York, NY, 2005.

Santillo, Humbart, MH, ND. *Food Enzymes: The Missing Link to Radiant Health,* Hohm Press: Prescott, AZ, 1987.

Schaeffer, Severen L. *Instinctive Nutrition,* Celestial Arts: Berkeley, CA, 1987.

Schauss, Alexander. *Diet, Crime and Delinquency,* Parker House: Berkeley, CA, 1980.

Schmid, Ronald F., MD. *Native Nutrition: Eating According to Ancestral Wisdom,* Healing Arts Press: Rochester, VT, 1994.

Schmid, Ronald F., MD. *Traditional Foods Are Your Best Medicine: Health and Longevity with the Animal, Sea, and Vegetable Foods of our Ancestors,* Ocean View Publications: Stratford, CT, 1987.

Scott, William D. *In the Beginning God Said: Eat Raw Food: Genesis 1:29, a Closer Look*, North Idaho Publishing: Coeur d'Alene, ID, 1999.

Seignalet, Jean. *L'Alimentation ou la Troisième Médecine [Nutrition or the Third Medicine]*, Édition François-Xavier de Guilbert: Paris, 2004.

Shelton, Herbert M., DC. *Food Combining Made Easy*, Willow Publishing, Inc.: San Antonio, TX, 1982.

Shelton, Herbert M., DC. *The Science and Fine Art of Fasting*, Natural Hygiene Press: Chicago, 1978.

Shelton, Herbert M., DC. *Fasting Can Save Your Life*, Natural Hygiene Press: Chicago, IL, 1964.

Shelton, Herbert M., DC. *The Hygienic System, Vol. 1: Orthobionomics*, Dr. Shelton's Health School: San Antonio, TX, 1934.

Simontacchi, Carol. *The Crazy Makers: How the Food Industry Is Destroying Our Minds and Harming Our Children*, Tarcher/Putnam: New York, NY, 2000.

Smith, Jeffrey M. *Seeds of Deception: Exposing Industry and Government Lies about the Safety of the Genetically Engineered Foods You're Eating*. Yes! Books: Fairfield, IA, 2003.

Smith, Lendon H. *Dr. Lendon Smith's Low-Stress Diet Book*, McGraw-Hill: Blacklick, OH, 1988.

Somers, Suzanne. *The Sexy Years: Discover the Natural Hormone Connection — the Secret to Fabulous Sex, Great Health, and Vitality for Women and Men*, Random House Large Print: New York, NY, 2004.

Sommers, Craig, ND, CN. *Raw Foods Bible*, Guru Beant Press, 2004.

Stitt, Barbara Reed. *Food & Behavior*, Natural Press: Manitowoc, WI, 1997.

Stoycoff, Cheryl. *Raw Kids: Transitioning Children to a Raw Food Diet*, Living Spirit Press: Stockton, CA, 2000.

Szekely, Edmond Bordeaux, Ed. and Trans. *The Essene Gospel of Peace*, International Biogenic Society: Nelson, BC, Canada, 1981.

Szekely, Edmond Bordeaux. *The Chemistry of Youth*, Academy Books: San Diego, CA, 1977.

Teitel, Martin, PhD and Wilson, Kimberly. *Genetically Engineered Food: Changing the Nature of Nature*, Park Street Press: Rochester, VT, 2001.

Tilden, John H., MD. *Toxemia, the Basic Cause of Disease: An Antidote to Fear, Frenzy and the Popular Mania of Chasing after So-Called Cures*, Natural Hygiene Press: Chicago, IL, 1974.

Trudeau, Kevin. *Natural Cures "They" Don't Want You to Know About*, Alliance Publishing Group, Inc: Hinsdale, IL, 2004.

Vetrano, Vivian Virginia, DC, hMD, PhD. *Errors in Hygiene?!!?* GIH Publishing: Barksdale, TX, 1999.

Vonderplanitz, Aajonus. *We Want to Live*, Carnelian Bay Castle Press: Santa Monica, CA, 1997.

Walford, Roy L., MD. *Maximum Life Span*, Norton: New York, NY, 1983.

Walker, Norman, DSc. *Fresh Vegetable and Fruit Juices: What's Missing in Your Body?* Norwalk Press: Prescott, AZ, 1970.

Wigmore, Ann, DD, ND. *Overcoming AIDS and Other "Incurable Diseases" the Attunitive Way through Nature*, Copen Press: New York, NY, 1987.

Wigmore, Ann, DD, ND. *The Wheatgrass Book*, Avery Publishing Group, Inc.: Wayne, NJ, 1985.

Wigmore, Ann, DD, ND. *The Hippocrates Diet and Health Program*, Avery Publishing Group, Inc: Wayne, NJ, 1984.

Wigmore, Ann, DD, ND. *Be Your Own Doctor: A Positive Guide to Natural Living*, Avery Publishing Group, Inc: Garden City Park, NY, 1982.

Wiley, T. S. *Lights Out: Sleep, Sugar and Survival*, Pocket Books, New York, NY, 2000.

Wolcott, William L. and Fahey, Trish. *The Metabolic Typing Diet: Customize Your Diet to Your Own Unique & Ever Changing Nutritional Needs*, Doubleday: New York, NY, 2000.

Wolfe, David. *Eating for Beauty: For Women and Men: Introducing a Whole New Concept of Beauty: What It Is, and How*

You Can Achieve It, Maul Brothers Publishing: San Diego, CA, 2002.

Wolfe, David. *The Sunfood Diet Success System: 36 Lessons in Health Transformation*, Maul Brothers Publishing: San Diego, CA, 1999.

Wolfe, David and Holdstock, Shazzie. *Naked Chocolate: The Astonishing Truth about the World's Greatest Food*, Maul Brothers Publishing: San Diego, CA, 2005.

Yiamouyiannis, John. *Fluoride the Aging Factor: How to Recognize and Avoid the Devastating Effects of Fluoride;* Health Action Press: Delaware, OH, 1993.

Young, Robert O., PhD, DSc and Young, Shelley Redford. *The pH Miracle: Balance Your Diet, Reclaim Your Health*, Warner Books: New York, NY, 2002.

Young, Robert O., PhD, DSc. and Young, Shelley Redford. *Sick and Tired? Reclaim Your Inner Terrain*, Woodland Publishing: Pleasant Grove, UT, 2001.

Zavasta, Tonya. *Beautiful on Raw: Uncooked Creations*, BR Publishing: Cordova, TN, 2005.

Zavasta, Tonya. *Your Right to Be Beautiful: How to Halt the Train of Aging & Meet the Most Beautiful You*, BR Publishing: Cordova, TN, 2003.

Zephyr. *Instinctive Eating: The Lost Knowledge of Optimum Nutrition*, Pan Piper Press: Pahoa, HI, 1996.

Recipe Book Bibliography

Au, Bryan. *Raw in Ten Minutes*, Trafford Publishing: Victoria, BC, Canada, 2005.

Baird, Lori, Ed. *The Complete Book of Raw Food: Healthy, Delicious Vegetarian Cuisine Made with Living Foods, Includes Over 350 Recipes from the World's Top Raw Food Chefs*, Healthy Living Books: Long Island City, NY, 2004.

Baker, Elizabeth. *The Uncook Book: Raw Food Adventures to a New Health High*, Drelwood Publications: Saguache, CO, 1980.

Boutenko, Sergei and Boutenko, Valya. *Eating without Heating: Favorite Recipes from Teens Who Love Raw Food*, Raw Family Publishing: Ashland, OR, 2002.

Brotman, Juliano. *Raw: The Uncook Book: New Vegetarian Food for Life*, Regan Books: New York, NY, 1999.

Chavez, Gabrielle. *The Raw Food Gourmet: Going Raw for Total Well-Being*, North Atlantic Books, Berkeley, CA, 2005.

Cornbleet, Jennifer. *Raw Food Made Easy for 1 or 2 People*, Book Publishing Company, Summertown, TN, 2005.

Cousens, Gabriel, MD. *Rainbow Green Live-Food Cuisine*, North Atlantic Books: Berkeley, CA, 2003.

Ferrara, Suzanne Alex. *The Raw Food Primer*, Council Oak Books: Tulsa, OK, 2003.

Graham, Doug. *The High Energy Diet Recipe Guide*, Nature's First Law: San Diego, CA, 1996.

Jubb, Annie Padden and Jubb, David, PhD. *LifeFood Recipe Book: Living on Life Force*, Jubbs Longevity Inc.: New York, NY, 2002.

Kendall, Frances Lillian. *Sweet Temptations Natural Dessert Book: Delicious Desserts That Need No Cooking*, Avery Publishing Group, Inc: Garden City Park, NY, 1988.

Kenney, Matthew and Melngailis, Sarma. *Raw Food/Real World: 100 Simple to Sophisticated Recipes*, Regan Books: New York, NY, 2005.

Kulvinskas, Viktoras. *Love Your Body: Live Food Recipes, or How to Be a Live Food Lover*, Hippocrates Health Institute: Boston, MA, 1972.

Levin, James, MD, and Cederquist, Natalie. *Vibrant Living*, GLO, Inc.: La Jolla, CA, 1993.

Maerin, Jordan. *Raw Foods for Busy People: Simple and Machine-Free Recipes for Every Day*, Lulu Press Inc.: Morrisville, NC, 2004.

Malkmus, Rhonda J. *Recipes for Life from God's Garden,* Hallelujah Acres Publishing: Shelby, NC, 1998.

Markowitz, Elysa. *Warming Up to Living Foods*, Book Publishing Company: Summertown, TN, 1998.

Mars, Brigitte. *Rawsome! Maximizing Health, Energy and Culinary Delight with the Raw Foods Diet,* Basic Health Publications, Inc: North Bergen, NJ, 2004.

Patenaude, Frédéric. *Instant Raw Sensations: The Easiest, Simplest, Most Delicious Raw Food Recipes Ever!* Raw Vegan: Montreal, Quebec, Canada, 2005.

Patenaude, Frédéric. *The Sunfood Cuisine: A Gourmet Guide to Raw-Food Vegan Eating*, Genesis 1:29 Publishing: San Diego, CA, 2002.

Rhio. *Hooked on Raw: Rejuvenate Your Body and Soul with Nature's Living Foods*, Beso Entertainment: New York, NY, 2000.

Rogers, Jeff. *Vice Cream, Over 70 Sinfully Delicious Dairy-Free Delights*, Celestial Arts: Berkeley, CA, 2004.

Safron, Jeremy A. *The Raw Truth: The Art of Preparing Live Foods*, Celestial Arts: Berkeley, CA, 2003.

Scott-Aitken, Lynelle. *Raw Food Recipes: No Meat, No Heat,* Green Frog Publishers, 2005.

Shannon, Nomi. *The Raw Gourmet: Simple Recipes for Living Well*, Alive Books: Burnaby, BC, Canada, 1998.

Sheridan, Jameth, ND and Sheridan, Kim, ND. *Uncooking with Jameth & Kim: All Original, Vegan & Raw Recipes & Unique Information about Raw Vegan Foods*, HealthForce Publishing: Escondido, CA, 1991.

Trotter, Charlie & Klein, Roxanne. *Raw*, Ten Speed Press: Berkeley, CA. 2003.

Underkoffler, Renée Loux. *Living Cuisine: The Art and Spirit of Raw Food*, Avery: New York, NY, 2003.

Vonderplanitz, Aajonus. *The Recipe for Living without Disease*, Carnelian Bay Castle Press: Santa Monica, CA, 2002.

Wandling, Julie. *Thank God for Raw: Recipes for Raw*, Hallelujah Acres Publishing: Shelby, NC, 2002.

Wigmore, Ann. *Recipes for Longer Life*, Rising Sun Publications: Boston, MA, 1978.

Related Web Sites

As those of you who are used to the Internet know, web sites come and go. By the time you read this book, some of these sites may no longer be up. But these are the current ones I have found very useful.

www.alissacohen.com
This site sells Alissa's book, *Living on Live Food*. Additionally, there are several "before" and "after" photos of people on the raw diet. There is also a chat room for discussion.

www.annettelarkins.com
This web site belongs to Annette Larkins, who gave her testimony in Chapter 2. It has more about her and the products she offers.

www.buildfreedom.com/rawmain.htm
This is a very interesting site with links to other major raw food sites. It includes information about the instinctive raw diet and the raw animal food diet (see Appendix C). It has a paragraph about each site and a sort of "who's who" in the raw food world.

www.doctoryourself.com
This site has a lot of informative articles to help you take responsibility for your health and become your own doctor. It sells an eponymous book.

www.drday.com
Anyone who is still skeptical about the power of a raw diet should check out this site. It includes Dr. Day's photos of a very protruding breast tumor while she was busy trying out every sort of alternative health therapy for it. After trying dozens of things, she came upon juice cleansing, wheatgrass and a raw food diet, which cured her completely. The site sells her numerous videos on the topic.

www.foodnsport.com
This site has a lot of interesting articles by notable raw food doctor Doug Graham and word of his upcoming events and lecture appearances, which include a yearly fasting retreat.

www.fredericpatenaude.com
This is an informative site with interviews and articles on

the subject of raw eating. Site owner Frédéric Patenaude also sells his books, including an excellent and informative recipe book, *Sunfood Cuisine*, and *The Raw Secrets*. His most recent book, *Instant Raw Sensations*, includes fast, delicious recipes that are low in fat. You can also subscribe to his weekly newsletter, which is very informative and has useful tips.

www.fresh-network.com

This is a UK-based site; so it may not be practical to buy anything here if you live in the US, but it does have some good recipes and articles.

www.fromsadtoraw.com

This site offers a lot of information: recipes, answers to frequently asked questions, links, books and magazines, facts and tips.

www.getwellstaywellamerica.com

This is another Natural Hygiene site, with articles by Victoria Bidwell. It includes very informative articles on diet and other health topics, testimonials, as well as books and tapes for sale.

www.greenpeople.org

This site will link you to your local community supported agriculture (CSA) biodynamic farm, food co-op and health food stores, along with other local resources for obtaining good organic food and ecology-friendly products.

www.healself.org

This has numerous articles by Dr. Bernarr Zovluck, DD, DC. You can click on just about any illness or other health topic and read his very informative articles. He has been eating raw foods exclusively for over 50 years and is quite strong and youthful-looking!

www.health101.org

This site has a lot of powerful articles on health in addition to sales of books, products and classes. If you click on "articles," I especially recommend the article called, "Raw Foods: What Some People Don't Know," which quotes misinformed and ignorant health professionals about the futility of the raw diet, together with Don Bennett's responses clarifying their misconceptions.

www.livefoodfactor.com

The web site for this book, it has post-publication updates and additions to the book, as well as articles on the raw food diet.

www.livingnutrition.com

This site is by noted raw fooder and author David Klein. He publishes the raw food magazine *Living Nutrition*, which you can subscribe to on this site. The site includes a bookstore, health shop and listing of raw food events.

www.mercola.com

This site is run by a doctor who is full of cutting edge knowledge in nutrition and other areas of taking control of your health. You can get on his semi-weekly mailing list, which contains numerous articles. It also has a health information blog.

www.milksucks.com

This site is by People for the Ethical Treatment of Animals (PETA) and details how harmful dairy is not only to people, but also to the dairy cows, due to the way they are reared. It includes "Scary Dairy Tales" with testimonials to the perils of a white moustache.

www.notmilk.com

Named as a play on the "Got Milk?" dairy ads, this site has dozens of very interesting articles dispelling the milk myth and showing how very hazardous dairy is to our health. The site is by Robert Cohen, who sells his book (also available on audiotape), *Milk the Deadly Poison*, which is loaded with scientific data on the health hazards of dairy consumption.

www.paulnison.com

This is the official web site of author and raw food chef Paul Nison, with various resources relating to Paul's health and healing teachings, his lecture schedule, great links and much more.

www.purehealthandnutrition.com

This is a great free online newsletter that comes out every Thursday and features tips, tools and advice on the raw-food diet, health and more.

www.rawandjuicy.com

This site is by Shelly Keck-Borsits, author of the book *Dying to Get Well*. You can buy the book here or download it for free! The author needs the money from the book sales but is so intent on getting the word out that she freely gives away the book. The site includes a raw chat room, raw recipes and a "raw artist" link.

www.rawfamily.com

This is the Boutenkos' site and lists free recipes, frequently asked questions (FAQs), articles, testimonials and links. It also has the Boutenkos' books, DVDs and videos for sale.

www.rawfood.com

This is the largest raw food online store, owned by David Wolfe and Stephen Arlin. The items are 100% raw, as they are 100% raw fooders themselves. Imported from all around the world, many of these items are not available anywhere else in the USA. They also have the largest selection of raw food books available. In addition, the store sells natural beauty products, tapes, CDs and videos, and lists raw food events hosted by Wolfe. The site also includes links to articles on the raw food diet and related topics, as well as a personals section.

www.rawfoodlife.com

This is a very informative site, with links to other raw food sites and related articles published in magazines and professional journals.

www.rawfoodnews.com

This site has only some links.

www.rawfoodplanet.com

One of the creators of this site is pioneer raw fooder Viktoras Kulvinskas. It is truly a mega-site that is a fantastic resource, especially for travelers since it includes a map of the USA you can click on to find local raw food resources. It even covers quite a few other countries you can click on! Resources on this site include recipes, events calendar, schools, online courses, support and chat groups, books, articles and much, much more.

www.rawfoods.com (or www.living-foods.com)

This site has plenty of articles, including FAQs about the raw diet, a raw personals for connecting with other raw fooders, a store, free recipes and a chat room.

www.rawfoodteens.com

This site is a bulletin board for teenagers going on a raw

food diet. There is support for teens, with such issues as eating disorders, weight management, beauty and the struggles of going raw. There will be a chat room later.

www.rawfoodwiki.org

This site offers recipes, testimonials, equipment for sale and links.

www.rawfriends.com

This web site offers recipes and connections to housing with fellow raw fooders and even organizes scholarships and fund raising associated with the raw lifestyle.

www.rawgourmet.com

This site is by Nomi Shannon, author of the beautiful recipe book *The Raw Gourmet*, which abounds with color photos of her delicious raw food creations. The site has links, recipes, events, kitchen gadgets and books for sale, as well as an opportunity to sign up for her free seven-part course on eating raw.

www.rawguru.com

This site lists raw food leaders and recipes, articles, jokes, games and frequently asked questions. It also sells raw foods, books and equipment. You can also sign up for a newsletter.

www.rawlife.com

This is raw food author and lecturer Paul Nison's store. Along with free information, FAQs and recipes, the site sells books, raw food (some hard to find, such as raw cashews), raw chocolates, juicers and other kitchen equipment.

www.rawreform.com

This site belongs to Angela Stokes, who presented her testimony in Chapter 2. It includes her E-book for sale, as well as articles.

www.rawtimes.com

This site has links to nationwide raw restaurants, raw food stores, raw food machines and supplies, as well as book reviews and other items.

www.rawvegan.com

Go to this web site to sign up for a free 7-day e-course (e-mail course) on the raw food diet and learn practical ways to increase your energy and look younger by using the power of raw foods.

www.rawveganbooks.com

As the name suggests, this site sells a wide variety of books on the topic of raw veganism. Phone: 800-642-4113.

www.shazzie.com

This site has all sorts of information for the raw journey, as well as before and after photos. Shazzie wrote the book *Detox Your World,* which gives information on detoxifying one's environment, as well as on eating raw.

www.soilandhealth.org

This online library site contains a wealth of information, including entire books on health that can be downloaded for free.

www.superbeing.com

Raw fooder site owner Roger Haeske offers special reports, articles, books, testimonials and a free e-mail newsletter geared to the beginning raw fooder you can sign up to receive.

www.thegardendiet.com

This web site offers e-books, DVDs, retreats and photos of the author, a very muscular bodybuilder who has been on a raw vegan diet for many years.

www.iamhealthyinc.com

This site is run, in part, by Paula Wood, who gave her testimony in Chapter 2. It includes articles and recipes and offers courses.

www.totalhealthsecrets.com

This site offers information on internal cleansing techniques.

www.transformationinstitute.org

This site is a school for Natural Hygiene by Dr. Robert Sniadach. You can purchase his comprehensive correspondence course on this site. It has free FAQs and interviews as well.

Raw Food Chat Groups

The various raw food Internet chat groups are fluid and changeable; they come and go frequently; so this is just a sample of what was available at press time:

http://groups.yahoo.com/group/rawfood/

http://groups.yahoo.com/group/rawfoodsbeginners/

http://groups.yahoo.com/group/12stepstorawfood/

http://groups.yahoo.com/group/freshnetgroup/

http://groups.yahoo.com/group/hallelujahdiet/

http://groups.yahoo.com/group/rawfoodpower/

http://groups.yahoo.com/group/rawfoodeaters/

http://health.groups.yahoo.com/group/rawfoodarticlesarchive/

http://health.groups.yahoo.com/group/100_percent_raw

Resources for Food and Kitchen Supplies

Some raw foods are difficult to find, even at your local health store. It may therefore be necessary to shop online for certain items, such as raw nut butters, sun-dried fruits, unpasteurized oils, raw cacao beans and others. Kitchen gadgets needed for gourmet dishes (see Chapter 10) are also available at many of these sites. The following lists will also include phone numbers for those who do not have Internet access.

Acres USA

P. O. Box 91299, Austin, TX 78709. Phones: 800-355-5313, 512-892-4400, 512-892-4448 (fax). Web site: www.acres usa.com. This is an excellent source of books, tapes and videos for organic farmers and home gardeners. They also publish a monthly magazine. Send for their free catalog.

Alive Foods

Web site: www.alivefoods.com. This is an Australian company that sells bee pollen, supplements, hemp oil, books and DVDs about raw food and nutrition.

Biodynamic Farming and Gardening Association, Inc.

25844 Butler Rd., Junction City, OR 97448. Phones: 888-516-7797, 541-998-0105, 541-998-0106 (fax). Web site: www.biodynamics.com. E-mail: biodynamic@aol.com. This organization coordinates Community Supported Agriculture (CSA) farms throughout the USA. CSAs supply locally grown organic foods direct from farm to consumer. Call their toll-free number to locate one in your area.

Country Life Natural Foods

P. O. Box 489 52nd St., Pullman, MI 49450. Phones: 800-456-7694, 269-236-5011 and 269-236-8357 (fax). Web site: www.clnf.org. This company sells raw, organic nuts and nut butters, dried organic fruits (some of which are sun-dried and therefore raw) and organic seeds.

EatRaw

125 Second St, Brooklyn, NY 11231. Phones: 866-4EATRAW, 866-432-8729, 718-210-0048 and 718-802-0116 (fax). Web site: www.eatraw.com. This company sells

raw food, natural beauty and skin care, kitchen appliances, books, videos and natural cleaning supplies.

Excalibur Dehydrators

Excalibur Products, A Division of KBI, 6083 Power Inn Road, Sacramento, CA 95824. Phone: 800-875-4254. Web site: www.excaliburdehydrator.com. They sell the best temperature-controlled dehydrators on the market.

Go Raw

6313 University Ave, San Diego, CA 92115. Phones: 619-286-2446 and 619-286-2446 (fax). Web site: www.goraw.com. This company sells lots of raw crackers, cookies, sprouted and dehydrated seeds, raw granola and more.

HealthForce Nutritionals

1835A S. Centre City Pkwy, #411, Escondido, CA 92025-6505. Phones: 800-357-2717, 760-747-8922 (fax also). Web site: www.healthforce.com. This company sells Greener Grasses and Vitamineral Green, both of which are living dehydrated grasses. If you don't have time to make your own wheatgrass, this is the next best thing.

High Vibe

Phone: 888-554-6645. Web site: www.highvibe.com. They sell raw foods, books and videos concerning the raw lifestyle, natural beauty products and much more.

Jaffe Brothers Natural Foods

28560 Lilac Road, Valley Center, CA 92082. Phone: 760-749-1133, 760-749-1282 (fax). Web site: www.organicfruits andnuts.com. In business for over 50 years, this company sells organic nuts, fruits and other dry goods.

K-Tec USA

1206 South 1680 West, Orem, UT 84058. Phones: 800-748-5400, 801-222-0888 and 801-802-8585 (fax). Web site: www.ktecusa.com. This is the company that makes the K-Tec heavy-duty blender.

Living Nuts

Phone: 207-780-1101. Web site: www.livingnutz.com. For people who are used to eating chips and popcorn with different flavors, these flavored nuts make a great transition food, as well as a great treat for the long-term raw fooder.

Living Tree Community Foods

P. O. Box 10082, Berkeley, CA 94709. Phones: 800-260-5534, 510-526-7106 and 510-526-9516 (fax). Web site: www.livingtreecommunity.com. E-mail: info@livingtreecommunity.com. Not everything is raw, and since things are always changing, you have to e-mail them or call them. They have a large selection of truly raw nuts and truly raw dried fruits. They have a very wide assortment of raw nut and seed butters, raw cacao beans, coconut butter and olive oil.

Macaweb

Phone: 888-645-4282. Web site: www.macaweb.com. This company sells various raw, organic foods, including maca, the super food from Peru.

NatuRAW

851 Irwin Street, Suite 304, San Rafael, CA 94901. Phones: 800-NATURAW (800-628-8729), 415-456-1719 (office), 775-587-8613 (fax). Web site: www.naturaw.com. This company sells raw treats and goodies, supplements, raw cacao (chocolate), body care and more.

Nature's First Law

Phone: 800-205-2350. Web site: www.rawfood.com. This store carries lots of raw food items you can't find elsewhere, items from all over the world, all organic and 100% raw.

Orkos

Web site: www.orkos.com/home_EN.php. Within Europe only, these distributors sell instinctive quality, organic produce, nuts, seeds, honey and more.

Peace Pies

Phone: 760-805-5315. Web site: www.rawpie.com. You certainly don't have to give up pies to be a raw food eater! They sell plenty of raw vegan pies.

Raw Life

P. O. Box 16156, West Palm Beach, FL 33416. Phone: 866-RAW-PAUL, 866-729-7285. Web site: www.rawlife.com. Paul Nison sells raw food, books, tapes and videos.

Seeds of Change

P. O. Box 15700, Santa Fe, NM 87506-5700. Phones: 505-438-8080 and 505-438-7052 (fax). Web site: www.seedsofchange.com. This company sells organic seeds and seeds that have been less hybridized than usual (see Chapter 12).

SunOrganic Farm

411 S. Las Pasas Road, San Marcos, CA 92078. Phone: 888-269-9888, 760-510-8077 and 760-510-9996 (fax). Web site: www.sunorganicfarm.com. This company sells raw nuts, nut and seed butters and dehydrated fruits. Circumstances are always changing; so it is best to call before placing an order to discover which items are truly raw.

The Raw Bakery

Phone: 800-571-8369. Web site: www.rawbakery.com. This is the only place (at the time of this writing) where I have found truly raw, shredded coconut. It also sells raw cakes and other goodies.

The Raw Gourmet

P. O. Box 21097, Sedona, AZ 86341. Phone: 888-316-4611. Web site: www.rawgourmet.com. Nomi Shannon sells books, including her highly recommended raw recipe book, as well as useful kitchen gadgets. For more information, see the web site summary at the site listed above.

The Raw Life

The Raw World, 322 South Padre Juan, Ojai, CA 93023. Phones: 866-RAW-PAUL (866-729-7285) and 818-832-0007 (fax). Web site: www.rawlife.com. Raw food, books, tapes and videos are for sale.

The Raway

P. O. Box 600422, San Diego, CA 92160. Phones: 619-795-9647 and 315-410-3873 (fax). Web site: www.theraway. com. They sell great gourmet raw food.

The Supermarket Coalition

A Project of The Rural Coalition, 1012 14th St., Suite 1100, Washington, DC 20005. Phones: 866-RURAL-80, 202-628-7160, 202-628-7165 (fax). Web site: www.supermarketcoop. com. This web site links to an on-line retail storefront and to various local produce suppliers, such as www.growing power.org for Milwaukee and Chicago.

USDA Farmers National Market Directory

Web site: www.ams.usda.gov/farmersmarkets/map.htm. Locate a farmers market in your area.

Resources for Healing and Fasting Supervision

Pcople who are seriously ill may wish to go to a cleansing center where they can fast under professional supervision and learn how to eat and prepare live food.

The facilities listed below offer some form of supervised fasting, sometimes on an outpatient basis only, as with Dr. Zovluck. Most of them also offer various educational programs.

Web sites that list doctors who have experience in supervising fasts include www.orthopathy.net/doctors/ and www.natu ralhygienesociety.org/doctors.html. Some international contacts may be found at http://sci.pam.szczecin.pl/~fasting/.

Ann Wigmore Foundation

P. O. Box 399, San Fidel, NM 87049-0399. Phone: 505-552-0595. E-mail: info@wigmore.org. Founded by Ann Wigmore and operated in Boston for 32 years, they are now located in a radiant oasis, high in the desert of enchanting New Mexico.

Creative Health Institute

112 West Union City Road, Union City, MI 49094. Phones: 866-426-1213, 517-278-6260, 517-278-5837 (fax). E-mail: info@creativehealthinstitute.us. Web site: www.creative healthinstitute.us. This natural health teaching center, based upon Ann Wigmore's teachings, provides a natural program of body purification, nutrition and rejuvenation through the use of fresh raw fruits, vegetables, juices, nuts, sprouted seeds, grains, beans, chlorophyll rich greens and wheatgrass juice.

Dr. Anthony Penepent, MD, MPH

439 125th Street, 1270 Broadway #10011, New York, NY 10027. Phone: 212-316-9775. Web site: www.birdflusur vive.com. Dr. Penepent graduated in 1981 from the Grenadan medical school at St. George's University and has a Master of Public Health degree in nutrition from Loma Linda University in California. He studied alternative medicine and Natural Hygiene under Dr. Christopher Gian-Cursio, ND, in New York and began his Natural Hygiene-based practice there in 1986. He was IAHP certified in water

fasting and dietary healing in 1989 and is a Member of the International Natural Hygiene Society.

Dr. Ben Kim

147 Anne St. N, Barrie, ON, Canada L4N2B9. Phone: 705-733-0030. If you are looking for a natural solution to your health condition(s) but cannot visit the clinic, you can receive personalized guidance from Dr. Kim through his comprehensive consulting service.

Dr. Bernarr Zovluck, DC, DD

P. O. Box 1523, Santa Monica CA 90406. Phone: 310-396-2914. E-mail: drbernarr@aol.com Web site: www.healself. org. Dr. Bernarr offers fasting supervision via telephone consultation for those choosing to fast at home, as well as general health consultations.

Dr. Cinqué's Health Retreat

305 Verdin St., Buda, TX 78610. Phone: 512-295-4256. Dr. Ralph Cinqué operates a fasting retreat at his home. He interned with both Dr. Shelton in the USA and Dr. Alec Burton of Australia and has been working in the health retreat and spa business all of his adult life.

Dr. Dimitri Karalis

Hermanus, Cape Province, South Africa. Phones: 27+(0) 2854759901, 27+(0)283162978, 27+(0)283161299 (fax). Dr. Karalis has been a naturopathic physician since 1973. He opened the first biologically-oriented healing clinic in South Africa and now has a clinic on the coast. He has had great success with diseases like arthritis, neuritis, prostate enlargement, migraines, chronic fatigue, insomnia, dyspepsia, diabetes, cancers, depressions, fears, lung disorders, obesity, dermatitis and many other metabolic diseases.

Dr. Joel Fuhrman, MD

4 Walter E. Foran Blvd., Suite 409, Flemington, NJ 08822 Phones: 908-237-0200. 908-237-0210 (fax). E-mail: info@ drfuhrman.com. Web site: www.drfuhrman.com. Dr. Fuhrman is a board-certified family physician who specializes in preventing and reversing disease through nutritional and natural methods, has published several books, and publishes an online, monthly newsletter.

Dr. John Fielder, DO, DC, ND

P. O. Box 901, Cairns, Queensland 4870, Australia. Phones: 07-4093-7989 (617-4093-7989 from outside of Australia). Web site: www.ig.com.au/anl/fielder.html. E-mail: academy.naturalliving@iig.com.au. A practitioner of Natural Hygiene, Dr. Fielder is a graduate of the Naturopathic College of South Australia in osteopathy, chiropractic and naturopathy. He also offers a comprehensive correspondence course in Natural Hygiene.

Dr. Keki R. Sidhwa, ND, DO

Shalimar 14, The Weavers, Newark-on-Trent, Notts NG2 4RY, England. Phone: 01636-682-941 (011-44-1636-682-941 from the USA). Dr. Sidhwa is the founder and director of Shalimar Health Home, where he has helped over 25,000 people to overcome their ailments by fasting and following a Hygienic lifestyle. Dr. Sidhwa's fasting center is now closed, but he still offers telephone and office consultations.

Dr. Maya Nicole Baylac

Phone: 808-982-8202. E-mail: contact@mindyourbody.info. Web site: www.mindyourbody.info. Dr. Baylac practices privately on the Big Island of Hawaii. She is a hygienic doctor and psychotherapist. She has practiced Reichian breath work, Gestalt therapy, bioenergetics and meditation in individual sessions and in groups for 25 years, blending her psychological background and her hygienic practice into a unique mind/body/spirit approach. She supervises detoxification and rebuilding programs with water fasting, juice fasting and raw foods during long-term retreats.

Dr. Stanley S. Bass, ND, DC, PhC, PhD, DO, DSc, DD

3119 Coney Island Ave, Brooklyn, NY 11235. Phone: 718-648-1500. Web site: www.drbass.com. Dr. Bass was certified by the IAHP (International Association of Hygienic Physicians) as a "specialist in fasting supervision and hygienic care" and is a founding board member of the INHS (International Natural Hygiene Society). He has supervised over 30,000 fasts and health recoveries using diet.

Dr. Virginia Vetrano, DC, hMD

Dr. Vetrano's Health Information Service, P. O. Box 190, Barksdale, TX 78828. Phones: 830-234-3499, 830-234-3599 (fax). E-mail: vvvetrano@rionet.cc. Dr. Vetrano worked with Dr. Shelton for many years in the practice of Natural

Hygiene and has been a doctor and educator since 1964. She currently does telephone consultations.

Fasting Center International

Phone: 818-590-2536. E-mail: FastMaster@Fasting.com. Their 20- to 120-day fasts include personal online supervision.

Hallelujah Acres

P. O. Box 2388, Shelby, NC 28151. Phones: 704-481-1700, 704-481-0345 (fax). E-mail: info@hacres.com. Web site: www.hacres.com. They publish a free health newsletter that you can sign up to receive. They also offer classes, including online health education courses to learn about health and nutrition from a Biblical perspective.

Hippocrates Health Institute

1443 Palmdale Court, West Palm Beach, FL 33411. Phone: 561-471-8876. E-mail: info@hippocratesinst.org. Web site: www.hippocratesinst.org. Operated by Brian Clement for the past 25 years, this 70-person, in-residence health facility was originally founded by Dr. Ann Wigmore.

Hummingbird Homestead

22732 NW Gillihan Road, Sauvie Island, OR 97231-3781. Phones: 503-621-3897, 503-621-3781 (fax). E-mail: Jayne@earthworld.com. Hummingbird Homestead, a place of solitude, peace and joy, was founded by Victoria Jayne, LCSW, Reiki Master, NLP Master Programmer, Essene Minister and spiritual seeker. A retreat can include workshops, therapeutic counseling, detoxifying juice fasts, live foods education, as well as other services and products.

Living Foods Centre

Holmleigh, Gravel Hill, Ludlow SY81QS, UK, Phones: 00944(0)1584 875308, 00944(0)1584 875778 (fax). Run by Elaine Bruce, author of *Living Foods for Radiant Health*, Elaine Bruce is an experienced naturopath teaching residential Living Foods courses, tailored for a UK audience.

Optimum Health Institute

There are two Optimum Health Institutes (OHIs):
- OHI San Diego, 6970 Central Ave, Lemon Grove, CA 91945. Phones: 619-464-3346, 619-589-4098 (fax).
- OHI Austin, 265 Cedar Lane, Cedar Creek, TX 78612. Phones: 512-303-4817, 512-303-1239 (fax).

They share the web site www.optimumhealthinstitute.org.

Rest Of Your Life Health Retreat

P. O. Box 1056, La Vernia, TX 78121. Phones: 830-779-2655, 830-779-2655 (fax). E-mail: drhaag@roylretreat.com. Web site: www.roylretreat.com. Tosca Haag, MD, was an assistant editor and contributing writer for *Dr. Shelton's Hygienic Review* for many years. She was tutored by Dr. Shelton and Dr. Vetrano and has been supervising director of several Health Retreats. Her husband, Gregory Haag, MD, also works there.

Sacred Space Healing Center

776 Haight Street (at Scott), San Francisco, CA 94117. Phone: 415-431-0878. E-mail: info@sacredspace-sf.com. Offers live blood analysis, nutritional counseling and fasting retreats in Puerto Vallarta, Mexico.

Scott's Natural Health Institute

P. O. Box 361095, Strongsville, OH 44136. Phone: 440-238-3003. Web site: www.fastingbydesign.com. Dr. D. J. Scott, DM, ND, DC, offers therapeutic fasting under professional, scientific supervision, using weekly, precise, scientific, monitoring of disease processes until healing or remission measurably occurs, accomplished by his very advanced, federally licensed, diagnostic laboratory, of which he is the director. He has been in practice for over 50 years and has personally supervised the care of over 40,000 patients. He has fasted, under direct supervision, some 20,000 patients, many of whom were of international origin.

Tanglewood Wellness Center

Phone: 301-637-4657. E-mail: info@tangelwoodwellness center.com. Formerly in Bethesda, MD, this fasting center is now located in the Republic of Panama.

The Arcadia Health Centre

31 Cobah Road, Arcadia, NSW 2159, Australia. Phones: 61-2-9653-1115, 61-2-9653-2678. Web site: www.alecburton. com. Run by Drs. Alec and Nejla Burton, the Arcadia Health Centre is the first and only clinic practicing Natural Hygiene in Australia that is conducted by licensed and certified members of the IAHP (established in 1961). Dr. Burton graduated in chiropractic and osteopathy in England. He is a co-founder of the British Natural Hygiene Society,

The Australian Natural Hygiene Society and the International Association of Hygienic Physicians.

The Gerson Institute

Administrative Office: 316 East Olive #A, Redlands, CA 92373. Phone: 888-792-0077. E-mail: Mail@wholelifelearn ingcenter.org. Those at the Gerson Institute have been assisting detox and nutritional healing for decades. They also have a new Hawaiian retreat center: 17-502 Ipuaiwaha St., Kea'au, HI 96749. Phone: 808-982-8202 (fax also), 808-280-2537 (cell).

The Goldberg Clinic

2480 Windy Hill Road, Ste. 203, Marietta, GA 30067. Phone: 770-974-7470. Additional location: 9121 North Military Trail, Ste. 308, Palm Beach Gardens, FL. 33410. Phone: 561-722-9637. Dr. Goldberg is a Clinical Nutritionist, Clinical Epidemiologist, Diplomate of The American Clinical Board of Nutrition and Certified Natural Hygiene Practitioner.

Tree of Life Foundation

P. O. Box 778, Patagonia, AZ 85624. Phone: 520-394-2520. Web site: www.treeoflife.nu. The Tree of Life Foundation is headed by Dr. Gabriel Cousens. It also offers seminars, workshops and a master's degree in living foods.

TrueNorth Health Outpatient Clinic

6010 Commerce Blvd. #152, Rohert Park, CA 94928. Phone: 707-586-5555. Web site: www.healthpromoting. com. TrueNorth Health, also known as the Center for Conservative Therapy, has operated its residential health education Center in Penngrove, California since 1984. Their views are best described in their book, *The Pleasure Trap: Mastering the Hidden Force That Undermines Health & Happiness*, by Douglas J. Lisle and Alan Goldhamer.

Raw Restaurants

The number of raw restaurants in the USA and Canada has increased so dramatically over the past five years that now there are over 60, I am told. Because there are so many, and they come and go with such fluidity, this listing may not be up-to-date. However, there is a web site that tries to keep up-to-date with the listings of raw food restaurants by state: www.rawfoodinfo.com/directories/dir_rawrests.html.

Another site that contains raw restaurant listings by state (and even by country!) is www.rawfoodplanet.com.

I wish to express my sincere thanks to the owners of www.rawfoodplanet.com for giving me permission to reprint their raw restaurant listing at the time of the publication of this book. Please refer to their web site for any updates, as we are sure to see more and more raw food restaurants, just as happened with the vegetarian movement.

I have also added a few restaurants that I knew of which the web site did not have at the time.

Note that some upscale grocery stores, like Whole Foods and Wild Oats, offer seating for eaters, juice and salad/deli bars and of course the produce section, where you can buy fresh fruits to enhance your meal. Check their web sites, or see their telephone numbers listed in the "Raw Franchises" section that follows, to locate one near you.

In the listings that follow, one star means vegetarian; two stars means vegan; and three stars means raw foods.

United States

Arizona

Rawsome! Café ***
234 W. University Drive, Tempe, AZ 85044. 480-496-5959 or 866-RAW-4-LIFE (729-4543). E-mail: info@rawforlife. com.

Supreme Master Ching Hai Vegetarian House *

> 3239 E. Indian School Rd., Phoenix, AZ 85108. 602-264-3480. Hours: Tu-Sat 11AM-2:30PM & 5-9PM; closed Sun & M.

Tree of Life Café ***

> 771 Harshaw Road — P.O. Box 1080, Patagonia, AZ 85624. Café: 520-394-2589. Café E-mail: cafe@treeoflife.nu.

California

Alive Café ***

> 1972 Lombard St. (near Webster), San Francisco, CA 94123. 415-923-1052. Hours: W-Sun 12PM-9PM. Live food cuisine, featuring appetizers, snacks, salads, soups, entrees, desserts, teas and beverages.

Au Lac Vegetarian Restaurant */**/***

> Mile Square Plaza, 16563 Brookhurst, Fountain Valley, CA. 714-418-0658. Hours: Tu-Sun 10:30AM-9:00PM. Au Lac is a vegetarian restaurant featuring Vietnamese and Chinese cuisine. Au Lac now offers vegan, raw food dishes.

Back to the Garden ***

> 21065 Bush St., Middletown, CA 95461. 707-987-8303 or 707-987-8315. Offers gourmet dining and catering featuring high-quality, organic, vegan, living cuisine. Also offers a selection of raw vegan crackers and other delicious dehydrated items for pickup or for shipping via UPS.

Café Gratitude **/***

> 2400 Harrison St., San Francisco, CA. 415-824-4652. Serving all organic, vegan and mostly live foods! They support local farmers, sustainable agriculture and environmentally friendly products and invite you to "step inside and enjoy being someone who chooses loving your life, adoring yourself, accepting the world, being generous and grateful every day."

Café Sangha ***

> 31 Bolinas Rd., Fairfax, CA. 94930. 415-456-5300. Local, seasonal, organic, vegan ingredients. Raw gourmet.

Cilantro Live ***

> There are two locations in the San Diego area:

- 315½ 3rd Avenue, Chula Vista, CA 91910. 619-827-7401. Hours: M-Th 11-8, F 11-9, Sat 12-9, Sun 12-8.

- Carlsbad Village Faire, 300 Carlsbad Village Drive, Ste. 106 Carlsbad, CA 92008. 760-858-0136, 760-858-0138 (fax). Hours: M-Th 11-8, F 11-9, Sat 12-9, Sun 12-8.

San Diego County's organic, vegan and 100% raw restaurant.

Inn of the Seventh Ray */**/***
128 Old Topanga Canyon Rd., Topanga, CA 90290. 310-455-1311. Features a live foods chef, Angja Aditi. Live food cooking lessons available; call for details.

Juliano's Raw Planet ***
609 Broadway (corner of 6th and Broadway), Santa Monica, CA 90401. 310-587-1552. Online catalog "Raw Superstore," "University of Raw" (classes) and the "World's first organic restaurant certified by QAI (Quality Assurance International), the world leader in organic certification," located at 609 Broadway in Santa Monica. Hours: M-Th 11AM-10PM, F 11AM-11PM, Sat 10AM-11PM, Sun 10AM-10PM.

Kung Food **/***
2949 5th Ave., San Diego, CA 92103. 619-298-7302. 100% vegan, fast casual, buffet style restaurant. "We also have some raw food."

Leaf Cuisine ***
11938 West Washington Blvd., Los Angeles, CA 90066. 310-390-6005. Their food is "organic (certified by QAI), vegan, raw, kosher (certified by KCS)."

Lydia's Lovin' Foods /***
Fairfax, CA. Raw and cooked meals.

Ranchos Natural Foods **/***
3918 30th St., San Diego, CA 92104. 619-298-3339. San Diego's only all-vegan grocery. Raw food deli, vegan deli, juice bar. Technically, this is a health food grocery, not a restaurant, but their deli includes lots of live vegan foods, and seating is provided.

Raw Energy Organic Juice Café ***
2050 Addison St. (between Shattuck & Milvia), Berkeley, CA 94704. 510-665-9464. "We only use organic produce; we make our own 'milk' from nuts; we recycle your cups and

utensils; and our compost goes to a community garden where organic farming is taught.

Taste of the Goddess ***
7253 Santa Monica Blvd., Santa Monica, CA. 323-874-7700.

District of Columbia

Source of Life Juice Bar & Deli: Everlasting Life Community Co-Op ** / ***
2928 Georgia Ave. NW, Washington, DC 20001. 202-232-1700. Hours: M-Sat 9-9, Sun 11-9. Lectures and cooking classes. Live food and vegan cuisine.

Florida

Rhythm 'N Roots Raw Food Restaurant & Juice Bar ***
111 North M Street, Lake Worth, FL 33460. 561-588-2801. As far as we know, Rhythm 'N Roots has temporarily closed. If you live in the West Palm Beach area and are interested in joining a raw food group, please sign up for our West Palm Beach living foods Yahoo group. We are especially interested in getting something going for raw potlucks in the North Palm Beach area. This group has been formed in order to achieve a raw food community in the West Palm Beach area. For more information, you may also contact Viveca at 561-748-5258 and leave a message, or you may e-mail vivecapark@juno.com.

Tree of Zion ** / ***
2426 NE 2nd Ave., Miami, FL 33137. 305-573-5874. Natural juice and smoothie bar, daily Italian (vegan) dishes, raw food dishes, raw desserts, metaphysical and spiritual books, Ethiopian garments and Rastafari artifacts, African and Indian crafts, vintage clothing. Hours: M-W 11AM-10PM, Th-Sat 11AM-11PM, Sun 11AM-3PM.

Georgia

A Taste of Life ** / ***
1427 S. Gordon St., Atlanta, GA 30310. Raw Foods. Different menus each day.

Cameli's Vegan Vegetarian */**/***

1263 Glenwood Ave. SE, Atlanta, GA 30316. 404-622-9926.

Here to Heal ***

2113 Pace St., Covington, GA 30014. 770-385-5273. Call for hours. "100% Raw and Organic! No Bragg's Liquid Aminos, dehydration, honey, maple syrup or nutritional yeast whatsoever!"

Mutana's Marketplace & Juice Bar */**/***

1388 Ralph David Abernathy Blvd., Atlanta, GA 30310. 404-753-5252.

Raw Foods Kafé ***

Everlasting Life Natural Foods Market, 878 Ralph David Abernathy Blvd., Atlanta, GA 30310. 404-758-1110.

Hawaii

Note: See the Vegetarian Society of Honolulu Hawaii Vegetarian Dining Guide, featuring over 70 listings (restaurants, health food stores, etc.).

Joy's Place */**/***

1993 South Kihei Rd., Kihei, Maui, HI. 808-879-9258. Café with raw foods options.

Mandala Garden Juice Bar and Deli */**/***

29 Baldwin Ave., Paia, Maui, HI 96779. 808-579-9500. Indian and live food.

Veg Out */**/***

Haiku Town Center, 810 Kokomo Rd., Haiku, Maui, HI 96708. 100% vegetarian with vegan, raw and wheat-free options.

Idaho

Akasha Organics */**/***

Chapter One Bookstore, 160 North Main St., Ketchum, ID 83340. 208-726-4777. Market and raw food café. E-mail: akasha@svidaho.net

Illinois

Charlie Trotter's /**/***
816 West Armitage, Chicago, IL 60614. 773-248-6228, 773-6088 (fax). Hours: Tu-Th 6PM-10PM, F-Sat 5:30PM-10PM, occasionally open M. Mostly cooked, expensive gourmet food, but offers raw dishes upon request. E-mail: info@charlietrotters.com. Web address: www.charlietrotters.com.

Cousin's Incredible Vitality ***
3038 W. Irving Park Rd., Chicago, IL 60618. 773-478-6868, 773-478-6888 (fax). Hours: Sun, M, W, Th 4:30PM-10PM, F, Sat 4:30PM-11PM. Raw, all vegan, organic restaurant with a Mediterranean flair.

Karyn's Fresh Corner & Karyn's Inner Beauty Center **/***
1901 North Halsted St., Chicago, IL 60614. 312-255-1590. Hours: M-Sun 9AM-9PM. Mostly raw, all vegan restaurant.

Maine

Eden Vegetarian Café **/***
78 West St., Bar Harbor, ME 04609. 207-288-4422. "Mt. Desert Island's only vegan restaurant, focusing on serving mostly organic ingredients from the area's many farms and small growers." Salads and raw food options available.

Little Lad's Café & Restaurant **/***
58 Exchange St., Portland, ME 04101. 207-871-1636.

Little Lad's Café & Restaurant **/***
128 Main St., Bangor, ME. 207-942-5482. "Bangor's only total vegetarian restaurant." Hours: Sun 11-5, M-Th 7-7, F 7-2. Sat Closed. They serve "no meat, no fish, no eggs and no dairy." Salads and raw food options available.

Maryland

Everlasting Life Health Food Super Market */**/***
9185 Central Ave., Capitol Heights, MD. 202-232-1700. Catering available.

Massachusetts

Body & Soul **/***
13R Bessom St. (Village Plaza Shopping Center), Marblehead, MA 01945. 781-631-7286.

The Organic Garden **/***
294 Cabot St., Beverly (NE of Boston on the coast), MA 01915. 978-922-0004. Hours: Tu 11-8, W-Th 11-9, F-Sat 11-10, Sun 3-7. 45 min. to 1-hour drive from Boston. Features a great selection of raw food items on the menu.

Michigan

People's Food Co-op **/***
216 N. Fourth Ave., Ann Arbor, MI 48104. 734-994-9174. Salad bar hours: M-Sat 9AM-9PM, Sun 9AM-8PM. Organic produce plus soup/salad bar. Web site: www.peoplesfood. coop.

Seva **/***
314 E. Liberty St., Ann Arbor, MI 48107. 734-662-1111. Hours: M-Th 11AM-9PM, F-Sat 11AM-10PM, Sun 10AM-9PM, with brunch served 10AM-3PM. Cooked vegetarian fare with raw salad plates and juices/smoothies.

Minnesota

Ecopolitan **/***
2409 Lyndale Ave., South, Minneapolis, MN 55405. 612-87-GREEN. Ecopolitan is a completely organic, vegan and raw restaurant and an ecological shop selling natural, non-toxic home and body goods.

Nevada

Go Raw Café ***
2910 Lake East Dr., Las Vegas, NV 89117. 702-254-5382. Live food cuisine.

New York

Angelica Kitchen **/***
300 E. 12th St. (between 1st and 2nd Ave.), New York, NY 10003. 212-228-2909. Hours: 11:30-10:30 daily. "A minimum of 95% of all food used to prepare our menu has been grown ecologically. In addition, we use no refined sugars, no preservatives, no dairy, no eggs, no animal products whatsoever." Salads, juices and gourmet raw food entrées on menu.

Bonobos Restaurant **/***
18 E. 23rd St. (at Madison Avenue overlooking Madison Square Park), New York, NY. 212-505-1200. All food is served with live enzymes intact as Mother Nature intended. We support local farmers. Take out, delivery, catering, skylight, dining room, events. Coming soon Bonobo's Annex, 156 West 20th Street, NYC.

Caravan of Dreams **/***
405 E. 6th St. (between 1st Ave. and Ave. A), New York, NY 10009-6303. 212-254-1613. Kosher. Good raw food selection.

Green Paradise ***
609 Vanderbilt Ave. (between St. Marks Ave. and Bergen St.), Park Slope (Brooklyn), NY. 718-230-5177. Organic, vegan, raw food restaurant and juice bar.

In the Raw **/***
65 Tinker St., Woodstock, NY 12498. 845-679-9494. Organic, vegetarian deli, juice and smoothie bar, specializing in raw food.

Quintessence ***
263 E. 10th St. (between 1st Ave. and Ave. A), New York, NY 10009. 646-654-1823. Quintessence is "a gourmet dining retreat that relaxes and rejuvenates beyond belief. Our food is comprised of some of the most rare and exotic ingredients found on earth, which combine to form the elegant, innovative dishes that have been celebrated as some of the very best found in New York City. But more than just great tasting food, everything served at Quintessence is 100% organic, vegan and raw. We understand you seek more from your food than is offered at most restaurants, and our commitment to both flavor and health has created an un-

paralleled dining experience that will both satisfy your appetite and energize, revitalize and refresh from the inside out. So join us. Take a break from the city to enjoy our spa-like environment and experience the essence of food with Quintessence."

Quintessence ***
566 Amsterdam Ave. (between 87th and 88th St.), New York, NY 10024. 212-501-9700.

Soul Restaurant ***
In the Spirit New York Night Club, 530 W. 27th St., New York, NY. 212-268-9477. Night Club. Restaurant with raw menu created by raw chef Chad Sarno.

Ohio

Squeaker's Café & Health Food Store **/***
175 N. Main St., Bowling Green, OH 43402. 419-354-7000. Vegan and raw foods.

Squeaker's Café & Health Food Store **/***
601 N. Main St., Findlay, OH 45840. 419-424-3990. Vegan and raw foods.

Oregon

Calendula — A Natural Café **/***
3257 SE Hawthorne Blvd., Portland, OR 97214. 503-235-6800. Vegan/organic, with living foods options.

Omega Gardens */**/***
4036 SE Hawthorne, Portland, OR. 503-235-2551. Super salad bar. Features raw, vegan, gourmet dinners. Tu 6-8PM. Call for reservations.

Pennsylvania

Arnold's Way ***
319 West Main St. Store #4 Rear, Lansdale (40 miles N. of Philadelphia), PA 19446. 215-361-0116. The only raw, vegetarian hamburger and steaks! Also: pies, salads, soups, pâtés, wraps, juices and ice creams. Classes and events.

Kind Café ** / ***
724 North 3rd St., Philadelphia, PA 19123. 215-922-KIND (5463). 100% vegan, 50% raw and mostly organic. Hours: M-Sat 11-8. Menu features: Live lo mein, happy chicken wrap, raw pizza, chili, living lasagna, raw pies and vegan smoothies. Books on the shelves, art on the wall and educational classes.

Maggie's Mercantile * / ** / ***
320 Atwood St., Pittsburgh, PA 15213. 724-593-5056. Hours: M-F 11:30AM-9:00PM. Deli style. Raw, live and organic vegetarian and vegan foods. They say: "Our produce is 90-95% organic. Eat well, live compassionately!" Additional location: 1262 Route 711, Stahlstown, PA 15687. 724-593-5056. Hours: M-F 11:30AM-9:00PM.

Oasis Living Cuisine ** / ***
81 Lancaster Ave. (Rt. 30 and Rt. 401, Great Valley Center), Malvern, PA 19355. 610-647-9797. Cooked and raw foods. Not completely vegetarian.

Texas

Pure – A Living Foods Café ***
2720 Greenville Ave., Dallas, TX 75206. 214-824-7776. GRAND OPENING: Fall 2005. Check web site for date! We at Pure are doing everything in our power to make the opening happen ASAP. Texas' first raw restaurant serving organic, living cuisine. Foods in their pure, vibrant and natural state. Live foods loaded with enzymes create life, youth, beauty, peace, vitality and perfect weight. So, try Pure and experience how amazing the food tastes!

Canada

British Columbia

RAW * / ** / ***
1849 West 1st Ave., Vancouver, BC, Canada. 604-737-0420. Location map and hours on web site. Raw is a progressive health café committed to supplying you with the freshest, certified organic ingredients. Using natural, raw materials

and infusing them with a modern urban edge, you will be mesmerized by this beautiful example of Feng Shui design. Cuisines: Raw foods, salads, vegetarian, organic. Casual, feng shui ambiance. Outdoor dining patio. Entertainment.

Ontario

Heart's Joy Living Foods Garden Restaurant ***
250-598-7718. Planning to open in 2005. We are actively searching for a great location; if you have any leads, please let us know! Give us a call at 250-598-7718. The Heart's Joy menu will offer "the ultimate in healthy eating live food." Silkily subtle soups, power juices, made-on-the-premises crackers and pâtés, satisfying salads, pizzas with pizzazz, pastas, wraps and burritos, nourishing nut loaves with gourmet gravy, not-your-usual nori rolls and exotic sorbets, pies and cakes; all are prepared fresh, fresh, fresh from organic or local, ethically-grown produce.

Live Health Cafe ***/***
264 Dupont St., Toronto, Ontario. 416-515-2002. Vegan, organic and raw foods. Fresh organic juices, gourmet entrees and raw food desserts. Raw products available. Catering and delivery upon request.

ra ra raw! **/***
319 Augusta Ave. (in Kensington Market), Toronto M5T 2M2 Canada. 416-961-2727. An organic, raw food restaurant. Choose from a wide variety of dairy-free, wheat-free, sugar-free and preservative-free main courses, soups, appetizers, desserts and drinks. This vegan restaurant, in Toronto's cosmopolitan Kensington Market, proves that you can create a sumptuous, gourmet meal from all natural ingredients. Take out and catering are available as well. Open 7 days a week, 11AM to 8PM. Ra ra raw! also carries a wide range of supplements, Nature's super foods and organic produce and grocery.

Raw Franchises

Some nationwide franchises for raw, organic produce include Whole Foods Market and Wild Oats. Jamba Juice is a franchised juice bar. Many of the drinks contain concentrates, but you can request a pure one. The carrot juice is a safe bet.

Check their web sites to find the ones closest to where you live or along the routes you will be traveling. Or you may call their national centers.

For Whole Foods, www.wholefoodsmarket.com, call 512-477-4455.

For Wild Oats, www.wildoats.com, call 800-494-9453.

For Jamba Juice, www.jambajuice.com, call 800-545-9972.

Glossary

ahimsa	the Hindu/Buddhist philosophy of non-violence toward any living being
alliesthethic response	a change of taste that occurs when one has eaten an initial food to repletion
allopathic	pertaining to allopathy, or the use of pharmaceutical drugs to relieve disease symptoms by producing opposite symptoms, as practiced by conventional medical practitioners
amenorrhea	the unusual absence of menstruation
ankylosing spondylitis	a disease of the spine that causes the vertebrae to form a solid inflexible column
antioxidant	any chemical thought to protect living organisms from the damaging effects of oxidation
arrhythmia	a condition in which the heart beats with an irregular or abnormal rhythm
bioavailability	the degree to which, or rate at which, a chemical is absorbed or becomes available at the site of physiological activity after ingestion
biophotons	a particle of light (photon) emitted in some fashion from a biological system
Candida albicans	a type of parasitic fungus that can infect human tissues when present in excessive amounts
carcinogen	a cancer-causing agent
Crohn's disease	a chronic disease of the intestines, especially the colon and ileum, often characterized by abdominal pains, bleeding, diarrhea and ruptures
cross-links	abnormal chemical combinations of sugars and proteins that occur in the presence of heat, either from cooking or within the body as it ages

diverticulosis an intestinal condition characterized by the presence of numerous *diverticula* (pouches or sacs branching out from the intestinal walls)

E. coli the bacterium *Escherichia coli*, commonly found in the intestines of humans and other animals, at least one strain of which can cause severe food poisoning

eczema a non-contagious inflammation of the skin, characterized chiefly by redness, itching, and the outbreak of lesions that may discharge serous matter and become encrusted and scaly

edema an excessive accumulation of fluid in the body

enzyme a biologically produced catalyst, a chemical causing a particular chemical reaction to occur while not being changed itself

fibromyalgia a syndrome characterized by chronic pain in the muscles and soft tissues surrounding joints, fatigue and also tenderness at specific sites in the body; also called fibromyalgia syndrome, fibromyositis or fibrositis

free radical an atom or molecule missing an electron, a condition that causes it to react with and destroy other molecules it comes into contact with

frugivore an animal that subsists chiefly on fruits

fruitarian a human frugivore

glycemic index a ranking of the rise in blood glucose from various foodstuffs

goiter a non-cancerous enlargement of the thyroid gland, visible as a swelling at the front of the neck, often associated with iodine deficiency

graminivore an animal that chiefly consumes grains

hydrogenated combined with hydrogen, especially an unsaturated oil combined with hydrogen to produce a solid fat

hyperthyroidism excessive thyroid function, resulting in increased metabolic rate, enlargement of the thyroid gland, rapid heart rate and high blood pressure

immunomodulatory affecting the functioning of the immune system

initial food a food that is primordially suited to one's biology, usually meaning non-hybridized, not over-cultivated and in an unprocessed condition

instinctive eater one who selects which foods to eat chiefly by smell and taste from among initial foods

jaundice a yellowed skin condition resulting from liver dysfunction

liquidarian one who subsists chiefly on a liquid diet

liver cleanse also called *liver flush* or *gallbladder flush*, may refer to: (1) an equal mixture of vegetable oil and citrus juice, often including various herbs or spices, that causes the liver and gallbladder to spasm, possibly releasing stored stones; or (2) a coffee enema used for the same purpose

Maillard molecule any unnatural chemical produced by cooking food, named after French chemist Louis Maillard

mutagen an agent or substance that is capable of increasing the frequency of mutation, or change in the DNA sequence of a gene or chromosome

myasthenia gravis a disease characterized by progressive fatigue and generalized weakness of the skeletal muscles, especially those of the face, neck, arms and legs, caused by impaired transmission of nerve impulses following an autoimmune attack on acetylcholine receptors

Natural Hygiene a natural healing system based on adherence to the biological laws of life, chief of which is that biological organisms are self-healing entities and that disease symptoms are remedial in nature and should therefore be permitted to run their course, not suppressed by or ameliorated with drugs or unnecessary surgeries

osteoporosis a decrease in bone mass resulting in decreased density and enlargement of bone spaces producing porosity and fragility

Parkinson's disease a degenerative disorder of the central nervous system characterized by tremor and impaired muscular coordination

peroxidation over-saturation with oxygen resulting in the formation of destructive chemicals known as free radicals

phytochemical any chemical found in plants

phytonutrient any phytochemical having a beneficial effect upon health or playing an active role in the amelioration of disease

pyrolysis the transformation of a substance by the application of heat, as in cooking

SAD Standard American Diet — the highly processed, refined and predominantly cooked diet consumed by the typical American

SARS Severe Acute Respiratory Syndrome — a serious and highly contagious type of pneumonia

trans fatty acid a biologically abnormal saturated or partly saturated fatty acid produced by the hydrogenation of vegetable oils and present in hardened vegetable oils, most margarines, commercial baked foods and many fried foods

triglyceride a naturally occurring fat consisting of three individual fatty acids bound together into a single large molecule; an important energy source forming much of the fat stored by the body, an excess of which in the bloodstream is considered to be a marker for heart disease

ulcerative colitis inflammation of the walls of the bowel accompanied by the formation of ulcers, a condition which can result in permanent bowel damage

Glossary

vegan
one who consumes no animal products, including meat, dairy, eggs and honey, and may even refuse to use anything coming from an animal source, such as leather shoes

vegetarian
from the Latin *vegetus*, meaning "whole, sound, fresh, lively"; one who typically eschews animal flesh consumption, but may consume bee products, eggs (*ovo-vegetarian*), dairy (*lacto-vegetarian*) or both (*ovo-lacto-vegetarian*)

Index

Norway, 188
Null, Dr. Gary, 389, 390
nutmeg, 346, 349
nutrition, non-food sources, 63
nuts, 35, 60, 166, 176, 200, 205,
206, 210, 211, 212, 214, 216,
221, 224, 225, 227, 228, 234,
236, 240, 257, 262, 276, 283,
297, 303, 304, 308, 324, 325,
345, 348, 349, 354, 403, 404,
408, 409, 423, 467, 483
acidic, 9, 265
benefits, 11, 25, 126, 129, 131,
169
cholesterol, 138, 143
butter, 210, 216, 227, 284, 286,
325, 338, 463, 465
almond, 336, 347, 351, 352,
361, 438
coconut, 11, 215, 308, 344,
345, 347, 381, 465
calcium, 216, 372, 373
almond, 216
cheese, 335, 355
macadamia, 343, 354, 355,
438
cream, 211
coconut, 211, 279
digestibility, 208, 215, 251, 279,
325, 415, 425
environmental impact, 23
hazelnut, 262
milk, 51, 210, 323, 345, 349,
350, 354, 475
almond, 338
coconut, 36, 211, 321, 348
oil, coconut, 215, 345, 358
overeating, 280, 281, 282, 284
peanut, 224, 262, 325
protein, 155, 235, 279, 283,
301, 302
sources, 463, 464, 465, 466
storage, 211, 216, 286
freezing, 215, 276, 324
varieties

almond, 143, 251, 262, 336,
338, 340, 341, 346, 348, 349,
362
Brazil, 215, 256, 262, 348
cashew, 262, 276, 337, 340,
348, 381, 460
coconut, 36, 345, 347, 348,
362, 381, 466
macadamia, 143, 251, 262,
354, 355, 360
cheese, 343
pecan, 262, 348, 355, 358,
359
pine, 360
pistachio, 143
walnut, 143, 213, 262, 346,
348, 358, 439
weight gain, 296
weight loss, 11, 93
obesity, xxiv, 6, 9, 11, 27, 34, 81,
82, 136, 191, 203, 224, 249, 364,
468
cats, 306
causes, 12, 127, 149, 157, 267,
318, 368, 375, 377
statistics, 292
odor, 413, 417
body, 7, 59, 64, 190, 219, 231,
232, 373
oil, 159, 243, 256, 270, 370, 384
canola, 380
coconut, 215, 345, 358
cod liver, 123
fish, 434
flaxseed, 167, 211
heated, 35, 116, 150, 227, 236,
276, 284, 366, 379, 433, 434,
486, 488
hemp, 463
mineral, 369
olive, 203, 204, 214, 217, 264,
276, 336, 337, 341, 343, 351,
352, 353, 354, 355, 356, 357,
358, 359, 465
palm, 379

To contact the author, write to:

sschenck@alumni.indiana.edu
or LiveFoodFactor@yahoo.com

Alternatively, the author may be contacted via the publisher's mailing address.

Your victories and testimonials relating to your own raw journey are welcome, as are any comments. Maybe you would like to contribute to my next book.

While the author welcomes all reader feedback, please be advised that personal replies are not guaranteed.

Additional copies of *The Live Food Factor* may be ordered directly from the publisher. Single copies are US$27.95 plus $4.50 shipping and handling via Priority Mail. For each additional copy, add $2.00 shipping and handling. California residents should add 7.75% sales tax.

Orders to Canada and Mexico require $7.00 shipping and handling for the first copy, $4.00 for each additional copy.

For other countries, enclose $9.00 shipping and handling for the first copy and $6.00 for each additional copy.

Contact the publisher for bulk discount prices.

Send check or money order to:

Awakenings Publications
P. O. Box 712423
San Diego, CA 92171-2423

Printed in the United States
56257LVS00003B/7

9 780977 679508